Volume I

Tonality and Design in Music Theory

Earl Henry
Webster University, St. Louis

Michael Rogers
University of Oklahoma, Norman

PEARSON
Prentice Hall

Upper Saddle River
New Jersey 07458

Library of Congress Cataloging-in-Publication Data

Henry, Earl.
   Tonality and design in music theory / Earl Henry, Michael Rogers.
     p. cm.
   Includes index.
   ISBN 0-13-081128-9
   1. Music theory—Textbooks. I. Rogers, Michael R. II. Title.

MT6.H526 2004
781.2—dc22

2004052228

Editor-in-Chief: Sarah Touborg
Senior Acquisitions Editor: Christopher Johnson
Editorial Assistant: Evette Dickerson
Marketing Manager: Sheryl Adams
Marketing Assistant: Cherron Gardner
Managing Editor: Joanne Riker
Production Editor: Randy Pettit
Manufacturing Buyer: Benjamin D. Smith
Cover Design: Kiwi Design
Composition: Preparé
Printer/Binder: Courier Companies, Inc.
Cover Printer: Lehigh

Credits and acknowledgments borrowed from other sources and reproduced, with permission, in this textbook appear on appropriate page within text (or on page x).

Pearson Education LTD.
Pearson Education Australia PTY, Limited
Pearson Education Singapore, Pte. Ltd
Pearson Education North Asia Ltd
Pearson Education, Canada, Ltd
Pearson Educación de Mexico, S.A. de C.V.
Pearson Education–Japan
Pearson Education Malaysia, Pte. Ltd

10 9 8 7 6 5 4 3 2 1
ISBN 0-13-081128-9

Contents

Preface

Music Theory is the study of how and why music works. This suggests that understanding the subject consists of something more than data bits, definitions, or a body of prescribed knowledge. While this set of textbooks offers plenty of instruction about names, labels, and an appropriate vocabulary for effective communication among musicians, we have designed the series to offer a good deal more. Without being dangerously speculative, we have tried to propose, where possible, the *reasons* which lie behind principles and procedures of aesthetically stimulating musical constructions—that is, an explanation for just how the rules came about and how they have influenced changing musical styles.

We have also approached theoretical study from the listener's perspective, so that our discussions and analyses refer not only to the printed notation of scores, but also to the reactions of educated audiences to the individual sounds and larger patterns of music. By alluding frequently to the aesthetic involvement of music and the psychological manipulation of master composers, for example, we have endeavored to enrich cognitive and perceptual experiences; these are simultaneously the byproducts of informed listening and the foundation of performing, composing, and teaching music.

Presented in proper manner and spirit, these books can enable theory teachers to not only foster intellectual development and aural growth for their students, but also to advance beyond that stage into the ambitious realms of changing opinions and attitudes, reworking beliefs and habits, judging sides of a controversy, and refining a set of values. Students may come to develop a sense of wonder about the mysteries and forces of music itself. In other words, training in music theory can support learning how to think and learning how to respond—the twin sides of a true musical education.

We draw from the well-established tradition of Comprehensive Musicianship in choosing and organizing topics for these books. Lessons and assignments are presented not only in basic tonal harmony, but also in fundamentals, concepts of melody, counterpoint, form, analysis, composition, writing essays, and various aspects of contemporary music—all within a stylistic and historical context. Although our emphasis is on Western musical art, text material is amplified by the music of both men and women, differing styles, various cultures, and examples drawn from popular and ethnic sources. Distinctive features as well as commonalities and universals are identified in comparing works.

The methodology of *Tonality and Design in Music Theory* is intentionally eclectic. We present a wide variety of analytic techniques, including both traditional approaches (harmony and form, for example) and also a generous representation of linear analysis. We introduced the latter topic without any formal or restrictive adherence to Schenkerian principles because we feel that these topics are a worthy subject for advanced study in their own right, but only after a beginning groundwork has been established. Our book will not, for example, teach students to draw elaborate graphs. Instead, it will enable them to not only appreciate the long-range attractions and links that pitches have for one another, but also to understand and create graphic representations of these relationships in a variety of ways. Single-line melodic study is covered along with selective representations of structural reductions (as simplified notation) in both harmonic and contrapuntal settings in order to clarify the skeleton and scaffolding of music. These reductions permit distinctions to be made between events that give meaning and those that take meaning.

One of the most challenging aspects of writing the actual words, sentences, and paragraphs for an introductory theory course is to establish an appropriate tone, style, and level of readability for students of varying backgrounds—one that is forceful and clear for the learner while being engaging and thought-provoking for the facilitator. In short, we have written a book that we hope is simple and direct, but at the same time, properly sophisticated and nuanced so that while concepts are not diluted, there is no underestimation or dishonoring of the profusion of music itself. We have devoted special care and attention to the problem of writing a text for readers who are coming to a topic for the first time, and can only hope that a satisfying and challenging balance has been achieved so that the books will have appeal as well for the teacher.

ACKNOWLEDGMENTS

We are indebted to numerous individuals who provided valuable assistance in the preparation of this book. Kendall Stallings, Glen Bauer, Robert Chamberlin, Gay Spears, and Karen Trinkle used the book in class testing and provided many invaluable suggestions and corrections. Carole Gaspar and Kathryn Stieler assisted with text translations. In addition, we thank the students at Webster University who used various transformations of these materials over several years. The involvement of students in pointing out typographical errors, unwieldy exercise problems, and ambiguous explanations has helped us produce a more useful book. The books are *for* students, after all, and we have profited greatly from their input on virtually every page.

Earl Henry
Michael Rogers

USING THE TEXT

To Students

Tonality and Design in Music Theory is the final manuscript version of a two-volume textbook to be published by Prentice Hall with a January, 2005, copyright date. We hope that you will enjoy using this book and will find it helpful in your studies. Please note how the text has been organized to facilitate study and comprehension.

Organization

Each chapter centers on a full and detailed discussion of one major aspect of traditional Western music. These prose discussions are then divided into two, three, or four smaller parts that likewise present self-contained topics. There are over thirty of these smaller divisions in each volume, so that while the chapters cover a broad aspect of Western musical art, chapter divisions progress in "bite-sized" pieces. Each chapter division ends with a *Review and Application* consisting of important terms, class and individual exercise problems, and music for analysis. Be sure that you understand each of the terms and its relationship to the central topic. The exercises can be completed either in class or at home, as directed by your instructor. *Chapter Projects* conclude each broad area of study. These projects include analysis, composition, essay, and a wide range of other endeavors that will help you apply the knowledge you have gained to a wider range of interests and studies.

Following each *Review and Application*, chapter divisions contain *Self-Tests*. These quizzes are short, and center on objective questions about the material concerned. You should take each self-test at home in a *timed* situation. The time limits in the text are only suggestions; you may want to allow yourself more time, but note carefully how much of the self-test you have covered in the prescribed time. Remember that in many aspects of music theory, *speed* in analysis and construction is as important as a knowledge of procedure. The answers to self tests can be found on the website for both volumes (www.prehall.com/henry). Where questions are objective, the given answers can be scored correct or incorrect; in other situations, however, you will find an answer given, but with the indication that other correct answers are possible. When in doubt, check your answers with your instructor. Score each self test as directed on the basis of 100 points and note your progress.

Workbook/Anthology.   The two Workbook/Anthologies that accompany the texts are optional at the discretion of institutions and individual instructors. These volumes contain a wide range of problems, drill exercises, composition activities, and music for analysis. As you progress through the text, you will note references to specific pages in the Workbook/Anthology that correspond to the text material. Your instructor will assign some or all of these materials as supplementary studies. Each chapter of the Workbook/Anthology contains one or more complete works of movements for study and analysis.

Compact Disc Recordings.   Each volume corresponds to two compact discs that contain recorded examples of text material. Another CD corresponds to each volume of the workbook/anthology. These recordings will assist you in your study when a keyboard is not avaible. As shown in the next example, a logo lets you know when a text or workbook passage is recorded.

CD 1, TRACK 04
Robert Schumann, "Träumerei" (Dreams) from *Scenes from Childhood* Simple Beat Division

CD 1, TRACK 6-1 MIXED VALUES (2 PARTS)
**Ludwig van Beethoven, Quartet,
Op. 18
Rhythmic Variety**

If the caption indicates that the example is in multiple parts ("2 parts," "3 Parts," and so on), you will need to pause the CD at the end of the first passage, and then resume the same track when you are ready to listen to the next example.

(pause CD)

TRACK 6-2 MIXED VALUES
**Robert Schumann, Trio, Op. 110
Rhythmic Economy**

While a few of the recorded examples are synthesized, most are live acoustic performances by both student and professional musicians.

Website.   From the Internet, you can connect easily to Prentice Hall's website for this book at www.prehall.com/henry. On this site (available 2005), you will find additional study suggestions and materials that correlate with every chapter of *Tonality and Design.* As you work through the problems on the website, the correct answers and supplementary commentary are available at any time you choose. In addition, a student-centered forum will permit you to discuss related topics and swap ideas with other students, with professional musicians, and with the authors.

Occasionally, when an inspired composer chooses acclaimed poetry as the basis of an original musical work, the results are monumental—greater, perhaps, than either of the two works taken separately. Such is the case with the final movement of Ludwig van Beethoven's Ninth Symphony. In an unusual approach to an instrumental work, Beethoven (1770–1827) added a chorus and chose as a text the poem "Ode to Joy" by the German dramatist Friederich Schiller (1759–1804). Beethoven set the opening stanza of Schiller's poem as a simple, but exquisite melody that has been revered by generations since. In our time, "Ode to Joy" has been sung, played, studied, recorded, arranged, and borrowed for use in *new* original music in styles ranging from serious art to commercial pop.

As we review music fundamentals in Chapters 1, 2, and 3, we will refer often to Beethoven's "Ode to Joy." Despite its remarkable simplicity, the melody offers an expert and consummate blending of the basic elements of music. This synthesis of sound, time, texture, and shape characterizes traditional Western artistic principles in their highest order.

CD 1, TRACK 02
Ludwig van Beethoven,
Theme from Symphony No. 9
in D Minor "Ode to Joy"

Freu-de schö-ner Göt-ter-funk-en Toch-ter aus E - ly - si-um, wir be-tre-ten feu-er-trunk-en

Him - mli-sche dein Hei - lig tum! Dei - ne Zau - ber bin-den wie - der was die - Mo-de

steng-ge-teilt; al - le Men-schen wer-den Brü - der wo dein sanf-ter Flü - gel weilt.

Joy, thou goddess, fair, immortal	Custom's laws indeed may sever,
Offspring of Elysium,	But thy magic joins again;
Mad with rapture to the portal	All mankind are brethren ever
Of thy holy fane we come.	'Neath thy mild and gentle reign.

Printed music may be referred to as a SCORE. In the last example, we see only the vocal line with the original German text. An ARRANGEMENT is a version of a work that may differ substantially from the original. The notes in an arrangement may be the same as the original ones, but with a completely different instrumentation. In other arrangements, new accompaniment and other figures may be added. The score below is a piano arrangement of Beethoven's melody. In piano music, two staffs are connected with a brace at the left. In Unit I, we will discuss numerous aspects of music notation that appear in the examples on these pages.

Piano Arrangement of "Ode to Joy"
from Beethoven's Symphony No. 9 in D Minor

A REDUCTION is an arrangement for piano of a work originally conceived for a larger ensemble. In the passage below, Beethoven's orchestral score has been reduced for voice and piano.

Reduction for Voice and Piano

A FULL SCORE (also termed CONDUCTOR'S SCORE) shows each instrument or voice category in the ensemble and the notes that they are assigned to play. When instruments or voices have extended rests, they are often omitted from a full score for purposes of clarity. Beethoven's Symphony No. 9 in D Minor, which includes the "Ode to Joy" melody, is scored for flutes, oboes, clarinets, bassoons, horns, trumpets, percussion, and strings. When the voice enters in the final movement of the work, however, only the oboes (*hoboen*), clarinets (*klarinetten*), and strings are accompanying; other instruments are omitted from the full score.

Orcherstral Score

An AUTOGRAPH SCORE is one in the composer's own calligraphy. Throughout history, some composers have exhibited better "penmanship" than others. The original autograph score of Beethoven's Symphony No. 9 is in the Prussian State Library in Berlin. A photographic reproduction of this autograph, called a FACSIMILE, was published in 1924. Compare the previous page with Beethoven's autograph of a similar passage shown here.

MUSIC THEORY is the study of the materials of music and how those materials have been organized by composers throughout Western history. The "rules" of theoretical study acquaint you with procedures by which composers have created music of lasting value. In virtually all cases, however, the music itself preceded any specifications for producing a given style or effect. The guidelines for analysis and composition given throughout this text are not arbitrary restrictions intended to stifle the creativity of young musicians (as composers from Debussy to Stockhausen have contended). Rather, the "rules" of music theory comprise a discussion and documentation of music that has endured the test of time.

CHAPTER *1*

Fundamentals of Pitch and Rhythm

MUSIC, often defined as organized sound and silence, has served for centuries as a primary means of artistic expression in the Western world. When we speak of "traditional" or "common-practice" music, we usually mean works composed around 1650 to 1900. Central to traditional Western music is NOTATION—the process of representing sounds. The historical insistence on precise notation helps distinguish Western music from that of many other world cultures.

THE NOTATION OF PITCH

NOTES occur in a variety of shapes and comprise the basic symbols for sound. The relative highness or lowness of sound is termed PITCH and is notated upon a grid of five lines and four spaces called a STAFF.

The Clef

The seven BASIC PITCHES (conveniently represented by the white keys of the piano keyboard) are identified with letters of the alphabet: A, B, C, D, E, F, and G. Using a symbol called a CLEF, we can designate a particular line or space on the staff as the location of one of these basic pitches. Pitches fall in sequence from A to G ascending or G to A descending. By locating any one pitch on the staff, therefore, we have identified them all.

A musical REGISTER is a high, low, or mid-range set of pitches. A treble (higher) register is usually notated with a treble clef; the tenor register, with the tenor clef, and so on. Although many different clefs have been employed by

Western musicians since the Middle Ages, only three are common in modern editions.

The TREBLE CLEF (𝄞) identifies relatively higher tones and fixes the second staff line as the position of the pitch G. Lower tones are notated in the BASS CLEF (𝄢) which names a note on the fourth staff line as F.

The MOVABLE C-CLEF (𝄡) locates the pitch C, appears in two different locations in modern editions, and is found today chiefly in instrumental music. The ALTO CLEF sets the third line as the position of the pitch C; in the TENOR CLEF, the fourth line is C.

Observe that the note specified by a given clef refers also to a precise register. For now, compare the pitch "middle C" (at the center of the piano keyboard) as it is notated in treble, bass, alto, and tenor clefs.

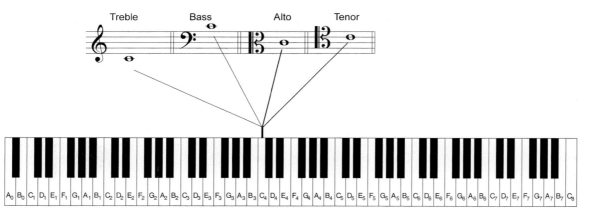

When the staff location of one pitch (G, F, or C) is fixed by a clef, we also know the names and locations of *every* note on the staff. If the clef changes, the sequence of note names (A-G) remains the same, although the specific pitches represented by different lines and spaces will vary.

Ledger Lines.   When higher pitches exceed the five lines of the staff, LEDGER LINES provide a temporary extension. Notice that while each of the passages below sounds the same, the notation is different.

Until the nineteenth century, clefs were employed in many different staff positions to avoid ledger lines. Although the clef positions shown in the next example are no longer familiar to most performers, the principle of note identification remains the same: the C-clef identifies C; the bass clef shows the position of F. The soprano, mezzo-soprano, and baritone clefs are found in original editions of both vocal and instrumental music.

| soprano clef | mezzo-soprano clef | baritone clef |

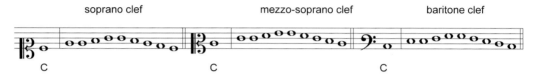

The staff and clef, invented around 1000 C.E., standardized Western musical notation. In the ten centuries since these symbols were introduced, music has undergone constant change. The fact that we continue to express our musical art with the same line and space grid—illuminated by a clef—is evidence of the flexibility of these symbols.

WORKBOOK/ANTHOLOGY I
I. Note Names, page 1

The Octave

When different notes on the staff have the same letter name, they are by definition one or more *octaves* apart. An OCTAVE is a natural phenomenon that causes us to hear two different pitches as nearly identical. In the next passage, the first pitch G is an octave below the second. Likewise, the second frame shows the notation of pitches F that are one and two octaves apart, respectively.

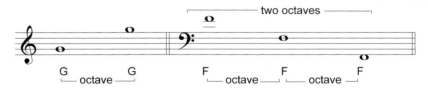

The Octave Sign.   Performers on some orchestral instruments (violin, flute, and tuba, for example) are accustomed to reading ledger lines above or below the staff. For many other instruments however, composers use an altered notation to avoid more than one or two ledger lines. The OCTAVE SIGN (8va) specifies that a pitch or series of pitches is to be performed an octave higher or lower than written. The octave sign appears above the notes affected if they are to be played higher; below, for notes sounding an octave lower. The word *bassa* (or 8^b) is usually added when the sounding pitches are an octave lower than written.

Notice that a dashed line delineates the *ottava* passage in the previous example. As shown below, the word *loco* ("in place") appears above the first note that follows the *ottava* passage.

Clefs also facilitate octave transposition. In addition to those already discussed, the symbol 𝄢 indicates pitches sounding an octave lower than written and is often employed for the tenor voice.

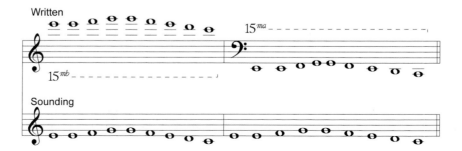

Quindicesima.   Occasionally, a passage is notated *two* octaves above or below sounding pitch. The designation *15ma* stands for the Italian word *QUINDICESIMA* ("fifteenth") and indicates a two-octave difference between written and sounding pitch.

The Unison.   An INTERVAL is defined as the difference (or distance) between two pitches. The octave is an interval that occurs when pitches in different staff locations share a letter name. Another interval, the UNISON, describes two *identical* pitches. As shown in the next example, intervals like the octave and unison may be MELODIC (pitches heard consecutively) or HARMONIC (pitches sounded simultaneously).

Octave Designations

With many different pitches sharing a single letter name, traditional notation includes a means of referring to notes in a specific octave. OCTAVE DESIGNATION assigns a number to each register on the standard piano keyboard. The pitch C is the lowest in each octave; pitches above C carry the same octave designation.

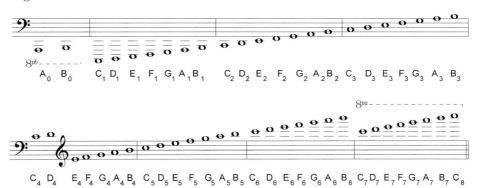

Although several systems of octave designation are in use today, the one explained here is the simplest. In a spoken reference, identify an entire octave range by its lowest pitch ("the C-four octave," for example). Specify an individual pitch as "C-five," "D-flat-two," or whatever the case may be.

WORKBOOK/ANTHOLOGY I
II. The Octave and Octave Designations, page 7

The Keyboard

Intervals such as the octave and the unison are easily identified on the piano keyboard. The pitch C is the white key to the left of the two adjacent black keys; to the immediate left of the three black keys is the pitch F. The seven basic pitches fall sequentially across the white keys as shown in the next example.

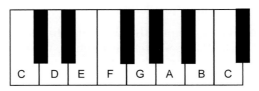

Half and Whole Steps.   The octave, with its sensation of stability and culmination, is an essential interval in virtually all world cultures. One of several differences between Western and other musical systems, however, concerns the *smallest* interval. In the West, we divide the octave into twelve equal smaller parts called half steps. The HALF STEP is the smallest (most narrow) interval in Western music. On the keyboard, the distance from one key to the next closest key above or below is a half step. Two half steps combine to form a WHOLE STEP—another defining interval.

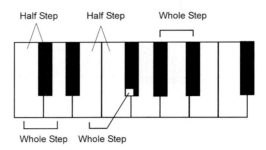

Accidentals

Symbols called ACCIDENTALS are used to represent basic pitches that have been raised or lowered. A SHARP (♯), for example, indicates a pitch that is raised a half step. A basic pitch lowered a half step, on the other hand, is indicated with the FLAT symbol (♭). Use a NATURAL (♮) to cancel the effect of a flat or a sharp. Accidentals come before the pitch they affect; in a written reference, the accidental follows the note name.

Double Sharps and Flats.   Basic pitches may be raised and lowered *two* half steps with the DOUBLE SHARP (𝄪) and DOUBLE FLAT (♭♭) signs, respectively. In the first frame below, pitches ascend by half step; in the second frame, the line descends.

Enharmonic Equivalents

In the last example, the third and fourth pitches (F𝄪 and G) sound the same. Pitches that are written differently, yet have the same sound are termed ENHARMONIC EQUIVALENTS (or just "enharmonics"). When we include double flats and double sharps, each of the twelve pitches in every octave has two different alternate notations.[1] Three of the twelve pitches, along with their enharmonic equivalents, are shown in the next example.

Pitch Class.   While the term "enharmonic" connotes pitches in the same octave, PITCH CLASS is a broader designation encompassing a given pitch, all of its enharmonic equivalents, *and* all possible octave duplications. In the previous example, the three pitches in each frame sound in unison and are all in the same pitch class. Each frame in the next example, on the other hand, displays pitches in a single pitch class, but in different octaves.

Musical notation is precise in that composers generally do not use pitch names interchangeably. As we will discuss in later chapters, while the pitches C♯

WORKBOOK/ANTHOLOGY I
III. The Keyboard and
Accidentals, page 9

and D♭ may be enharmonic equivalents (and, of course, assigned to the same pitch class), musical context in tonal music *always* dictates one notation or the other.

REVIEW AND APPLICATION 1–1

Pitch Names, Clefs, and Octaves

Essential Terms

accidental	enharmonic	ledger line	notation	staff
basic pitch	flat	octave	pitch class	unison
clef	interval	natural	sharp	

1. Identify the pitches below in treble and bass clefs. Include octave designation.

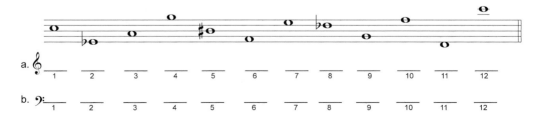

---

[1] The pitches G♯ and A♭ have only one enharmonic equivalent.

2. The pitches below are notated in alto and tenor clefs. Identify both note names and octave designations.

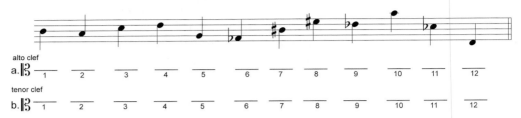

alto clef

a.

tenor clef

b.

3. The line below is a Medieval melody notated here to include *ottava* passages and a clef change. Use the lower staff to write all pitches as they will sound in the bass clef. Notate the different pitch shapes as they appear in the upper line. Be prepared to name and designate the octave of each pitch.

4. Write the designated interval above or below the given pitch. Name both pitches and provide the octave designation. In some cases, two or more answers are correct.

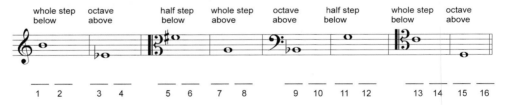

5. For each given pitch, provide another that is an enharmonic equivalent. Identify both pitches with letter name and octave designation. Two different answers are correct in each instance.

SELF-TEST 1–1

Time Limit: 5 Minutes

1. Write each pitch specified in the clef provided. *Scoring: Subtract 5 points for each incorrect pitch.*

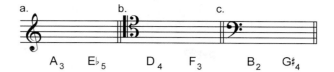

A_3 $E\flat_5$ D_4 F_3 B_2 $G\sharp_4$

2. Write pitches as directed, above or below the given notes. *Scoring: Subtract 9 points for each incorrect pitch.* Considering enharmonics, two answers are possible.

Whole Step   Half Step   Whole Step
Above   Above   Below

3. Provide one enharmonic equivalent for each pitch shown. More than one correct answer may be possible. *Scoring: Subtract 9 points for each incorrect answer.*

4. *If necessary,* add an accidental to the *second* pitch so that the interval conforms to its description. *Scoring: Subtract 7 points for each incorrect answer.*

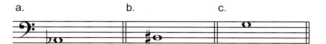

Half Step   Whole Step   Half Step   Whole Step

5. Provide the term that is used to end an *ottava* passage. *Scoring: subtract 2 points for an incorrect answer.*

————————————

Total Possible: 100   Your Score_____

THE NOTATION OF RHYTHM AND METER

RHYTHM concerns the duration of sounds and silences. In most world cultures—including the West—musical time is measured in even pulses called BEATS. TEMPO, the speed of the beat, affects pacing, but is not a factor in rhythmic notation. Rhythm centers on durational relationships. This important structural parameter causes us to perceive an ebb and flow of motion or stillness in the course of a musical work.

Traditional Note Symbols

Western rhythmic notation centers on a system of fractional relationships among note values. Any rhythmic symbol can represent one beat in time; once that unit has been established, however, all other rhythmic symbols are interpreted accordingly either as multiples or as fractions of the beat. The symbols for silence are called RESTS and have values that correspond to notes.

The basic note symbol (○) is termed a WHOLE NOTE. As shown in the following example, other values are represented graphically as variations of this shape: The DOUBLE WHOLE NOTE or BREVE includes two vertical bars, the HALF NOTE has a STEM (vertical attachment), and the QUARTER NOTE is blackened.

RHYTHMIC SYMBOLS OF GREATER VALUE

Note	Rest	Name	Value
‖O‖	▪	Double Whole	Double value of whole
O	▬	Whole	Whole
♩	▬	Half	1/2 value of whole
♩	❩	Quarter	1/4 value of whole

The double-whole rest fills the third space.[2] Whole and half rests, on the other hand, associated with lines on the staff, are distinguished by their respective positions. As shown in the next example, the quarter rest is centered across the five lines.

double-whole rest   whole rest   half rest   quarter rest

Lesser Rhythmic Values.   Symbols of less than a quarter note in value include one or more FLAGS (↿)—curved lines that extend from the stem. With rest symbols, flags are replaced by HOOKS (•). Each flag or hook decreases durational value by one half.

RHYTHMIC SYMBOLS OF LESSER VALUE

Note	Rest	Name	Value
♪	♪	Eighth	1/8 value of whole
♬	♪	Sixteenth	1/16 value of whole
♬	♪	Thirty-second	1/32 value of whole
♬	♪	Sixty-fourth	1/64 value of whole

Once a composer identifies the rhythmic symbol that represents one beat, the relative values of all other symbols are fixed as well. Observe the lengths in beats or beat fractions of the durational symbols in the next example. The quarter, half, and eighth notes, respectively, are designated as the beat unit.

---

[2]The designations "double whole" and "breve" are synonymous. The former will be employed in this text.

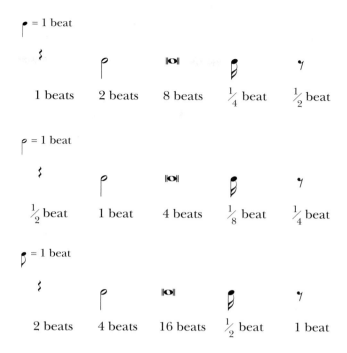

Flags and Beams.   In some cases, flags are replaced with BEAMS—broad horizontal lines that connect note stems. When beams are used, the number of beams corresponds to the number of flags: Two eighth notes are connected by one beam; sixteenths are connected by two beams, and so on.

Especially in instrumental music, beat groups are beamed together for additional clarity. When groups are beamed correctly, they are easier to read; if the beaming is not typical, however, the passage may appear *more* difficult.

Correct Beaming
Beats Grouped by Beams

Incorrect Beaming
Beat Groups Ambiguous

In vocal music, beams are used for multiple notes on the same syllable. In this event, these notes are also grouped with a slur.

Modest Mussorgsky, *Boris Godunov*

Your pro - fessed de - vo - tion,— sir, I trust not, all in vain your — sol - emn — oaths.

The Augmentation Dot.   Composers may use an AUGMENTATION DOT (or just "dot") to extend a note or rest by one-half. If the quarter note has the value of one beat, for example, the *dotted-quarter note* receives one and one-half beats. With a half-note beat, on the other hand, the dotted-quarter note would receive three-fourths of a beat. Finally, the same dotted-quarter note has the value of three beats if the eighth note is set as one beat.

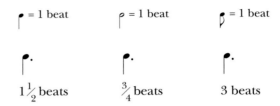

The dot principle is often extended to include two, three, and even four augmentation dots after notes or rests. Each succeeding dot receives one-half the value of the symbol or dot that precedes it.

The Tie.   The dot may be employed with rests and with notes of any pitch, but the TIE is a symbol that combines the values of two notes *of identical pitch.*

Notes and rests of various durations occur in Western music over an underlying beat. As long as the tempo remains unchanged, the beat moves forward relentlessly. As we will discuss in the next section, when some of the beats are heard as more important than others, the parameter of rhythm takes on a new dimension called *meter.*

Meter

Effective musical lines generate momentum. Regular patterns of strong and weak beats—called METER—not only help provide this energy, but also aid in defining simultaneous voices. In a series of strong and weak beats that creates the effect of meter, the first beat has an ACCENT or musical stress. One or more weak beats follows to complete the pattern. Different meters exhibit individual schemes of weak and accented pulses; we hear the first accented beat as the strongest.

Barlines.   Complete metric patterns are called MEASURES; in traditional notation, the beginning of each measure is identified by a BARLINE (|). A DOUBLE BARLINE (‖), on the other hand, signals the endpoint of a group of measures (used at the end of a composition or major section). The FINAL BAR-LINE (‖) is a thin-thick symbol that identifies the end of a composition or movement.

Duple and Triple Meters. Two of the most common meters, illustrated in the next example, are DUPLE (strong-weak) and TRIPLE (strong-weak-weak).

The familiar Mexican dance tune shown below is in a triple meter and employs numerous rests. Notice, however, that rests *do not* occur on the first (accented) beat of the measure. In the notation below, the quarter note is the unit of beat.

We could also notate the same tune with a half- or eighth-note beat as shown in the next example. Given a constant tempo, the two lines below (as well as the quarter-note version in the last passage) all sound the same.

The French folk song, *Frère Jacques* (which we know as *Are You Sleeping, Brother John?*), is in a duple meter that might be notated with any one of several different beat units.

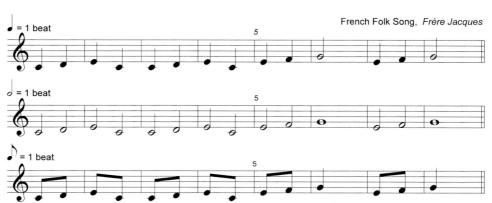

Beethoven's "Ode to Joy" is cast in QUADRUPLE METER—four beats per measure. The first beat receives the traditional metric accent; the third beat (–) is also accented, but less so than the first (<). Both the second and fourth beats are unaccented (with the second slightly stronger than the fourth).

Quadruple Meter

Quadruple meter differs from duple and triple in that it includes two different levels of accent (along with two unaccented beats).

Quadruple Metric Plan

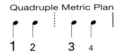

Anacrusis.   Beethoven began his setting of Schiller's poem with a strong beat; many other compositions, however, begin with a weak beat or a weak group of beats. An incomplete measure that begins a composition or section is termed an ANACRUSIS (also called a "pick up"). Any missing beat or beats stand alone at the end of the composition to complete the first measure. In the passage below, by the German composer Louise Reichardt (1779–1826), the meter is quadruple with a half-note beat. The opening quarter note is an anacrusis and receives one-half beat. Accordingly, the final measure shown here has only three and one-half beats.

Meter is one of several elements that makes Western music sound the way it does. Accented beats are separated by only one to three lesser pulses. In other cultures, complex and lengthy patterns with numerous levels of accent are common. Metric accents also govern our traditional reaction to music in the West. Hearing a triple meter, we may feel like swaying from side to side on accented beats; a duple accent in a bright tempo may be appropriate for marching. Most commercial music today is duple or quadruple while in the nineteenth century, many folk and popular tunes were in triple meters.

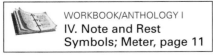

REVIEW AND APPLICATION 1–2 ━━━━━━━━━━━━

Rhythmic Values and Meter

Essential Terms

anacrusis	beat	meter
augmentation dot	barline	rhythm
beam	measure	tempo

1. Given three different beat units, provide the values of the notes or rests in beats or fractions of beats ($\frac{1}{2}$ beat, 2 beats, 4 beats, and so on).

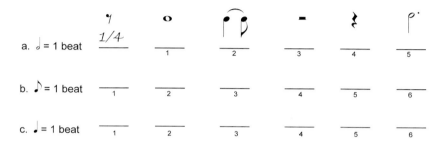

a. $\,\half\,$ = 1 beat   1/4   ___ 1   ___ 2   ___ 3   ___ 4   ___ 5

b. $\,\eighth\,$ = 1 beat   ___ 1   ___ 2   ___ 3   ___ 4   ___ 5   ___ 6

c. $\,\quarter\,$ = 1 beat   ___ 1   ___ 2   ___ 3   ___ 4   ___ 5   ___ 6

2. Add barlines to the two passages below. Study the specified meter and unit of beat, then count numbers of beats before each barline.

a. **Triple Meter**　　　　　　　　　　　　　　　Henry Mancini, "Charade"

b. **Quadruple Meter**　　　　　　　L. van Beethoven, Sonata No. 21, Op. 53 [3]

---

[3] *Opus* (abbreviated "Op.") is Latin for "work." In the time of Bach, Haydn, and Mozart, opus numbers were most often assigned by the publisher and they provide information on the chronological order in which music was distributed to the public (not necessarily the order in which works were composed). Publishers often contracted with composers for *sets* of sonatas or other works. "Opus 13," for example, might include six different sonatas which would be designated as "Opus 13, No. 1," "Opus 13, No. 2," and so on.

SELF-TEST 1–2

Time Limit: 5 Minutes

1. With the given unit of beat (quarter note, half note, and so on), write *one note* that has the specified value. *Scoring: Subtract 4 points for each incorrect answer.*

a. ♩ = 1 beat

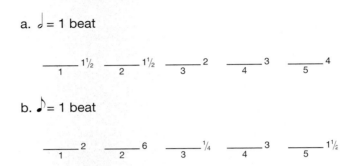

b. ♪ = 1 beat

2. If the quarter note has the value of one beat, provide the values in beats or fractions of beats of the dotted and double-dotted notes below. *Scoring: Subtract 6 points for each incorrect answer.*

♩ = 1 beat

3. Some of the measures below are incomplete. The meter is triple and the quarter note is the beat. Where measures are incomplete, add *one note* symbol (it may be dotted) at the end of the measure. If the measure is complete, leave it unchanged. Pitch is not a consideration in this problem. *Scoring: Subtract 6 points for each incorrect answer.*

Triple Meter
♩ = 1 beat

Total Possible: 100   Your Score_____

Beat Division

In addition to the accent pattern, BEAT DIVISION (the way in which the beat divides into smaller note values) distinguishes among different meters. When composers choose notes smaller than one beat in value, they divide the beat in one of two ways. In SIMPLE METERS, the beat is always an undotted (simple) note and it divides into two equal parts. If the meter is COMPOUND, on the other hand, the beat is a dotted note and the division will be into three smaller parts.

Simple Beat Division

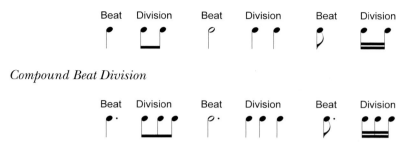

Compound Beat Division

In addition to the beat and a natural accent pattern, music often moves along in divided-beat pulses as well. The following melody by Robert Schumann (1810–1856) makes consistent use of the simple beat division. As shown below, even on beats where no division occurs in the music, performers often *feel* the lesser pulses to help ensure accuracy and precision.

CD 1, TRACK 04
Robert Schumann, "Träumerei" (Dreams) from *Scenes from Childhood*
Simple Beat Division

Observe the underlying *compound* beat division in the show tune, "Seventy-Six Trombones." The beat here is the dotted-quarter note; the division, the eighth note. Remember, however, that just as easily, the dotted-half or dotted-eighth notes could serve as the beat.

CD 1, TRACK 05
Meredith Wilson, "Seventy-Six Trombones" from *The Music Man*
Compound Beat Division

Since the fifteenth century, meter in Western music has centered upon an accent pattern (generally duple, triple, or quadruple) and the choice between the simple or the compound beat divisions. Once a meter is chosen, that scheme is usually employed for an entire movement or section. In other world societies (Africa, for example), duple and triple accent patterns, as well as simple and compound beat divisions are employed *simultaneously* in different voices. While our musical notation includes symbols that permit a high degree of complexity (see page 33), Western composers have preferred the regularity and the simplicity of a single metric effect.

Meter Signatures

Accent pattern and the manner of beat division (simple or compound) are the two essential elements of a meter. The METER (or TIME) SIGNATURE conveys this information with two numerals placed at the beginning of a movement or sectional division.[4] If the meter is simple, the upper numeral indicates the number of beats in a measure (2, 3, 4, or whatever). The lower numeral in a simple meter signature stands for a simple note value:

Lower Numeral	Beat	Lower Numeral	Beat	Lower Numeral	Beat	Lower Numeral	Beat
2	𝅗𝅥	8	♪	4	♩	16	𝅘𝅥𝅯

Simple Meters.   Signatures that represent simple meters are easily recognized since, with one exception, the upper numeral is *not* divisible by 3. The numeral 3 is the exception and also designates a simple meter (with a two-part beat division). All of the meters in the next example are simple.

Quarter-Note Beat			Half-Note Beat		Eighth-Note Beat	
$\frac{2}{4}$	$\frac{3}{4}$	$\frac{4}{4}$	$\frac{2}{2}$	$\frac{4}{2}$	$\frac{3}{8}$	$\frac{4}{8}$

Notice that the meter signature identifies not only the accent pattern and beat division, but also the value of every rhythmic symbol. In a meter like $\frac{3}{4}$, the numeral 4 indicates that the quarter note usually receives the beat. When we have this information, we know that the half note receives two beats, the eighth note, a half beat, and so on. The time signature $\frac{4}{4}$ relays similar information to the performer. Beethoven's "Ode to Joy" is cast in a simple meter with four beats per measure and a quarter-note beat.

Quadruple-Simple Meter

***Common Time* and Alla Breve.**   Two symbols, with origins in the Middle Ages, are still sometimes employed today in place of numerical time signatures. The symbol **C** is the equivalent of $\frac{4}{4}$; a duple-simple meter with half-note beat $\left(\frac{2}{2}\right)$ may be designated with the symbol **¢**. The latter meter is often designated

---

[4]The meter signature is provided at the beginning of a composition and is *not* repeated unless the meter changes.

ALLA BREVE. The German composer Gustav Mahler (1860–1911) uses *alla breve* for the first theme of his Symphony No. 1 in D Major.

Gustav Mahler, Symphony No. 1 in D Major
First Movement

Sing through Mahler's melody using *alla breve*, then perform the line in $\frac{4}{4}$. Where the *alla breve* melody (as Mahler wrote it) is lilting and folklike in its simplicity, the quadruple-simple meter is labored. Sing the melody a final time in the original duple meter and feel the divided-beat pulse.

Compound Meter Signatures. If a meter is compound, the upper numeral of the meter signature is divisible by 3 (3 itself, of course, is always simple). Use the following rule to differentiate between simple and compound meters:

If the upper numeral of the meter signature is divisible by 3 (and not 3 itself), the meter is compound; all other numerals represent simple meters.

We need not be concerned with whether an upper numeral is divisible by both 3 and 2 ($\frac{6}{4}$, for example). The fact that the upper numeral is divisible by 3 identifies the meter as compound. The beat in a compound meter is a *dotted note* (because we need a three-part beat division).

Unfortunately, our system of rhythmic notation lacks a numeral to designate a dotted note as the lower numeral of a meter signature.

Simple Meters		*Compound Meters*	
2 = 2	3 = 3	2 = 2	3 = 3
♩ 4	♩ 2	♩· ?	♩· ?

In a compound meter, the lower numeral of the time signature represents not the beat, but the *beat division*. If the beat in a compound meter is a dotted-quarter note, for example, the lower numeral in the meter signature is 8 (one-third of a dotted-quarter note).

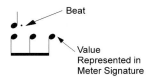

Where the lower numeral in a compound meter signature is 16, the beat is a dotted-eighth note (three times the value of the sixteenth note). A dotted-half note beat is specified by the numeral 4.

Compound Meters

Lower Numeral	Beat
8	𝅘𝅥𝅭·
16	𝅘𝅥𝅮·
4	𝅗𝅥·

Just as we cannot be direct in our designation of the beat in a compound meter, we must also adjust the upper numeral of a compound meter signature as well. The upper numeral represents *three times* the beat-level pulse. If a compound meter is duple, therefore, the upper numeral will be 6; if triple, 9; if quadruple, 12. The following table illustrates meter signatures for the most common simple and compound meters with duple, triple, and quadruple accent patterns.

Simple Meters		Compound Meters	
$\frac{2}{4}$	Duple, 𝅘𝅥 beat	$\frac{6}{8}$	Duple, 𝅘𝅥𝅭 beat
$\frac{3}{2}$	Triple, 𝅗𝅥 beat	$\frac{9}{4}$	Triple, 𝅗𝅥· beat
$\frac{4}{8}$	Quadruple, 𝅘𝅥𝅮 beat	$\frac{12}{16}$	Quadruple, 𝅘𝅥𝅮· beat

Metric Classification.   We classify the meter according to the accent pattern (duple, triple, or whatever) and the manner of beat division (simple or compound).

$\frac{3}{4}$	triple-simple	$\frac{4}{4}$ (**c**)	quadruple-simple
$\frac{9}{8}$	triple-compound	$\frac{2}{2}$ (**¢**)	duple-simple
$\frac{12}{8}$	quadruple-compound	$\frac{6}{8}$	duple-compound

With the exception of music before about 1250 and some innovative works in the twentieth and twenty-first centuries, Western music is metric. The contrast between simple and compound meters is heard in simple folk songs like *Grandfather's Clock* (duple-simple) on the one hand and *Three Blind Mice* (duple-compound) on the other. These same metric plans are mirrored in more lengthy and complex works since the sixteenth century. Likewise, a triple accent pattern (underlying the song *Take Me Out To the Ball Game*) contrasts with the duple and quadruple meters seen in Beethoven's "Ode to Joy" and countless other works.

WORKBOOK/ANTHOLOGY I
V. Beat Division; Meter
Signatures, page 15

ADDITIONAL RHYTHMIC RESOURCES

Meter establishes the framework for the rhythmic parameter of a piece, but composers may employ additional values and figures to create variety. Chief among these are the beat subdivision, the borrowed division, "irregular" note groups, mixed meter, and syncopation.

Beat Subdivision

The beat may be subdivided to produce values even smaller than the division. BEAT SUBDIVISION is the same in both simple and compound meters: The note value designated as the beat division *subdivides* into two parts.

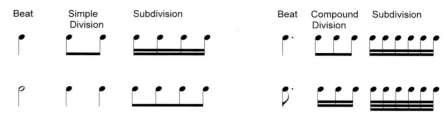

A mixture of beat, divided-beat and subdivided-beat values is shown in the next example. Observe that while several different note values are employed, one rhythmic figure unifies the phrase. Most traditional composers create distinctive rhythmic patterns, then repeat and vary those figures.

CD 1, TRACK 6-1 MIXED VALUES (2 PARTS)
Ludwig van Beethoven, Quartet, Op. 18
Rhythmic Variety

Robert Schumann cast the eight-measure phrase below in duple-compound meter. Unlike Beethoven's economical writing (shown in the previous example), however, Schumann's melody offers a different rhythmic figure in every measure.

TRACK 6-2 MIXED VALUES
Robert Schumann , Trio, Op. 110 (Edited)
Rhythmic Economy

Both the limited Beethoven and the more varied Schumann melodies "work" and show us that problems of proportion and balance can be solved successfully in various ways.

Borrowed Division

While a composer might employ a simple meter *primarily*, within this framework, we may also divide the beat into *three parts* for variety. The BORROWED DIVISION permits a composer to use a three-part beat division in a simple meter or a two-part beat division in compound meters. In effect, the alternate division is "borrowed" from the corresponding simple or compound meter.

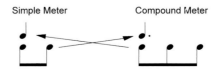

The Triplet and Duplet.   Shown in the next example, the TRIPLET is a special marking that indicates three notes played in the time of two. The three notes of the triplet occur faster than the two notes that constitute the natural (simple) beat division.

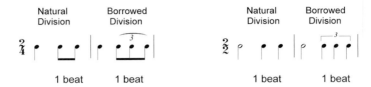

Although less common, the DUPLET provides a similar two-part beat division within a compound meter.

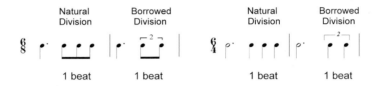

CD 1, TRACK 7-1 BORROWED DIVISION (3 PARTS)
Richard Wagner, *Tannhäuser*
Simple Meter

In the next examples, notice how composers employ the borrowed division to create variety in both simple and compound meters.

TRACK 7-2 BORROWED DIVISION
William Schuman, Symphony for Strings
Compound Meter

TRACK 7-3 BORROWED DIVISION
Carlos Chavez, *Sinfonia India*
Unequal Groupings

Unequal groupings of the borrowed division are common.

Carlos Chavez, *Sinfonia India*

The borrowed division principle can be extended to beat subdivisions (Chopin) and multiple beats (Marx).

Equivalent Meters.   When two meters have the same accent patterns, but contrasting modes of beat division, they are termed EQUIVALENT. The meter $\frac{2}{4}$ has a duple accent pattern and a simple beat division; $\frac{6}{8}$ is the equivalent meter (with a compound beat division and duple accent pattern). Likewise, $\frac{3}{4}$ and $\frac{9}{8}$ are equivalent meters as are $\frac{4}{4}$ and $\frac{12}{8}$. Metric equivalence is important when composers maintain the accent pattern, but shift to the alternate beat division. Employing the equivalent meter within a melody (shown below) varies the rhythmic framework significantly without changing the accent pattern. In addition, composers often follow a movement in one meter with an equivalent meter for the second or subsequent movement.

Carl Pandolfi, Quartet

Two-Against-Three.   The use of the natural and borrowed divisions simultaneously is known as TWO-AGAINST-THREE. Nathaniel Dett (1881–1943) was

a Black Canadian composer who studied, taught, and composed in the United States. In the opening measures of his piano work, *Parade of the Jasmine Banners,* Dett combines the natural three-part division in $\frac{6}{8}$ with the duplet. The two-against-three effect is both intense and distinctive.

└── Two-Against-Three ──┘

While two-against-three is an important structural element in many world musics, its use in traditional Western music is limited to shorter passages as shown in the previous example.

Irregular Groups

Composers sometimes divide the beat into groups of five, seven, ten, and eleven or more equal (or unequal) note values. Such arrangements are termed IRREGULAR GROUPS and are indicated on the score with a bracket or slur. An irregular grouping has the same value as the natural division or subdivision; the numeral indicates that all notes in the group are to be performed on a single beat (as in the next example).

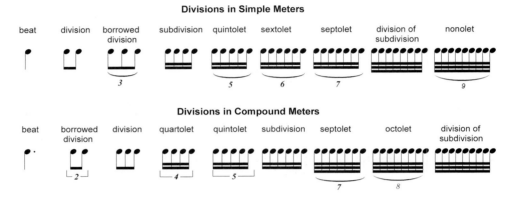

In the next example, the American composer Charles Tomlinson Griffes (1884–1920) chose distinctive pitch patterns and irregular groupings of seven (*septolet*) to the half note to suggest an exotic bird: *The White Peacock*.

Charles Tomlinson Griffes, *The White Peacock*

Other uses of irregular groupings are less structural than Griffes' and a matter of embellishment or notational convenience. Clara Wieck Schumann (1819–1896), in addition to promoting and performing her husband's music, was a gifted composer in her own right. In her song, "*Ich stand in dunklen Träumen*" (*I Stood in Dark Dreams*), a *quintolet* embellishes the pitch D.

TRACK 9-2 RHYTHMIC VARIETY
Clara Schumann, "I Stood in Dark Dreams"
Quintolet

In Claude Debussy's (1862–1918) orchestral work *La Mer*, the division of a quarter note into ten thirty-seconds appears to be motivated more by filling in between starting and ending pitches than any precise metric effect. Observe also that like the *decuplet* in the first measure, the final flourish (measure 3, on page 29) is a *metrically regular* group of ten notes.

Claude Debussy, *La Mer*

Asymmetrical and Mixed Meters

Especially since about 1875, some composers have chosen ASYMMETRICAL METERS—accent plans that include a combination of duple *and* triple patterns. QUINTUPLE METER, for example, has five beats: one triple pattern and one duple pattern. A meter is SEPTUPLE if each measure has seven beats (divided various ways between duple and triple). The first beat is the strongest accent in the measure; secondary accents receive a lesser emphasis in performance.

A main theme from Peter Illyich Tchaikovsky's Symphony No. 6 is in a quintuple meter with quarter-note beat.

CD 1, TRACK 10-1 ASYMMETRICAL METERS (3 PARTS)
Peter Illyich Tchaikovsky, Symphony No. 6 (III) Quintuple Meter

While Tchaikovsky (1840–1893) chose a 2 + 3 quintuple arrangement (a secondary accent on each third beat in the last example), the alternate plan (3 + 2) also constitutes a quintuple meter.

Quintuple Metric Plans

2 + 3 (Tchaikovsky)   3 + 2

Asymmetrical meters have distinctive accent patterns that appealed to composers in the late nineteenth and early twentieth centuries. Sing or play Tchaikovsky's melody in a quadruple meter (with a quarter note in place of the half) and note the dark, labored spirit of the original. Likewise, try Beethoven's "Ode to Joy" (as shown below) with an extra beat in each measure.

TRACK 10-2 ASYMMETRICAL METER
Tchaikovsky Melody in Quadruple Meter
Metric Effects

Tchaikovsky Melody in Quadruple Meter

"Ode to Joy" in Quintuple Meter

TRACK 10-3 ASYMMETRICAL METER
Kenyan Song, *When the Lion Coughs*
Quintuple Meter

Asymmetrical meters are uncommon in Western folk music, but they occur often in other parts of the world. The Kenyan Song *Sukuru Ito* (*When the Lion Coughs*) is in a quintuple meter. The version shown below has an eighth-note beat.

When the lion coughs, the medicine men will dance,
Jungle trees will shake, for they fear his terrible glance.

Mixed Meter.   When meters change frequently—so that the prevailing pattern of accents is disrupted—the meter is said to be MIXED. Mixed meter has been a staple of the twentieth-century vocabulary. The Nationalistic fervor of the late nineteenth century caused some composers like the Hungarian Béla Bartók (1881–1945) to employ authentic folk elements that often lacked symmetry in the Western sense. The Russian folk tune *Song of Volochebniki* exemplifies the type of mixed meter that was influential throughout the twentieth century.

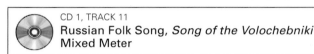

CD 1, TRACK 11
Russian Folk Song, *Song of the Volochebniki*
Mixed Meter

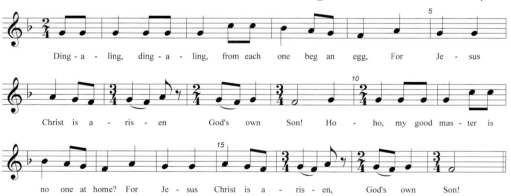

The Russian composer Modest Mussorgsky (1839–1881) often employed mixed meter in his music. The "Promenade" theme from *Pictures at an Exhibition* (1874) alternates $\frac{5}{4}$ and $\frac{6}{4}$ meters and bears a striking resemblance to *Song of the Volochebniki* with its repeated and varied melodic cells.

Modest Mussorgsky, "Promemade" from
Pictures at an Exhibition

Alternate Meter Signatures. Mussorgsky could have employed a number of alternate meter signatures for the passage from *Pictures At An Exhibition.* The eleven-beat phrase could have been notated as $\frac{11}{4}$. With this notation, a composer would probably use a dotted barline to indicate the internal division.

Mussorgsky, Renotated

Composite Meters. Especially in the twentieth century, composers sometimes use two upper numerals in the time signature (representing two different alternating accent patterns) over a single beat unit. Meters such as $\frac{3+2}{4}$ or $\frac{3+4}{8}$ are termed COMPOSITE. Notice that Mussorgsky could have notated the first few measures of *Pictures At An Exhibition* in $\frac{5+6}{4}$—a composite meter.

Mussorgsky, Composite Meter

Musical Accent

As we have discussed, an accent is a musical stress. Metric accent is important in establishing patterns of strong and weak beats that form our expectations for the rhythmic flow. Composers also use other types of accent to complement (or to contradict) these anticipated metric patterns. Principal among these are *dynamic, tonal,* and *agogic* accents.

Dynamic Accent. The symbol > placed above or below a note head directs the performer to sing or play that note relatively louder than others surrounding it. In a Mazurka (Polish dance) by Frédéric Chopin (1810-1849), the composer employs dynamic accents on the third beat of each measure. These accents contradict the natural metric emphasis on the first beat.

CD 1, TRACK 12-1 MUSICAL ACCENT (3 PARTS)
Frédéric Chopin, Mazurka, Op. 6, No. 3
Dynamic Accent

Tonal Accent. A TONAL or TONIC ACCENT occurs when a note is relatively higher or lower than neighboring pitches. In the passage for strings by the

Bohemian composer Antonín Dvořák (1841–1904) quoted below, the pitch D$_5$ has a tonal accent, being higher than other notes in the passage. Traced over several adjacent measures, a series of pitches with tonic accents often lends direction to a melody in either ascending or descending motion.

TRACK 12-2 MUSICAL ACCENT
Antonin Dvořák, Sextet, Op. 48
Tonal Accent

Agogic Accent.   A pitch that has relatively *greater duration* than others surrounding it has an AGOGIC ACCENT. In the opening melody of Debussy's *Rêverie*, agogic accents create longer values that span two measures. Such techniques of metric obscurity are common both to Debussy and to many other late nineteenth-century composers.

TRACK 12-3 MUSICAL ACCENT
Claude Debussy, *Rêverie*
Agogic Accent

Syncopation

If agogic accents are repeated regularly, they may create a special effect called *syncopation.* SYNCOPATION is the intentional disruption of the natural metric flow. As we have discussed, the regular patterns of strong and weak beats establish the metric framework; any deviation is quickly recognized as exceptional. In a quadruple meter, for example, we expect an accent on beat 1 and a lesser accent on beat 3. As seen in the passage below by the French composer César Franck (1822–1890), a *series* of misplaced (agogic) accents contradicts the meter and centers interest on a weak pulse. As in this passage, syncopation often involves one or more long notes between two shorter ones.

CD 1, TRACK 13-1 SYNCOPATION (3 PARTS)
César Franck, Symphony in D Minor
Syncopated Beat

TRACK 13-2 SYNCOPATION
Virgil Thompson, Quartet
Syncopated Beat Division

In the next example, tied notes disrupt the duple-compound meter and create a syncopated effect.

Finally, special rhythmic effects such as syncopation are often important elements in individual and historical styles. A syncopated beat subdivision com-

TRACK 13–3 SYNCOPATION
Scott Joplin, *The Entertainer*
Syncopated Beat Subdivision

bined with frequent tied notes, for example, is characteristic of the music called "ragtime." The Black American composer Scott Joplin (1868–1917) is especially associated with this lively style.

Hemiola. A special type of syncopation called HEMIOLA temporarily converts a duple meter to triple or a triple meter to a duple one. Composers create the special effect of hemiola by changing the natural metric stresses so that the alternate accent pattern emerges. In $\frac{2}{4}$, for example, the first beat of each measure is accented; the second, unaccented. If we employ ties and dynamic accents, $\frac{3}{4}$ emerges briefly.

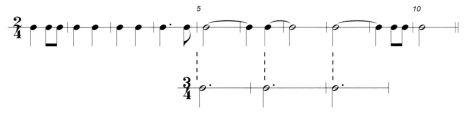

Hemiola is such a striking effect that composers rarely employ it for more than a few measures. In the Sonata for Violin, Johannes Brahms (1833–1897)

CD 1 TRACK 14–1 HEMIOLA (2 PARTS)
Johannes Brahms, Sonata for Violin, Op. 100 (I)
Simple Meter

uses hemiola to effect $\frac{2}{4}$ within the notated triple-simple meter. Notice that Brahms employed a beaming in the violin part that accentuates the hemiola (measures 95–96).

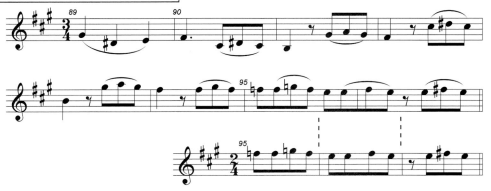

Hemiola patterns also occur in compound meters. After establishing the duple-compound meter over the first eighty measures of the C Major Sonata, Brahms ties the third and fourth eighth notes to create the effect of $\frac{3}{4}$.

HEMIOLA TRACK 14–2
Johannes Brahms, Sonata in C Major, Op. 1 (III)
Compound Meter

While Western rhythm is more limited than the systems employed in Africa and other cultures, special effects such as hemiola, borrowed division, and two-against-three provide limitless variety within our traditional framework. In Volume II of this text, we will explore exceptional uses of traditional rhythmic materials as well as new resources devised by innovative composers in the twentieth and twenty-first centuries.

WORKBOOK/ANTHOLOGY I
Metric and Rhythmic
Resources, page 17

REVIEW AND APPLICATION 1–3

Metric Resources

Essential Terms

agogic accent	composite meter	irregular groups	triplet
asymmetrical meter	duplet	meter signature	tonal accent
beat division	dynamic accent	metric accent	syncopation
beat subdivision	equivalent meter	mixed meter	
borrowed division	hemiola		

1. When complete, the table below will show all relevant information about a given meter signature. Observe the given information, then complete the table.

Meter Signature	Beat	Division	Subdivision	Borrowed Divison	Accent Pattern
a. $\frac{4}{4}$	_____ 1	_____ 2	♬♬	_____ 3	_____ 4
b. $\frac{12}{8}$	_____ 1	_____ 2	_____ 3	♫♩ 2	_____ 4
c. $\frac{2}{2}$	_____ 1	♩ ♩	_____ 2	_____ 3	_____ 4
d. _____ 1	♪.	_____ 2	_____ 3	_____ 4	Triple

2. Provide a meter signature that conforms to the given information.

Meter Signature	Beat	Accent Pattern
a. _____	𝅘𝅥𝅭.	duple
b. _____	♪	quadruple
c. _____	𝅘𝅥	quintuple
d. _____	♪.	triple
e. _____	♪.	duple

3. Provide barlines for the following passages.

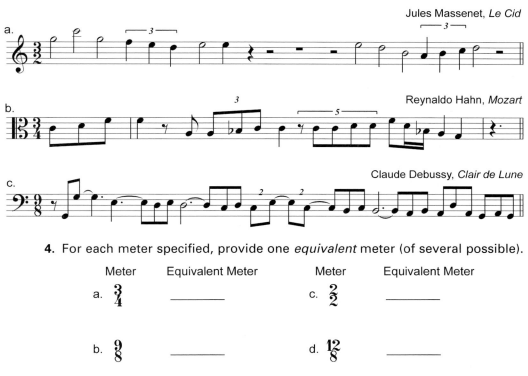

Jules Massenet, *Le Cid*

Reynaldo Hahn, *Mozart*

Claude Debussy, *Clair de Lune*

4. For each meter specified, provide one *equivalent* meter (of several possible).

Meter	Equivalent Meter	Meter	Equivalent Meter
a. $\frac{3}{4}$	_____	c. $\frac{3}{2}$	_____
b. $\frac{9}{8}$	_____	d. $\frac{12}{8}$	_____

5. The passage that follows is in duple meter and includes triplets. In the space provided, rewrite the passage in one of the equivalent meters so that it will be notated differently, but sound exactly the same.

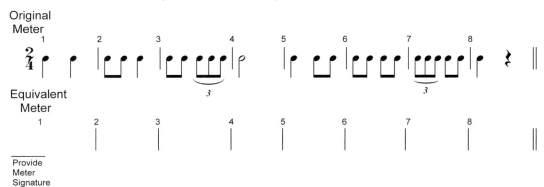

Original Meter

Equivalent Meter

Provide Meter Signature

SELF-TEST 1–3

Time Limit: 5 Minutes

1. Within each unit of beat specified, provide one *rest* (it may have one or more dots) that has the given value. *Scoring: subtract 3 points for each incorrect answer.*

a. ♩. = 1 beat

<u>   </u> 2   <u>   </u> ⅓   <u>   </u> 1   <u>   </u> ⅔   <u>   </u> 4
   1   2   3   4   5

b. ♩. = 1 beat

<u>   </u> ⅓   <u>   </u> 2   <u>   </u> ⅔   <u>   </u> 1   <u>   </u> ⅙
   1   2   3   4   5

2. For each collection of symbols below, provide the total number of beats and fractions of beats (2, $3\frac{1}{3}$, $2\frac{2}{3}$, and so on). *Scoring: Subtract 8 points for each incorrect answer.* Note: no barlines are provided in these examples.

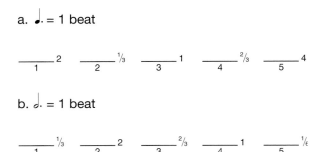

Total Beats _____   Total Beats _____   Total Beats _____
           1   2   3

3. Study the descriptions of musical techniques or effects and match each with a term from the list below. In some cases, two answers are correct (full credit for supplying *either*). *Scoring: Subtract 3 points for each incorrect answer.*

a. Hemiola   e. Syncopation
b. Mixed Meter   f. Two-Against-Three
c. Borrowed Division   g. Agogic Accent
d. Irregular grouping   h. Tonal (Tonic) Accent

(1) _____ A group of five notes played on one beat.

(2) _____ The use of a duplet in a compound meter.

(3) _____ The intentional misplacement of accents.

(4) _____ A pitch that is accented due to relative staff placement.

(5) _____ A syncopation that creates the effect of a triple meter within a notated duple meter (for example).

(6) _____ The simultaneous use of both the borrowed and natural beat divisions.

(7) _____ An accent that is created from relatively greater length.

(8) _____ The use of two or more different meters sequentially.

4. Provide a meter signature that conforms to the given characteristics. *Scoring: Subtract 5 points for each incorrect answer.*

   a. _____ Triple accents, ♪ is the beat *division.*

   b. _____ Quadruple accents, ♩ is the beat.

   c. _____ Duple accents, ♩. is the beat.

   d. _____ Triple accents; ⌐3¬ ♪♪♪ is the *borrowed division.*

5. Provide the appropriate term. *Subtract 2 points for an error.*

   An interruption of the natural metric flow is termed _____.

   Total Possible: 100   Your Score_____

PROJECTS

Analysis

Projects for analysis begin in Chapter 3.

Composition

Percussion Ensemble.   Compose an ensemble for 4-6 percussion instruments of your own invention. Prepare a full score (as shown in the example). The composition should be at least 16 measures of $\frac{4}{4}$ or the equivalent in another meter of your choice (32 measures of $\frac{6}{8}$, for example). Put another way, your composition should be one to two minutes in length. The repetition of measures, phrases, and even complete sections however, is an integral part of music composition and is entirely acceptable for this project.

Design your own instruments of indefinite pitch. For variety, one of your instruments should be capable of two different indefinite pitches (high-low). Find interesting objects that can be beaten, shaken, blown, tapped, whirled, smashed, dropped, broken, turned on/off, slapped, cut, torn, punctured, or pounded. Include instructions on how your instruments should be performed (as in the example).

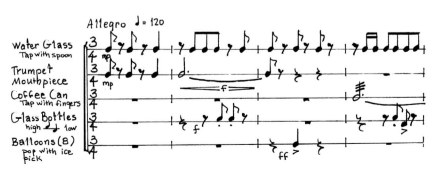

Fill water glass ⅓ full. Tap with spoon. Fill one soda bottle ½ full of water. Leave the other empty. Place bottles close together, then achieve tremolo effect with spoon. Fill balloons, fix to board at lip with thumbtack. Pop with needle or ice pick. Trumpet players buzzes lips on mouthpiece.

For Further Study

Composers and Their Notation. Why would a composer choose one note symbol over another as the unit of beat? Given our familiarity with the quarter-note beat, why would a composer use anything else?

The answer to these questions lies at least partly in the art of composition itself. Composers do not often begin a new work with a blank piece of paper. They have thought long and hard about the music—perhaps for months or years. Most composers develop the ability to hear the sounds in their heads and "see" the notated page as they want it to sound. Accordingly, a composer may just "feel" a melody with a half- or eighth-note beat.

Transcribe Beethoven's "Ode to Joy" melody (page 2) from $\mathbf{c}$ to $\frac{4}{8}$ and $\frac{4}{2}$. Assuming correct notation, the two new versions will sound identical to the original, but how do they look? Write a paragraph or two explaining how the revision in notation might affect your performance. Would you tend to employ a faster beat in $\frac{4}{8}$ and a slower one in $\frac{4}{2}$? Does one notation imply a legato performance?

2

Scales and Intervals

A SCALE (It. *scala,* "ladder") is an abstract inventory of pitches that displays the melodic and harmonic material for a musical composition. Arranged typically from low to high, the first, or TONIC pitch represents the musical center of gravity. While traditional melodies may include scalar (stepwise) patterns, a scale is extracted from a melody after the fact through careful listening and observation of fundamental melodic and harmonic patterns. A scale, then, is just a summary of the main pitches that a composer used to write a piece. But when we are careful to arrange this pitch collection in a proper order, certain important relationships can be visually displayed and symbolized.

The three lines that follow are all based on the same scale (to be discussed). Each line also fits the most broad definition of MELODY—a pattern of pitches and rhythms arranged logically so that the listener perceives organization into longer and more complete sections. All three phrases are distinct and reflect not only the composer's individual style, but that of his or her historical era.

 CD 1, TRACK 15-1 MELODIES (3 PARTS)
W. A. Mozart, *La Clemenza di Tito*

 MELODIES TRACK 15-2
Clara Shumann, "If You Love Because of Beauty" (edited)

MELODIES TRACK 15-3
George Gershwin, *Someone to Watch Over Me*

Although based on the same scale, the three melodies in the last example are different in many ways. Clearly, rhythm and meter vary from one line to another, but other differences are more subtle and require analysis. We study traditional compositions, like those above, both through their scales and also by reckoning the intervals formed between pairs of adjacent pitches. As we examine the intervals present in a melody, we can better understand its uniqueness; in turn, this information enables us to comprehend style and interpretation as they relate to musical performance.

Our studies in Chapter 2 will center not only on the two most important scales employed by traditional composers (major and minor), but also on other melodic resources that have been popular outside the traditional practices. In addition, we will examine both scales and melodies through essential interval types and qualities.

MAJOR SCALES

Throughout our musical history, Western composers have preferred scales with seven different pitches. This preference is clear in the construction of the piano keyboard itself. Beginning on any one white key, for example, an octave series always includes five whole steps and two half steps. With each unique series, however, the two half steps are placed differently.

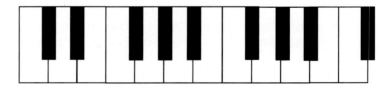

While a MAJOR SCALE may begin on any pitch, it is most simply illustrated beginning on the pitch C. The ascending major scale always follows the interval sequence: Whole, Whole, Half, Whole, Whole, Whole, Half. The pitches of a major scale are traditionally written in ascending or descending order and within a single octave.

Major Scale

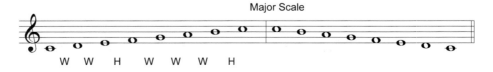

W   W   H   W   W   W   H

Scales are constructed of two superimposed TETRACHORDS (groups of four adjacent pitches). In the major scale, both the upper and the lower tetrachords are W–W–H in construction. The two tetrachords are connected by a whole step.

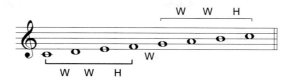

Scale Degrees.   Because the relationships among pitches in a scale are so important in traditional music, each pitch is assigned a number. The tonic is the first scale degree; others reflect their relationships to the tonic in steps above it. The tonic is a priority pitch in a composition; it is the most stable melodic and harmonic goal and it carries greater weight than any other pitch. In fact, the term "tonic" derives from the Greek word for "weight."

scale degree: **1**   **2**   **3**   **4**   **5**   **6**   **7**   **8 (1)**

In writing about music, scale-degree references are so common that we give them a special symbol. The caret (ˆ) placed above a number refers to a particular pitch in a specified scale. In C major, for example, the designations $\hat{3}$ and $\hat{6}$ denote the pitches E and A, respectively. We might discuss the first phrases of *Amazing Grace,* as follows:

- the melody begins on $\hat{5}$
- $\hat{5}$ is also the highest pitch
- $\hat{1}$, $\hat{3}$, and $\hat{5}$ are the most prominent pitches

Hymn, *Amazing Grace*
text by John Newton

A - maz - ing   grace, how   sweet the   sound that   saved a - wretch like   me. _____

Scale-Degree Names.   In addition to scale-degree numbers, musicians use words both to specify particular pitches and to define and emphasize their relationships to the tonic. The DOMINANT pitch ($\hat{5}$) for example, is five steps above the tonic; the SUBDOMINANT ($\hat{4}$), five steps *below* the tonic.

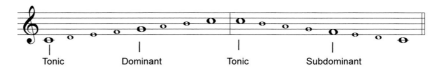

Tonic   Dominant   Tonic   Subdominant

Likewise, the MEDIANT ($\hat{3}$) relationship designates a pitch three steps above the tonic. The SUBMEDIANT ($\hat{6}$) lies three steps below the tonic.

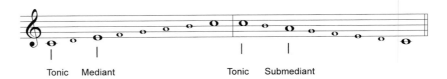

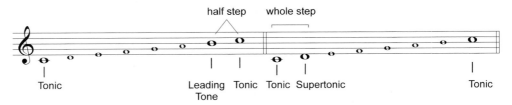

Pitches immediately above and below the tonic are the SUPERTONIC ($\hat{2}$) and the LEADING TONE ($\hat{7}$), respectively. The leading tone is the seventh degree of a major scale. In emphasizing the tonic through ascending half-step motion, the leading tone is one of the most powerful forces in traditional music. On the other hand, the supertonic ($\hat{2}$) often gravitates to tonic, but lacks the strong tendencies associated with $\hat{7}$.

Used in carefully planned melodies, less stable pitches such as $\hat{7}$ and $\hat{4}$ cause us to perceive the tonic as a focal point. Treated fully in later chapters, this effect is termed *tonality* and has been *the* defining element in most Western music since about 1680. While alternate systems of organization have been used in the twentieth and twenty-first centuries, many successful tonal composers today continue to establish and maintain tonal relationships among pitches. As we will discuss throughout many chapters of this text, these relationships, shown complete in the figure below, play a role in governing not only melody, but harmony and form as well.

Diatonic and Chromatic

The term DIATONIC identifies pitches within a given scale system. In the C major scale, for example, the pitches C, D, E, F, G, A, and B are *diatonic*; all other pitches are outside the scale and are *nondiatonic*. Another term commonly used for pitches outside a scale system is CHROMATIC (from *chromos*, Gk. for "color").

Just as we differentiate between diatonic and chromatic pitches, a distinction between two types of half step is crucial. A DIATONIC HALF STEP is one that includes two *different* letter names (such as F♯ and G). If a half step is CHROMATIC, on the other hand, the two pitches have the *same* letter name (G♭ and G♮, for example). In our study of scales, the distinction between types of half step is easily stated: *diatonic* half steps occur in traditional scales; *chromatic* half steps do not. In all diatonic scales (arrangements of the seven white keys and all of their transpositions) each letter name is represented only once.

Diatonic Half Steps   Chromatic Half Steps

To achieve technical facility, performers frequently practice scales mechanically—in ascending and descending patterns. In actual music, however, we must be conscious of the varying roles of scale degrees in creating the effect of tonality as will be explored in subsequent chapters. In the next section, we will survey how successful composers have achieved variety within the tonal system.

WORKBOOK/ANTHOLOGY I
I. Major Scales, page 19

Mode

In the Western system of music, MODE is an effect that "flavors" a melody as either major or minor. The mediant pitch of a scale ($\hat{3}$) is a MODAL DEGREE; its distance from tonic defines the mode. If the mode is MAJOR (as in the C major scale), the mediant pitch lies two whole steps above the tonic. If this same distance is a whole step plus diatonic half step, the mode is MINOR (discussed beginning on page 59).

The French folk song *Frère Jacques* is major in mode. In the second movement of his first symphony, however, the German composer Gustav Mahler wrote a parody of the familiar tune in minor. As notated below with C as the tonic, the version in minor requires E♭ to create the characteristic step-and-a-half interval between $\hat{1}$ and $\hat{3}$.

CD 1, TRACK 16-1 MODE (2 PARTS)
French Folk Song, *Frère Jacques*
Major Mode

TRACK 16-2 MODE
Gustav Mahler, Symphony No. 1 in D Major (edited)
Minor Mode

Tonality, Key, and Mode.   The term KEY refers to the organization of a scale or melody so that pitches gravitate toward a given tonic. If the tonic is C, the *key* is C; in the key of F, F is the tonic. In discussing traditional Western music, TONALITY often reflects the selection of a tonal center—a key—*and also* the choice between the major or the minor mode.[1] We may describe music of the Middle Ages and Renaissance, on the other hand, as being MODAL in that many possibilities were common within any one "key" besides just major and minor.[2] In addition, however, the word "modal" is used in context. As a noun, "modality" usually refers to the choice between major or minor. Used as an adjective, "modal" may connote music outside the tonal system (see page 68).

Transposed Major Scales

TRANSPOSITION is the process of beginning melodic material on a different pitch, but without changing the original pattern of intervals. We can transpose a C major scale to begin on F, for example, simply by duplicating the whole- and half-step pattern learned earlier. The result is an F major scale.

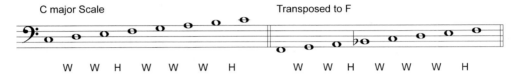

Notice that the F major and C major scales shown in the last example have all pitches but one in common. In the F major scale, the pitch B♭ is diatonic; the basic pitch B (B♮) is chromatic. In C major, on the other hand, B is diatonic and B♭ is chromatic.

Scale-Degree Relationships. When a scale or melody is transposed, the scale-degree relationships are realigned as well. In C major, C is the tonic and F is $\hat{4}$ (the subdominant). If the scale is F major, F is now the tonic and the pitch C is $\hat{5}$ (the dominant). In the key of G major, C is the subdominant, but F♯ is a nondiatonic pitch and has no primary functional role. As we will discuss in later chapters, musical context clarifies the functional roles.

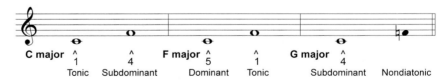

Key Signatures

While a transposition of F major requires only one accidental (B♭), if the tonic of a major scale is F♯, all of the pitches are sharped except B. Likewise, five flats are necessary to create a major scale on D♭.

---

[1] The term "Common-Practice Period" designates music that was written between about 1680 and 1900—the tonal era in Western music.
[2] In the broadest sense, music before about 1450 is characterized as Medieval; the Renaissance era spans the period 1450–1600.

```
W    W   H   W    W    W   H          W    W   H   W    W    W   H
```

Except for C, every major key requires at least one accidental. A KEY SIG-NATURE is a listing of the accidentals necessary to create the effect of a particular mode (major, for example) beginning on a given tonic. Instead of notating the individual sharps or flats (as in the scales above), they are grouped at the beginning of the composition and repeated on every succeeding line.

The sharps or flats specified by a key signature are in force for the entire composition and must be canceled measure by measure (in most cases, using the natural sign) if a basic pitch is needed. We will begin our survey of transposition with a phrase from "Solitude" by Edward "Duke" Ellington (1899-1974) who achieved international popularity as a "big band" composer in the era preceding World War II.

Duke Ellington, Solitude
Words by Eddie de Lange and Irving Mills

In my sol - i - tude _____ you haunt me, with rev - er - ies _____ of days gone by. _____

In the next example, Ellington's phrase is transposed to F♯ major. In the first line, accidentals are used; in the second, a key signature shows the clear advantages of that notation.

F♯ Major with Accidentals

F♯ Major with Key Signature

Order of Flats and Sharps. The sharps or flats used in a key signature do not appear in a random order. The sequence of flats spells out the word "BEAD" plus the letters G, C, and F. The first flat is always B♭; if there is a sixth flat, it will be C♭.

Order of Flats

1	2	3	4	5	6	7
B♭	E♭	A♭	D♭	G♭	C♭	F♭

Flats alternate higher and lower positions on the staff.

The order of sharps is the reverse of that for flats: F♯ is the first; B♯ is the seventh and last.

Order of Sharps

1	2	3	4	5	6	7
F♯	C♯	G♯	D♯	A♯	E♯	B♯

On the staff, sharps alternate higher and lower positions as flats do. In the treble clef, we position A♯ below D♯, however, to avoid a ledger line in the higher position. For consistency, the same arrangement is followed in the bass clef.

Key Signatures on Alto and Tenor Staves.   When key signatures appear on alto, tenor, or any other clef, place accidentals amid the lines and spaces, alternating higher and lower positions. Do not place an accidental on a ledger line.

Because of enharmonic duplications, we employ fifteen, rather than twelve different major keys.

Major Keys

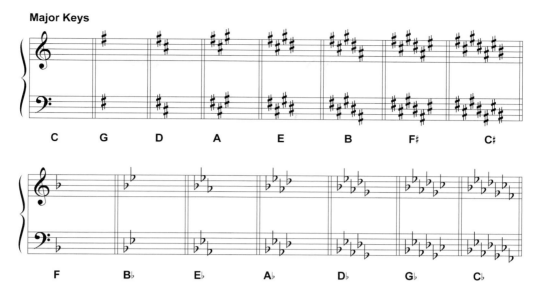

Just as you once memorized the multiplication tables, the names of the states, and other important facts, you should consider learning the major key signatures through memorization. Consider using flash cards, associating the order of keys with the circle of fifths (see page 64), or any other method that is convenient. Instant recall of scales and other basic materials will be greatly facilitated if you have memorized the key signatures.

WORKBOOK/ANTHOLOGY I
II. Major Keys, page 23

REVIEW AND APPLICATION 2–1

Major Scales and Keys

Essential Terms

chromatic	key signature	mode	tetrachord
diatonic	melody	scale	tonality
key	modal degree	scale degree	tonic

1. Identify the intervals below as diatonic half step (**D**), chromatic half step (**C**), whole step (**W**), or none of these (**N**).

2. Given the major key, write the pitch requested. Add any necessary accidental.

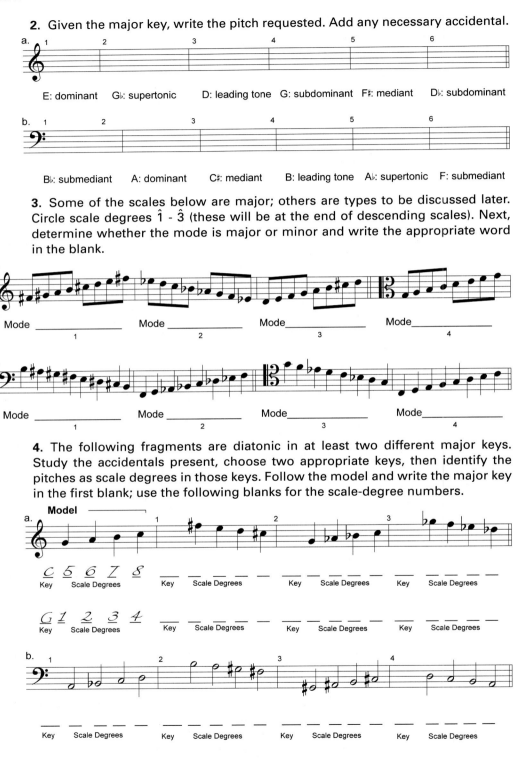

a.

1   2   3   4   5   6

E: dominant   G♭: supertonic   D: leading tone   G: subdominant   F♯: mediant   D♭: subdominant

b.

1   2   3   4   5   6

B♭: submediant   A: dominant   C♯: mediant   B: leading tone   A♭: supertonic   F: submediant

3. Some of the scales below are major; others are types to be discussed later. Circle scale degrees 1̂ - 3̂ (these will be at the end of descending scales). Next, determine whether the mode is major or minor and write the appropriate word in the blank.

a.

Mode _____   Mode _____   Mode _____   Mode _____
   1   2   3   4

b.

Mode _____   Mode _____   Mode _____   Mode _____
   1   2   3   4

4. The following fragments are diatonic in at least two different major keys. Study the accidentals present, choose two appropriate keys, then identify the pitches as scale degrees in those keys. Follow the model and write the major key in the first blank; use the following blanks for the scale-degree numbers.

a.   **Model**

1   2   3

C *5* *6* *7* *8* ___ ___ ___ ___   ___ ___ ___ ___   ___ ___ ___ ___
Key Scale Degrees   Key Scale Degrees   Key Scale Degrees   Key Scale Degrees

G *1* *2* *3* *4* ___ ___ ___ ___   ___ ___ ___ ___   ___ ___ ___ ___
Key Scale Degrees   Key Scale Degrees   Key Scale Degrees   Key Scale Degrees

b.   1   2   3   4

___ ___ ___ ___   ___ ___ ___ ___   ___ ___ ___ ___   ___ ___ ___ ___
Key Scale Degrees   Key Scale Degrees   Key Scale Degrees   Key Scale Degrees

___ ___ ___ ___   ___ ___ ___ ___   ___ ___ ___ ___   ___ ___ ___ ___
Key Scale Degrees   Key Scale Degrees   Key Scale Degrees   Key Scale Degrees

SELF-TEST 2–1

Time Limit: 7 Minutes

1. Write chromatic half steps above the given pitches. Scoring: *Subtract 6 points for each error.*

2. Identify major key signatures shown. *Subtract 6 points for each error.*

3. Write the pitches specified. Include any necessary accidental. *Subtract 6 points for each error.*

| D major | E♭ major | F♯ major | B major | G♭ major |
| Subdominant | Supertonic | Mediant | Submediant | Dominant |

4. Write ascending major scales on the given tonics. *Subtract 11 points for an incorrect scale.*

Total Possible: 100   Your Score _____

INTERVALS

An INTERVAL is the distance (or difference) between two pitches. While interval construction is important in its own right, the classification of intervals is central to understanding more complex musical materials such as triads and seventh chords. We might study and classify all of the intervals in a melody or harmonic series, for example, just a few of them, or we might search for the occurrence of one particular interval category. In all cases, the process of interval construction or analysis centers on recognizing *size*. Likewise, when we construct intervals as basic musical materials, they are categorized by *type* in a general way and more exactly by calculating the *quality*.

Interval Type

INTERVAL TYPE is a measurement in diatonic steps (lines and spaces between two adjacent pitches). Determine size by simply beginning with the lower pitch and counting upward.

Notice that while even-numbered interval types (second, fourth, and the like) always involve a line and a space, odd-numbered types span lines *or* spaces.

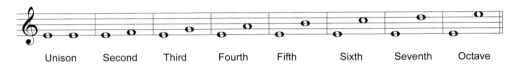

In the last example, pitches occur consecutively (MELODIC INTERVALS); in the line below, the same pitches sound simultaneously as harmonic intervals.

The analysis of interval content often reveals valuable information about the structure of a composition. Although Beethoven's "Ode to Joy" serves as the basis of an entire movement, the first two phrases include only two different interval types: unisons and seconds.

Beethoven, *Ode to Joy*

D major

Return to page 39-40 at the beginning of this chapter and compare the Mozart, Schumann, and Gershwin melodies in terms of their interval content. In the Mozart melody, thirds and fourths are common as are seconds and unisons. Clara Schumann's song is, like Beethoven's "Ode to Joy," limited almost exclusively to seconds and unisons (the fourths in measures 2–3 are notable exceptions). Finally, Gershwin's tune also moves basically stepwise, although we find a third in the first measure and leaps of a fifth and an octave toward the end of the phrase.

A first step in musical analysis may be the accumulation of data. The table below, comparing Beethoven's "Ode to Joy" and the three compositions on page 39-40 by interval content, is an example of data that might be used in forming conclusions.

Melody	Total Intervals	Unison	Second	Third	Fourth	Fifth	Sixth	Seventh	Octave
Beethoven	29	9	20	0	0	0	0	0	0
Mozart	23	5	9	5	3	0	0	0	1
Schumann	20	10	7	0	3	0	0	0	0
Gershwin	24	3	17	2	0	1	0	0	1

Both interpreting data and devising appropriate analytical methods will be discussed in detail in later chapters. For now, we may conclude that traditional Western melody centers on stepwise movement, but that in many compositions, frequent or strategically placed leaps provide variety and balance.

Compound Intervals. If an interval is larger than an octave, it is termed COMPOUND. The two pitches that comprise a ninth, tenth, eleventh, and so on, however, are more commonly analyzed simply as compound second, compound third, or compound fourth, respectively. Notice in the next line that two octaves comprise fifteen—not sixteen steps.

| Ninth | Tenth | Eleventh | Fifteenth |
| (Compound Second) | (Compound Third) | (Compound Fourth) | (Two Octaves) |

Intervals are central to understanding scales, melodies, and harmonic materials. The recognition of interval type centers on counting lines and spaces. In the next section, we will discuss interval *quality*—a more precise measurement that explains how intervals of the same type may produce quite different sounds.

Interval Quality

Earlier, you learned about the half step and the whole step. These intervals, though different in size, are both categorized as seconds. Other seconds have three and even four half steps between pitches. The melodic intervals below, for example, are all seconds, yet each is different in size and each has a distinctive sound.

Type:	Second	Second	Second	Second
Half Steps:	1	2	3	4

For some purposes, interval type alone adequately describes a pair of pitches; for others, QUALITY is a more precise measurement that reflects interval size in half steps. We classify interval quality in two generic categories: *Perfect* and *Major/Minor.* Several different qualities are possible within either the perfect or the major/minor category. Octaves, unisons, fourths, and fifths fall into the perfect category; seconds, thirds, sixths, and sevenths may be major or minor.

Perfect Intervals.   While interval quality can be determined by calculating the number of half steps between pitches, we obtain the same result more quickly by comparing the upper note to the major scale represented by the lower. When the upper pitch is diatonic in the key represented by the lower, unisons, fourths, fifths, and octaves are *perfect* in quality. We often employ abbreviations for intervals ("P5" rather than "perfect fifth," for example) when both type and quality are identified.

| P1 | P4 | P5 | P8 | P1 | P4 | P5 | P8 |

If the upper pitch of an interval is *not* diatonic (that is, outside the major scale represented by the lower pitch), the interval is *not* perfect.[3] Intervals that are one half step smaller than perfect are DIMINISHED ("d") in quality; if one half step larger, the quality is AUGMENTED ("A").

Study the following table that shows various qualities of unison, fourth, fifth, and octave by half-step content.[4] Notice that while two intervals may contain the same number of half steps and, accordingly, have the same sound (a d5 and an A4, for example), the notation and identification must reflect the appropriate interval *type*.

Intervals in Perfect Category					
Interval	**Quality**	**Half-Step Content**	**Interval**	**Quality**	**Half-Step Content**
Unison	Perfect	0	Fifth	Perfect	7
	Augmented	1		Diminished	6
Fourth	Perfect	5		Augmented	8
	Diminished	4	Octave	Perfect	12
	Augmented	6		Diminished	11
				Augmented	13

Major/Minor Intervals.   When the upper note of a second, third, sixth, or seventh corresponds to the scale or key represented by the lower pitch, that interval is MAJOR ("M") in quality.

| M2 | M3 | M6 | M7 | M2 | M3 | M6 | M7 |

---

[3]Intervals are compared to major scales for convenience only. There is nothing "normal" or "preferable" about major scales.

[4]By definition, an octave has twelve half steps between pitches just as a unison is the sounding of two identical pitches. In music outside the tonal system, however, (as in some twentieth-century styles), we may encounter unusual intervals such as a "diminished octave" or "augmented unison."

A second, third, sixth, or seventh that is one half step more narrow than major ("m") in quality; if *two* half steps smaller, the quality is diminished. Likewise, if an interval is larger than major by one half step, the quality is augmented. Seconds, thirds, sixths, and sevenths can *never* be correctly described as perfect in quality (and perfect intervals can never be classified as major or minor).

Doubly-Augmented and Doubly-Diminished Intervals.   Regardless of type, if an interval is a half step larger than augmented or a half step smaller than diminished, the quality is DOUBLY-AUGMENTED ("AA") or DOUBLY-DIMINISHED ("dd"), respectively. Doubly augmented and diminished intervals do not occur diatonically in traditional scales.

Compound intervals are analyzed and constructed as corresponding simple intervals plus an octave.

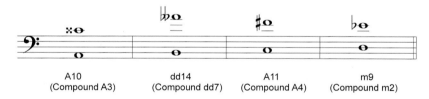

Discerning quality is a precise measurement in half steps that accounts for differences between intervals of the same type. In most traditional melodies, major and minor seconds predominate. We should note, however, that major and minor sixths and sevenths, as well as some augmented and diminished intervals are available in the diatonic inventory for dramatic and other purposes. Still other intervals (an augmented sixth or a doubly-diminished seventh, for example) occur primarily as embellishing figures.

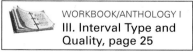

WORKBOOK/ANTHOLOGY I
III. Interval Type and Quality, page 25

Constructing Intervals Below a Given Pitch

The BASS (the lowest sounding pitch) is so important in traditional Western music that we typically rely on the lower of the two pitches in identifying quality. In constructing triads and chords, however, we may need to construct intervals of a specific type and quality *below* a given pitch. In this case, interval type may be determined in the usual way (simply by counting lines and spaces). Quality, however, is reckoned through one (or both) of two methods: *lower-pitch* adjustment and *interval inversion.*

Lower-Pitch Adjustment.   Previously, we have relied upon the lower of two pitches as a standard in determining interval quality. In constructing an interval below a given pitch, however, we do not know the scale or key of the lower pitch. Instead, you can use a three-step method of adjustment to realize the appropriate lower pitch.

1. Calculate interval type in the usual way.
2. Identify the resulting quality.
3. Adjust the *lower* pitch as necessary.

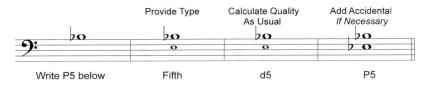

Be aware that in adjusting the lower pitch of an interval, a flat *increases* interval size (as above) while a sharp *narrows* the interval by one half step.

Interval Inversion.   An interval is INVERTED when the lower pitch is raised an octave to become the upper pitch; likewise, an upper pitch may be lowered an octave to become the lower pitch.

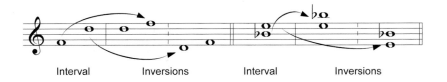

When intervals are inverted, type and quality change in a way that allows us to write pitches below one given while retaining the familiar scale or key reference. Interval types are complementary when inverted: seconds invert to sevenths; sevenths, to seconds; fifths invert to fourths; fourths, to fifths; and so on. The interval and its inversion always add up to nine.

Interval	Inversion	Interval	Inversion
Second	Seventh	Seventh	Second
Third	Sixth	Sixth	Third
Fourth	Fifth	Fifth	Fourth

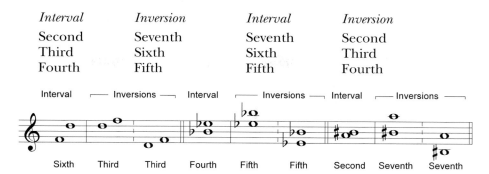

Interval qualities that are major or minor, or that are diminished or augmented are likewise complementary. Inverted, major intervals become minor; diminished intervals change to augmented; augmented becomes diminished. If an interval is perfect in quality, however, the inversion remains perfect.

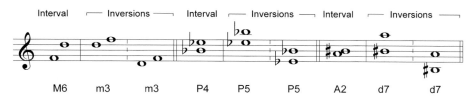

As shown in the next table, except for perfect qualities (that remain perfect when inverted), an inverted interval assumes the quality that is complementary to the original.

Quality	Inversion	Quality	Inversion
Perfect	Perfect		
Major	Minor	Minor	Major
Diminished	Augmented	Augmented	Diminished
Doubly-Diminished	Doubly-Augmented	Doubly-Augmented	Doubly-Diminished

Use interval inversion to write a pitch below one given. First, construct the inversion *above* the given pitch (in the usual way); next, lower the derived pitch an octave. No further calculations are necessary.

Consonance and Dissonance

Early Western music theorists were captivated by the stable (consonant) and active (dissonant) properties of intervals. Even before the eleventh century, textbooks provided clear rules for the intervals that should be used on strong and weak beats, respectively. These early concepts are obsolete in today's music, but we continue to classify intervals just as Medieval theorists did.

Intervals are traditionally classified in one of three categories: *perfect consonance, imperfect consonance,* or *dissonance.* PERFECT CONSONANCES are the perfect octave, fifth, fourth, and unison respectively. These intervals were used at the most important metric points in early music. According to early theorists, intervals represent "perfection" when the relationship between the two pitches is simple. If two strings are sounded (by bowing or plucking, for example) and one string is exactly half the length of the other, the interval will be a perfect octave; the ratio of string lengths is 2:1. Where strings are exactly the same length, the interval is a perfect unison and the ratio is 1:1. Likewise, the perfect fifth occurs when sounds (frequencies) are in the ratio 3:2; the perfect fourth results from a 4:3 ratio.

Perfect Consonances

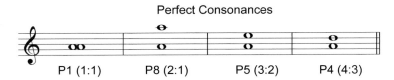

P1 (1:1)   P8 (2:1)   P5 (3:2)   P4 (4:3)

While perfect consonances were employed on strong beats, IMPERFECT CONSONANCES (major and minor thirds and major and minor sixths) have less simple ratios between pitches and were employed freely on weaker beats.

Imperfect Consonances

m3   M3   m6   M6

As we will discuss further in Chapter 6, DISSONANCES such as major and minor seconds and major and minor sevenths are reserved for weak metric positions and carefully resolved to a consonance.

Dissonances

M2   m2   M7   m7

A second traditional category of dissonance, the *tritone,* is treated with utmost care—even today.

The Tritone.   The augmented fourth and its inversion, the diminished fifth, are so important in the history of Western music that they are known by a special designation—TRITONE. The interval name is derived from the three whole steps between the lower and upper pitches in the augmented fourth. While early theorists used a different term to refer to the diminished fifth, today we know both intervals as "tritone." We will discuss the special nature of the tritone in several different chapters.

Interval patterns are extracted through analysis to form scales. In turn, scales enable us to identify the most important pitches in a composition and the

WORKBOOK/ANTHOLOGY I
IV. Interval Inversion,
page 27

ways in which other pitches gravitate toward them. In the next section, we will discuss how traditional composers varied melodic choices by employing the *minor* scale.

REVIEW AND APPLICATION 2–2

Intervals

Essential Terms

compound interval	interval inversion	interval type	tritone
harmonic interval	interval quality	melodic interval	

1. Identify the intervals below by type and quality. Begin with the lower pitch—regardless of order.

a.

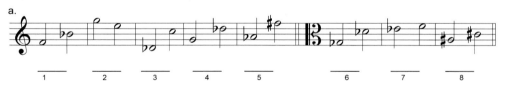

2. Identify the intervals in the passages below by type and quality. Work left to right from each pitch to the next.

Paul Hindemith, Sonata No. 2

a.

Franz Schubert, Symphony No. 4

b.

3. Write intervals *below* the given pitch as designated.

m7   P4   M3   P11   A6   m3

4. Write the specified interval above the given pitch.

a.

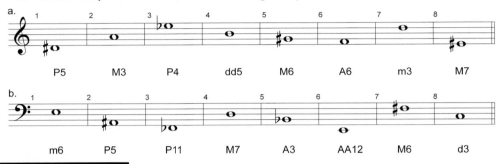

P5   M3   P4   dd5   M6   A6   m3   M7

b.

P11 below...

m6   P5   P11   M7   A3   AA12   M6   d3

SELF-TEST 2–2

Time Limit: 7 Minutes

1. Write the specified interval above or below the given pitch. *Subtract 6 points for each incorrect response.*

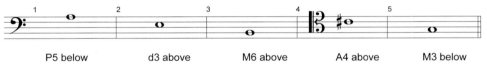

P5 below   d3 above   M6 above   A4 above   M3 below

2. Identify the intervals below by type and quality. *Subtract 6 points for each error.*

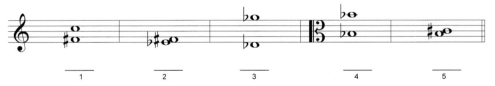

___1___   ___2___   ___3___   ___4___   ___5___

3. Provide the inversion for the given intervals. Identify all four intervals by type and quality. *Subtract 6 points for any incorrect interval label; subtract 8 points if either of the inverted intervals is incorrectly notated.*

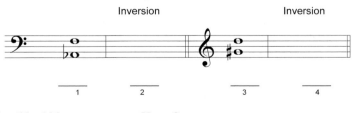

Inversion   Inversion

___1___   ___2___   ___3___   ___4___

Total Possible: 100   Your Score _____

MINOR SCALES

For a period of over two hundred years (ca. 1650–1900), Western composers centered their music on a single pitch and chose either the major or the minor mode. This practice is still followed in most of today's popular and commercial music. We have studied the major scale as easily represented by a series of basic pitches beginning on C. The series that represents MINOR is a "white-key" scale beginning on the pitch A. Like major scales, those that are minor may be transposed to begin on any pitch. Ascending, the NATURAL (or PURE) MINOR SCALE has the sequence Whole, Half, Whole, Whole, Half, Whole, Whole.[5]

CD 1, TRACK 17-1 MINOR SCALES
(3 PARTS)
Natural Minor Scale

W   H   W   W   H   W   W

Transposition. Transpose natural minor scales to begin on any pitch by employing the interval sequence W H W W H W W. Notice in the next example that as in major, chromatic half steps are not used in writing natural minor scales.

A Natural Minor   C Natural Minor   F# Natural Minor

We often speak about minor scales as if they were somehow in opposition to major. In fact, however, as we will discuss in this chapter, the two scales are more alike than they are different. The positions of the half steps, however, are dissimilar. In minor, half steps occur between $\hat{2}$ and $\hat{3}$ and between $\hat{5}$ and $\hat{6}$. Compare this to major scales where $\hat{3}$–$\hat{4}$ and $\hat{7}$–$\hat{8}$ are half steps.

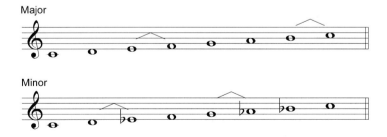

Major

Minor

Beginning on the same tonic, notice that $\hat{2}$, $\hat{4}$, and $\hat{5}$ are identical in major and minor. With the tonic itself, four of the seven diatonic pitches are the same in major and minor.

---

[5]The term "natural" distinguishes the white-key series beginning on the pitch A from other varieties of minor to be discussed later in this chapter.

Major

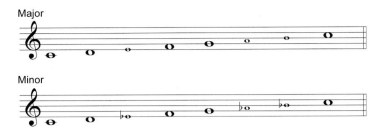

Minor

Finally, observe the two tetrachords, joined by a whole step, that form the natural minor scale (W–H–W and H–W–W). Comparing major and minor, only $\hat{3}$ is different in the lower tetrachord. In the upper tetrachord, however, there are significant differences that will be discussed later in this chapter.

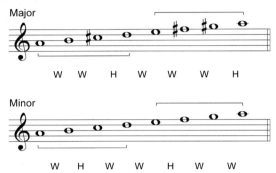

Minor Key Signatures.   We can create natural minor scales through duplicating the whole- and half-step series, but this method is burdensome. As is the case with major scales and keys, key signatures in minor list all of the sharps or flats necessary to produce the appropriate pattern. Key signatures for the three scales shown on page 59 are given below. Consult page 64 of this chapter for a complete listing of minor key signatures.

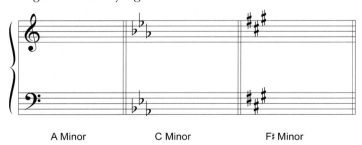

A Minor   C Minor   F♯ Minor

Variations in the Minor Scale

Among the differences between the major and the natural minor scale is the interval formed between ↑$\hat{7}$ and $\hat{8}$. In major, ↑$\hat{7}$ is a leading tone and lies a half step below the tonic. In natural minor, however, the seventh scale degree is a SUBTONIC (↓$\hat{7}$)—a pitch a whole step below the tonic.[6]

---

[6]When we discuss scale degrees and use the caret references ($\hat{3}$, $\hat{5}$, and so on), the symbol $\hat{7}$ designates the *leading tone*. We can use an arrow to connote the subtonic: ↓$\hat{7}$. When both leading tone and subtonic pitches are discussed in the same sentence or paragraph in this text, an arrow may be added to the leading-tone symbol for clarity (↑$\hat{7}$). In other texts, a flat sign may accompany $\hat{7}$ to indicate the subtonic (♭$\hat{7}$).

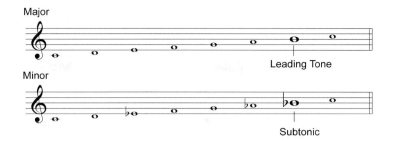

Major

Leading Tone

Minor

Subtonic

Lacking the ascending half-step motion that we associate with a leading tone, the listener's attention is not centered as forcefully with a subtonic. Accordingly, traditional composers altered the minor scale to strengthen its tonal implications. These alterations resulted in two new scale forms that we know today as *harmonic* and *melodic* minor, respectively. Although performers learn and practice the three forms of minor as if they were alternate materials, natural, harmonic, and melodic minor represent only three common choices within the minor mode. Composers regularly use different forms of minor within the same composition, the same phrase, and even within the same measure.

Harmonic Minor.   If the absence of a leading tone in minor was a problem for common-practice composers, it was one easily solved: they simply raised ↓$\hat{7}$ (subtonic) a half step in passages where $\hat{8}$ was the melodic goal. The new scale, with raised ↑$\hat{7}$, is known as HARMONIC MINOR.

TRACK 17-2 MINOR SCALES
Natural and Harmonic Minor

Natural Minor   Harmonic Minor

Harmonic minor is written the same ascending and descending. To construct a harmonic minor scale, employ the key signature for natural minor (or the appropriate accidentals), then raise ↓$\hat{7}$ a half step to create a leading tone.

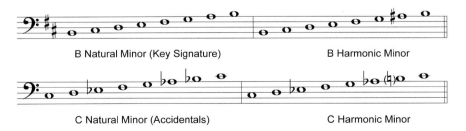

B Natural Minor (Key Signature)   B Harmonic Minor

C Natural Minor (Accidentals)   C Harmonic Minor

Melodic Minor.   While adding the leading tone (↑$\hat{7}$) has the desired effect of reinforcing the tonal center in minor, the interval between $\hat{6}$ and ↑$\hat{7}$, an AUGMENTED SECOND, was viewed by traditional composers as awkward and stylistically unacceptable.[7] To avoid the augmented second, a third form of

---

[7]In caret references to the sixth scale degree in this text, the symbol $\hat{6}$ refers to the pitch specified by the key signature. If $\hat{6}$ is raised (as in melodic minor), the arrow is added (↑$\hat{6}$) to indicate a chromatic alteration.

minor emerged for passages in which ↑6̂ and ↑7̂ appeared consecutively. In MELODIC MINOR, both ↑6̂ and ↑7̂ are raised ascending—a choice that offers the strength of the leading tone, but without the difficult augmented second.

Because ↑6̂ is needed only in ascending passages in minor (where 8̂ is the melodic goal and is most likely preceded by ↑7̂), we write descending melodic minor with (↓)6̂ and ↓7̂ to emphasize the gravitational pull toward 5̂.

Johann Sebastian Bach (1685–1750) was a German composer whose music, while not widely known during his lifetime, underwent a revival during the mid-nineteenth century. Today, Bach is considered both a paragon of traditional Western music and a model of the Baroque style. The following melody from his Cantata No. 78 begins in the key of G and in the minor mode. The first occurrence of 6̂ (E♭) conforms to the key signature since 7̂ is not an adjacent pitch. In the second measure, however, where 6̂, 7̂, and 8̂ all occur consecutively, Bach used both E♮ and F♯ (the melodic form). As the line continues through the fifth measure, ↑6̂ and 7̂ are employed consistently.

Observe that Bach's melody is in neither natural nor melodic minor; it is simply *minor*. The composer chooses 6̂ and ↑6̂, respectively in different measures according to the immediate melodic goals.

Relationships in Major and Minor

A series of pitches like C D E F G A and B is merely theoretical material until one pitch is established—through its context with other surrounding notes—as the tonic. When C is the tonic, we hear major; if we employ the same pitches but instead cause them to gravitate toward A, the effect of minor results. Throughout this text, we will study the myriad of techniques used by traditional composers to create a feeling of key. For now, we will explore two important relationships between major and minor: *Relative* and *Parallel*.

The Relative Relationship.   When major and minor keys have the same pitches (key signature), the relationship between them is termed RELATIVE. Because they share a common pitch inventory, C major and A minor are complementary. C major is the relative major of A minor; A minor is the relative minor of C major.

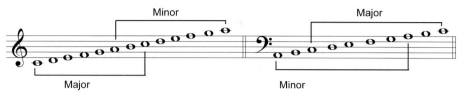

The Relative Relationship

The same relative relationship exists between each comparable pair of major and minor keys. The tonic of the relative minor is found as $\hat{6}$ in the major scale. As shown in the previous example, the pitch A is $\hat{6}$ in C major; it is also the tonic of the relative minor. Two additional major/relative minor key pairs are shown in the next example. The relative minor of G major is E minor; F minor and A♭ major share a relative relationship.

The simplest approach to identifying relative major and minor keys relies on the minor third between their tonics. The tonic of a relative minor is found a minor third *below* the tonic of the relative major key.

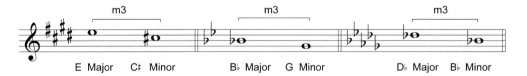

We can reverse the process to find the relative major of a given minor. The tonic of a relative major key lies a minor third *above* the tonic of the minor.

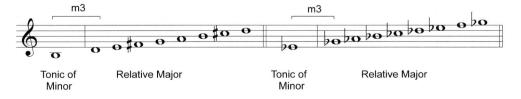

The following example shows all fifteen major keys together with their relative minors.

Major and Relative Minor Keys

| C Major | G Major | D Major | A Major | E Major | B Major | F♯ Major | C♯ Major |
| A Minor | E Minor | B Minor | F♯ Minor | C♯ Minor | G♯ Minor | D♯ Minor | A♯ Minor |

| F Major | B♭ Major | E♭ Major | A♭ Major | D♭ Major | G♭ Major | C♭ Major |
| D Minor | G Minor | C Minor | F Minor | B♭ Minor | E♭ Minor | A♭ Minor |

The Circle of Fifths.   A useful characteristic of the Western tonal system is the fact that keys with successive numbers of flats or sharps are separated by the interval of a perfect fifth. This progressive arrangement of keys is called the CIRCLE OF FIFTHS. In the following diagram, notice that a progression around the circle in a clockwise direction produces keys with increasing numbers of sharps. If we consider counter-clockwise movement around the circle, on the other hand, each new key is a perfect fifth *lower* than the one preceding it and has one more flat in its signature.

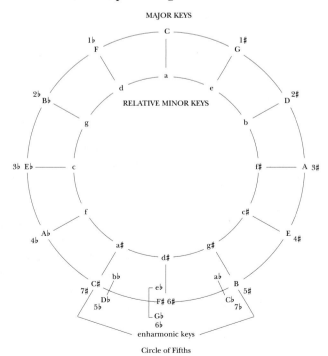

Circle of Fifths

The circle of fifths is helpful not only in remembering major and minor keys, but in predicting key relationships within the course of a traditional composition.

The Parallel Relationship.   The second important relationship between major and minor keys concerns those with the same tonic pitch—termed PARALLEL. As with the relative relationship, parallel majors and minors are complementary: C major is the parallel major of C minor; C minor is the parallel minor of C major. While parallel major and minor keys have the same tonic, the key signatures are different.

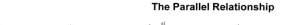

The Parallel Relationship

C Major   C Minor   E Major   E Minor   B♭ Major   B♭ Minor

As you may have noticed from the last example, adding three flats to the signature of the major key produces the signature of the parallel minor. Likewise, the signature of a parallel major can be determined by adding three sharps to the key signature of the minor.

Modal Degrees.   When we compare major and parallel harmonic minor scales as used by traditional composers (that is, with a leading tone in ascending passages), the most important pitches—$\hat{1}$, $\hat{5}$, and $\uparrow\hat{7}$ are the same. Likewise, $\hat{2}$ and $\hat{4}$ are identical.

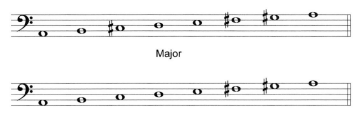

Major

Ascending Minor

Differences between major and parallel minor keys center on $\hat{3}$ (a minor third above tonic in minor) and $\hat{6}$ (a minor sixth above tonic in minor). These pitches are termed MODAL DEGREES. In addition, of course, natural minor has a subtonic rather than a leading tone.

Modal Shift.   Notice that because parallel majors and minors share a tonic pitch, changing from one to the other constitutes a MODAL SHIFT—not a change of key. In F minor for example, the key is F and the mode, minor. In F major, the key is still F; we have only shifted to the major mode. Likewise, modal shifts often occur from major to minor.

The next passage is from a piano sonata by Carl Phillipp Emanuel Bach (1714–1788), son of the great composer, J. S. Bach. Beginning in F major, we feel no tonal disorientation when the mode changes to minor in measures 4–6. After four measures in F minor, the major mode returns.

CD 1, TRACK 19
C.P.E. Bach, Sonata No. 1
Modal Shift

F Major   F Minor

F Minor   F Major

The minor mode constitutes a significant resource in traditional tonal music. Where eighteenth-century composers equated minor with sadness or melancholy (a tradition that has continued in modern commercial music), masters from Bach to Bernstein have employed the minor mode to structure works of great joy.

WORKBOOK/ANTHOLOGY I
V. Minor Scales and Keys, page 29

REVIEW AND APPLICATION 2–3 ━━━━━━━━━━━━━━━━━

Minor Scales and Keys

Essential Terms

circle of fifths	melodic minor	modal shift	subtonic
harmonic minor	modal degrees	parallel minor	
natural minor	minor	relative minor	

1. Provide an appropriate key signature, then write the ascending scale designated. If necessary, add one or more accidentals.

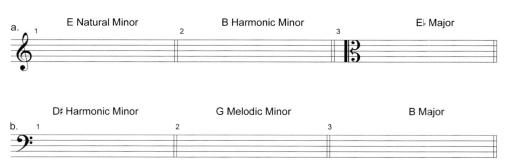

a.   E Natural Minor   B Harmonic Minor   E♭ Major

b.   D♯ Harmonic Minor   G Melodic Minor   B Major

2. Write ascending scales as you did for the last exercise. In these frames, however, the given pitch is *not* the tonic, but a specified scale degree. First, determine the tonic and the key signature, then complete the minor scale to the right of the given pitch. One or more accidentals may be necessary.

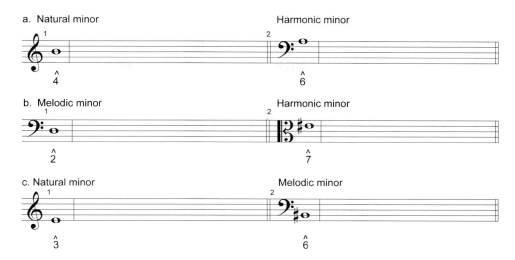

a. Natural minor   Harmonic minor

b. Melodic minor   Harmonic minor

c. Natural minor   Melodic minor

3. Where appropriate, determine one major and one minor key for each of the fragments below (more than one major and more than one minor key is possible in some cases). Note, however, that some fragments may be taken from an altered minor scale and *only one key is appropriate*. In this event, identify only the minor key (leave the major-key blank empty).

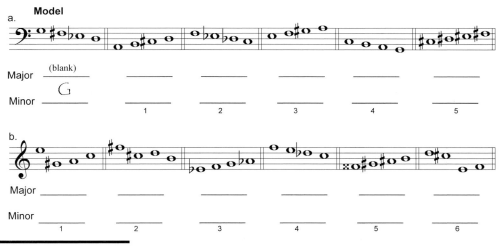

a. **Model**

Major ___(blank)___ _____ _____ _____ _____ _____

Minor ___G___ _____ _____ _____ _____ _____

                   1   2   3   4   5

b.

Major _____ _____ _____ _____ _____ _____

Minor _____ _____ _____ _____ _____ _____

           1   2   3   4   5   6

SELF-TEST 2–3

Time Limit: 7 Minutes

1. Write the following scales. Use a key signature and add accidentals as necessary. *Subtract 14 points for each wrong answer.*

    a. the relative natural minor of G major ascending.

    b. the parallel major of B♭minor descending.

c. the relative harmonic minor of B major ascending.

d. the parallel melodic minor of F major ascending.

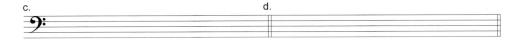

2. The scales below are major or one of the three forms of minor. Choose an appropriate letter from the list and enter on the blank. *Subtract 11 points for incorrect answers.*

a. major

b. natural minor

c. harmonic minor

d. melodic minor

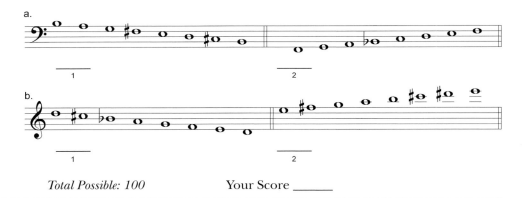

Total Possible: 100   Your Score _____

OTHER MODES AND SCALES

In addition to major and minor, several other scalar resources have been popular with Western composers—especially before 1650 and after about 1850. These scales include not only older forms such as the *pentatonic scale* and the *Church Modes,* but newer resources like the *whole-tone* scale.

The Church Modes

The predecessors of our major and minor scales are octave-wide series of whole and half steps called the CHURCH MODES. As they were employed originally, the Church Modes are quite complex with precise registers, characteristic melodic formulas, and a unique terminology. For our purposes, these modes represent white-note series on D, E, F, and G, respectively. Each mode has either a major or a minor effect (as determined by the distance between Î and 3̂).

The four Church Modes, named for ancient Grecian tribes, are DORIAN, PHRYGIAN, LYDIAN, and MIXOLYDIAN.[8] These scales begin on D, E, F, and G, respectively. Notice in the next example that Dorian and Phrygian are minor modes; Lydian and Mixolydian are major.[9]

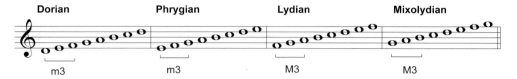

Each mode has a distinctive whole- and half-step pattern.

Name	Mode	Characteristic
Dorian	Minor	Natural minor scale with raised $\hat{6}$
Phrygian	Minor	Natural minor scale with lowered $\hat{2}$
Lydian	Major	Major scale with raised $\hat{4}$
Mixolydian	Major	Major scale with lowered $\hat{7}$

The characteristics in the last table are helpful in constructing modes from a key signature. In making modal adjustments, remember that an added sharp may cancel a flat; an added flat may nullify a sharp.

Mode	Key Signature
Dorian	Natural minor with *added sharp*
Phrygian	Natural minor with *added flat*
Lydian	Major with *added sharp*
Mixolydian	Major with *added flat*

Ionian and Aeolian Modes. While the four Church Modes just discussed formed the core of Medieval and Renaissance melodic materials, the modes that we know today as major (IONIAN) and minor (AEOLIAN) were added to the system in the sixteenth century. By 1700, Ionian and Aeolian had become the only two modes chosen by traditional composers.

---

[8]In the Medieval modal system, there were two modes named Dorian, two named Phrygian, and so on. The differences between the authentic modes (as described in this chapter) and their plagal counterparts are outside the scope of this text.

[9]The white-note series built on B, the *Locrian mode*, was unacceptable to composers due to the diminished fifth between $\hat{1}$ and $\hat{5}$. See page 71 for the use of the Locrian mode in the late nineteenth century.

Examples of Aeolian mode abound in late nineteenth-century literature because those patterns are common in Western folk songs. In addition, Western composers like Claude Debussy, Modest Mussorgsky, and the Frenchman Maurice Ravel (1875–1937) rediscovered other modes such as Lydian, Mixolydian, and Phrygian. Ravel, for example, based the second theme of his string quartet (1902–1903) on the Phrygian mode transposed to A.

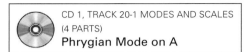

CD 1, TRACK 20-1 MODES AND SCALES (4 PARTS)
Phrygian Mode on A

TRACK 20-2 MODES AND SCALES
Maurice Ravel, Quartet (I)
Phrygian Melody

Ravel explores the tritone (augmented fourth) between $\hat{2}$ and $\hat{5}$ in the first phrase, then emphasizes the tonic pitch in the second.

Pentatonic Scale

One of the world's oldest and most common scales is the PENTATONIC, so-called because it has five discrete pitches. Theoretically, the pentatonic scale is a projection of perfect fifths, with those fifths arranged from low to high within an octave span.

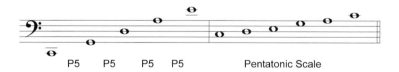

Notice that the pentatonic is a GAPPED SCALE that omits some lines or spaces on the staff. In addition, while we traditionally write the pentatonic as a major scale with $\hat{4}$ and $\hat{7}$ omitted (as above), various arrangements are common both in Western and world literature. Like other scales, the pentatonic may be transposed to begin on any pitch (on G in the next example).

TRACK 20-3 MODES AND SCALES
Pentatonic Scale on G

Pentatonic on G

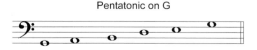

TRACK 20-4 MODES AND SCALES
English Folk Song, *The Green Bushes*
Pentatonic Melody

Like the folk songs of many world cultures, the English tune *The Green Bushes* is pentatonic.

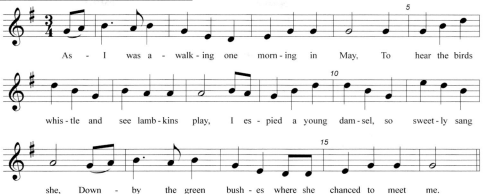

As - I was a - walk-ing one morn-ing in May, To hear the birds

whis-tle and see lamb-kins play, I es-pied a young dam-sel, so sweet-ly sang

she, Down - by the green bush-es where she chanced to meet me.

Other Scales

Alongside the church modes and the pentatonic scale that achieved popularity with innovative composers after about 1875, other scales were devised. Some of these, like the Locrian mode and the whole-tone scale, lack the functional tendencies associated with major and minor.

Locrian Mode. In addition to the white-note series already discussed, the one beginning on B, called the LOCRIAN MODE (SCALE), was only a theoretical possibility for traditional composers. The Locrian has half steps between $\hat{1}$ and $\hat{2}$ and between $\hat{4}$ and $\hat{5}$. The "flavor" is minor, but the interval between the tonic and dominant is a diminished fifth.

Locrian Mode   Locrian on D

While traditionalists were troubled by the diminished fifth between $\hat{1}$ and $\hat{5}$, later composers relished this unique effect. Especially in the early part of the twentieth century, several composers, including the American Carl Ruggles (1876–1971), were attracted to the melodic and harmonic possibilities.

The Locrian mode is a natural minor scale with lowered $\hat{2}$ and lowered $\hat{5}$; construct the scale from a key signature by adding two flats to the inventory of the corresponding natural minor.

B Minor   B Locrian   D Minor   D Locrian

Whole-Tone Scale. As composers began to tire of traditional tonal materials in the late nineteenth century, several entirely new scales were invented to produce innovative melodic patterns. Claude Debussy is associated with a series consisting of six whole steps called the WHOLE-TONE SCALE. The seventh pitch of a whole-tone scale duplicates the first. As shown in the next example, composers typically avoid double sharps in writing whole-tone scales; since the scale is not tonal, enharmonic equivalents may be employed as needed. All of the following notations, for example, are correct for a whole-tone scale on C.

TRACK 21-1 MODES AND SCALES, CONTINUED
(3 PARTS)
Whole-Tone Scale on C

Whole Tone Scales on C

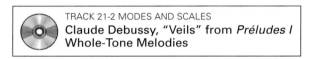

TRACK 21-2 MODES AND SCALES
Claude Debussy, "Veils" from *Préludes I*
Whole-Tone Melodies

Both major themes of Debussy's *Voiles* ("Veils") from the first book of *Préludes* are whole tone. The first centers on C; the second, on A♭.

First Theme

Second Theme

Chromatic Scale. A pattern that inventories all twelve half steps in the octave is the CHROMATIC SCALE. Traditionally, we write the scale ascending with sharps and descending with flats.

Chromatic Scale

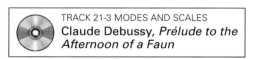

TRACK 21-3 MODES AND SCALES
Claude Debussy, *Prélude to the Afternoon of a Faun*

One of Debussy's best known works is *Prélude a l'Après-Midi d'un Faune* ("Prelude to the Afternoon of a Faun"). The opening flute solo illustrates the use of a chromatic scale fragment.

Traditional composers like Bach, Beethoven, and Brahms were largely content with the major or minor scale as a melodic resource. As the Romantic and nationalist movements moved composers toward folk materials in the late nine-teenth century, however, the Aeolian and other modes became increasingly pop-ular in concert works. In addition, composers like Debussy, Mussorgsky, Franz Liszt (1811–1886), and the American Charles Ives (1875–1954) experimented with new scales such as the pentatonic, whole tone, and devised "synthetic" series as well.

WORKBOOK/ANTHOLOGY I
VI. Modes and Other Scales, page 33

REVIEW AND APPLICATION 2–4

Modes and Scales

Essential Terms

Aeolian mode	Dorian mode	Locrian mode	Phrygian mode
chromatic scale	gapped scale	Lydian mode	pentatonic scale
Church Modes	Ionian mode	Mixolydian mode	whole-tone scale

1. Write the ascending scales or modes using the given pitch in the octave spec-ified as the first scale degree. Use the octave sign at your discretion.

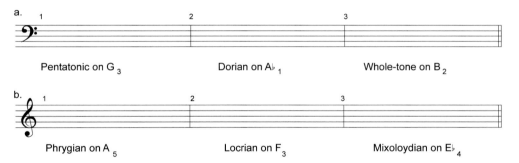

2. Complete the scales and modes below using the given pitch as a reference. These frames include all scales studied in this chapter: major, all forms of minor, modes, and other scales. Write the complete ascending scale to the right of the given pitch.

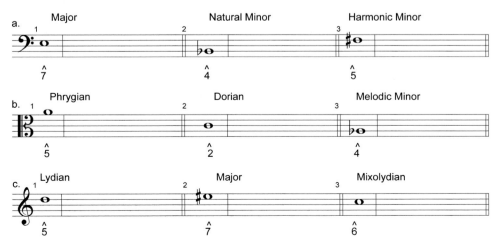

3. The scales and modes below, both ascending and descending, represent all of those covered in the present chapter. Identify each by type (major, harmonic minor, Dorian, and so on).

a.

_____ 1   _____ 2   _____ 3

b.

_____ 1   _____ 2   _____ 3

c.

_____ 1   _____ 2   _____ 3

SELF-TEST 2–4

Time Limit: 7 Minutes

1. For each characteristic given, write the name of the scale or mode that is closely associated with the specified trait. *Subtract 4 points for each incorrect response.*

_____ a. lowered $\hat{2}$.

_____ b. diminished fifth between $\hat{1}$ and $\hat{5}$.

_____ c. minor scale with raised $\hat{6}$.

_____ d. different in ascending and descending forms.

_____ e. raised $\hat{4}$.

_____ f. enharmonic spellings acceptable.

_____ g. gapped scale.

_____ h. major scale with lowered $\hat{7}$.

2. Supply key signatures for the scales or modes designated. *Deduct 8 points for incorrect answers.*

E Dorian   B Minor   G♭ Lydian   F Phrygian   E♭ Major

3. Write whole-tone and pentatonic scales beginning on the tonics provided. Subtract 14 points for an incorrect scale.

Whole Tone   Pentatonic

Total Possible: 100   Your Score _____

PROJECTS

Analysis

Projects for analysis begin in Chapter 3.

Composition

Modal Melodies.   The melody below is from Mozart's Sonata, K. 332 and is diatonic in F major.

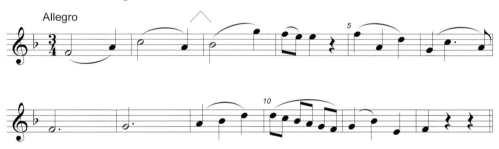

Discover how the melody can be transformed through changes in key and meter signatures. Equivalent metric plans will have no effect on the way the passage sounds, of course, but will result in a different appearance. Changing the key signature, on the other hand, will alter the melody profoundly.

Mark half steps in the original melody with the caret symbol ˆ (the first of these, in measure 2-3 is marked). On a separate sheet, transcribe and renotate the melody four times, but vary the meter and key signatures as follows:

	Meter Signature	*Key Signature*
First Copy	$\frac{3}{8}$	Three Flats
Second Copy	$\frac{3}{2}$	Two Flats
Third Copy	$\frac{3}{4}$	No Sharps/Flats
Fourth Copy	$\frac{3}{16}$	Two Flats

Identify half steps in the four copies as you did in the original. The key is still F in each version, but you will notice that half steps fall in different places. Between which scale degrees do half steps fall in the variations? What is the mode in each case? Do the new versions have a leading tone or a subtonic? Play or sing the original and the four versions and note the musical effect.

For Further Study

Accidentals and Key Signatures.   Looking at a modern piano keyboard or at the complex key mechanism of a clarinet or oboe, we might assume that Western music has always made use of all twelve chromatic pitches. At one time, however, the only pitches used were those that we refer to today as "the white notes" or "basic pitches." Accidentals came into use sometime around the tenth century to provide a perfect fourth above the pitch F; practically, this was a means of avoiding the tritone. In the passage below, for example, the diatonic pitch B would have been sung B♭—whether notated that way or not.

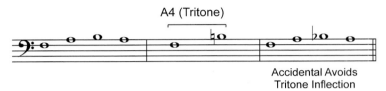

A4 (Tritone)

Accidental Avoids
Tritone Inflection

Investigate aspects of accidentals and key signatures through an outline for class discussion, notes for your own use, or as a more formal paper as directed by your instructor. Your sources might be a music dictionary, encyclopedia, or the Internet.

- How did our signs for accidentals originate? What is a "hard" B, for example? a "soft" B?

- About when were key signatures first used? What is a *partial key signature* (partial signature)? In which era were these incomplete signatures often found in Western music?

- Key names are not written the same way in other languages as they are in English. How are the keys we refer to as "F Major" and "F Minor" written in German, French, Italian, and Spanish?

- In German, how is the pitch B♮ represented with a letter? Which letter stands for the pitch B♭? Using the German system, we can notate a composition using the letters B-A-C-H. How is this done? Name at least one composer who wrote a composition on the name "Bach."

CHAPTER 3

Diatonic Triads and Chords

Beethoven wrote "Ode to Joy" nearly three hundred years after the principles of traditional Western music were first formulated in the late Renaissance. By Beethoven's time, composers and audiences alike were in general agreement about how music ought to sound. Indeed, the system of tonal music was so well understood and ingrained that a major challenge facing nineteenth-century composers was simply finding a way not to sound like every other composer.

Central to Western music are stereotypical vertical patterns called HARMONY. Melody and harmony are inseparable in our system; melody arises from harmonic principles; harmony supports and clarifies melody. In other words, melody actually generates the harmonic parameter as individual lines converge to form chords.

Outside the West, an independent harmony is uncommon. In Africa and Indonesia, for example, a thickening of texture is achieved not through harmonic principles, but by melodic and rhythmic lines of various complexities that are layered, one upon the other. In other cultures, a melody, learned from memory, is often accompanied by imitating that melody simultaneously a few steps above or below the original pitches. Although Western harmony evolved from just such an *improvised* practice, our preference for exactness eventually cultivated a balance between limited musical choices on the one hand, and the ability to notate our music with a modicum of accuracy on the other.

Two of the most basic harmonic sonorities of traditional Western music occur throughout Beethoven's "Ode to Joy." As shown in the next example, the simple melody is supported by an equally basic harmonic parameter that alternates between the effects of stability and momentum.

CD 1, TRACK 22
Ludwig van Beethoven, "Ode to Joy"
Harmony

Our studies in Chapter 3 center on traditional harmonic materials called *triads* or *chords*. While in later chapters we will explore the use of these materials in series or *progressions* that define tonality, we will first consider triads and chords as fundamental musical elements. This examination includes not only constructing and recognizing triads, but also learning the terminology and the analytical symbols that allow us to understand and replicate the tonal process.

TRIADS

The most basic element of traditional harmony is a group of three pitches called a TRIAD. Historically, Western composers have built triads from superimposed (consecutive) intervals of the same type. If the intervals between pitches are seconds, for example, the triad is SECUNDAL; fourths and fifths predominate in QUARTAL and QUINTAL triads, respectively.

Since the fifteenth century, traditional Western composers based their music on triads built of superimposed thirds. These TERTIAN TRIADS constitute the most important element of traditional tonal harmony. In their most basic form, tertian triads occur over consecutive lines or spaces. Except as noted, the term "triad" in this text will designate a tertian triad.

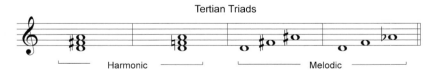

When a triad is arranged over consecutive thirds, the lowest pitch is called the ROOT. The pitch directly above the root is the THIRD; the FIFTH is the highest pitch of the triad. The terms "third" and "fifth" refer to the intervals these pitches form over the root.

Triads in Root Position.   We make an important distinction between the root of a triad and the *bass*. The BASS is simply the lowest pitch heard in a given triad. The *root* of a triad, on the other hand, is the lowest sounding pitch when the notes are arranged over consecutive lines and spaces. This arrangement is called ROOT POSITION. When a triad is in root position (as in the last example), the root and the bass are the same. Triads are identified according to the root. If the root is C, for example, the pitches constitute a *C triad*; in an E♭ triad, the root is E♭.

Triad Quality

Just as we measure intervals in several different ways (type, quality, simple/compound structure, and so on), so are triads identified by quality as well as root name. Four triad qualities are common: *major, minor, augmented,* and *diminished.*

Major and Minor Triads.   A root-position triad is MAJOR if the interval between the root and the third is a major third and if the fifth above the root is perfect. When these conditions are met, the upper third (between third and fifth) is minor.

Major Triad

MINOR TRIADS in root position have a minor third between the root and the third and a perfect fifth above the root. The upper third is major.

Minor Triad

Major and minor triads have in common a perfect fifth between root and fifth. As discussed below, other qualities of triad *lack* the perfect fifth.

Augmented and Diminished Triads.   A root-position triad is AUGMENTED in quality if the interval between the root and the third is a major third and if the fifth is augmented. The upper third will be major.

Augmented Triad

DIMINISHED triads in root position have thirds that are minor and a fifth that is diminished.

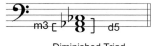

Diminished Triad

In the next example, root-position triads appear in all four traditional qualities with E and B♭ as roots. Notice that major and minor triads are named

for the qualities of their thirds; the classifications "diminished" and "augmented" refer to the quality of the fifth.

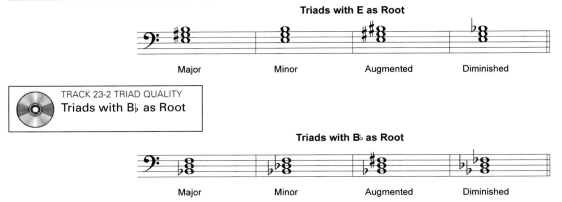

Inverted Triads

As we discussed, the root and the bass of a root-position triad are the same. If a triad is *not* in root position, it is INVERTED. In inverted triads, the root appears *above* the bass. Notice, however, that where intervals typically change in quality when inverted, triads do not. Inverted, a major triad remains major in quality.

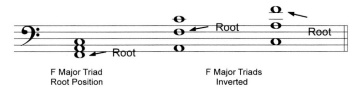

As long as all three pitches of a triad are present (and no new ones are added), the position of the root is not a factor in identifying the quality of inverted triads.

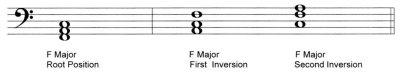

First and Second Inversions.   While the two inverted triads in the last example have the same root (F), their bass pitches are different. If the third is in the bass, the triad is in FIRST INVERSION. In SECOND INVERSION, the fifth is the lowest pitch.

We identify triads as being in root position, in first inversion, or in second inversion. This is because the interval content—and therefore the triad's relative stability—is different depending upon the BASS POSITION (the relative arrangement of the root and the bass). As we discussed earlier, root-position triads have a third and a fifth above the bass. With inverted triads, however, the perfect fifth is not present. In first inversion, the third is in the bass; the root and the fifth, above it. The fifth is the bass in second inversion.

CD 1, TRACK 24 BASS POSITION
Triads with F as Root

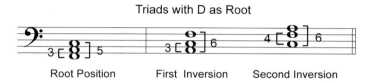

Triads with D as Root

Root Position   First Inversion   Second Inversion

Triads and Chords.   We often use the terms "triad" and "chord" more or less interchangeably. Like a triad, a CHORD is a group of pitches. While the term "chord" may designate various sonorities, however, "triad" is a special type of chord with pitches occurring over consecutive thirds. In another sense, "triad" might refer to three pitches comprising raw material; when those same three pitches appear in a musical work, we may properly employ the word "chord." A triad, in other words, may often be extracted from a chord as shown in the lowest line of the next example. All of the extracted triads are in root position.

Ludwig van Beethoven, Sonata in C Major, Op. 53

Chords

Triads
Extracted

Minor   Minor   Major   Major   Minor

The major and minor triads in the last example represent the raw material from which Beethoven created a composition of lasting value nearly two hundred years ago. In later chapters of this text, we will discuss tonal function, counterpoint, and voice leading—elements of the traditional Western style that must be balanced in a successful composition. For the present, we will continue our study of triads by learning to construct them in various qualities and bass positions.

WORKBOOK/ANTHOLOGY I
Root-Position and Inverted Triads, page 35

Triad Construction and Identification

We can determine triad quality by sizing up the component intervals, but this method is slow and tedious. Instead, simply compare the upper pitches of a triad to the key represented by the root. If the third and fifth are diatonic in the major key of the root, *a triad is major in quality*. Likewise, if either or both of the upper pitches are *not* diatonic in the major key of the root, the triad *cannot* be major.

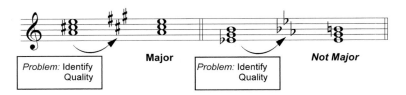

In this latter case, since there are only three other possibilities in traditional music, determine quality by comparing the given triad with one on the same root that is major.[1]

- a major triad becomes minor if the third is lowered a half step.
- a major triad becomes augmented if the fifth is raised a half step.
- a major triad becomes diminished if the third and the fifth are lowered a half step.

Each of the triads below has B♭ as its root. Accidentals (outside the key of B♭ major) create minor, augmented, and diminished qualities, respectively.

Triad Identification.   Since triads are identified from the root, rearrange an inverted triad to appear in root position before determining its quality. At first, you may want to do this on paper; the eventual goal, however, is to "juggle" the pitches mentally until you can visualize them in consecutive thirds. Where consecutive thirds appear, the triad is in root position and the root and the bass are the same. If an interval *other* than a third occurs between adjacent pitches, the triad is *inverted* and the root is above the bass.

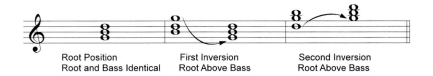

As illustrated in the last example, the first step in triad identification is determining the root. With the triad in root position, compare the third and the fifth to the major key signature represented by the root. Finally, document any nondiatonic pitches and assess their effect on triad quality.

---

[1]As with the construction and identification of intervals based on a major key signature, we should mention that building triads based from the key signature of the root is simply convenient. There is nothing inherently preferable about any quality of triad.

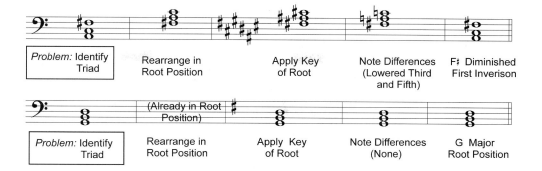

Problem: Identify Triad	Rearrange in Root Position	Apply Key of Root	Note Differences (Lowered Third and Fifth)	F♯ Diminished First Inverison

| Problem: Identify Triad | Rearrange in Root Position (Already in Root Position) | Apply Key of Root | Note Differences (None) | G Major Root Position |

Triad Construction

Triad construction typically begins with the root—including any accidental associated with it. Next, supply basic pitches above the root as the third and the fifth. Complete a major triad by altering these basic pitches as necessary to conform to the key signature represented by the root.

Problem: Construct Major Triad	Third and Fifth	Apply Key Signature	Add Accidentals (If Necessary)

For a minor, augmented, or diminished triad, begin by constructing a major triad as described in the last example, then adjust the third, the fifth, or the third *and* the fifth as necessary.

Problem: Construct Diminished Triad	Add Third and Fifth	Apply Key Signature	Major Triad	Lower Third Lower Fifth

Minor Key Signatures.   Use a shortcut to construct minor and diminished triads. Simply apply the *minor* key signature of the root and the triad will be minor in quality. Lower the fifth a half step to create a triad that is diminished.

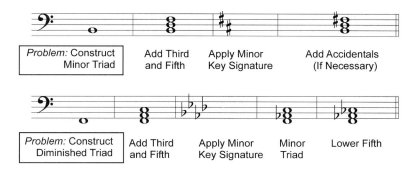

Problem: Construct Minor Triad	Add Third and Fifth	Apply Minor Key Signature	Add Accidentals (If Necessary)

Problem: Construct Diminished Triad	Add Third and Fifth	Apply Minor Key Signature	Minor Triad	Lower Fifth

If the desired triad is inverted, first build (or imagine) one in root position, then arrange the pitches with the third or the fifth in the bass as necessary.

| *Problem:* Construct Minor Triad in Second Inversion | Begin with Root Position | Fifth in Bass | *Problem:* Construct Major Triad in First Inversion | Begin with Root Position | Third in Bass |

Constructing Triads from Given Third or Fifth.   In analysis, we often visualize or construct a triad of a specified quality above a given *bass* (which may or may not be the root). In the latter case, we must first determine the root before building the complete triad. Construct root-position or inverted triads from a given bass note by adding one step to precede the process learned earlier:

- If the given pitch is the third, the root lies either a *major third* (major and augmented triads) or a *minor third* (minor and diminished triads) below the bass.

or

- If the given pitch is the fifth, the root will be a *perfect fifth* lower for major and minor triads, an *augmented fifth* lower for augmented triads, and a *diminished fifth* lower if the triad is diminished.

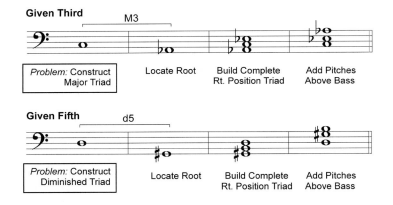

Given Third   M3

| *Problem:* Construct Major Triad | Locate Root | Build Complete Rt. Position Triad | Add Pitches Above Bass |

Given Fifth   d5

| *Problem:* Construct Diminished Triad | Locate Root | Build Complete Rt. Position Triad | Add Pitches Above Bass |

Triads are the basic building blocks of Western harmony. When we view them as theoretical materials, root-position triads fall into two categories: those with a perfect fifth (major and minor), and those that lack the perfect (diminished and augmented). In inverted triads, the position of the root above the bass lessens the effect of stability.

WORKBOOK/ANTHOLOGY I
II. Constructing and Identifying Triads, page 37

REVIEW AND APPLICATION 3–1 ——————————————————

Triads

Essential Terms

bass	first inversion	root position	triad
bass position	harmony	second inversion	triad quality
chord	root	tertian triad	

1. Construct root-position triads of the specified quality. The given pitch is the root.

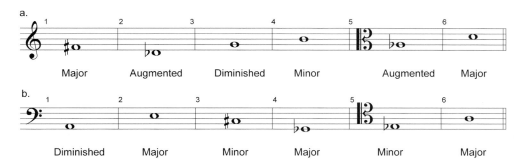

a.

1	2	3	4	5	6
Major	Augmented	Diminished	Minor	Augmented	Major

b.

1	2	3	4	5	6
Diminished	Major	Minor	Major	Minor	Major

2. Identify the following triads by root name, quality, and bass position (write "Root," "First," or "Second" in the last case).

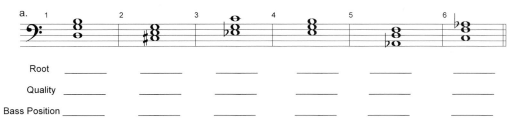

a.

Root _____   _____   _____   _____   _____   _____

Quality _____   _____   _____   _____   _____   _____

Bass Position _____   _____   _____   _____   _____   _____

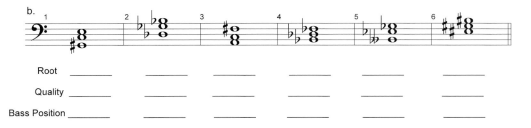

b.

Root _____   _____   _____   _____   _____   _____

Quality _____   _____   _____   _____   _____   _____

Bass Position _____   _____   _____   _____   _____   _____

3. Given the third or the fifth of a triad *as the bass,* add the other pitches above the bass as specified.

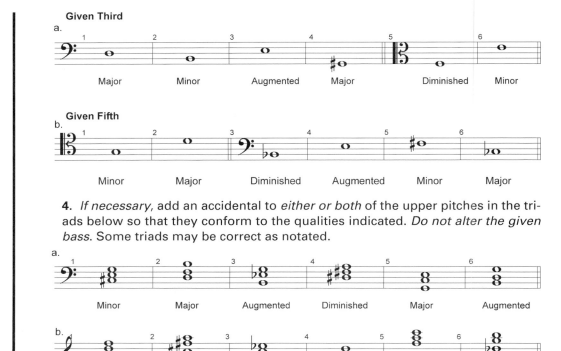

Given Third

a.

Major   Minor   Augmented   Major   Diminished   Minor

Given Fifth

b.

Minor   Major   Diminished   Augmented   Minor   Major

4. *If necessary*, add an accidental to *either or both* of the upper pitches in the triads below so that they conform to the qualities indicated. *Do not alter the given bass*. Some triads may be correct as notated.

a.

Minor   Major   Augmented   Diminished   Major   Augmented

b.

Minor   Major   Diminished   Augmented   Minor   Major

SELF-TEST 3–1

Time Limit: 5 Minutes

1. Identify the triads below by root name, quality, and bass position. *Scoring: Subtract 4 points for each error.*

Root   _____   _____   _____   _____

Quality   _____   _____   _____   _____

Bass Position   _____   _____   _____   _____

2. Construct root-position triads of the qualities specified. Please note whether the given pitch is the root, the third, or the fifth. *Scoring: Deduct 13 points for any incorrectly notated triad.*

Given Root   Given Third   Given Root   Given Fifth

Major   Minor   Augmented   Diminished

Total Possible: 100   Your Score _____

DIATONIC TRIADS IN MAJOR

Our studies in later chapters will center on how triads are used in progressions that establish a tonal center. For now, we will survey the inventory of DIATONIC TRIADS—those built upon successive degrees of a major or minor scale and conforming to the appropriate key signature. In Chapter 2, you learned the names for diatonic pitches. These names also designate the *triads* built upon each scale degree.

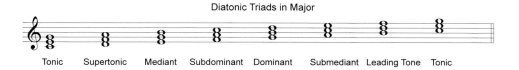

In major keys, diatonic triads occur in predictable qualities. Three are major, three are minor, and the leading-tone triad is diminished.

Grouped according to quality in the next example, the tonic, subdominant, and dominant are major; the supertonic, mediant, and submediant are minor; and the leading tone is the singular diminished triad.

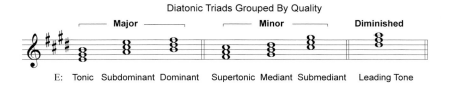

Designating Key in Analysis.   In the last example, notice that the key—E major—is designated with an uppercase letter "E" and a colon (**E:**). Triad names and other analytical data are understood to occur in this key. Likewise, the designation *B♭: supertonic* specifies the pitches C-E♭-G. In minor, lowercase letters indicate the key (see page 95).

Constructing Diatonic Triads

In major keys, DIATONIC TRIADS conform to the key signature (E major in the last example); triad qualities are inflexible. The dominant triad, for instance, will always be built upon $\hat{5}$ and will always be major in quality. Similarly, the submediant, with $\hat{6}$ as the root, is minor, and so on.

The predictability of diatonic triads allows us to construct them easily. Asked to write the root-position supertonic triad in F major, for example, begin with the appropriate scale, build a triad with basic pitches upon the second degree (G-B-D), then apply accidentals as necessary to reflect the key signature (necessitating B♭, rather than B♮ in this case).

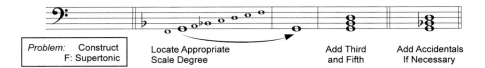

Problem: Construct F: Supertonic	Locate Appropriate Scale Degree	Add Third and Fifth	Add Accidentals If Necessary

Likewise, if we want to build the leading-tone triad in D♭ major, we can follow the same steps:

1. Locate the appropriate scale degree.
2. Add a third and a fifth.
3. Adjust the third and or fifth according to the key signature.

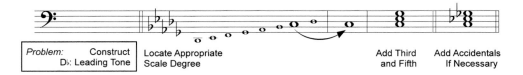

Problem: Construct D♭: Leading Tone	Locate Appropriate Scale Degree	Add Third and Fifth	Add Accidentals If Necessary

Construct an inverted diatonic triad with a *fourth* step: arrange the pitches with the third or the fifth in the bass as needed.

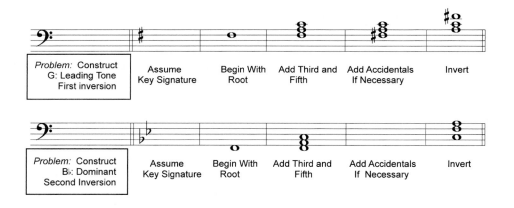

Problem: Construct G: Leading Tone First inversion	Assume Key Signature	Begin With Root	Add Third and Fifth	Add Accidentals If Necessary	Invert

Problem: Construct B♭: Dominant Second Inversion	Assume Key Signature	Begin With Root	Add Third and Fifth	Add Accidentals If Necessary	Invert

Identifying Diatonic Triads

By definition, diatonic triads in major keys conform to the key signature. This fact makes identification relatively simple. As a first step, make sure that the triad is in root position. Next, identify the root as a scale degree within the given key. Finally, assign the appropriate scale degree name and consider the bass position.

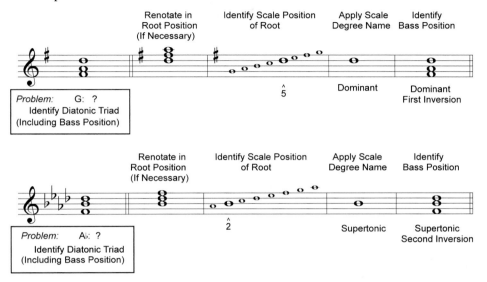

Analytical Symbols

While the words "tonic" and "dominant" in the last passage are helpful in understanding the harmony, triads and chords are more easily identified through a set of symbols. Roman and arabic numerals combine in analysis to convey important information:

- the scale-degree position of the root.
- the quality of the triad.
- the bass position.

Viewing a series of symbols (and not the score itself), for example, trained musicians can *hear* the movement of one chord to another. Analysis not only affirms the presence of tonal relationships visually, but clarifies a hierarchy that we will discuss further in later chapters.

Roman Numerals.   Roman numerals I–VII designate scale degrees $\hat{1}$–$\hat{7}$, respectively. In addition, modern analytical approach employs "uppercase" and "lowercase" roman numerals (I, ii, iii, IV, and so on) to reflect the quality of the triad. Uppercase roman numerals stand for the three major triads: I, IV, and V. Triads that are minor are represented by the (lowercase) numerals ii, iii, and vi. We use a circle symbol in addition to the lowercase numeral to distinguish a diminished triad such as the leading tone (vii°) because these triads are unstable and are afforded special handling in tonal music.

The symbols in the next example are appropriate for diatonic triads in *any* major key.

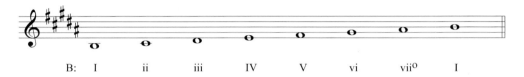

     B: I   ii   iii   IV   V   vi   vii°   I

Notice in the examples below that roman-numeral symbols are a visual representation of triad quality while with the functional names, quality is understood, but not displayed.

  B♭:   vi   A: iii   G: vii°   A♭: V
     Submediant   Mediant   Leading Tone   Dominant

Arabic Numerals.   Just as roman numerals clarify the relationships among diatonic triads, arabic numerals designate a triad's bass position. A system of arabic-numeral labeling, called FIGURED BASS (discussed fully in Volume II), provides this information by listing the intervals sounding above a given bass note. If the triad is in root position, we hear a third and a fifth above the bass. The numerals $\frac{5}{3}$, therefore, specify a triad in root position.

        Triad   Component Intervals $\frac{5}{3}$

Likewise, in first and second inversions, intervals sounding above the bass are a sixth and a third ($\frac{6}{3}$) and a sixth and a fourth ($\frac{6}{4}$), respectively. These arabic numerals connote the two triad inversions.

    First   Component Intervals   6   Second   Component Intervals   6
    Inversion   3   Inversion   4

Abbreviated Designations.   In traditional analysis, we routinely abbreviate the arabic numerals. If a triad is in root position, for example, the numerals $\frac{5}{3}$

are omitted entirely. In first inversion, we omit the 3 and apply only the numeral 6. The full designation $^6_4$ appears with a triad in second inversion.

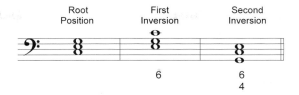

Together with the arabic numeral that identifies the bass position, an analytical symbol gives a helpful illustration of the way a passage sounds. Notice in the next example how tonic and dominant triads in various inversions are identified in the key of C major.

Returning to the Beethoven example, notice that roman and arabic numerals combine to clarify the diatonic origins, the triad qualities, and the bass positions. We know that all of the triads are major in quality since I and V are *always* major triads in a major key. We know as well, through the absence of arabic numerals, that all of the triads are in root position (remember: the tonic six-four in measure 4 is a cliché formula to be discussed later).

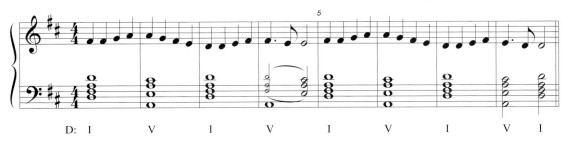

Even without the notes themselves, skilled musicians can read a series of roman and arabic numerals in tempo and understand how the harmony will sound. Listen to the Beethoven example two or three times, then read the following line of analytical symbols in tempo (the same ones that accompany the melody).

D: I | V | I | V | I | V | I | V | I ||

As you learn the traditional harmonic vocabulary, you will probably discover an increasing ability to recognize patterns aurally. Chords are not used in a random order, after all; the movement of tonic to dominant and back to tonic is only one of many chord sequences that defines key and mode.

Construction and Identification with Analytical Symbols. Use analytical symbols to identify diatonic triads in any major key. The roman numeral itself specifies the relationship between the root of the triad and the tonic of the given key; the form of the roman numeral (uppercase or lowercase) illustrates the quality. Finally, arabic numerals label the bass position. Remember that if a triad is diminished, the circle symbol accompanies a lowercase roman numeral.

A: IV   vi $_6$ I $^6_4$ D♭:   ii $_6$ V   vii $^o_6$

From a given analytical symbol, construct triads by following the procedure established earlier in the chapter. First, determine the root, third, and fifth; next, write the correct pitch in the bass according to the arabic-numeral directions. Finally, add pitches above the bass as necessary to complete the triad.

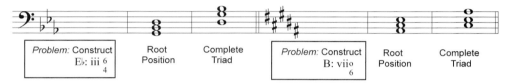

Problem: Construct E♭: iii $^6_4$ Root Position   Complete Triad   *Problem:* Construct B: vii $^o_6$ Root Position   Complete Triad

Diatonic triads occur on each degree of a major scale. Triad quality is invariable: tonic, subdominant, and dominant are always major; supertonic, mediant, and submediant are minor in quality. The leading-tone triad is diminished. In the next section, we will discuss the more colorful diatonic vocabulary of triads in minor.

WORKBOOK/ANTHOLOGY I
III. Diatonic Triads in Major, page 39

REVIEW AND APPLICATION 3–2 ━━━━━━━━━━

Diatonic Triads in Major

Essential Terms

arabic-numeral analysis   figured bass
diatonic triad   roman-numeral analysis

1. Begin with the appropriate key signature and construct triads as directed.

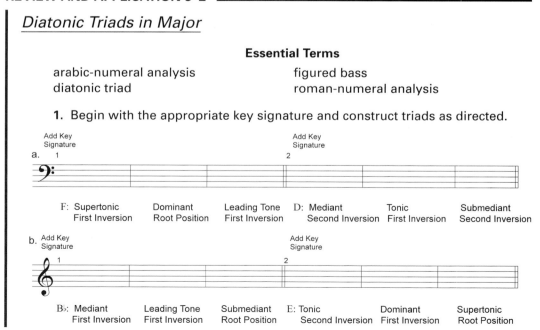

a.   Add Key Signature 1   Add Key Signature 2

F: Supertonic   Dominant   Leading Tone   D: Mediant   Tonic   Submediant
   First Inversion   Root Position   First Inversion   Second Inversion First Inversion Second Inversion

b.   Add Key Signature 1   Add Key Signature 2

B♭: Mediant   Leading Tone   Submediant   E: Tonic   Dominant   Supertonic
    First Inversion First Inversion Root Position   Second Inversion First Inversion Root Position

2. Use diatonic scale-degree names (as in the previous exercise) to identify the given triad in the specified key. Next, use the blank measures to construct first and second inversions of the same triad.

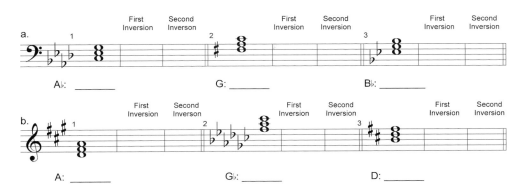

3. In the given major keys, construct diatonic triads as specified by the roman and arabic numerals.

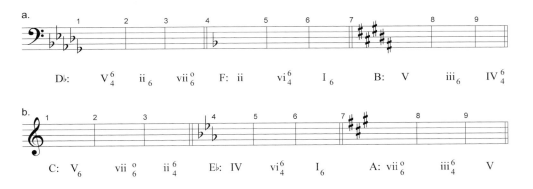

4. Use roman and arabic numerals (plus additional symbols as appropriate) to identify diatonic triads in the major keys suggested. Begin by supplying the relevant key signature.

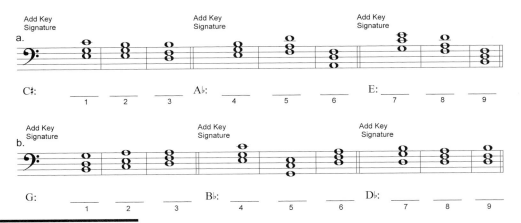

SELF-TEST 3–2

Time Limit: 7 Minutes

1. Indicate the quality of diatonic triads in major by writing the appropriate word in the blank (major, minor, diminished, or augmented). *Scoring: Subtract 5 points for each error.*

   a. Tonic   _____   e. Dominant   _____

   b. Supertonic   _____   f. Submediant   _____

   c. Mediant   _____   g. Leading tone   _____

   d. Subdominant   _____

2. Use roman and arabic numerals (plus any additional symbol necessary) to identify the diatonic triads in the keys indicated. *Scoring: Subtract 8 points for an incorrect response.*

   B♭: _____   A: _____   F: _____   F♯: _____
       1   2   3   4

3. In E major, construct the triads specified. *Scoring: Subtract 9 points for an incorrect answer (consider the notation entirely correct or entirely incorrect).*

   E: IV   E: vii°₆   E: V⁶₄

4. Provide the term that specifies a type of triad constructed of superimposed thirds. *Scoring: subtract 6 points for an incorrect answer.*

   _____

   Total Possible: 100   Your Score _____

DIATONIC TRIADS IN MINOR

Unlike the major scale, the minor scale is not limited to a single pattern. In minor, composers use natural, harmonic, and melodic forms side by side and even simultaneously. Accordingly, the diatonic triads in minor are more varied and more numerous. For theoretical purposes, we might write a "complete" minor scale that includes both ↓$\hat{6}$ and $\hat{6}$ as well as both ↓$\hat{7}$ (subtonic) and (↑)$\hat{7}$ (the leading tone).

G Minor Scale (All Possibilities)

If we construct diatonic triads on each degree of the minor scale, we must take into account all of the possibilities represented by our theoretical "complete" minor scale. As we will discuss, some of the triads were more useful to tonal composers than others. For now, however, we will consider only the theoretical possibilities presented by ↑6̂, ↓6̂, ↓7̂ and 7̂.

Triads with 6̂ and ↓7̂.   Study the analytical symbols in the next example and compare the qualities of diatonic triads within the natural form of minor. In analysis, the designation **g:** indicates G minor. In prose writing, however, the keys are specified as "G major" or "G minor."

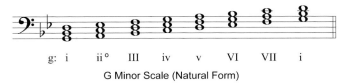

g: i   ii°   III   iv   v   VI   VII   i

G Minor Scale (Natural Form)

With no altered pitches, three triads are major in quality, three are minor, and one is diminished. Notice, however, that now, the tonic, subdominant, and dominant are the minor triads. The supertonic triad is diminished. Finally, in addition to the mediant and submediant, the SUBTONIC TRIAD (built on the subtonic pitch) is major.

Triads with ↑7̂ (Leading Tone).   If we raise the leading tone (↑7̂) wherever it occurs, a new set of triads in minor emerges. Now, the dominant and leading-tone triads are the same in quality as they are as in major (major and diminished, respectively). The mediant triad is *augmented.* In analysis, we add a plus sign (+) to an uppercase roman-numeral symbol that stands for an augmented triad.

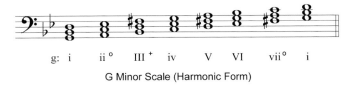

g: i   ii°   III⁺   iv   V   VI   vii°   i

G Minor Scale (Harmonic Form)

In the next example, we can see the harmonic form of minor as it occurs typically in a musical setting. In a series of chords like iv–V–i, 6̂ (E♭) and ↑7̂ (F♯) appear in consecutive chords. While the augmented second between these two pitches is present theoretically, however, a skilled composer would assign them to two different voices (as in the next example). The E♭ appears in the alto; the F♯ in the soprano. Thus, in the harmonic setting, both musical lines are smooth and representative of common-practice ideals.

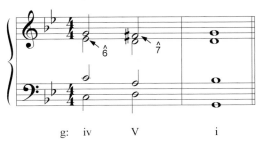

g: iv   V   i

Triads with ↑6̂ and ↑7̂.   A third set of triad qualities emerges when both raised sixth (↑6̂) and leading-tone ↑7̂ are employed. Notice that both the sub-dominant and the dominant triads are major in quality; the supertonic is minor; and *both* the submediant and the leading-tone triads are diminished.

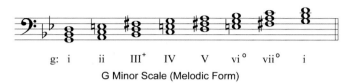

g: i   ii   III⁺   IV   V   vi°   vii°   i

G Minor Scale (Melodic Form)

Any of the triads in the last three examples is possible within the minor mode. When we construct diatonic triads using a "complete" minor scale, thirteen different chords exist. In fact, the only triad that is completely *unaffected* by ↑6̂ and (↑)7̂ is the tonic.

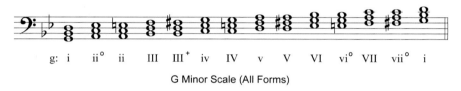

g: i   ii°   ii   III   III⁺   iv   IV   v   V   VI   vi°   VII   vii°   i

G Minor Scale (All Forms)

Typical Diatonic Triads in Minor.   Despite a colorful range of diatonic possi-bilities, traditional composers regarded some triad qualities as useful in defining key and mode; others were reserved to accompany stereotypical melodic pat-terns or used simply for their color. We can make several conclusions about the *most typical* triad qualities in minor. The tonic and the subdominant triads are usually minor. The dominant and leading-tone triads, on the other hand, em-ploy ↑7̂ (an accidental) to provide tonal emphasis. The dominant triad is major in quality; the leading tone, diminished. Finally, while ↑6̂ frequently appears in melodies, the supertonic and the submediant triads include ↓6̂ and are dimin-ished and major, respectively.

While we must be prepared to construct or identify all of the diatonic pos-sibilities in minor, the following qualities emerge as the most common.

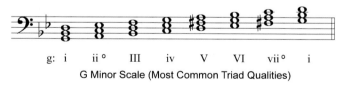

g: i   ii°   III   iv   V   VI   vii°   i

G Minor Scale (Most Common Triad Qualities)

Notice that accidentals are necessary to create a major triad on the domi-nant and to provide a leading-tone triad on ↑7̂ (as opposed to a subtonic). Re-member: the key signature in minor *does not* reflect the most common choices for V and vii°; these qualities are created with accidentals.

c: v   V   b: VII   vii°   c♯: v   V   d: VII   vii°

WORKBOOK/ANTHOLOGY I
IV. Diatonic Triads in Minor,
page 41

Various possibilities are presented by diatonic triads with their optional alterations in minor. In the next section, we will introduce another common chord, but one that has four different pitches: the *dominant seventh chord.*

THE DOMINANT SEVENTH CHORD

As we have learned, a root-position triad is comprised of three pitches that are arranged in consecutive thirds. If, in addition to the third and the fifth, we add a *seventh* above the root, the resulting sonority is called a SEVENTH CHORD.

Seventh chords remain tertian, but a dissonant element (the seventh) requires special treatment in traditional harmony. In this section we will discuss diatonic seventh chords built upon $\hat{5}$—a DOMINANT SEVENTH. We will talk about the use of the dominant seventh in Chapter 6; other types of seventh chords will be covered in Chapter 8.

The Root-Position Dominant Seventh

We identify quality in seventh chords in two ways:

1. The quality of the triad.
2. The quality of the seventh above the root.

The dominant seventh is also known as a MAJOR-MINOR SEVENTH CHORD because the triad is major; the seventh, minor.

Dominant seventh chords are crucial to the development of tonal harmony as we will consider in Chapter 6. For now, our goal is both to recognize the basic sonority and to construct dominant seventh chords on any given root.

Construction of Dominant Sevenths.   Construct a dominant seventh chord in major or minor keys by adding a third above the fifth of the dominant triad. Notice in the next example that dominant triads and dominant seventh chords are identical in major and parallel minor keys.

Identification of Dominant Sevenths. In analysis, identify the root-position dominant seventh with the roman numeral V (denoting the triad) and an arabic numeral 7 that emphasizes the dissonant interval.

Inverted Dominant Sevenths

In addition to root position, a triad has two possible inversions. A seventh chord, with four discrete pitches, has three different inversions. Seventh chords in first and second inversions occur with the third and the fifth, respectively, in the bass. The seventh chord is in THIRD INVERSION if the seventh itself is the lowest sounding pitch. Dominant seventh chords in root position and in all three inversions are shown in the next example.

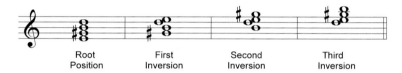

The arabic-numeral symbols for inverted dominant sevenths reflect the position of the dissonant element. Inverted, the seventh becomes a second.

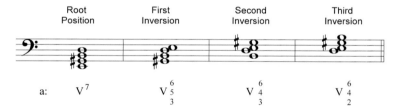

As with triads, arabic numerals are typically abbreviated (shown in the next example).

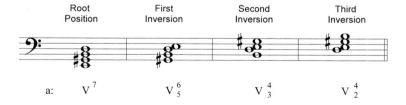

Constructing Dominant Seventh Chords

In major keys, construct a dominant seventh chord by beginning with the dominant triad and adding a seventh above this root. No accidentals are necessary. If an inverted chord is needed, construct the sonority first in root position, then rearrange the pitches as necessary.

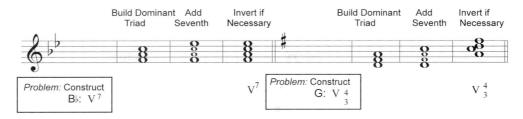

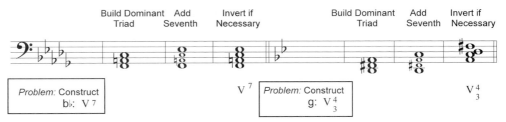

If the key is minor, raise the third of the dominant triad, then add a seventh above the root. This alteration both creates the major-minor quality and provides a leading tone in the given key.

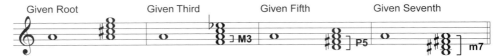

Given Third, Fifth, or Seventh. When constructing chords from a given roman numeral, we know the pitch name of the root (since that is the purpose of the roman numeral itself). Sometimes, however, we need to construct a dominant seventh chord with the third, fifth, or seventh as the given pitch. In this case, the first step in chord construction is locating the root.

- If the *third* is the given pitch, the root lies a major third lower.
- With a given *fifth*, find the root a perfect fifth lower.
- When the given pitch is the *seventh*, the root is a minor seventh lower.

The dominant seventh chord is one of the most important sonorities in the common-practice vocabulary. We are so accustomed to the unique balance of stable and active intervals that we hear the root of *any* major-minor seventh chord as the dominant pitch.

> WORKBOOK/ANTHOLOGY I
> V. Seventh Chords, page 43

REVIEW AND APPLICATION 3–3

Triads in Minor; Dominant Seventh Chords

Essential Terms

dominant seventh chord	subtonic
major-minor seventh chord	third inversion

1. Use roman and arabic numerals to analyze the triads below in the given major or minor key. Note the occurrence of any accidental and its effect on the appropriate analytical symbol.

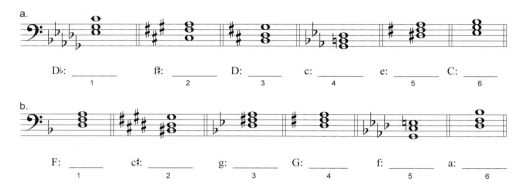

Dβ: _____   fβ: _____   D: _____   c: _____   e: _____   C: _____
      1   2   3   4   5   6

F: _____   cβ: _____   g: _____   G: _____   f: _____   a: _____
      1   2   3   4   5   6

2. In minor keys, dominant and leading-tone triads require an accidental. In addition, other triad qualities in minor necessitate ↑6̂ or (↑)7̂ (IV in a minor key, for instance). Construct basic triads in root position or inversion as suggested by the analytical symbols.

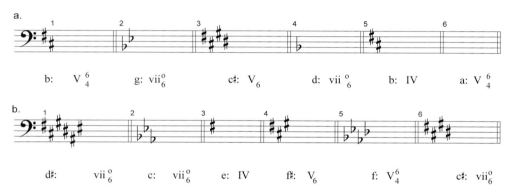

b: V$_4^6$ g: vii°$_6$ cβ: V$_6$ d: vii°$_6$ b: IV   a: V$_4^6$

dβ: vii°$_6$ c: vii°$_6$ e: IV   fβ: V$_6$ f: V$_4^6$ cβ: vii°$_6$

3. Begin by providing the key signature of the major or minor key suggested. Next, construct root-position or inverted *dominant* seventh chords as indicated. Be sure to add the leading tone to the dominant triad in minor keys.

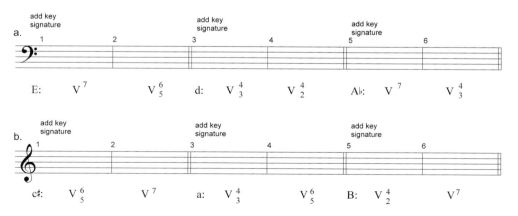

add key signature / add key signature / add key signature

E: V^7 V$_5^6$ d: V$_3^4$ V$_2^4$ Aβ: V^7 V$_3^4$

cβ: V$_5^6$ V^7 a: V$_3^4$ V$_5^6$ B: V$_2^4$ V^7

4. For each root-position or inverted triad below, indicate two different keys in which that chord might appear and also the two different diatonic positions (I, ii, iii, and so on). *Do not* list both major and parallel minor keys (*i.e.*, D major and D minor). In each case, keys with at least two different diatonic positions are possible.

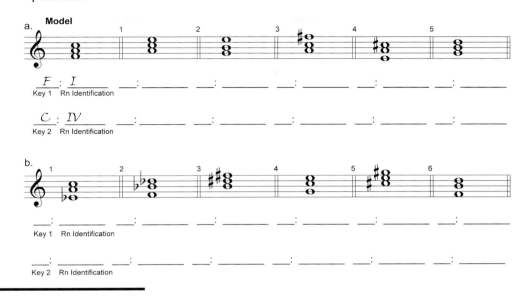

SELF-TEST 3–3

Time Limit: 10 Minutes

1. Provide a word (major, minor, diminished, or augmented) that identifies triad quality as used *most commonly* by traditional composers. *Scoring: Subtract 4 points for each incorrect response.*

   Qualities in Minor

   a. Tonic _____   e. Dominant _____

   b. Supertonic _____   f. Submediant _____

   c. Mediant _____   g. Leading tone _____

   d. Subdominant _____

2. Provide a key signature and construct triads or dominant seventh chords as prescribed by the roman numerals and other symbols. Be sure to add accidentals as necessary. *Scoring: Subtract 3 points for an incorrect key signature; subtract 7 points for each incorrect chord.*

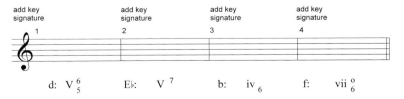

3. Use roman numerals and other symbols to identify the chords below. *Scoring: Subtract 8 points for incorrect responses (any spelling error, missing accidental, or incorrect bass position constitute an error).*

B: _____ g: _____ e: _____ b♭: _____
     1   2   3   4

Total Possible: 100   Your Score _____

FOUR-PART FORMAT

Principles of harmony and chord connection are typically taught and learned through a four-part vocal style. In several chapters of this text, we will study chord sequence and connection as they combine to create a smooth, tonal effect. In the present chapter, our introduction to four-part writing will center on the construction, spacing, and doubling of individual chords.

Spacing in Four Voices

The four natural voice categories are SOPRANO, ALTO, TENOR, and BASS. In the four-part style, we employ a grand staff and write the soprano and alto in the treble clef; the tenor and bass in the bass clef. In another sense, however, we tend to group the soprano, alto, and tenor as one entity identified as the UPPER VOICES; the bass typically moves independently of these upper voices.

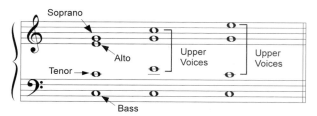

Each of the chords above is C major with the root doubled, yet each has a different sound. In a structural sense, we can explain these differences by comparing the spatial position of the four voices in each chord. The first and second chords are *close* in spatial position; the third chord is in *open position*.

Open and Close Position. Spatial position concerns the closeness of the upper three voices; the bass voice is not a factor. A chord is in CLOSE POSITION when the upper three voices are as close together as possible. In close position, no chord tones appear between soprano and alto or between alto and tenor. Viewed in another way, in close position, the tenor and the soprano will be separated by *less than an octave*. If the spatial position is not close, on the other hand, it is *open*. In OPEN POSITION, the tenor and the soprano are *an octave or more* apart and one or more chord tones will be missing between adjacent upper voices. Notice that while spatial arrangement affects the sound (as in the last example), neither the chord quality nor the bass position is changed.

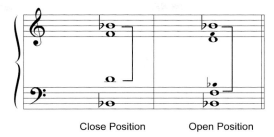

Close Position   Open Position

Spacing in the Upper Voices.   An additional guideline for traditional four-part writing centers on the intervals between tenor and alto and between alto and soprano (adjacent upper voices). No two adjacent upper voices should be separated by *more* then an octave. Wider intervals sound better when they are in the lower voices; upper voices are most often spaced more closely.

Study the chords in the next example. Despite differences in spatial position, each has the same identity (A minor), each is in root position, and the root is doubled in each case.

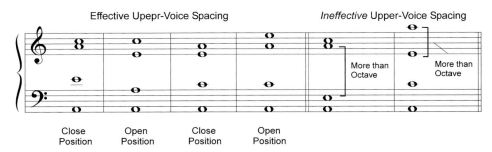

Close   Open   Close   Open
Position   Position   Position   Position

Voice Ranges.   While individual singers have various ranges, you should generally adhere to the limits for each voice range given below.

Doubling in Major and Minor Triads

When a triad is arranged for four voices, one of the pitches must be duplicated or DOUBLED. Conventional approaches to doubling are largely dependent upon musical context. For now, we will employ the most general guidelines for doubling one of the pitches in a major or minor triad:

- If a major or minor triad is in root position, *double the root.*

- In first inversion, *double the highest pitch.* This may the root, the third, or the fifth.

- *Double the bass* of a triad in second inversion.

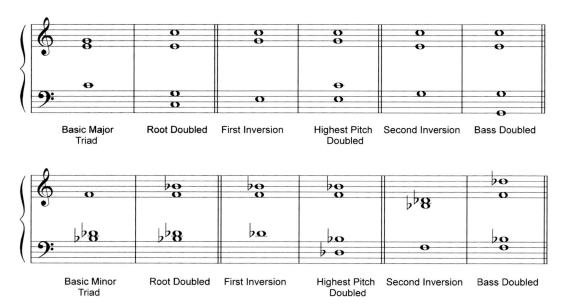

Basic Major Triad — Root Doubled — First Inversion — Highest Pitch Doubled — Second Inversion — Bass Doubled

Basic Minor Triad — Root Doubled — First Inversion — Highest Pitch Doubled — Second Inversion — Bass Doubled

Exception 1: Doubling and the Leading-Tone Pitch. An important exception to the doubling guidelines cited above is actually an outgrowth of good musical sense. As we will discuss further in later chapters, the leading tone has a strong tendency to move to the tonic ($\uparrow\hat{7}-\hat{8}$). Active tones like $\uparrow\hat{7}$ are important in tonal music, but due to their strong tendencies, one occurrence is sufficient in any one chord. As a general principle, never double the leading tone. Because doubling the leading tone would *increase* this momentum, traditional composers choose another pitch (usually the third of the triad) in a four-voice setting.

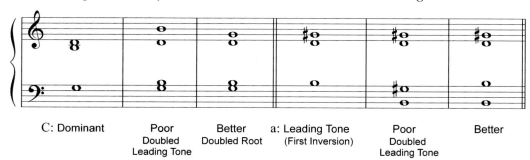

C: Dominant — Poor Doubled Leading Tone — Better Doubled Root — a: Leading Tone (First Inversion) — Poor Doubled Leading Tone — Better

Exception 2: Doubling in Diminished Triads. Because they are less stable than major or minor triads, composers typically double the third of a diminished triad. Moreover, diminished triads occur most often in first inversion.

Diminished Triad — Close Position Third Doubled — Open Position Third Doubled — Diminished Triad — Close Position Third Doubled — Open Position Third Doubled

Constructing Triads in Four Parts

At this point in our studies, we are in a position to create a musical setting, albeit one chord at a time. If the spatial arrangement and doubling are specified, make sure that your chord scoring conforms to the conventions of the four-part style (depending upon the given quality and bass position). When you are not directed to employ a certain spatial arrangement or doubling, of course, you have more freedom.

Asked to score a G minor triad in first inversion, four of the many different possibilities are shown in the next example.

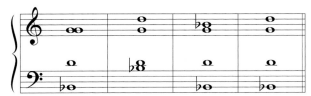

Because the spatial arrangement was not specified, each of the chords in the previous example is correct. In each case, all three pitches of the triad are present (root, third, and fifth), the third is in the bass as directed, and the pitch in the soprano is also the one doubled. Had close position been specified, however, only the first chord would have adhered to this arrangement. In the second, third, and fourth chords, the tenor and soprano are separated by an octave or more and are in open position.

While the chords in the last example all exhibit correct "spelling" and four-part procedure, each of the G minor, first inversion chords below is incorrect in some way (as noted in the caption).

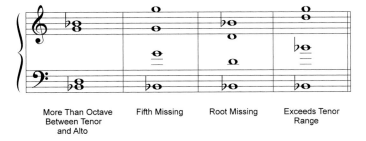

| More Than Octave Between Tenor and Alto | Fifth Missing | Root Missing | Exceeds Tenor Range |

Construct four-part chords from a given analytical symbol first by interpreting that symbol within the given key, choosing an appropriate doubling and spacing, and then completing the notation in soprano, alto, tenor, and bass voices. Remember that in minor, $\uparrow\hat{7}$ in the leading-tone triad (vii$^{\circ}_6$) is *an accidental* just as $\uparrow\hat{7}$ is an accidental in the corresponding scale. Especially with the dominant and leading-tone triads in minor, you must add the accidental that creates the specified quality.

Dominant Seventh Chords in Four Parts

In root position, space the four pitches of a dominant seventh chord just as you would a triad. Notate the root as the bass and arrange the third, fifth, and seventh above the bass in either open or close position. Likewise, for inverted dominant sevenths, provide the appropriate pitch as the bass note and choose among the remaining pitches for the tenor, alto, and soprano. Adhere to the principles of spacing and vocal range discussed earlier.

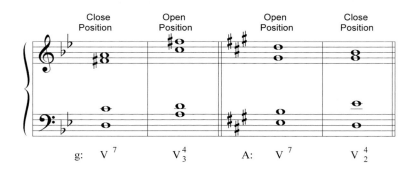

Fifth Omitted in Root Position. Composers often strengthen the root of a root-position dominant seventh chord by omitting the fifth and doubling the root. Notice that this option is appropriate *only* for chords in root position; inverted seventh chords should have all four pitches present. In the next example, compare acceptable doubling and spacing in dominant sevenths in D major and F minor.

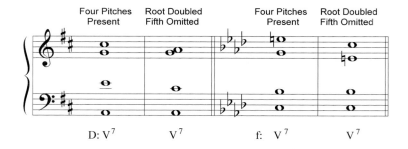

Construction Checklist. Music of lasting value is created by an inspired composer—not through adherence to a set of rules or guidelines. Because studies in music theory typically center on the tonal system, however, successful composers must consider not only listener and performer expectations, but the melodic and harmonic tendencies of tonal materials as well. The conventions explained in this text reflect the practice of celebrated tonal composers from the mid-seventeenth century to the present day. Moreover, in the vocal style, certain patterns prove more natural than others; composers who intend to write within this style must avoid awkward intervals, unnecessary leaps, and other faults that detract from the musical effect.

Use the following checklist to eliminate problems in doubling, spacing, and voicing in constructing individual triads and dominant seventh chords. In later chapters additions to the checklist will highlight new materials and guidelines for using them within a tonal context.

CHECKLIST FOR CHORD CONSTRUCTION IN FOUR-PART STYLE

Material	Bass-position Preference	Doubling	Upper Voices within Octave or Less	Voices within Natural Ranges	Avoid Doubled Leading Tone	Root/Third and Fifth Present
			General Guidelines			
Major Triad	none					
Root Position		Root	✓	✓	✓	✓
First Inversion		Soprano	✓	✓	✓	✓
Second Inversion		Bass (fifth)	✓	✓	✓	✓
Minor Triad	none					
Root Position		Root	✓	✓	✓	✓
First Inversion		Soprano	✓	✓	✓	✓
Second Inversion		Bass (fifth)	✓	✓	✓	✓
Diminished Triad	First inversion	Third (bass)	✓	✓	✓	✓
Augmented Triad	First inversion	Third (bass)	✓	✓	✓	✓
Dominant Seventh Root Position	none	none	✓	✓	✓	All four pitches present
First inversion		none	✓	✓	✓	All four pitches present
Second inversion		none	✓	✓	✓	All four pitches present
Third Inversion		none	✓	✓	✓	All four pitches present

Identifying Diatonic Chords in Four Parts

Identifying basic triadic material from a four-voice musical score is only slightly more complex than the task of discerning quality and bass position in triads. As we have discussed, once any doubled pitch has been eliminated, the basic root-position or inverted triad remains. If four different pitches are present, consider the chord to be a dominant seventh.[2] At first, you may find it helpful to employ a work staff to reduce the chord to its triadic basis (as in the next example).

---

[2]Several different types of seventh chords are common in the traditional harmonic vocabulary. These chords will be discussed in later chapters; for now, only the dominant seventh is included in examples and exercises.

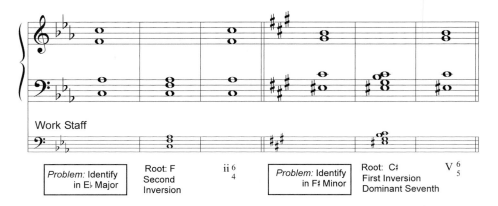

| Problem: Identify in E♭ Major | Root: F
Second
Inversion | ii $^6_4$ | Problem: Identify in F♯ Minor | Root: C♯
First Inversion
Dominant Seventh | V $^6_5$ |

In this chapter we have studied triads—both as fundamental materials and as the diatonic building blocks of tonal harmony. In four-part settings, conventional approaches to doublings, spacings, and other factors arise entirely from musical considerations. In later chapters of this text, we will explore the use of triads and chords in progressions—series of chords that define and embellish tonality.

 WORKBOOK/ANTHOLOGY I
VI. Chords in Four Parts, page 45

REVIEW AND APPLICATION 3–4

The Four-Part Style

Essential Terms

close position   doubling   open position   subtonic triad   upper voices

1. As suggested by the analytical symbols, construct chords in four parts. Begin by providing a key signature; then, write the chords specified. In the first line, employ close spatial position; use open position in the second line. Add accidentals as necessary in minor keys. Chord connection (voice leading) is *not* a factor in this exercise.

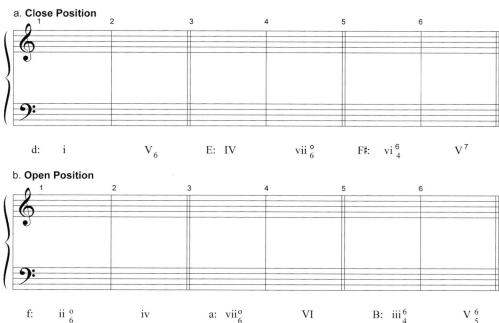

a. **Close Position**

d: i   V $_6$ E: IV   vii $^o_6$ F♯: vi $^6_4$ V ^{7}

b. **Open Position**

f: ii $^o_6$ iv   a: vii^o VI   B: iii $^6_4$ V $^6_5$

2. Locate one error in each of the following chords. Consider adherence to conventional doubling, spatial position (as indicated), the absence of an accidental in minor, improper spacing in the upper voices, or missing root or third. Write your answers in the spaces below the score.

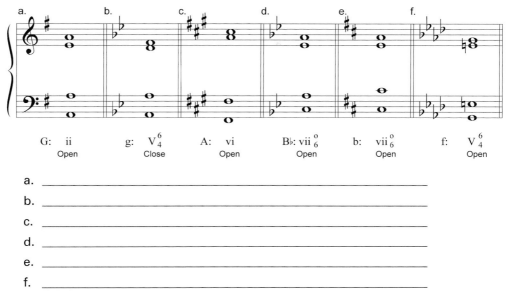

a. _____

b. _____

c. _____

d. _____

e. _____

f. _____

3. Rewrite the chords in the last problem (above) to eliminate all errors.

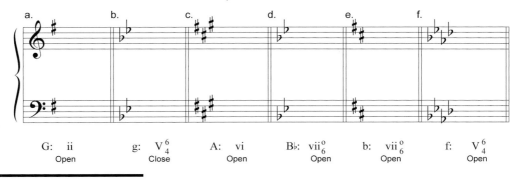

SELF-TEST 3–4

Time Limit: 10 Minutes

1. Make a check beside the correct statement in each of the following groups. *Scoring: Subtract 5 points for each incorrect answer.*

    a. Which of the following pitches is *outside* the range of the alto voice?

        ___ (1) B_3

        ___ (2) A_4

        ___ (3) C_3

        ___ (4) C_4

b. Which of the following is *not* typically doubled in four-voice vocal writing?

___ (1) the bass

___ (2) the leading tone

___ (3) the dominant

___ (4) the soprano

c. Which of the following is *not* true of close spatial position?

___ (1) the tenor and soprano are separated by an octave or more

___ (2) the voices are as close together as possible.

___ (3) the soprano and alto are separated by less than an octave.

___ (4) the position of the bass voice is not a consideration.

d. In diminished triads, which of the following statements represents common voicing in four parts?

___ (1) double the root

___ (2) double the third

___ (3) double the fifth

___ (4) double the soprano

2. Identify the spatial position of each chord. Write "open" or "close" in the blank. *Scoring: Subtract 5 points for each incorrect answer.*

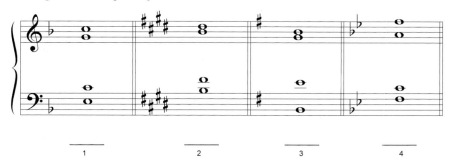

      1   2   3   4

3. Add alto and tenor voices to complete the given chords in four parts *and in the spacing designated*. Add any necessary accidentals. Use conventional spacing, doubling, and bass positions. *Scoring: Subtract 10 points for each incorrect chord; subtract 5 points for an incorrect spacing.*

F♯:   ii   d: V^7 B♭: I$^6_4$ g♯: vii$^{o}_6$

     Close   Open   Close   Close

Total Possible: 100   Your Score _____

PROJECTS

Analysis

In this text, our aim is to explain the harmonic, melodic, and rhythmic materials of traditional music through examples from the literature. While this choice sets fundamental and theoretical materials in the context of a musical work, it also necessitates that music be edited to remove materials not yet studied, or that these chords and pitches be discounted in analysis. Both of these possibilities occur in the examples for analysis in the present chapter (and also in several other chapters throughout this volume). Where chords are marked "to be studied in later chapter," simply move on to the next chord in the score. Individual pitches that are printed in cue-size are likewise to be ignored for the present.

Text

Joseph Haydn, Serenade from Quartet, Op. 3, No. 5 (II), text pages 113-114. Chords have been extracted from this favorite Haydn work for string quartet. Study the lowest line and provide roman- and arabic-numeral analysis. Ignore all smaller notes; these are pitches outside the harmony or chords to be studied in later chapters. Measures 29-53 of the serenade are provided here. Measures 54-67 (to the end) of this same work appear in the Workbook/Anthology.

Workbook/Anthology I

Joseph Haydn, Serenade from Quartet, Op. 3, No. 5 (II), workbook page 49.
Ludwig van Beethoven, Sonatina in G Major, Op. 36, No. 2, workbook page 50.

Composition

Duet for Flute and Bassoon. Many traditional melodies are little more than arpeggiated triads and dominant seventh chords such as those we have studied in Chapter 3. Your assignment here is to write three short compositions for flute and bassoon (both nontransposing instruments) and base these duets on given chord progressions. Consult Appendix A on page 483 for instrument ranges.

Assign the bassoon the lowest pitch of each chord exactly as it appears in the progression that follow. For the flute, however, create a melody by arranging the chord tones in various ascending and descending patterns and with different rhythmic values.

Consider the following progression as an example. The first passage is set in a triple meter; the second, in duple.

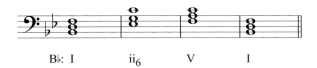

B♭: I   ii₆   V   I

Use the progressions below as the basis of the first, second, and third duets, respectively. Adhere to the score format shown. Strive for clear calligraphy with dynamics and articulations added. Duplicate the roman-numeral analysis below the bassoon line in each case.

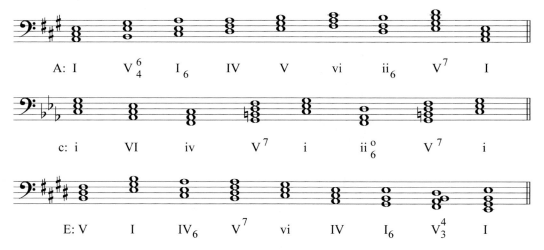

For Further Study

Chord Symbols. Chord symbols such as C^7 or GMI^7 have been in use in jazz and popular music for decades. While far from standardized, these symbols convey much of the same information seen through roman- and arabic-numeral labels. On the other hand, because popular music and jazz have a melodic basis, the soprano-bass framework—so crucial in traditional music—cannot be represented easily through chord symbols. In addition, the numeral basis of the roman-numeral system permits a ready association with degrees of a scale. These associations are equally important in a popular style, but not immediately apparent with chord symbols.

After providing a roman- and arabic-numeral analysis of the Haydn Serenade passage below, make a lead sheet of the same measures that provides melody and chord symbols (you may also want to consult Appendix B on page 485). Begin by copying the melody of the Serenade on another sheet. This done, add chord symbols above the melody to create a LEAD SHEET that reproduces the original harmony as closely as possible. If a chord is in second inversion, for example, show both the basic triad and the bass note with your symbol (C/G for the I$_4^6$ in measure 30) as discussed in Appendix B. Ignore chords identified on the score as "covered in later chapters." Your lead sheet for the Serenade will look something like this:

G major   C major with   G dominant   C major   G major
               G as bass   seventh

When you have completed a lead sheet (measures 20-53 of the Haydn Serenade), perform the melody with an improvised keyboard accompaniment, together with guitar and drum rhythm section (if available). Compare the lead-sheet (popular style) performance with a keyboard reading of the Serenade passage as originally written. Write a brief summary of your reactions to both versions of the notation and performance. You might answer questions such as these:

- Does a performance of the lead-sheet version of the Serenade constitute a new musical composition, or is it an arrangement of the original?

- In the lead-sheet performance (assuming adequate improvisation), how much do we miss the bass of the original? the inner voices?

- Is the lead-sheet rendition of Haydn's Serenade preferable to the original in any way? If you are a fan of jazz and popular music, of course, the style will be familiar.

Joseph Haydn, Serenade
from Quartet, Op. 3, No. 5

Chord to be studied in
a later chapter

Chord to be studied
in a later chapter

UNIT *2*

Introduction to Tonal Principles

Mozart, Adagio from Concerto for Clarinet and Orchestra K. 622[1]

Chapter 4
Melodic Structure

Chapter 5
Harmonic Function

S cholars of music in the West generally recognize three basic categories: *folk, pop,* and *art.* FOLK MUSIC documents the human experience with songs and instrumental pieces that are often composed on the spur of the moment, memorized, and then passed along from one generation to the next. Because precise notation has not been an important characteristic of Western folk music, the same song may exist in several different versions.

Music that is POPULAR may have appeal to a wide range of individuals—including those with modest levels of artistic understanding. A pop (commercial) composition may have tremendous acclaim with one societal or regional

---

[1]Designations such as "K. 622" are composer-catalog numbers that place a particular work in historical perspective—often with detailed biographical information and a thematic index. The letter "K" refers to the Austrian scholar, Ludwig von Köchel (1800–1877), who compiled and edited a definitive chronological catalog of Mozart's complete works (published in 1862). In Mozart's case, compositions are listed from K. 1 (a juvenile minuet) to K. 626 (the powerful *Requiem Mass*) that was completed by a student after the composer's death in 1791. Other thematic catalogs include the *Bach Werke Verzeichnis* (*B W V*), Otto Deutsch's commentary and chronological listing of Schubert's music (*D.*), the Anthony van Hoboken thematic compendium of Haydn's works (*Hb.*), and Ralph Kirkpatrick's volume on the music of Domenico Scarlatti (*K.*).

group, but the luster may fade quickly. Popular music not only provides momentary diversion in our daily lives, but it generates income for the composer, concert promoters, performers, recording companies, advertising agencies, the media, and so on.

A composer of ART MUSIC, on the other hand, aspires to exhilarate the listener intellectually and emotionally. King George II of England once remarked to George Frideric Handel (1685–1759) that the composer had "entertained the entire kingdom." "I do not wish to entertain them, milord," Handel said boldly to his monarch, " I wish to make them *better*."

Naturally, not all composers of art music are equally successful. But when a phrase, a melody, or an entire composition elevates and expands our senses and creates within us the passion for greater attainment on our own part, that work has the potential to endure. One such composition is the second movement of the concerto that Wolfgang Amadeus Mozart (1756–1791) wrote for the famous Viennese clarinet player Aton Stadler. The melody that opens the adagio has been described as having "supernatural serenity." In addition, many of the melodic and harmonic principles by which we in the West measure music as *great art* are also embodied in Mozart's melody as they are in the movement, and in the concerto as a whole.

CD 1, TRACK 25
W.A. Mozart, Concerto for Clarinet, K. 622 (II)

The first thirty-two measures of Mozart's concerto are given here in a piano arrangement (the complete movement appears in the Workbook/Anthology, page 194).

4

Melodic Structure

From time to time in the early chapters of this text, we will talk about the melodic and harmonic parameters of Western music as if they were separate entities. In reality, of course, the two realms exist in a close partnership. Since the late Renaissance, melodic principles have derived from harmonic choices; a convincing harmony, on the other hand, supports inherent tonal tendencies in the melody. With this understanding, our focus in the present chapter is on traditional means of melodic structure. In Chapter 5, we will survey harmonic relationships that govern tonal music.

PITCH CENTRICITY

Randomness is *not* a characteristic of traditional Western music. While there are only seven different pitch classes in a diatonic scale, writing a strong tonal melody is no simple task. Both pitch and rhythm are important in effective tonal composition, yet is one more important than the other? We can answer our question using the melody that opens the menuet (minuet) from Joseph Haydn's *Divertimento in C Major*. While imparting a sense of key and mode was a primary concern for virtually all common practice composers, Haydn centers our interest on the pitch C in a compelling way that remains a model of traditional practice and classical style even today.

CD 1, TRACK 26
Joseph Haydn, Divertimento in C Major

Not surprisingly for a work in C major, the pitch C occurs most frequently (8 times — including the first pitch); E and G are the next most common (7 and 6 occurrences, respectively). In comparison, $\hat{4}$, $\uparrow\hat{7}$, and $\hat{6}$ are employed less often. The melody is incomplete as shown (ending on $\hat{2}$ to assure the listener that more will follow).

If we test the melody by imposing a different set of rhythmic values—even a random one—will the pitches of Haydn's menuet still impart a tonal effect? In the next example, observe that the notes are the same, but the rhythms are a re-

CD 1, TRACK 27-1 PITCH CENTRICITY (2 PARTS)
Haydn Menuet
Reversed Rhythmic Values

verse ordering. Pitches in the revision no longer coincide with strong and weak metric positions as Haydn conceived them and agogic accents now emphasize different pitches.

While we would not claim that the new version of Haydn's melody is equivalent aesthetically (with reversed accents and an ambiguous metric plan), play the previous line and see if you agree that the tonal effect is still reasonably clear. Anchored by the beginning and ending pitches ($\hat{1}$ and $\hat{2}$), we continue to feel the effect of the major mode with C as the tonic.

Next, we might test the consequences of pitch *order* by choosing a similar balance of ascending and descending motion, employing the same pitches and rhythms, but arranging the pitches randomly (in this case, except for first and final pitches, in a computer-generated order).

Listen to the new version of the melody and compare it with the original. Even with an identical pitch content and the same rhythms, you will have little sense of C major in the revision. While different arrangements of the pitches will vary in their tonal effect, we can conclude that the order is more important in establishing a feeling for key than duration or emphasis.

Pitches in an effective tonal melody are *not* equal in importance. In a well-crafted tonal melody, we hear some scale degrees as stable, while others are active and tend to RESOLVE (that is, to move) to one of the more stable pitches. Put another way, pitches in a scale have a CENTRICITY or a clearly defined hierarchy that focuses interest upon the tonic pitch. Centricity, present in the original Haydn melody (and absent in the reordering), creates the effect of tonality.

Tendency Tones

Less stable pitches are drawn inexorably toward stronger ones—much as the earth's gravity causes objects in the physical world to behave as they do. Pitches that musically gravitate are called TENDENCY TONES. Without tendency tones to identify them, we could not so easily discern that some pitches are structural.

Active and Stable Pitches.   We classify the pitches in a scale as being either ACTIVE (having a tendency to move toward another pitch) or STABLE (pitches without such tendencies). In major keys, $\hat{1}$, $\hat{3}$, and $\hat{5}$ are stable; other pitches are tendency tones and have active roles. Notice in the next example that the stable pitches in a major scale outline a tonic triad while tendency tones ascend or descend by step to stable pitches. In any major key, $\hat{2}$ gravitates toward $\hat{1}$ while $\hat{4}$ descends to $\hat{3}$. Likewise, $\hat{6}$ may descend to $\hat{5}$ or it may ascend through $\uparrow\hat{7}$ to $\hat{8}$ (the alternate possibility shown).

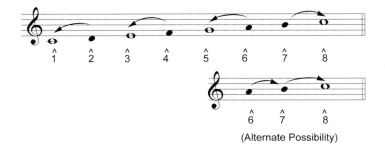

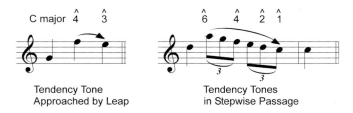

Tendency tones are most pronounced when approached by leap or when they are accented. If a melody moves in stepwise patterns, on the other hand, we hear the end of a scale fragment as the focal point and we expect the last tone, if active, to resolve characteristically.

Tendency Tone   Tendency Tones
Approached by Leap   in Stepwise Passage

Both of the last examples are from Haydn's menuet melody (page 120). In the seventh measure, $\hat{4}$ is approached by leap; the subsequent resolution to $\hat{3}$ is crucial to maintain tonal centricity. In measure 5, however, the stepwise descent from A to C focuses our attention on the tonic pitch—the goal of the scale. The intervening tendency tones ($\hat{6}$, $\hat{4}$, and $\hat{2}$) all resolve characteristically, but our sense of tonality comes mainly from the momentum of the scale.

Listen to Haydn's melody again and concentrate on the resolution of tendency tones. Next, listen a second time to the random ordering of pitches (page 121) and note that in many places, the natural tendencies of active tones are ignored. The fourth scale degrees in measures 4 and 8 are approached by leap and their lack of resolution is especially disorienting in this random ordering.

While intuitive composers often write successful melodies that include exceptions to the guidelines we have discussed, just as often tonal melodies show careful attention to the resolution of tendency tones. In a phrase from Virgil Thompson's opera, *Mother of Us All* (1947), $\hat{4}$ resolves to $\hat{3}$ to create a strong phrase ending.

CD 1, TRACK 28-1 TENDENCY TONES (3 PARTS)
Virgil Thompson, *Mother of Us All*
Fourth Scale Degree

So   beau - ti - ful.   It   was   so   beau - ti - ful   to   meet   you   here,

A♭ major

Notice how the dramatic leap to $\hat{6}$ and a subsequent descent to $\hat{5}$ shape the entire phrase in Sonata in B♭ Major, Op. 2, No. 5 by the Italian Archangelo Corelli (1653–1713).

TRACK 28-2 TENDENCY TONES
Archangelo Corelli, Sonata in B♭ Major, Op. 2, No.5
Sixth Scale Degree

B♭ major

TRACK 28-3 TENDENCY TONES
American Folk Song, *Shenandoah*
Consecutive Tendency Tones

Two or more tendency tones sometimes occur consecutively. In this event, as seen in the next passage, the *last* of the pitches is heard as a resolution.

O   Shen-en-doah.____ I long to hear you, a - way, ____ you roll-ing riv - er.____
D major

In another example of tonal centricity, an aria from *The Barber of Seville* by Gioacchino Rossini (1792–1868) provides an example of tendency tones that ascend or descend by step.

CD 1, TRACK 29-1 MELODIC EMBELLISHMENT (2 PARTS)
Giacomo Rossini, *The Barber of Seville*
Embellished Melody

Quan - do mi sei vi - ci - na, a - ma - bi - le Ro - si - na
G major

In addition to creating the effect of tonality, active tones smooth the melodic line and strengthen our perception of meter. If we substitute addition-

TRACK 29-2 MELODIC EMBELLISHMENT
Rossini Melody without
Embellishments

al stable pitches for the active tones in Rossini's aria phrase, the musical effect is that of an instrumental fanfare—not a lilting vocal line. In addition, tonality in the revised version is actually *less* clear.

Active and stable tones are both essential to a strong melody. In *Frühlingslied* (*Spring Song*), by the German composer Felix Mendelssohn (1805–1847), there are no active tones in the first two measures. This arpeggiated structure (that is, sounded sequentially in the manner of a harp) of the first part of the phrase is balanced, with stepwise movement — including active tones—in the second. Of the twelve non consecutive pitches in the line, only three are tendency tones and they occur as the phrase concludes on $\hat{3}$.

CD 2, TRACK 30
Felix Mendelssohn, *Frühlingslied* (*Spring Song*)
Active and Stable Tones

G major

Melodic Tendencies in Minor.   In minor keys, scale-degree tendencies are similar to those in major, but the composer may choose the natural or raised $\hat{6}$ and $\hat{7}$. As in major, $\hat{1}$, $\hat{3}$, and $\hat{5}$ are stable pitches in minor. Likewise, the tendencies of $\hat{2}$ and $\hat{4}$ are basically the same in both modes. Natural $\downarrow\hat{7}$ (the subtonic) often descends to $\downarrow\hat{6}$; in turn, $\downarrow\hat{6}$ has a strong tendency to descend to $\hat{5}$.

Melodic Tendencies in Minor

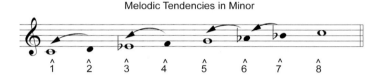

When raised, $\uparrow\hat{6}$ and $\uparrow\hat{7}$ most typically ascend by step.

Melodic Tendencies in Minor
(Raised 6 and 7)

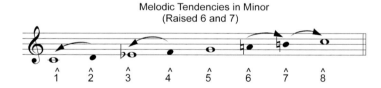

The choice in minor of pitches from the upper tetrachord is illustrated through *The Lonely Wanderer*, a piano work by the Norwegian composer Edvard Grieg (1843–1907). The opening line descends twice from $\hat{8}$ down to $\hat{5}$, before ascending back to $\hat{8}$. In the descending passages, where $\hat{5}$ is the goal, Grieg used $\downarrow\hat{6}$ and $\downarrow\hat{7}$; ascending to $\hat{8}$, however, he employed the leading tone ($\uparrow\hat{7}$) and chose not to use ($\uparrow\hat{6}$) at all.

CD 1, TRACK 31-1 MELODIC TENDENCIES (2 PARTS)
Edvard Grieg, *The Lonely Wanderer*
Melodic Tendencies in Minor

B minor

Melodic Goals

Tonal composers manipulate melodic tendencies not only to emphasize key and mode, but also to focus listener attention on the *goal* of the line. In an example where the tonic is the goal, the line ascends; $\uparrow\hat{7}$ and $\uparrow\hat{6}$ are convenient means of emphasizing this pitch (measure 3 of the previous example). If the goal of the passage is $\hat{5}$, on the other hand (as in measures 1 and 2 of the Grieg passage), $\uparrow\hat{7}$ is unnecessary.

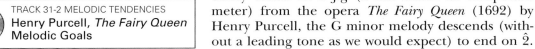

B minor

Melodic goals define passages that may feature leaps and consecutive tendency tones. In a jig (a fast dance in compound meter) from the opera *The Fairy Queen* (1692) by Henry Purcell, the G minor melody descends (without a leading tone as we would expect) to end on $\hat{2}$.

TRACK 31-2 MELODIC TENDENCIES
Henry Purcell, *The Fairy Queen*
Melodic Goals

G minor

Purcell (1659–1695), perhaps the greatest of English composers, seems to ignore the natural tendencies of several pitches in the preceding melody. Nonetheless, the melodic outline of pitches on strong beats suggests a gentle descent from G_3 in measure 1 to A_2 in the final measure.

Purcell, Melodic Tendencies

G minor $\hat{8}$ $\downarrow\hat{7}$ $\downarrow\hat{6}$ $\hat{5}$ $\hat{3}$ $\hat{2}$

Points of stability are not always immediate in the short term, but by the end of a phrase, the relationships among diatonic pitches are usually clear. Composers define intermediate tonal goals through *melodic cadences.*

Melodic Cadences

A PHRASE is a complete musical thought that culminates with an ending formula called a CADENCE – a temporary or permanent resting point. In a melody, the pitch that ends a phrase is known as the MELODIC CADENCE. We can identify two different types of melodic cadence: *terminal* and *progressive.*

Terminal Melodic Cadence.   When a phrase ends with $\hat{1}$ or $\hat{3}$, the effect is conclusive and is known as a TERMINAL MELODIC CADENCE. The initial phrase of Beethoven's first symphony, for example, ends with a terminal melodic cadence. Notice that the strong ↑$\hat{7}$–$\hat{8}$ melodic pattern occurs five times within the four-measure phrase.

Ludwig van Beethoven, Symphony No. 1
First Movement

C major

Terminal Melodic
Cadence

Commercial music has remained tonal throughout the twentieth century (and gives no evidence of straying from this system in the future). The theme from the film *Pretty Woman* ends decisively on $\hat{1}$. Unlike the phrase in the last passage, however, the cadence in "Oh, Pretty Woman" occurs on a weak beat.

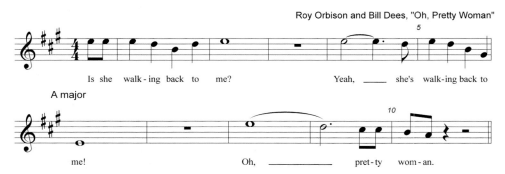

Roy Orbison and Bill Dees, "Oh, Pretty Woman"

A major

Is she walk-ing back to   me?   Yeah, _____ she's walk-ing back to

me!   Oh, _____ pret-ty wom-an.

The third scale degree is also heard as a terminal melodic cadence, although it is weaker than a cadence on the tonic. For the last scene of his opera *Four Saints in Three Acts,* the American composer Virgil Thompson (1896–1989) employs a four-measure phrase that is almost entirely stepwise in F major. The terminal melodic cadence ends on $\hat{3}$.

Virgil Thompson, *Four Saints in Three Acts*

F major

Terminal Melodic
Cadence

Progressive Melodic Cadence.   When a phrase ends with a pitch *other* than $\hat{1}$ or $\hat{3}$, the cadence is known as PROGRESSIVE. The effect of a progressive cadence suggests that another phrase will follow. As illustrated in the next two examples, $\hat{2}$ and $\hat{5}$ often serve as intermediate cadential points in a melody.

In the opening of his Symphony No. 6, Beethoven ended the first phrase on $\hat{2}$.

Ludwig van Beethoven, Symphony No. 6
First Movement

F major

Progressive Melodic
Cadence

Samuel Coleridge-Taylor (1875–1912) was a Black English composer who gained wide popularity in the United States at the turn of the twentieth century. The initial phrase of his popular piano work, *Three-Fours* (1909), ends with a progressive melodic cadence to $\hat{5}$.

Samuel Coleridge-Taylor, *Three-Fours* Op. 71

B♭ major

$\overset{\wedge}{5}$

Progressive Melodic
Cadence

The leading tone sometimes serves as a point of progressive melodic cadence. In the eighteenth-century American tune *Yankee Doodle* (shown in the next example), a progressive cadence on $\uparrow\hat{7}$ ends the first phrase. The following phrase concludes in a terminal cadence ($\hat{8}$) and causes us to hear both phrases—all eight measures—as a single musical idea.

CD 1, TRACK 32-1 PROGRESSIVE AND TERMINAL CADENCES (2 PARTS)
American Folk Song, *Yankee Doodle*

D major

$\overset{\wedge}{7}$

$\overset{\wedge}{1}$

On the surface, the pop song *Yankee Doodle* and Beethoven's elegant "Ode to Joy" would seem to have very little in common. Notice, however, that the two melodies share an identical phrase structure (a progressive, followed by a terminal melodic cadence), identical metric plans, a consistent range of temporal values, and a uniformity in style.

CD 1, TRACK 32-2 PROGRESSIVE AND TERMINAL CADENCES
Ludwig van Beethoven, "Ode to Joy"

$\overset{\wedge}{2}$

$\overset{\wedge}{1}$

Traditional composers create pitch centricity by adhering to natural scale tendencies, through conclusive melodic goals, and by means of convincing cadences. In a later section, we will discuss ways of discerning effective (or less successful) melodic construction through *reduction*—a dissection of melody to reveal structural and embellishing pitches.

WORKBOOK/ANTHOLOGY I
I. Melodic Tendencies, page 51

REVIEW AND APPLICATION 4–1

Melodic Tendencies and Cadences

Essential Terms

active pitch	phrase melodic cadence	progressive cadence	tendency tone
cadence	pitch centricity	stable pitch	terminal cadence

1. Study the two melodies below and classify each pitch as either stable (S) or active (A). Be prepared to identify the final cadences as terminal or progressive.

2. In each segment below, the last pitch is active. In the blank space, provide an appropriate stable pitch that would logically follow according to tonal tendencies in major or minor (as appropriate). In some cases, two or more pitches will be correct.

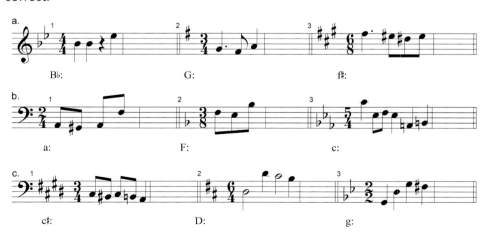

3. Each of the lines below includes at least one point at which a melodic tendency is ignored, resulting in a weakened tonal effect. Play or sing the melodies, locate these points, and be prepared to recommend alternate pitches that follow traditional melodic guidelines.

a.

F♯ Minor

b.

F Major

SELF-TEST 4–1

Time Limit: 5 Minutes

1. Make a check mark by the correct answer for each of the following. *Scoring: Subtract 9 points for each incorrect answer.*

a. Which of the following is *not* associated with pitch centricity.

_____ (1) active and stable pitches.

_____ (2) establishment of a tonal center.

_____ (3) figured bass.

_____ (4) tendency tones.

b. Melodic tendencies are especially important

_____ (1) when approached by leap.

_____ (2) when approached by step.

_____ (3) in melodic minor.

_____ (4) when part of a scale passage.

c. Which of the following scale degrees is *not* an example of a progressive melodic cadence?

_____ (1) $\hat{3}$

_____ (2) $\hat{5}$

_____ (3) $\hat{2}$

_____ (4) $\hat{7}$

d. Which of the following is *not* true of a melodic cadence in traditional music?

_____ (1) a cadence may be terminal or progressive.

_____ (2) a cadence does not occur on $\hat{3}$ or $\hat{7}$

_____ (3) a cadence defines a melodic goal.

_____ (4) a cadence occurs on a strong or a weak beat.

2. Considering natural melodic tendencies in the keys suggested, provide a pitch that would represent a tonal resolution. Use the note value of your choice. *Scoring: Subtract 9 points for each error.*

E minor   E♭ major   C♯ minor   D major

3. Identify the melodic cadences as terminal or progressive by writing the appropriate word in the blank. *Scoring: Subtract 14 points for each inaccurate response.*

CD 1, TRACK 33-1 IDENTIFICATION OF MELODIC CADENCES (2 PARTS)
Muzio Clementi, *Sonatina in C Major*

a.

C major

_____
1

TRACK 33-2 IDENTIFICATION OF MELODIC CADENCES
George Gershwin, *'S Wonderful!*

b.

S'Won-der-ful! _____ S'Mar-vel-ous! _____ You should care _____ for   me!

E♭ major

_____
2

Total Possible: 100   Your Score _____

MOTIVIC CONSTRUCTION

Traditional melody is inherently tonal. Stable and active tones, melodic cadences, and other factors, center our attention on a single pitch. Yet even with a clear tonality, other considerations affect our perceptions of melodic design. Chief among these is motivic development.

Whether folk, art, or pop, Western music is constructed so that the listener perceives both smaller and larger formal divisions as the work progresses. As we have discussed, composers achieve such balance by varying cadences (terminal or progressive). In addition, from the first to the final pitch, melodies are written in phrases and groups of phrases. Phrases and linked-phrase groups are connected through one of two methods: *motivic* or *periodic.*[1] Motivic design is discussed in the next section. See Chapter 9 for information on periodic melody.

Motives

A MOTIVE is a group of pitches (usually two to five) that is memorable in rhythm, interval pattern, or both. By definition, a motive is incomplete; motives generate and unify longer musical lines. MOTIVIC CONSTRUCTION describes the process by which motives are manipulated to form phrases and groups of related phrases.

One of the most famous motives in Western music literature is the one that begins Beethoven's Symphony No. 5 in C Minor. Opening with a rest, the reiterated eighth notes generate momentum that culminates in the memorable descending major third and dramatic fermata.

L. van Beethoven, Symphony No. 5
First Movement

C minor

Using techniques such as repetition, variation, and transformation, Beethoven manipulates this motive to unify a thirty-minute work. Likewise, in his popular opera, *Carmen*, the French composer Georges Bizet (1838–1875) threads the "fate motive" (shown in the next example) throughout each act as a harbinger of the drama's eventual tragic outcome. Notice the augmented second between C♯ and B♭. Since the goal of the opening motive is A_3, we would expect both C♮ and B♭. In this case, however, Bizet creates an exotic effect by employing—and even emphasizing—the augmented second.

Georges Bizet, *Carmen*

D minor

Especially in the 1990s, most popular music has been based on the repetition and variation of simple motives. Listen to the ascending half-step motive that opens *One of Us* and follow its variation in measures 3 and 5. The motive becomes an anchor that reinforces tonality and draws our attention to internal divisions. In addition, observe that the material in measures 2, 4, 6, and 7 is not really "new," but rather an inversion (descending stepwise) of the original.

---

[1] Some phrases show the influence of both techniques.

CD 1, TRACK 34
Eric Bazilian, *One of Us*
Eighth-Note Motive

Johann Sebastian Bach was a master at crafting complex compositions from simple motives. His Fugue No. 2 from the *Well-Tempered Clavier* (Volume I) begins with a figure that emphasizes the tonic pitch (C) and the minor mode (with $\downarrow\hat{6}$).

J. S. Bach, Fugue No. 2 in C Minor
Well-Tempered Clavier I

C minor

The descending perfect fourth dominates Bach's motive, but as the phrase continues, he expands the perfect fourth to a perfect fifth and to a major sixth before closing with a terminal cadence on $\hat{3}$. The persistent rhythmic figure centers our interest on the melody and its development into a phrase.

CD 1, TRACK 35-1 MOTIVES (2 PARTS)
J.S. Bach, Fugue in C Minor
Expanded Motive

Identifying Motives in Analysis. In writing about music, reduction and abbreviation are often helpful to clarify structure. We can identify a motive, for example, with the letter "m." Should a passage include more than one motive, you may use "1m" for the first motive, "2m" for the second, and so on. If a motive is varied, use superscripts to identify the first ($2m^1$), second ($2m^2$), and third ($2m^3$) variants as needed.

Motivic Phrases

Combining two different motives to form a phrase is a common technique in

TRACK 35-2 MOTIVES
Joseph Haydn, Sonata in D Major (I)
Repetition and Contrast

many styles of traditional Western music. In his Sonata in D Major, for example, Haydn introduces a motive (1m), repeats that motive, and then ends the phrase with new material (2m).

While most authorities would identify the motive in measure 3 as new material, notice that in its descending stepwise motion, 2m is clearly related to 1m. Further, the eighth notes in measure 4 can be heard as an expansion of 2m (and also of 1m, of course).

Jazz is especially rich in motivic design. Ann Ronell (1906–1993) begins her ballad *Willow Weep for Me* with a juxtaposition of the natural and the borrowed divisions. Notice that a tie weakens the metric strength of the third beat.

As we have discussed, simply repeating a memorable motive is an effective means of generating a complete phrase. Especially when repetition is combined with expansion (as seen in the Bach fugue on page 132), the design of a single motive helps the listener to follow organization over a longer time span. In *Willow Weep for Me,* Ann Ronell repeats the opening five-note motive (measure 1–2), expands it into a pattern of nine notes (measure 3), and concludes the phrase with a final statement of the triplet figure. In other styles, the syncopation that obscures the meter would be less pronounced; in jazz, however, an emphasis on accented beats is more the exception than the rule.

Ronell, Motivic Structure

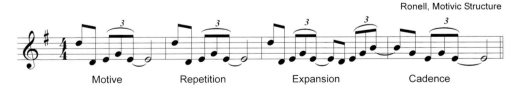

Subphrase.   While we identify the four measures in the last example as a phrase, smaller internal divisions are also present. A SUBPHRASE is one section of a phrase—often two or three measures in length. While longer than a motive, subphrases usually lack the cadential security of a phrase. In Ronell's melody, we have identified the first five pitches as a motive. Subphrases in the melody are two measures in length and the entire phrase is four measures.

Motive and Subphrase Construction

Having employed the triplet motive (1m) in every measure of the melody, Ronell introduces a new motive (2m) in measure 5. Motive 2m is followed by a variation that ends the second phrase with a recollection of the first motive (1m). The unusual progressive cadence ending on 6̂, as well as the use of both B♮ and B♭, are elements of twentieth-century styles that we will talk about in later chapters.

CD 1, TRACK 36
Ann Ronell, *Willow Weep for Me*
Repetition, Variation, and Contrast

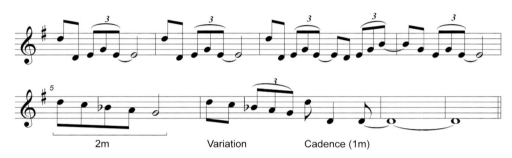

2m   Variation   Cadence (1m)

Sequence

SEQUENCE is a special type of repetition in which a motive is heard successively higher or lower. The most characteristic type of sequence involves three or more successive melodic and rhythmic patterns. Each statement (or LEG) is clearly a derivative of the generating motive (although some insignificant differences may exist). In the next example, the superscripts identify motive "1m," in two different variations (sequences of the original).

CD 1, TRACK 37-1 PHRASES EMPLOYING SEQUENCE (2 PARTS)
Sequence by Ascending Second

1m	1m¹	1m²	2m
Motive	Sequential Repetition	Sequential Repetition	Cadence

Sequence may be ascending or descending and by any constant interval. In the next example, the sequence is by descending third. The absence of the second eighth note in the second leg (measure 2) is insignificant. While alterations in the initial pitches of a motive may blur the sequential organization, changes later on rarely do.

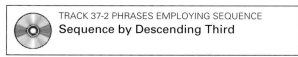

TRACK 37-2 PHRASES EMPLOYING SEQUENCE
Sequence by Descending Third

| 1m | 1m¹ | 1m² | Progressive |
Motive | Sequential Repetition | Sequential Repetition | Cadence

CD 1, TRACK 38-1 DIATONIC AND CHROMATIC
SEQUENCE (2 PARTS)
Neil Hefti, *In Veradero*
Diatonic Sequence

In his 1958 jazz standard, *In Veradero,* Neil Hefty uses a two-measure descending motive, then moves into a progressive cadence on the dominant.

Diatonic and Chromatic Sequence.   The sequence in the last example is DIATONIC because all of the pitches belong to the same key. In a CHROMATIC SEQUENCE, the note names would be the same, but one or more accidentals would be used. Both diatonic and chromatic sequences are common and a single phrase may contain both types. If Hefti had used chromatic sequence for *In Veradero,* the melody might have unfolded differently and toward a new key.

TRACK 38-2
Edited Hefti Melody
Chromatic Sequence

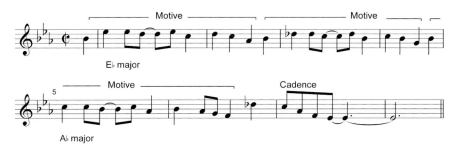

In the last example, the chromatic pitch D♭ serves to turn the melody from E♭ major to a new key: A♭ major. While diatonic sequence is common in tonal melodies, chromatic sequence often facilitates changes of key.[2]

---

[2]Modulation, the process of key change, is the subject of Chapter 11 of this volume.

J. S. Bach wrote six concertos for the Duke of Brandenburg. The opening phrase of the second of these works (third movement) begins with two related motives, repetitions, and diatonic sequence by descending step. There are four legs in this sequence, but as is often the case, the last of them is altered to form the cadence.

J. S. Bach, Brandenberg Concerto No. 2
Third Movement

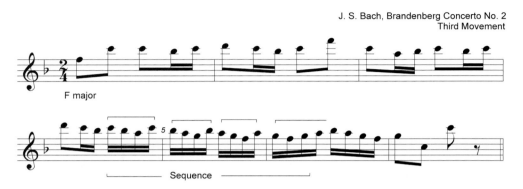

Chromatic sequence often follows the exact pattern of intervals in some legs with an alteration of that pattern in others. In the following passage from Beethoven's Quartet in F Major (Op. 18, No.1), the sequence ascends by step. The second leg includes F♯ to duplicate the original pattern (and to create a brief tonal orientation to G minor). The third leg is diatonic in F major, but is altered to form a terminal cadence.

Ludwig van Beethoven, Quartet Op. 18, No. 1
First Movement

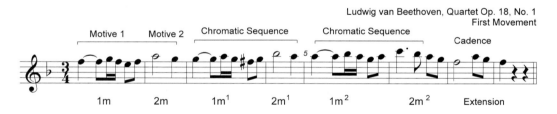

Diatonic sequence by step occurs in Mozart's *Symphonie Concertante* in E♭ Major. A motive of three legs culminates with a descending scalar pattern.

W. A. Mozart, *Symphonie Concertante* K. 364

Another example of diatonic sequence—this time by descending third—is the basis of an eight-measure phrase in Mozart's Quartet in G Major (shown in the next example).

W. A. Mozart, Quartet in G Major K. 80

Sequential Principle.   Even when three or more complete sequential legs are not present, many melodies are based on the sequence principle. Legs may be altered, for example, to suit the needs of a given passage. In the Irish folk song, *Molly Malone,* the third leg of a sequence begins like the first two, but more frequent pitch changes anticipate the progressive melodic cadence.

Irish Folk Song, "Molly Malone"

In Dublin's fair cit-y, where girls are so pret-ty I first set my eyes on sweet Mol-ly Ma-lone.

G major

In the third phrase of Mozart's Adagio from the Concerto for Clarinet, the third leg of a two-measure sequence increases in momentum to end in a terminal cadence.

W. A. Mozart, Adagio

D major

Even if chromatic or diatonic sequence is not employed, composers may use *sequence-like* figures to generate momentum through changing harmonies. In his Sonata, Op. 10 (third movement) Beethoven presents a simple motive, combined with reiterated tendency tones, to strengthen the C minor tonality. While the second phrase of the melody is a transposition of the first (a perfect fourth lower), the line ends with a return to C minor and a terminal cadence.

Ludwig van Beethoven, Sonata Op. 10, No. 1
Third Movement

Compound Melody.   Especially in melodies that are motivic in design, two distinctly different lines may evolve simultaneously in a single voice. This effect is called COMPOUND MELODY and is evident in the Beethoven sonata quoted above. The opening motive remains stationary (driving home the tonic pitch) while a second motive ascends, emphasizing pitches in the tonic triad through tendency tones $\hat{4}$–$\hat{3}$ and $\downarrow\hat{6}$–$\hat{5}$.

Compound Melody

Passages of compound melody appear in the works of many composers. In the final movement of his Suite No. 6 for Unaccompanied Cello, J. S. Bach creates the effect of two different instruments performing simultaneously by employing repeated notes and changes of register.

CD 1, TRACK 39
J. S. Bach, Suite for Unaccompanied Cello No. 6 (Gigue)
Compound Melody

In addition to developing melodic and harmonic parameters, composers typically lead the listener through the formal design of a work. Motives grow into phrases through repetition, transposition, sequence, and other techniques. As we will discuss in Chapter 9, these phrases develop into longer formal divisions called *periods* and *phrase groups*. In the next section of the present chapter, however, we will discuss musical style—the use of traditional materials to create varied effects.

WORKBOOK/ANTHOLOGY I
II Motives and Phrases, page 53

REVIEW AND APPLICATION 4–2

Motives, Phrases, and Sequence

Essential Terms

compound melody	motivic construction	sequence
leg	motive	subphrase

1. In the following melodies, be prepared to identify the motive (or motives), the type of any sequence present, and the final melodic cadence (progressive or terminal).

J. S. Bach, Suite in B Minor

B minor

César Franck, Fugue Theme Op. 18

D Major

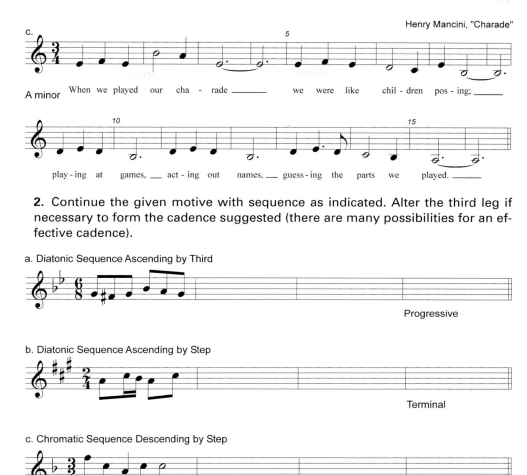

Henry Mancini, "Charade"

A minor When we played our cha - rade _____ we were like chil - dren pos - ing; _____

play - ing at games, __ act - ing out names, __ guess - ing the parts we played. _____

2. Continue the given motive with sequence as indicated. Alter the third leg if necessary to form the cadence suggested (there are many possibilities for an effective cadence).

a. Diatonic Sequence Ascending by Third

Progressive

b. Diatonic Sequence Ascending by Step

Terminal

c. Chromatic Sequence Descending by Step

Progressive

SELF-TEST 4–2

Time Limit: 5 Minutes

1. Match a term from the list with the definition given. Write the letter representing the term in the blank. *Scoring: Subtract 8 points for each error.*

   A. Compound melody   D. Subphrase

   B. Diatonic sequence   E. Chromatic sequence

   C. Motive   F. Sequential leg

   _____ (1) One repetition of a motivic pattern.

   _____ (2) An incomplete musical fragment of two to eight pitches.

   _____ (3) The repetition of an initial melodic and rhythmic pattern at another pitch level, but conforming to the prevailing key signature.

_____ (4) An element of melodic construction that is longer than a motive, but which lacks the cadential identity of a phrase.

_____ (5) A type of melodic variation that involves repetition of a given pattern, but with alterations outside the key.

_____ (6) The simultaneous presentation of two different melodic ideas within a single voice.

2. The following five questions concern the example below. *Scoring: Subtract 9 points for each incorrect answer.*

CD 1, TRACK 40
Self-Test 4-2
Melody for Analysis

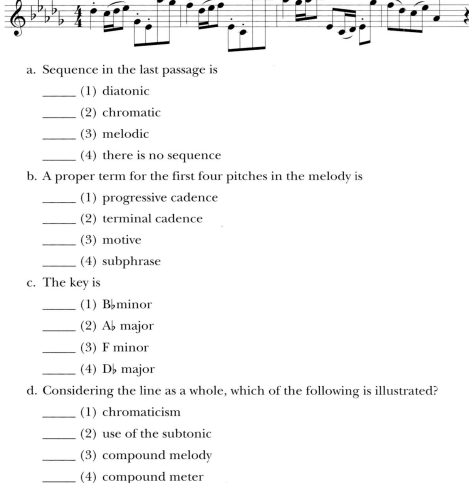

a. Sequence in the last passage is

_____ (1) diatonic

_____ (2) chromatic

_____ (3) melodic

_____ (4) there is no sequence

b. A proper term for the first four pitches in the melody is

_____ (1) progressive cadence

_____ (2) terminal cadence

_____ (3) motive

_____ (4) subphrase

c. The key is

_____ (1) B♭ minor

_____ (2) A♭ major

_____ (3) F minor

_____ (4) D♭ major

d. Considering the line as a whole, which of the following is illustrated?

_____ (1) chromaticism

_____ (2) use of the subtonic

_____ (3) compound melody

_____ (4) compound meter

e. We can describe the last pitch of the melody as

_____ (1) a progressive cadence

_____ (2) a terminal cadence

_____ (3) chromatic sequence

_____ (4) a new motive

3. Provide the term that refers to a melodic and rhythmic fragment that is heard successively higher or lower. *Scoring: subtract 7 points for an incorrect answer.*

_____

Total Possible: 100   Your Score _____

MELODIC STYLE

Why do Mozart's Adagio (page 116), *Oh, Pretty Woman* (126), and *Willow Weep for Me* (page 133) all sound so different, even though they are based on identical melodic, rhythmic, and harmonic principles? One answer is that the three melodies are different in MELODIC STYLE. Mozart's melody is elegant and timeless; the repetitive *Pretty Woman* theme is catchy; and Ann Ronell's "Willow," while syncopated, is melancholy in effect. In this section, we will discuss several factors that influence melodic style: range, instrumental or vocal concept, melodic motion, and contour.

Melodic Motion

Even though Mozart's Adagio was written for the clarinet, it is singable and thus VOCAL in concept. In traditional Western music, passages that are intended for vocal performance feature a preponderance of CONJUNCT MOTION—that is, melodies that progress basically by step. A passage may still be described as conjunct if leaps are present, yet not prominent. This is especially true if melodic tendencies are closely adhered to following leaps.

If a melody is not conjunct, it is *disjunct*. In DISJUNCT melodies, leaps predominate (although there may also be some stepwise motion). In addition, many of the leaps may be triad arpeggiations. We associate disjunct melodies with an INSTRUMENTAL STYLE—music for keyboard or an orchestral instrument.

Conjunct motion might be illustrated through many of the melodies in this chapter (including the Mozart Adagio). In addition, the two complementary phrases below are conjunct in melodic motion and vocal in concept.

CD 1, TRACK 41-1 MUSICAL STYLE (2 PARTS)
Ludwig van Beethoven, Sonata in E Minor
Vocal Style

Notice that the conjunct melody in the last example was written for piano—not voice. As Beethoven did, instrumental composers use a vocal style when appropriate just as composers of vocal music may sometimes write disjunct melodies (as in the next example).

TRACK 41-2 MUSICAL STYLE
George Frideric Handel, *Acis and Galatea*
Instrumental Style

O rud - dier than the cher - ry   O sweet - er than the   ber - ry.

The previous phrase, from Handel's opera, *Acis and Galatea*, might also have been written for cello, bassoon, or trombone. Skillful composers employ a predominantly conjunct or disjunct line for many reasons including ease of performance, dramatic effect, contrast with other material, and the like.

Range and Tessitura

The RANGE of a melody is the interval formed between the highest and the lowest pitches. The range of the Handel melody in the last passage, for example, is a major tenth ($B\flat_2$–D_4). In the Beethoven melody, the range is narrower—an octave (B_3–B_4). The standard piano keyboard has a range of over seven octaves; most singers have practical ranges of only about two octaves. For performers of average ability, the ranges for stringed and wind instruments vary from two octaves (the trumpet) to nearly three octaves (the violin).[3]

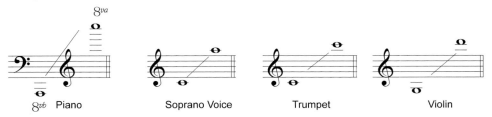

8vb Piano   Soprano Voice   Trumpet   Violin

Tessitura.   In addition to range, the TESSITURA—where *most* of the pitches lie—is a helpful standard of melodic construction. We can measure the range of a melody simply by comparing the highest and lowest pitches. The tessitura, however, is subjective. In some melodies, the range and the tessitura might be about the same. In others, a few notes are exceptionally higher or lower than others and are excluded from the tessitura. The next melody, by French composer Christoph Gluck (1714–1787), has the range of a minor ninth ($F\sharp_4$–G_5). In determining the tessitura, however, we would exclude the G_5 since it is higher than most of the other pitches. Likewise, because the $F\sharp_4$ and D_5 occur only once each, we might exclude these pitches from the tessitura as well.

Christoph Gluck, *Air de Ballet*

Range   Tessitura

[3]For more information on instrument ranges and transposition, see Appendix A on page 477.

Whether the concept is vocal or instrumental, some melodies have wide ranges (as in Bruce Broughton's theme from the 1985 film *Silverado*), while in other works, such as the Renaissance popular tune *La Folia* ("The Fool"), both range and tessitura are narrow.

Bruce Broughton, Theme from *Silverado*

C major

Range

M10

Renaissance Melody, "The Fool"

D minor

Range

d5

Contour

Most traditional melodies have a definitive profile of ascending and descending motion, called the CONTOUR. Some phrases ascend; others descend. Traditional melodies may have an arch (or inverted arch) shape that balances gradual (or sudden) ascent and descent.

A comparison of melodies may include a graphic representation of the melodic contours—as specifically or as generally as necessary to convey the most meaningful information. Measure numbers, of course, are useful points of reference. The gentle arch-shape of the Renaissance melody (*The Fool*) in the last example is apparent in a graphic representation. Likewise, the contour of the Beethoven quartet phrase on page 136 is shown as an ascending line with a sudden descent at the cadence.

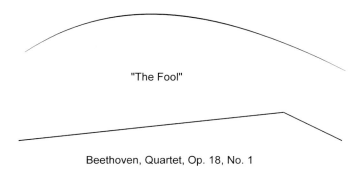

"The Fool"

Beethoven, Quartet, Op. 18, No. 1

While a graphic representation of phrase shape may be helpful in understanding segments of a melody, plotting a melodic contour is usually more useful in examining longer melodic divisions.

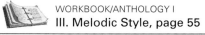

WORKBOOK/ANTHOLOGY I
III. Melodic Style, page 55

LINEAR ANALYSIS

Music moves in time from one point of stability to another. Sometimes, as in the case of melodic goals, these points of emphasis are close together. We can usually trace a series of cadences, for example, within the span of a few measures. Other structural points in a composition may be quite distant, however. The progression from the tonic key to another key and back again may be separated by dozens—even hundreds—of measures. One of the ways that we understand traditional melody and harmony is through LINEAR ANALYSIS—a classification of pitches in terms of their essential or embellishing roles.

To one extent or another, linear analysis today is based upon the theories and teachings of the Austrian Heinrich Schenker (1868–1935). Linear "reductions" of works emphasize the relationship between harmony and voice leading and often result in complex and arguably subjective diagrams that trace the melodic and harmonic flow throughout an entire composition or during a phrase or two. The diagram below, for example, traces such relationships in a large-scale symphonic movement.[4]

Tchaikovsky, Symphony No. 1
(First Movement)

On the other hand, linear analysis permits a study of these same melodic and harmonic relationships over just a few measures. This passage from Felix Mendelssohn's chorale "Behold A Star from Jacob Shining" is not difficult to understand from an analysis with traditional roman numerals (as we will discuss in this and later chapters).

Felix Mendelssohn, "Behold A Star from Jacob Shining"
from *Christus*

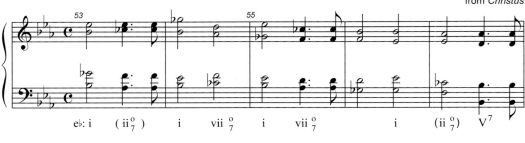

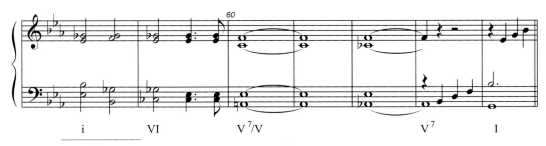

---

[4]These diagrams are taken from *Harmonic Practice in Tonal Music* (1997) by Robert Gauldin.

A linear analysis of the same twelve-measure passage conveys similar information in a different way.

While Schenkerian analysis has enjoyed a resurgence in the past decade, opinion regarding its proper place in an undergraduate music curriculum varies. At many institutions, Schenkerian analysis is limited to upper-division and graduate-level courses. But while some schools include little or no linear analysis in the undergraduate curriculum, there are still others at which virtually every aspect of the theory program revolves around graphic representations of a musical work. Our purpose in this text is to survey several principles of graphic analysis, but in such a way as to make it applicable to a wide range of analytical methods.

Melodic Reduction

MELODIC REDUCTION is the process of classifying the pitches of a melodic line into structural, secondary, or embellishing roles while at the same time, making note of the importance of various pitches over a given time span.

Structural Pitches.   As we discussed briefly in Chapter 3, many melodies center upon pitches in the tonic and dominant triads. Especially when they occur on strong beats, members of the tonic or dominant triads are STRUCTURAL PITCHES. If our purpose is to represent the pitches of a melody according to their relative importance (and not rhythmic value), structural pitches are represented as stemmed notes with open heads (♩).[5] Pitches that are heard as cadential or otherwise as the goal of a melodic line are also typically structural.

Secondary Pitches.   When members of the tonic, dominant, or another diatonic triad are unaccented, their role in the development of melody is often SECONDARY. In an analysis, we can show these pitches with solid note heads and stems (♩). A scale is a series of secondary pitches anchored by structural tones at the beginning and the end. In this case, the first and the last pitches have open noteheads; the secondary pitches have solid heads and stems.

Because the tonic is emphasized throughout the scale (by definition), we might use a slur to connect tonic pitches and emphasize their ongoing importance.

---

[5]We have not used the term "half note" because the various symbols in a structural reduction show relative melodic importance—not rhythmic value.

For the present, we can view the melody *Twinkle, Twinkle, Little Star* as comprised entirely of structural and secondary pitches (although we might disagree on the respective categories). In the example below, the pitches A and D (measures 2 and 4) are melodic goals (the D is also a terminal cadence).

Embellishing Pitches.   An EMBELLISHING PITCH has neither a structural nor a secondary role; rather, it decorates an essential pitch in one of several stereotypical ways. When a pitch is embellished, its structural importance increases. Depending upon the degree of detail involved in an analysis, embellishing pitches may be omitted from a melodic reduction, or they may be included as solid, unstemmed noteheads (.). Of the many different embellishing roles used by traditional composers, we will introduce one type here: the *neighboring tone*. Other types of embellishing pitches will be discussed in later chapters.

Neighboring Tone.   A NEIGHBORING TONE embellishes and emphasizes a structural or secondary pitch by step from above or below. Neighboring tones (abbreviated "NT") may be accented or unaccented; upper or lower; diatonic or chromatic. Embellishing pitches such as the neighboring tone are not always included in a reduction. When they do appear, however, a slur is often used to connect the embellishing and the embellished pitches.

Neighboring Tones

Looking again at *Twinkle, Twinkle, Little Star*, notice that the pitch B in the second measure fulfills the role of neighboring tone.

This variation of *Twinkle, Twinkle, Little Star* includes a variety of neighboring tones. These embellishing pitches are shown on the reduction as unstemmed noteheads. Here, the pitch B in measure 2 (identified as embellishing in the last example) has added importance because it is itself embellished. A structural reduction of the embellished melody is not particularly different from that of the original (last example). In the following reduction, however, embellishing pitches and their relationships to structural and secondary pitches are emphasized.

Twinkle, Twinkle, Little Star
Variation

Reduction

The Passing Tone.   A PASSING TONE ("PT") fills in the interval of a third between two chord tones. Passing tones may be accented or unaccented, ascending or descending. Occasionally, two consecutive passing tones fill in the interval of a fourth between two chord tones. Note that passing tones are *not* embellishing pitches. Since their role is to smooth a melodic line, diatonic passing tones lack an embellishing function. In the melodic reduction below, passing tones are indicated by a slur. In these examples, consider the chord to be E major in each case.

Passing Tones

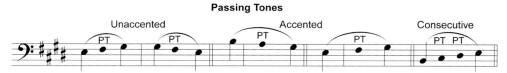

Returning to *Twinkle, Twinkle, Little Star,* we can see that the pitch G in measure 3 and the E in measure 4 are passing tones.

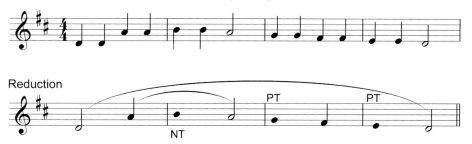

Because passing tones merely smooth the melodic line and have little significance otherwise, they are often omitted from a reduction. In this case, note the even more obvious structure of *Twinkle, Twinkle, Little Star* as a D major triad.

Reduction

Henry Mancini (1924–1994) was one of the most successful film composers after 1950. "The Sweetheart Tree," from the 1965 Warner Brothers comedy *The Great Race,* is a simple waltz that includes a number of passing and neighboring tones in the melody. With an analysis of the harmony (provided through roman numerals in the next example), we can make a reduction to show structural and secondary pitches as well as neighboring and passing tones.

Johnny Mercer and Henry Mancini, "The Sweetheart Tree"
from *The Great Race*

The reduction of "The Sweetheart Tree" is not too different from the original notation; this tells us that the melody is constructed mainly of chord tones. A further reduction, showing only structural pitches, is more helpful in understanding the melodic construction.

In 1728, John Gay (1685–1732) and Johann Pepusch (1667–1752) adapted a number of popular tunes interspersed with spoken dialogue into *The Beggar's Opera*—a spoof of Italian *opera seria* that was intended not for the aristocracy, but for the working class of London. The story of thieves, prostitutes, and murderers, combined with simple, popular melodies, was a huge success and helped launch a new era in the development of opera. An aria from *The Beggar's Opera*, "Courtiers Think It No Harm," appears in the next example along with a reduction (on the lower staff) that shows structural, secondary, and embellishing pitches. Passing tones are omitted from the reduction.

Johann Pepsuch and John Gay,
"Courtiers Think It No Harm" from *The Beggar's Opera*

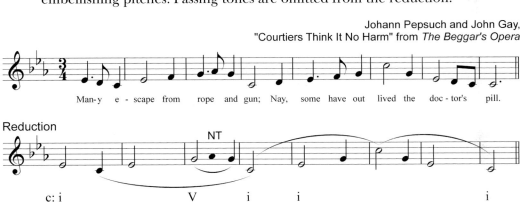

Like many traditional melodies, "Courtiers Think It No Harm" revolves around pitches in the tonic (C-minor) triad. Slurs highlight the continuing influence of the pitch C throughout the melody.

Prolongation

Many Western melodies, especially those associated with jazz and popular styles, are constructed so that one pitch—not necessarily the tonic—plays an important role over the span of several measures, or even over the course of an entire composition. This dominance of one pitch is called PROLONGATION. In tonal works, we often find prolongations of pitches in the tonic or dominant triads. William ("Count") Basie (1904–1984) was the leader of "Barons of Rhythm," a major influence in the Big Band Era of the 1930s and 1940s. In his *Rockabye Basie,* notice the continuing influence (prolongation) of the pitch A throughout the melody. The pitches A♭, on the other hand, are embellishing. As with other melodies we have studied in this section, the framework of *Rockabye Basie* is a tonic triad. Remember, however, that we have included these reductions to show how traditional melody is constructed. Do not be reluctant to try reductions of your own, but know that without a deeper knowledge of harmony, you may find your decisions quite subjective.

CD 1, TRACK 42
Count Basie, Shad Collins and Lester Young,
Rockabye Basie
Prolongation

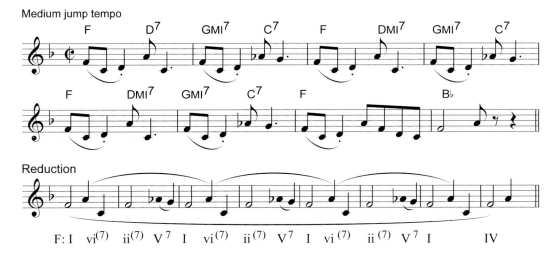

Arpeggiation

A sequence of several pitches within a single chord is called an ARPEGGIATION. The melody from Haydn's Menuet includes an arpeggiation of the tonic triad. In a reduction, you might show such an arpeggiation as a series of stemless notes, anchored by stemmed notes at the beginning and end of the series.

Reduction (Piano Score on page 120)

While those who espouse Schenker's theories work from a fairly rigid set of graphic guidelines, the same principles can be applied to supplement our understanding of melodic construction. We might undertake the analysis of a particular melody, for example, and in addition to a study of centricity, cadence, range, style, and motivic basis, include a melodic reduction. Another type of melodic analysis that is often valuable in studying traditional melody is *step progression.*

Step Progression

Many successful melodies are designed (consciously or otherwise) with series of three or more structural or secondary pitches in ascending or descending stepwise motion. These series, called STEP PROGRESSIONS, help organize a melody and *do not* typically occur among adjacent pitches. As shown in the next example, the folk song *My Old Kentucky Home,* includes several three-pitch step progressions.

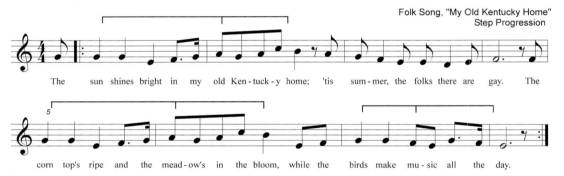

Folk Song, "My Old Kentucky Home"
Step Progression

The sun shines bright in my old Ken-tuck-y home; 'tis sum-mer, the folks there are gay. The

corn top's ripe and the mead-ow's in the bloom, while the birds make mu-sic all the day.

In many traditional melodies, a descending $\hat{3}$–$\hat{2}$–$\hat{1}$ pattern can be traced over the course of one or more phrases. The connection of stems, as shown here, is an alternate representation of step progression.

Step Progression

Two different step progressions ascend simultaneously in the theme from Haydn's Sonata in G Major (third movement). Notice that octave distribution is not normally a factor in defining step progressions. Any one of several methods may be used to identify step progressions in a formal analysis, but styles should not be mixed in the same study.

Joseph Haydn, Sonata in G Major
Third Movement

As with melodic reduction, defining step progression is subjective. They occur somewhere in virtually all Western melodies, but may or may not be significant. More effectively, melodic analysis enhances our performance potential by focusing attention on details that may be structural, but not readily apparent. Incorporating these details into performance will enhance an individual interpretation.

WORKBOOK/ANTHOLOGY I
IV. Melodic Reduction, page 57

REVIEW AND APPLICATION 4–3

Linear Analysis

Essential Terms

arpeggiation	linear analysis	range
conjunct motion	melodic reduction	secondary pitch
contour	neighboring tone	step progression
disjunct motion	passing tone	structural pitch
embellishing pitch	prolongation	tessitura

1. Circle structural pitches in the phrases below.

2. Complete a melodic reduction of the melody below. Isolate structural and secondary pitches, indicate embellishing tones, and step progressions. Note: reductions that are different in some respects may still reflect an appropriate representation of the melodic construction.

CD 1, TRACK 43
Joseph Haydn, "In Native Worth" from The Creation
Arpeggiation

rene,   He stands   A Man,   the Lord   and King   of   na - ture all.

*discount this
chord to be studied in
a later chapter

Reduction (melody only)

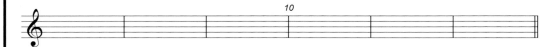

3. Determine the range and tessitura of the voice part in Haydn's "In Native Worth." Write the highest and lowest pitches on the staff below; then identify the interval. Likewise, compute the tessitura and express this as an interval as well.

Range   Tessitura

_____   _____
Interval   Interval

SELF-TEST 4–3

Time Limit: 5 Minutes

1. Choose a term from the list to match to each statement below. Write the letter of the correct answer in the blank.; *Scoring: Subtract 6 points for each error.*

A. Arpeggiation   E. Secondary pitch

B. Structural pitch   F. Melodic cadence

C. Embellishing pitch   G. Passing tone

D. Step progression   H. Linear Analysis

_____ (1) fills in the interval between two chord tones.

_____ (2) A study of pitches in various structural and embellishing roles.

_____ (3) pitches in a melody that are the most important.

_____ (4) may be terminal or progressive.

_____ (5) pitches in a melody that outline a chord.

_____ (6) pitches in a melody that focus attention on another, more important pitch.

_____ (7) chord tones that are in relatively weaker metric positions in a melody.

_____ (8) a movement of pitches in an ascending or descending scalar pattern, but not typically among adjacent tones.

2. Study the melody below, then in the blank staff, complete a reduction by eliminating passing tones and by showing neighboring tones as stemless solid notes with slur as appropriate. There are six such pitches in the melody. You need not differentiate between structural and secondary pitches. _Scoring: Subtract 8 points for any of the six reductions that is incorrectly reduced._

Revolutionary War Melody, "Chester"

Reduction

3. Use a specific term to describe the type of melodic cadence that occurs in measure 8 of _Chester_. _Scoring: subtract 4 points for an incorrect answer._

_____

Total Possible: 100   Your Score _____

PROJECTS

Analysis

As you progress through the chapters of this text, the analysis projects will naturally become longer and more complex. While it would be ideal to study melody and harmony at the same time, we will need to separate these parameters for the present. The melodies provided for study in the text and workbook are complete verses, sections, or movements and typical of various styles and eras. Pitches that lie outside the harmony have been identified and the underlying harmony has been extracted for you to identify. Center your studies on the melody now; in the next and later chapters, you will identify the harmony as well.

Text

Shaker Melody, "Simple Gifts," text, page 156. The Shakers were an eighteenth-century religious group (derived from the Quakers) that began in New York, but later spread throughout the United States. The sect died out in the late twentieth century, although elements of their uncomplicated, communal existence remains. The hymn "Simple Gifts" is still often heard today. It was used as the basis of a series of variations in Aaron Copland's popular ballet, _Appalachian Spring_ (1944).

The harmonization given on page 156 is entirely diatonic. Prepare an analysis of the melody that addresses some or all of the areas listed.

1. Provide a complete roman-numeral analysis.
2. Many neighboring and passing tones embellish or smooth the melody. Mark these pitches in the score ("NT" and "PT").
3. Comment on the resolution of tendency tones in the melody.
4. Locate and classify melodic cadences.
5. Mark any step progressions that are present and comment on melodic goals.
6. Determine the style, range, and tessitura of the melody.
7. Be prepared to discuss style and other aspects of melodic construction as directed.
8. Arrange the song as a lead sheet with melody, text, and popular-music chord symbols as suggested in the next example.

Workbook/Anthology II

George Frideric Handel, Largo from Xerxes, workbook page 59.
J.S. Bach, Menuet in G, workbook page 60.

Composition

Original Folk Song. Using "Simple Gifts" (page 156) as a model, set the following stanza as a folk song. Each line should be four measures long and adhere to the progression suggested (although if you choose minor, qualities will be adjusted accordingly).

Line	Progession			
Though you may think it best to scorn me,	I	I	V	I
I persist and love you still.	IV	I	V	V
For though the day's rebuffs have torn me,	VI	IV	I	V
Sleep will cure the ill.	I	V	I	I

Plan and compose a melody that accentuates the text, but is not complicated or irregular in rhythm and meter. Think of this melody as one that will be taught by rote, so your setting should be basically syllabic (one note to each syllable). Two different settings of the first two lines are provided as samples, but you should compose four lines that are entirely your own.

Sample 1: D Major

Sample 2: G Minor

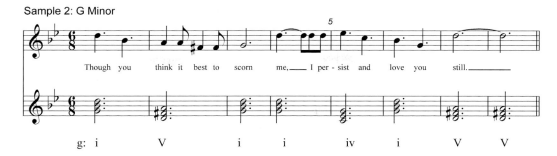

The first verse of your brief folk song will be only twice the length of the sample. If directed to do so, compose an additional four lines using the same progressions, Your melody for the second verse will be slightly different to accommodate the new words.

> And if the years find you unbending
> And I press my love in vain,
> Then life and love shall have one ending:
> Death will ease the pain.

For Further Study

Folk, Art, and Popular Music.   Folk, art, and popular music are all central to our Western culture. Together, the three categories fill our lives with enriching experiences, permit a moment of diversion, and foster community bonding. This theory text centers on Western art music. For a change of pace, you may find it interesting to investigate folk or popular music a bit deeper by writing a short paper (3-5 pages) or preparing an oral report of not more than five minutes. You can use a readily available source such as a music dictionary, encyclopedia, or the Internet, or you might consult books on folk and popular music, respectively, that will be available in your library.

Folk Music   What are the characteristics of Western folk music? Is it usually notated? How are folk songs learned and passed from one individual to another? Do we typically know the composer of an authentic folk song? What are some typical texts of folk songs? Are folk song composers trained musicians? Are there general melodic and harmonic characteristics for folk songs? What musical instruments are common?

Prepare a listening list of a least five representative folk songs including a stanza or two of lyrics if possible. Be sure to *exclude* pop music that is designed to mimic a folk style (Peter, Paul, and Mary, Joan Baez, and so on).

Popular Music   Popular music is written and performed for the "populace" which may have very little musical training or sophistication. Limit your study of popular music to America at the turn-of-the-century and later. What was "Tin Pan Alley," for example? How has the music of Black Americans been influential? What is ragtime? "the blues?" What are the characteristics of the music we call "Country and Western? *Exclude* jazz and all of its variants from your study, but investigate "rhythm and blues" as well as early rock.

Prepare a listening list that includes one excerpt from at least five of the categories you mention in your report or paper.

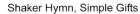

CHAPTER 5

Harmonic Function

Most of us have had the experience of listening to the performance of an original composition and perceiving a *wrong note*. Despite a lack of familiarity with the music, our sensitivity to the tonal system is so strong that we can usually hear deviations from it almost immediately. Play the first phrase of Mozart's Adagio, for

CD 1, TRACK 44
W. A. Mozart, Concerto for Clarinet, K. 622
Wrong Note

example, as notated below. Even if you had never heard the melody, you would probably realize that the A♯s in measures 3–4 do not "fit" with the other pitches.

For most listeners today, tonality is the only system of music. As children, we in the West sing tonal melodies in school; music for public consumption—radio, television, and film—invariably conforms to tonal principles. And if we sing, play, or compose "by ear," we naturally gravitate to familiar tonal patterns.

There is nothing inherently "better" about traditional Western music (as compared to Japanese, African, or Indonesian music, for example), but for several reasons, the tonal system has been popular with composers and audiences alike since the mid-seventeenth century. First, many aspects of pitch and duration can be notated in our system with great accuracy. Second, tonality has a solid theoretical basis in the harmonic series—the same natural sequence of pitch relationships that governs all world music.

In Chapter 5, we will examine several basic aspects of tonal harmony and discuss how melodic and harmonic elements combine to establish key and mode. Because the emergence of music as "melody with accompaniment" (*homophony*) facilitated the final evolution of the tonal system, we will begin with a historical look at *texture* in Western music.

TEXTURE

The number of voices (parts) and their relationships determine TEXTURE—the musical fabric. MONOPHONY, the earliest Western music, was written in one part and without accompaniment. While we might think that a central pitch reference is unique to traditional music, many medieval monophonic melodies are also organized around a single pitch. CHANT is a type of speech-song; GREGORIAN CHANT (after Pope Gregory) is music of the early Christian church. Chants such as *Victimae paschali laudes* (given below in part) help us to understand that virtually since its inception, Western music has included pitch "gravity." The pitch D_3 is clearly the center of interest in the phrases below.

Wipo of Burgundy, *Viictimae paschali laudes*
ca. 1050

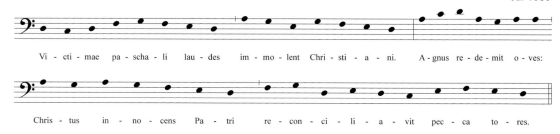

Let Christians dedicate their praises to the Easter Victim.

Polyphony

We know from the writings of early theorists that around 900 C.E., music began to be POLYPHONIC—that is, written with two or more distinct parts or voices. While the melodies of Gregorian chants like *Victimae paschali laudes* were performed in even pulses, early forms of meter, common by about 1250, allowed two or more voices to be delineated clearly through contrasting note values.

The two-voice composition shown in the next example was written about 1225 by a composer associated with the Cathedral of Notre Dame in Paris. The

CD 1, TRACK 45-1 FREE COUNTERPOINT (2 PARTS)
13th-Century France, Motet
Two-Voice Polyphony

work is a MOTET (a composition for voices) and illustrates an intermediate stage in the development of early Western polyphony.

Let the faithful devotion of all the faithful [call out in joy and praise to the Lord].

Counterpoint.   The combination of two or more equal voices is a type of polyphony called COUNTERPOINT. If the predominant texture of a work is counterpoint, that work is described as CONTRAPUNTAL. Early counterpoint, (as shown in the last example), was written primarily in two voices. The lower voice was a pre-existing chant melody called the *cantus firmus* (fixed melody); a newly composed voice was composed above the *cantus firmus*. By the beginning of the fourteenth century, however, a three-voice texture, in which *two* new melodies were composed, was common.

The four-voice texture (Soprano/Alto/Tenor/Bass) became standard in the fifteenth century and has been convenient for amateurs and professionals alike ever since. While most compositions were organized with a Gregorian chant as *cantus firmus*, popular melodies also appeared occasionally in the MASS (the principal Roman catholic service) and motets. The French monophonic song, *L'homme armé* (*The Soldier*) was especially popular. Shown below, the text relates the perils of life during the Hundred Years War (1337–1453).

French Medieval Song, *L'homme armé*

One must be on guard against the soldier.
Everywhere it has been announced
that everybody should arm himself with an iron hauberk [armored shirt]

The four-voice mass fragment in the next example is by the Burgundian composer, Guillaume Dufay (1400–1474). The *cantus firmus* is the secular melody *L'homme armé*. The first phrase of the tune appears in measure 5 in the tenor voice (which actually begins below the bass).

TRACK 45-2 FREE COUNTERPOINT
Guillaume Dufay, *Missa*
L'homme armé (*The Soldier*)
Four-Part Counterpoint

Guillaume Dufay, *Missa L'Homme Armé*

Imitative Counterpoint.   Counterpoint was an important texture for traditional composers like Bach and Mozart. Most often, however, their approach to contrapuntal composition was *imitative*. In IMITATIVE COUNTERPOINT, one voice enters with a melodic and rhythmic fragment and is followed by one or more additional voices that offer the same material (often transposed). Although Josquin Desprez is associated with the origin of imitative counterpoint (as opposed to FREE COUNTERPOINT which *lacks* direct imitation), the style was perfected by a later composer, Giovanni da Palestrina (1525–1594).

The *kyrie eleison* from Palestrina's *Missa Lauda Sion* is in four parts.[1] Notice that as voices enter, the first interval in each is an ascending perfect fourth; this motive unifies the thirteen-measure *kyrie* section and calls our attention to the imitative organization. The soprano is imitated by the tenor; the alto, by the bass. As is common in imitative writing, the first few pitches of the imitating voices are exact, but differences occur later in the line.

CD 1, TRACK 46
Giovanni da Palestrina, *Missa Lauda Sion* (Kyrie)
Imitative Counterpoint

Contrapuntal works like the Palestrina mass may appear to have been conceived as independent lines, but the composers were aware of chords created by the converging parts. In modern terms, we could describe the final three

---

[1]The text of this mass movement is *Kyrie eleison* ("Lord Have Mercy") and is repeated twice for a total of three statements.

chords of the *Missa Lauda Sion* passage as G: IV$_6$–V–I (as detailed below). With certain accommodations for style differences, this same harmonic formula could have ended a composition by Bach, Beethoven, or Brahms.

Homophony. In late-sixteenth-century Florence, a group of influential musicians, poets, performers, and intellectuals founded a new music that hastened the development of our traditional tonal system. The new approach to composition—called MONODY—centered on an embellished melodic line with a simple accompaniment of block tertian chords. Today, music composed in two or more parts, but with one part predominant, is called HOMOPHONY.

The next example is a fragment from the earliest extant opera, *Euridice* (1600), by Jacopo Peri (1561–1633). Notice that the vocal line (in Italian) is basically syllabic with a range and style not too different from a modern popular song. In Peri's day, the chordal accompaniment was performed on a harpsichord with a cello or lute doubling the bass line.

CD 1, TRACK 47-1 HOMOPHONY (2 PARTS)
Jacopo Peri, *Euridice*
Monody

Pre ga, so - spira e plo - ra, forse a - ver - ra che quel so - a - ve pian-to che mosse il ciel pieghi l'Infer no _ an - co - ra.

Venus
Pray, sigh and weep, perhaps it will come to pass that
that soft lament which moved Heaven may cause Hell yet to submit.

Chorale Style. While both contrapuntal and monophonic textures have continued to provide variety and contrast in longer works, the simplicity of homophony has attracted composers of Western popular, folk, and art music since the seventeenth century. We credit J. S. Bach with having perfected the four-part (SATB) Lutheran chorale *genre* (often referred to as the CHORALE or FAMILIAR STYLE). The brief four-part chorale offers a complete composition with many of the same inherent questions of balance and proportion that must be solved in more complex works. Because the harmonic and melodic design of a successful four-part chorale are clear and satisfying to both listener and performer, we continue to employ that style today as a means of studying and duplicating traditional harmony.[2]

The melody of "*Schmücke dich, o liebe Seele*" ("Deck Thyself, with Joy and Gladness") was written by the German composer Johann Crüger (1598–1662); nearly a century later, Bach harmonized the familiar melody in four parts for congregational performance (shown in part in the next example). Notice the traditional stemming patterns: soprano and tenor up; alto and bass down.

---

[2]For instructional purposes, we have omitted text from incomplete chorale phrases, but included the first stanza of the original German when a complete work is provided.

TRACK 47-2 HOMOPHONY
J. S. Bach, "Deck Thyself with Joy and Gladness"
Chorale Style

The graceful flow of melodic and harmonic tonal elements in chorales and other similar pieces allows us to study both the sequence of chords and the movement of individual lines. The process of chord connection (called *voice leading*) will be studied in Chapter 8; next, we will look at the tonal system and the relationships among chord roots.

WORKBOOK/ANTHOLOGY I
I. Texture, page 61

REVIEW AND APPLICATION 5–1

Texture

Essential Terms

chant   Gregorian chant   monophony
counterpoint   homophony   motet
familiar style   imitative counterpoint   polyphony
free counterpoint monody   texture

1. Five phrases are given below for analysis and discussion. Classify the texture of each into one of the categories listed. Be prepared to document your answers. Write your answer in the blank.

A. Monophony   C. Imitative Counterpoint
B. Free counterpoint   D. Homophony

Louise Reichardt, *From Ariel's Revelation*

Lil - ie, Geh' mich, Thau um blinkt dich, du bist traur - ig, bei dir fühl' ich Lei - den!

Lily, look at me!
You sparkle with dew;
You are sad, in you I sense suffering!

J. S. Bach, Fugue in E Major
Well-Tempered Clavier, II

b. _____

John Dunstable, Motet, *Veni Sancte Spiritus*

c. _____

George Gershwin and Ira Gershwin, "The Man I Love"

d. _____

Some-day he'll come a-long   the man I love;   And he'll be big and strong,   The man I love;

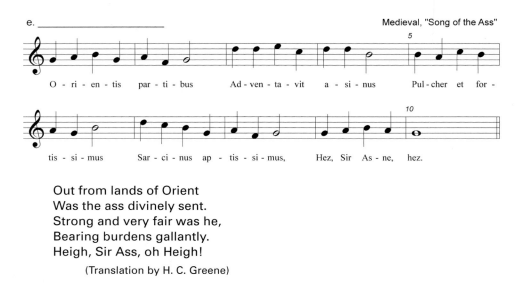

e. _____

Medieval, "Song of the Ass"

O - ri - en - tis   par - ti - bus   Ad - ven - ta - vit   a - si - nus   Pul - cher et for -

tis - si - mus   Sar - ci - nus ap - tis - si - mus,   Hez, Sir As - ne, hez.

Out from lands of Orient
Was the ass divinely sent.
Strong and very fair was he,
Bearing burdens gallantly.
Heigh, Sir Ass, oh Heigh!

(Translation by H. C. Greene)

SELF-TEST 5–1

Time Limit: 7 Minutes

1. Write one letter in the blank to associate the given description with an appropriate musical texture. Some letters may be used more than once. *Scoring: Subtract 7 points for each error.*

   A. Monophony   D. Imitative Counterpoint
   B. Monody   E. Homophony
   C. Free Counterpoint

   _____ (1) the texture found in modern popular songs

   _____ (2) originated in seventeenth-century Florence

   _____ (3) involves two independent voices that state the same basic musical material

   _____ (4) whistling a tune while walking down the street

   _____ (5) two or more independent voices without imitation

   _____ (6) the texture of Gregorian chant

   _____ (7) characteristic texture of music between about 1275 and 1400

   _____ (8) term used to describe early homophony

2. Study the score below; then answer the four questions. Adrian Willaert (1490–1562) was a Flemish composer who spent most of his career in Venice. *Scoring: Subtract 11 points for each error.*

   a. The most precise term for music like this is

      _____ (1) Counterpoint

      _____ (2) Free counterpoint

      _____ (3) Imitative counterpoint

      _____ (4) Baroque counterpoint

   b. The earliest date (C.E.) that a work like this might have been written is about

      _____ (1) 900

      _____ (2) 1200

      _____ (3) 1400

      _____ (4) 1500

   c. The second voice to enter is the

      _____ (1) soprano

      _____ (2) alto

      _____ (3) tenor

      _____ (4) bass

   d. Compare the second (measure 2) entry to the first (measure 1).

      _____ (1) the second entry is transposed a perfect fifth higher

      _____ (2) the second entry is identical to the first

_____ (3) the second entry is a perfect four higher than the first

_____ (4) the second entry begins with new material

_____

Total Possible: 100   Your Score _____

TONAL HARMONY

In the last chapter, we discussed melodic roles as stable ($\hat{1}$, $\hat{3}$, and $\hat{5}$) or active (all others) and learned how pitches in a major or minor key gravitate naturally toward the tonic. The same relationships exist in harmony. Just as we could not employ a random series of notes to establish a key, so do traditional composers choose chords carefully and with due attention to their natural tendencies. More specifically, tonal harmony centers on three choices made consistently by composers after about 1680:

1. The use of either major or minor mode
2. The choice of strong root movement
3. Conscious adherence to chord *function* in longer progressions and especially at cadences

Major and Minor

While young innovators of the Baroque Era such as Jacopo Peri were aware of their music's triadic effect, many never completely abandoned the modal system—one based upon several different scale possibilities. Early Baroque composers did not regularly employ strong harmonic formulas except at the ends of phrases. In addition, between cadences, harmonic choices were varied and drawn from the many different modes still in wide use in the early seventeenth century (Dorian, Phrygian, Lydian, Mixolydian, and so on).

The passage in the next example is a madrigal—a sixteenth-century secular vocal work in four to six voices and sung *a cappella* (unaccompanied by instruments). Claudio Monteverdi (1567–1643), a towering transitional figure between the Renaissance and Baroque eras, wrote *Dice La Mia Bellissima Licori* (*My Very Beautiful Licori Says*) in 1619. The harmonic vocabulary illustrates at one time the modality of the Renaissance (G Mixolydian in measures 1–6) and the more modern practice of adding the leading tone to create the effect we know as major (measures 7–12). Notice that the texture is basically homophonic with a brief passage of imitative counterpoint preceding the cadence.

CD 1, TRACK 49
Claudio Monteverdi, "My Very Beautiful Licori Says"
Major and Minor

Di - ce la mia bel-lis-si-ma Li-co-ri quan-do tal hor fa-vel-lo

G Mixolydian (with F♮)

se-co d'a - mor   ch'A-mor É un Spi-ri - tel - lo   ch'Amor É un Spi-ri - tel - lo
ch'Amor É un Spi-ri - tel- lo

G Major (with F♯)

Sometimes when I speak with her of love
my very beautiful Licori says
that Love is a small spirit

By the time of Bach's birth (1685), the system that we know as functional harmony had replaced the older modal approach. Composers chose either major or minor and focused the listener's attention on one pitch within this framework.

Root Movement

One of many important differences between modal and tonal music is reflected in the concept of ROOT MOVEMENT—the intervals formed between triad roots. As early as 1450, composers discovered that preceding the final tonic triad with the dominant—root movement by descending fifth— created a powerful effect in centering the listener's attention on one pitch.

The passage below, by the Englishman William Byrd (1543–1623), is a series of variations on a seventeenth-century pop tune, *The Carman's Whistle*. Root movement by descending fifth ends the phrase and illustrates an important progression of three chords that we will discuss at length in this chapter.

CD 1, TRACK 50
William Byrd, Variations on *The Carman's Whistle*
Root Movement

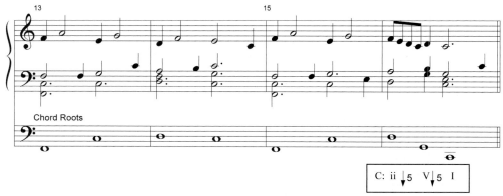

Jean-Philippe Rameau (1683–1764), a French theorist and composer, was among the first to explain the importance of root movement in the new system of music. In his book, *Treatise on Harmony* (1722), Rameau terms the sequence of chord roots the FUNDAMENTAL BASS (*basse fondamentale*). Examining the fundamental bass of the Byrd phrase in the last example, we see a variety of intervals between chord roots and both ascending and descending movement.

Root Movement: Byrd Variations

P5↑   M2↑   M2↓   P5↓   P5↑   M2↑   P5↓   P5↓

In Byrd's *The Carman's Whistle*, all chords in are in root position: the notated bass coincides with the fundamental bass. If inversions occur, however, the fundamental bass remains a theoretical line of chord *roots*. Looking at Bach's harmonization of "Deck Thyself with Joy and Gladness" in the next example, notice the difference between the fundamental bass and the much smoother bass voice that includes inverted triads. Roman numerals emphasize the relationship between chord roots.

Bach, "Deck Thyself with Joy and Gladness"

Fundamental Bass

F: I   V   vi V   I   V   I   V I IV I IV I   V   I

Categorizing Root Movement.   Interval inversion simplifies the classification of root movement. If we consider both ascending and descending motion, root movement by fifth, third, and second produces every diatonic chord (other root movement merely duplicates one of these). Traditionally, we classify root movement into one of three categories:

1. Ascending or descending second
2. Ascending or descending third
3. Ascending or descending fifth

In the next example, notice that root movement by ascending fourth produces the same triad as that derived by descending fifth; root movement by ascending sixth is the equivalent of descending third, and so on.

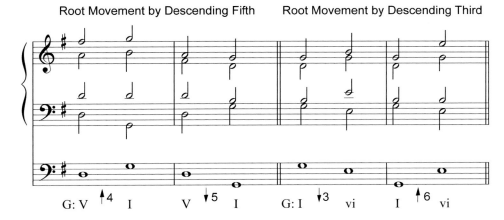

Study the root movement of the triad pairs shown in the next example. The basic classifications are ascending or descending fifth, third, or second.

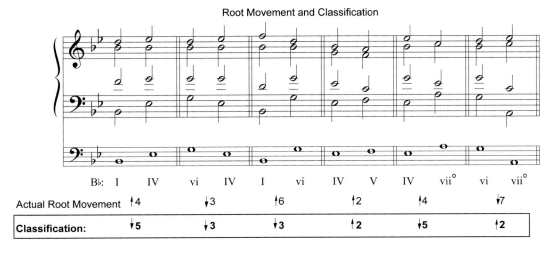

Strong Root Movement.   As noted by Rameau, root movement by descending fifth combines with melodic tendencies ($\uparrow\hat{7}-\hat{8}$) to produce a definitive feeling for key. Likewise, root movement by ascending second and by descending third also helps to define the tonic. As shown in the table on page 170, descending fifth, ascending second, and descending third are all strong root movements. Yet we might think of these three possibilities as having an internal hierarchy of strength as "strongest," "stronger," and "strong," respectively.

Categories of Strong Root Movement

Descending Fifth (↓5, ↑4)	Ascending Second (↑2, ↓7)	Descending Third (↓3, ↑6)
"Strongest"	"Stronger"	"Strong"

The three basic categories of strong root movement are shown in the next example. Progressions are always understood in a major or minor key, so specifying descending *perfect* fifth, ascending *major* second, and so on, is not necessary.

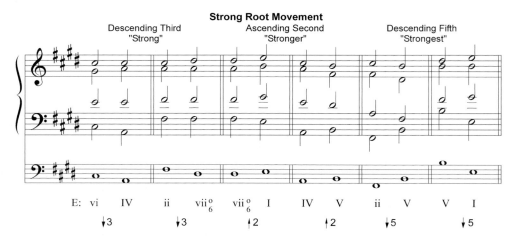

In addition to strong root movement, composers routinely make other choices. While these possibilities are weak theoretically, they often occur at opportune points in a composition to provide harmonic variety or to delay arrival at the tonic.

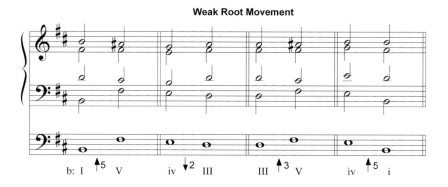

An important difference between modal and tonal music concerns root movement within a phrase and especially at the cadence. The logic underlying these choices in tonal music is called *function* and will be discussed in a later sec-

WORKBOOK/ANTHOLOGY I
II. Root Movement, page 65

tion of this chapter. Next, however, we will look at important tonal pillars—harmonic cadences—that continue to be employed by tonal composers today.

CADENCES

The harmonic formulas that shape phrases are crucial in defining tonality. We use the term "cadence" to refer both to the final pitch in a musical line and also to the last chords in a phrase. In reality, however, some or all of the defining forces in traditional music come together at cadential points. These influences may include the tendencies of ↑7̂–8̂, 4̂–3̂, or both; the melodic goal of a phrase; a strong metric effect; deliberate harmonic choices; and other musical considerations.

In traditional harmony, cadences are classified as terminal or progressive just as they are in a melodic sense (and with about the same meanings that we encountered in discussing melody). Terminal roles are most often fulfilled by *authentic* cadences; several different cadence types satisfy the progressive role.

Authentic Cadence

An AUTHENTIC CADENCE (abbreviated "AC") is a dominant to tonic (V–I) progression that ends a phrase. Because of the descending fifth root movement, authentic cadences create a feeling of finality in traditional music—much like the effect of a period in defining the end of a sentence. Listen to the

CD 1, TRACK 51
Authentic and Modal Cadences

authentic cadences in the next example. Remember that in minor keys, an accidental (F♯ in the second cadence) is necessary to create a major dominant. Otherwise, the cadence is *not* authentic and lacks key-defining strength.

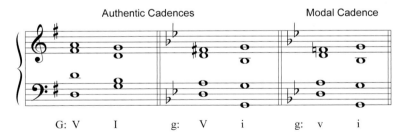

Perfect *Authentic Cadence.*   Both of the cadences in the last example are classified as *perfect authentic* (imparting a strong sense of finality).[3] By definition, an authentic cadence has a terminal effect. A cadence is PERFECT AUTHENTIC (abbreviated "PAC") if it meets *both* of two conditions:

1. Both the tonic and dominant chords are in root position.
2. The tonic pitch occurs in the soprano of the tonic chord.

---

[3]The term "perfect," means "definitive" in establishing a feeling for key. "Imperfect" (discussed on page 172) means "less definitive."

As early as the sixteenth century, composers employed authentic cadences to conclude phrases, sections, and entire compositions. The Palestrina mass phrase on page 160 and the phrase from *Euridice* (page 161), for example, both end with perfect authentic cadences. Later composers often made the final cadence of a work dramatic and repetitive. In his "Waldstein" piano sonata (1804), Beethoven ends the first movement with a flourish—and with a perfect authentic cadence.

CD 1, TRACK 52-1 AUTHENTIC CADENCES (2 PARTS)
Ludwig van Beethoven, Sonata, Op. 53 "Waldstein" (I)
Perfect Authentic

C: ii$_6$ V   I   V   I

Perfect Authentic
Cadence

Imperfect Authentic Cadence.   If an authentic cadence is not perfect, it is IMPERFECT and abbreviated "IAC." The effect of an imperfect authentic cadence is somewhat *less* final than those that are perfect and composers employ them both for variety and to separate levels of importance. We classify an authentic cadence as imperfect if *any one* of the following conditions is met:

1. *Either* the tonic or the dominant chord is inverted.

2. The leading-tone triad (vii°) substitutes for the dominant.

3. The soprano of the tonic chord is $\hat{3}$ or $\hat{5}$ (rather than $\hat{1}$ or $\hat{8}$).

TRACK 52-2 AUTHENTIC CADENCES
Imperfect Authentic Cadences

Used to conclude a phrase, any one of the five progressions in the next example would be classified as an imperfect authentic cadence.

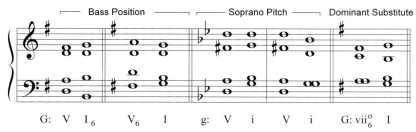

G: V I$_6$ V$_6$ I   g: V i   V i   G: vii°$_6$ I

Mozart used an imperfect authentic cadence to end the first phrase of his Adagio (with $\hat{5}$–$\hat{4}$–$\hat{3}$ melodic motion in the solo clarinet). The next passage is a full, or conductor's, score that shows the notation of each instrumental part. The solo line, originally written for a clarinet in the key of A, has been transposed a minor third lower as it sounds in performance.[4]

CD 1, TRACK 53-1 PERFECT AND IMPERFECT AUTHENTIC CADENCE (2 PARTS)
Imperfect Authentic

Composers make two phrases sound related by ending one with an imperfect authentic cadence and the next with the stronger effect of perfect authentic. In Bach's harmonization of Jakob Hintze's tune "*Alle Menschen müssen sterben*" ("All Men Living Are But Mortal"), for example, the first phrase ends with an imperfect authentic cadence (with $\hat{3}$ in the soprano); the second cadence is perfect authentic.

TRACK 53-2 PERFECT AND IMPERFECT AUTHENTIC CADENCE
J. S. Bach, "All Men Living Are But Mortal," melody by Jakob Hintze, ca. 1678
Imperfect and Perfect Authentic

[4]Many orchestral instruments sound pitches that are different from those on the notated part. Clarinets in the keys of A (sounding a minor third lower) and B♭ (sounding a major second lower then written) are common today. See Appendix A: Ranges and Transposition on page 477 for more information.

Notice that both cadences in the last example include a passing tone (the pitch G in both cases) that might also be considered the seventh of a dominant seventh chord. The use of a seventh—whether passing or chordal—increases the pull toward tonic.

Cadential Six-Four.   Cadences often involve a tonic chord in second inversion that resolves by step to the dominant. We will discuss six-four chords fully in Chapter 8, but the CADENTIAL SIX-FOUR is a common-practice cliché that is not actually a tonic at all, but an embellishment of the dominant. The cadential six-four is *not* itself a cadence, but it may constitute one of the chords in a cadence or cadence formula (see the Beethoven example on page 177).

Observe that the root and third of the tonic six-four (soprano and tenor in the last example) resolve in the same voices by descending step to the third and fifth of the dominant triad. The bass of the tonic six-four is doubled (bass and alto, above) and retained to become the doubled root of the dominant chord. The tonic six-four lacks the stability we associate with tonic triads. For this reason, we employ the special analytical symbol: $\mathrm{I}\,^6_4$ V

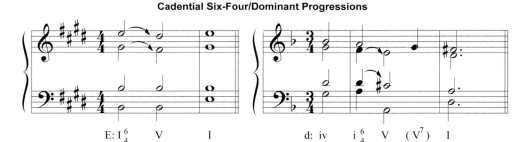

Regarding the cadential six-four in traditional progressions, we can make several observations:

1. The six-four chord is always tonic.
2. Two of the three upper voices in the tonic six-four resolve by descending step to the dominant or dominant seventh.
3. The bass remains stationary or leaps an octave.
4. The six-four chord usually occurs on a strong beat.

Joseph Haydn ends the third movement of his Sonata in D Major with a typical cadential six-four progression that is part of an authentic cadence (I_4^6–V–I).

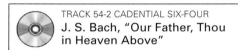

Bach's harmonization of an anonymous German melody concludes with a similar tonic six-four in C minor.

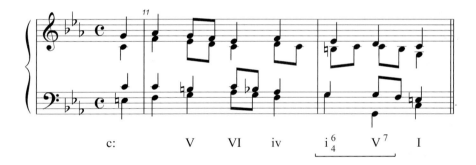

Picardy Third.   Notice in the last example that the final triad in C minor has a raised third (making the tonic major, rather than minor). The PICARDY THIRD (named for the region in France) is a major triad sometimes substituted as the tonic in a final cadence. While a picardy third rarely appears in an interior cadence, Baroque and later composers sometimes choose the major triad as the final sonority of a section or work in a minor key.[5]

Plagal Cadence

A PLAGAL CADENCE (abbreviated "PC") is subdominant to tonic. The effect, with ascending (rather than descending) fifth root movement, is relatively weak. Aside from the familiar "Amen" cliché at the end of a hymn, the plagal cadence is less common than other types.

---

[5]While many compositions in minor keys end with a minor tonic, in Mean-tone temperament (the most common method of tuning keyboard instruments during the Renaissance and Baroque periods), the major third was better in tune than the minor third.

CD 1, TRACK 55-1 AUTHENTIC AND PLAGAL CADENCES
(2 PARTS)
Plagal Cadences in Major and Minor

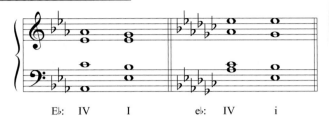

E♭: IV   I   e♭: IV   i

TRACK 55-2 AUTHENTIC AND PLAGAL CADENCES
J. S. Bach, "Now Thank We All Our God,"
melody by Johann Crüger, ca. 1647

A plagal cadence is often paired with one that is authentic as in Bach's harmonization of *"Nun danket alle Gott"* ("Now Thank We All Our God").

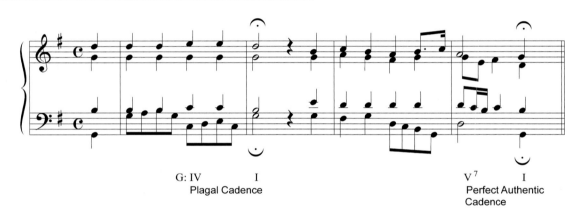

G: IV   I   V⁷   I

Plagal Cadence   Perfect Authentic Cadence

Half Cadence

A phrase ending with an authentic cadence is often preceded by one that ends in a HALF CADENCE ("HC")—a progression of two chords that ends on the dominant. The most common half cadences are IV–V, ii–V, and I–V as shown in the next example.

CD 1, TRACK 56-1 HALF CADENCES
(2 PARTS)
Half Cadences in Major and Minor

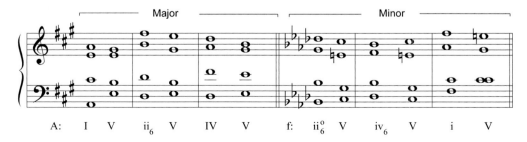

            Major   Minor

A: I   V   ii₆   V   IV   V   f: ii°₆   V   iv₆   V   i   V

Joseph Haydn ends the first phrase of a lively sonata movement with a I–V half cadence. The following phrase is perfect authentic.

HALF CADENCES, TRACK 56-2
Joseph Haydn, Sonata in D Major (I)
Half and Perfect Authentic Cadences

A tonic six-four may also figure into a half cadence. In earlier chapters, we discussed various aspects of Beethoven's "Ode to Joy." We can now describe the first cadence as half (I–V) with a cadential six-four. The second cadence is perfect authentic (V–I).

REPLAY CD 1, TRACK 22
Ludwig van Beethoven, "Ode to Joy"

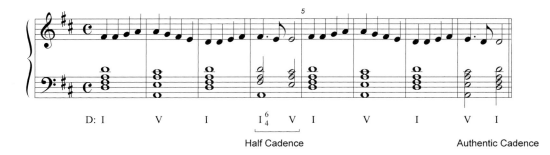

Phrygian Half Cadence. In minor keys, the half cadence has an especially colorful effect when $\hat{5}$ is approached by step in contrary motion in soprano and bass. This PHRYGIAN HALF CADENCE is so-called because of its similar effect to cadences in the Medieval Phrygian mode. The progression iv_6–V is the most common form of Phrygian half cadence.

In a passage from Bach's harmonization of the chorale melody, "*Wo soll ich fliehen hin*" ("Where Shall I Go?"), the first of the two half cadences is Phrygian due to the iv_6–V harmony and stepwise motion in bass and soprano. The second cadence shown is also half, but without the characteristic harmony and melodic motion associated with Phrygian.

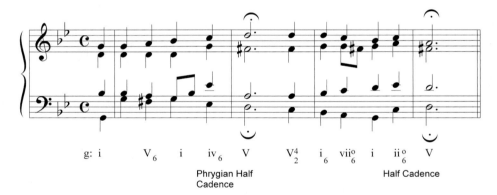

Deceptive Cadence

In a DECEPTIVE CADENCE, the dominant is followed by a tonic *substitute*. The most common deceptive cadence is V–vi (V–VI in minor), although other possibilities exist. Deceptive cadences are effective both in delaying the tonic and in unifying two or more phrases (the weaker deceptive cadence followed by an authentic cadence, for example).

In an early piano sonata, Haydn ends the first phrase with a deceptive cadence, then concludes the second phrase with a half cadence (I–V). Observe that the first (deceptive) cadence includes a dominant seventh chord.

CD 1, TRACK 58
Joseph Haydn, Sonata No. 4 in D Major (II)
Deceptive and Half Cadences

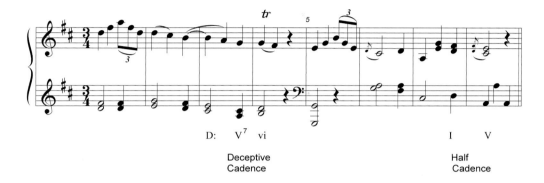

D: V⁷ vi

Deceptive
Cadence

I   V

Half
Cadence

Occurring at regular intervals, cadences combine with melodic tendencies to focus our attention on tonality at an immediate (or local) level. Throughout a work or section, different types of cadences constantly define and redefine the tonality while, at the same time, providing information about how phrases relate to one another. In many types of music today— especially popular and commercial music—composers employ exactly the same cadences that originated in the sixteenth and seventeenth centuries.

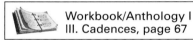

Workbook/Anthology I
III. Cadences, page 67

REVIEW AND APPLICATION 5–2

Cadences

Essential Terms

authentic cadence	fundamental bass	Phrygian half cadence
cadential six-four	half cadence	picardy third
deceptive cadence	plagal cadence	root movement

1. The following chords represent cadences in various keys. Begin by supplying roman numerals in the upper blanks. Next, use the lower blank to identify the cadence by writing the appropriate word or words. In the case of authentic cadences, specify "perfect" or "imperfect" and identify a Phrygian cadence as necessary.

a.

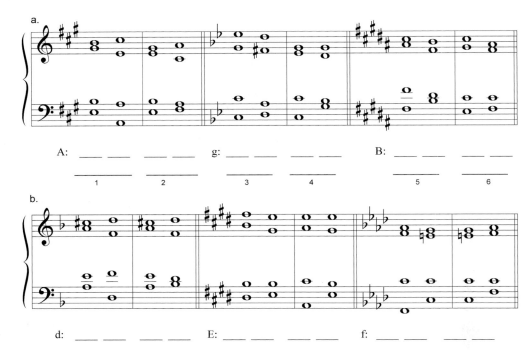

A: ___ ___ ___ ___ g: ___ ___ ___ ___ B: ___ ___ ___ ___

    1   2   3   4   5   6

b.

d: ___ ___ ___ ___ E: ___ ___ ___ ___ f: ___ ___ ___ ___

    1   2   3   4   5   6

2. Return to the previous exercise and classify the root movement of each cadence. Use the list below and enter a letter A–F to specify the category. In the second blank, indicate whether this root movement is strong (S) or weak (W).

A. Ascending	5		D. Descending	3
B. Descending	5		E. Ascending	2
C. Ascending	3		F. Descending	2

a. __ __   __ __   __ __   __ __   __ __   __ __
   Cadence 1 Cadence 2 Cadence 3 Cadence 4 Cadence 5 Cadence 6

b. __ __   __ __   __ __   __ __   __ __   __ __
   Cadence 1 Cadence 2 Cadence 3 Cadence 4 Cadence 5 Cadence 6

3. Identify the given root-position triad with an appropriate roman numeral. Next, observe the root movement to the next triad specified (ascending second, descending fifth, and so on). Construct the second triad and provide a roman numeral. In minor, add an accidental to any dominant or leading tone triad. Follow the model.

a. **Model**

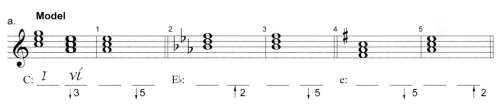

C: I vi __ __ E♭: __ __ __ __ e: __ __ __ __
   ↓3   ↓5   ↑2   ↓5   ↓5   ↑2

b.

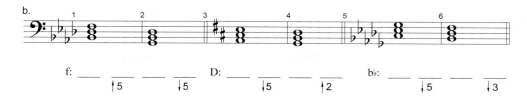

f: ___ ___ ___   D: ___ ___ ___   b♭: ___ ___ ___
        ↑5   ↑5   ↑5   ↑2   ↑5   ↑3

4. Two passages are given below. In the upper blanks, provide roman numerals to identify the two chords that comprise each cadence. In the lower blanks, identify the cadence using words, "imperfect authentic," "half," and so on.

CD 1, TRACK 59-1 REVIEW AND APPLICATION 5-2
(2 PARTS)
Ludwig van Beethoven, Sonata, Op. 7 (III)
Exercise 4-a

a.

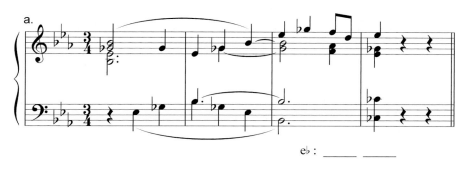

e♭ : _____ _____

_____

TRACK 59-2, REVIEW AND APPLICATION 5-2
Carl Maria von Weber, Theme, Op. 5
Exercise 4-b

b.

F: _____ _____   _____ _____
         1   2

SELF-TEST 5–2

Time Limit: 5 Minutes

1. Using roman numerals as well as the terms discussed in this chapter, identify each cadence as specifically as possible. While a complete phrase is given, you are asked to identify only the cadence. *Scoring: Subtract 3 points for each incorrect roman numeral; subtract 12 points for an incorrect cadence.*

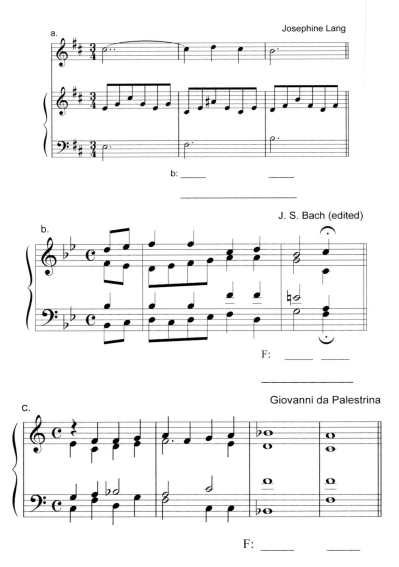

a.   Josephine Lang

b: _____   _____

_____

b.   J. S. Bach (edited)

F: _____ _____

_____

c.   Giovanni da Palestrina

F: _____   _____

_____

2. In block chords, construct the cadences suggested. Choose chords that create the cadence specified (more than one possibility exists in some cases). Provide roman numerals and add an accidental if necessary. You are not asked to differentiate between perfect and imperfect authentic cadences in this problem. *Scoring: Subtract 8 points for each incorrect roman numeral.*

e: _____   A♭: _____ _____   D: _____
Half   **Deceptive**   **Authentic**

Total Possible: 100   Your Score _____

HARMONIC FUNCTION

Cadences define tonality at the end of a phrase, but as we have seen, Renaissance composers also employed authentic and half cadences, yet produced a completely different kind of music. One of the most important differences between modal and tonal music concerns the relationships among chords not only at points of cadence, but *between* cadences. In modal compositions, chord sequence is not dictated by harmonic principles; root movement is often by second or third. In the tonal system, however, composers choose chords according to principles of HARMONIC FUNCTION—prescribed categories that are based largely on factors like the presence or absence of a leading tone, the effect of descending fifth root movement, and so on.

Tonal Context

Functional roles are defined through context—that is, the position of any one chord in a PROGRESSION (functional series) is defined by its relationship to other, adjacent chords. To illustrate the importance of context, consider the following triad:

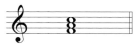

Is the preceding triad the tonic? the dominant? Is the key major? minor? When a triad is stripped of its defining context, we have no way of answering any of these questions. Still, because the triad is major in quality, we may make several assumptions about its diatonic role:

- The major triad in question is *not* a supertonic in major or minor (since those triads are minor or diminished).
- It is *not* a leading-tone triad (since the leading tone is always diminished).
- The triad is neither the submediant nor the mediant in major (as these triads are minor in quality).

CD 1, TRACK 60
Tonic Context

If we know the position of our F major triad in a progression, conclusions about its functional role are relatively simple. In the three examples shown below, the F major triad appears as the first, the second, and the final chord in a progression.

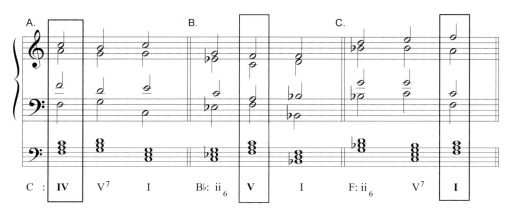

Play each of the three progressions in the last example (labeled A, B, and C) and notice that our F major triad is in a different position in each series. Because each progression establishes a different key, the role or FUNCTION of the F major triad is also different in each case.

Functional Roles

The chords in the preceding example illustrate the three functional roles in traditional harmony: *tonic, predominant,* and *dominant.* Each function has a clear purpose in the interplay of stability and tension that is central to a tonal effect.

Tonic Function.   The TONIC FUNCTION is one of stability and arrival. Chords of tonic function include $\hat{1}$ and $\hat{3}$ since these are the scale degrees most associated with stability. The tonic is often the first chord we hear in a composition and nearly always the last one. Once a chord is identified through context as the tonic (as in the third of the three progressions in the last example), any other chord may logically follow. While the tonic triad itself is the most common chord of tonic function, the submediant is a frequent tonic substitute (as in the deceptive cadence). In major keys, the mediant triad (including $\hat{3}$ and $\hat{5}$) is less effective in a role of stability because it also contains the leading tone—an inherently *unstable* pitch.

Tonic Function

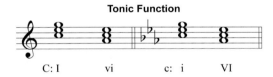

C: I   vi   c: i   VI

In order for a chord to be heard as tonic in function, it must be preceded by the dominant or a dominant substitute. The melodic tendencies and descending-fifth root movement focus our attention on the tonic. This is especially true if the dominant triad includes a seventh (as in the next example).

CD 1, TRACK 61
Tonic Function

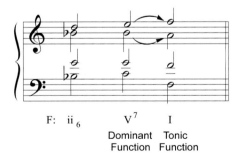

F: ii$_6$ V^7 I

Dominant   Tonic
Function   Function

Dominant Function.   Where chords of tonic function are heard as stable, the DOMINANT FUNCTION is one of momentum. Dominant-function chords contain the leading tone and allow us to hear the tonic as stable when the tendency of $\uparrow\hat{7}$ is resolved to $\hat{8}$. Both the dominant and leading-tone triads (containing the leading-tone pitch) have dominant functions in tonal music.

Dominant Function

C: V   vii°   c: V   vii°

The leading-tone triad and the dominant *seventh chord* contain both $\hat{4}$ and ↑$\hat{7}$—the two diatonic pitches with the strongest melodic tendencies. Together, these pitches form a tritone (an augmented fourth or a diminished fifth). Especially in a four-voice vocal style, a resolution of the leading-tone triad is dependent on the scoring of individual voices (called *voice leading* and discussed in Chapter 8). The tension of an augmented fourth often expands to the stability of a major or minor sixth in a triad of tonic function. Likewise, the voices that form a diminished fifth will normally contract to a major or minor third (note that these tendencies are the same in two, three, four, and more voices).

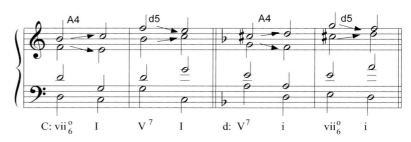

C: vii°₆   I   V⁷   I   d: V⁷   i   vii°₆   i

Returning to our discussion of chords in context, notice in the example on page 184 that the F major triad is heard as tonic in function due to the momentum created by the dominant seventh chord that precedes it.

We can hear our F major triad as dominant in function when it resolves to tonic. In this case, the key is B♭ (major or minor).

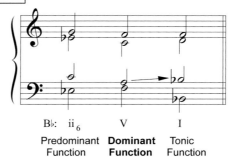

Bb: ii₆   V   I
Predominant   **Dominant**   Tonic
Function   **Function**   Function

Predominant Function. A third function, the PREDOMINANT, initiates the progression toward tonic by establishing an environment for the special relationship between the dominant and tonic.

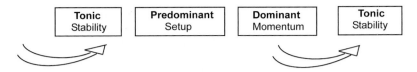

Predominant chords have neither the momentum of the dominant nor the stability of the tonic. The inverted supertonic triad in the next example has such a predominant role.

F: ii₆   V⁷   I

Predominant Dominant Tonic
Function Function Function

Supertonic and subdominant triads fulfill the predominant function in traditional music. Notice that in minor keys, two possibilities exist for the subdominant and supertonic triads depending on whether ↑$\hat{6}$ or ↓$\hat{6}$ is employed. All of the chords in the next example have roughly equivalent functions in C minor.

Predominant Function

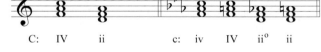

C: IV   ii   c: iv   IV   ii°   ii

Predominant triads contain $\hat{4}$ and $\hat{6}$, which often converge on $\hat{5}$ to articulate a chord of dominant function. We can make our F major triad sound like a predominant by following it with a chord of dominant function. If the F major triad in our example has predominant function, it will be followed by chords of dominant and tonic function, respectively. In addition, the predominant might well be preceded by a chord of tonic function.

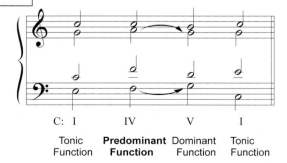

C: I   IV   V   I

Tonic   **Predominant** Dominant Tonic
Function   **Function**   Function Function

We can illustrate harmonic function in the last example as a circle. The tonic, the goal of a harmonic progression, is at twelve o'clock. Clockwise motion around the circle results in a heightened perception of tonality. Each departure from a chord of tonic function requires a movement around the circle and back to the stability of the home key. Remember, however, that after arrival at tonic, any chord may follow. Thus, tonic may progress to the dominant, and then back to tonic before beginning the process all over again.

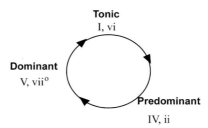

Tonic
I, vi

Dominant
V, vii°

Predominant
IV, ii

Cadence Formulas.   Systematic movement among the three harmonic functions forms the cornerstone of traditional composition. Especially at cadences, composers often employ all three functions to strengthen the effect of finality. While such CADENCE FORMULAS end with one of the cadence types we have discussed, a third chord may be added before the cadence. The progressions IV–V–I and ii₆–V–I are especially common cadence formulas. In the chorale below, Bach ends the first phrase of chorale *Dir, dir Jehova, will ich singen* ("Jehovah, Let Me Now Adore Thee") with IV–V–I all in root position.

CD 1, TRACK 63-1 CADENCE FORMULAS
(2 PARTS)
J. S. Bach, *Jehova, Let Me Now Adore Thee*

Bb: IV   V   I

Cadence Formula

In another of Haydn's keyboard sonatas, functional progressions occur both within the phrase and in the important cadential formula that ends it. Notice that while dominant-tonic progressions are frequent throughout, predominant function is reserved to emphasize the second of the two cadences (in measures 7–8). The lowest line is the fundamental bass extracted from Haydn's harmony.

TRACK 63-2 CADENCE FORMULAS
Joseph Haydn, Sonata in C Major

HARMONIC RHYTHM

The relative frequency of chord change is called the HARMONIC RHYTHM. We can represent harmonic rhythm by a specific time value such as a quarter or half note. Once a composer establishes a rate of harmonic rhythm, it is usually maintained for several measures. On the other hand, a change in harmonic rhythm may signal a cadence or another musical event. Composers frequently create contrast by varying the harmonic rhythm between adjacent sections (a faster rate of chord change, for example, contrasted with a slower one).

If we say "the harmonic rhythm is the eighth note," we mean that in general, chords change every eighth note (whether the eighth note is the beat, a unit of two beats, or a half beat). Further, our assessment of harmonic rhythm in these terms presupposes exceptions. Typically, a chorale harmonization has a rapid rate of harmonic rhythm—usually with chord changes every one or two beats. The first phrase of Bach's "*Aus meines Herzens Grunde*" ("My Inmost Heart Now Raises") illustrates a rather fast rate of chord change. Except for the repeated tonic chord at the beginning, chords change on every beat.

CD 1, TRACK 64-1 HARMONIC RHYTHM (2 PARTS)
J. S. Bach, "My Inmost Heart Now Raises"
One Chord Change per Beat

Works in other styles feature different rates of harmonic rhythm. The Austrian composer Franz Schubert (1797–1828) is known as a master of the *lied*—a German-language art song with piano accompaniment. The introduction to "*Ungeduld*" ("Pause") from Schubert's cycle *Die Schöne Müllerin* (*The Beautiful Miller Woman*) begins with a slow rate of chord change that contrasts with later harmonic complexities. Notice that roman numerals trace the rate of chord flow and make additional illustrations (as above) unnecessary.

TRACK 64-2 HARMONIC RHYTHM
Franz Schubert, "Undeduld"
from *Die Schöne Müllerin*
Slower Harmonic Rhythm

Harmonic rhythm is only one aspect of the tonal process that is carefully controlled by successful composers. As we have seen, cadences provide points of harmonic security; between cadences, harmonic flow is governed by functional relationships and inherent melodic tendencies. In Unit 3 we will study how tonal composers use *dissonance*—unstable chords and pitches—to actually strengthen a feeling for key.

WORKBOOK/ANTHOLOGY I
IV. Harmonic Function, page 69

REVIEW AND APPLICATION 5–3 ━━━━━━━━━━━━━━━━

Harmonic Function

Essential Terms

chord classification	harmonic function	progression
dominant function	harmonic rhythm	tonic function
function	predominant function	

1. For each of the following triads, begin by supplying an appropriate arabic and roman numeral in the keys indicated. Next, indicate the triad's function by writing **T** for tonic, **D** for dominant, and **P** for a chord of predominant function. For the present exercise, consider the mediant triad in major or minor to be tonic in function. Finally, provide the classification of the chord as tonic, first class, second class, third class, or fourth class.

2. Begin each frame by analyzing the two triads in the key indicated. Next, decide upon an appropriate function to follow the two given (tonic, predominant, or dominant). In some cases, two choices will be acceptable. Finally, notate a triad that has the function you chose (together with any necessary accidentals). Provide an analytical symbol.

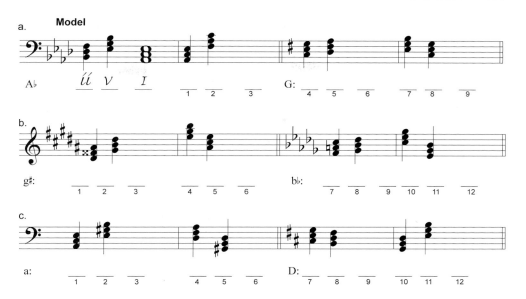

3. A major, minor, or diminished triad is given below. Provide up to three possible *major* keys in which that chord might function. In some cases, only *one* key will be possible.

a. Root Position

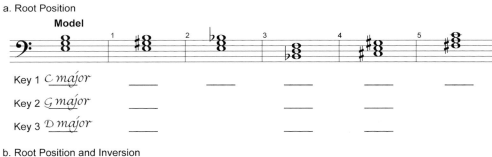

Key 1 *C major* ____   ____   ____
Key 2 *G major* ____   ____   ____
Key 3 *D major* ____   ____   ____

b. Root Position and Inversion

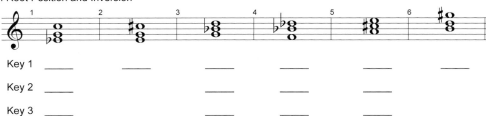

Key 1 ____   ____   ____   ____   ____
Key 2 ____   ____   ____   ____   ____
Key 3 ____   ____   ____   ____   ____

Consider the next series of chords in *minor* keys. Various possibilities presented by ↓6̂ and ↑6̂, and ↓7̂ and ↑7̂ make the choices more numerous than in major. Exclude chords that are rarely functional (the minor dominant, the subtonic triad, and the diminished submediant). At least two tonal possibilities exist for each chord; in other cases, three functional roles may be identified.

c. Root Position

Key 1 _____   _____   _____   _____   _____   _____

Key 2 _____   _____   _____   _____   _____   _____

Key 3 _____   _____   _____   _____

d. Root Position and Inversion

Key 1 _____   _____   _____   _____   _____   _____

Key 2 _____   _____   _____   _____   _____   _____

Key 3 _____   _____   _____   _____

SELF-TEST 5–3

Time Limit: 7 Minutes

1. Match a term from the list below with each of the statements that follows. *Scoring: subtract 7 points for each wrong answer.*

A. Harmonic function   E. Cadence formula

B. Tonic function   F. Chord classification

C. Dominant function   G. Harmonic rhythm

D. Predominant function

_____ (1) The subdominant and supertonic are examples.

_____ (2) The rate of chord change

_____ (3) The submediant is a substitute for this function.

_____ (4) The use of prescribed harmonic categories to establish a tonal center

_____ (5) Chords that create momentum

_____ (6) A system of looking at harmonic relationships governed by descending fifth root movement

_____ (7) A progression of chords that ends a phrase in an especially strong way

2. Study the chorale phrase below and provide information as requested. *Scoring: Subtract 2 points for each incorrect answer.*

(1) In the first blank under each beat, provide a roman numeral *including* arabic numeral identification and any other symbol necessary.

(2) In the "function" blank, write a letter ("T," "P," or "D") to identify the harmonic function of the chord as tonic, predominant, or dominant.

(3) In the "classification" blank, write "T" if the chord is tonic, or "1st," "2nd," "3rd," or "4th" if the chord is not tonic.

CD1, TRACK 65
J. S. Bach "O Sacred Head, Now Wounded" (Edited)
Self-Test 5–3, Question 2

Eb: ___ ___ ___ ___   ___ ___ ___ ___

Function: ___ ___ ___ ___   ___ ___ ___ ___

Classification: ___ ___ ___ ___   ___ ___ ___ ___
                 1   2   3   4   5   6   7   8

3. Provide the term that describes a melody/accompaniment texture. *Scoring: Subtract 3 points for an incorrect answer.*

_____

Total Possible: 100   Your Score _____

PROJECTS

Analysis

As an analytical approach, roman numerals have distinct limitations, but if determined correctly, they provide crucial data in understanding how tonality is established and maintained. Moreover, if analytical symbols for a given passage of tonal music do not provide this information (that is, if a consistent flow through the three functions is not apparent), you may have made an error in key. Consider the Bach chorale on text page 178 for example. As analyzed in the text, this passage is in G minor and the three functions fall in sequence as we would expect for a tonal work. If you had mistakenly begun the analysis in Bb major, however, notice the resulting lack of functional logic in the roman-numeral series:

Bb: vi | vi III vi ii | III III | vi ? vi vii | III |

Not only are there no cadences in Bb major, but neither tonic nor dominant chords is present at all. If a work is by a tonal composer, even an incorrect set of roman-numeral labels provides information (meaning that we must consider a new key for the passage).

Your analysis of the Mozart Concerto phrases (as well as the pieces included in the workbook) might center on some or all of the following areas:

a. provide roman-numeral analysis of chord roots (excluding inversions)
b. determine the functional role assignment for each chord as well as a chord classification of each sonority:
   1. which chords are used most (and least) frequently?
   2. how often does each functional category occur?
   3. are there occurrences of the mediant triad? the submediant?
c. study the types and frequencies of cadences
d. identify the prevailing harmonic rhythm in each work. Is it consistent throughout?

Text

W. A. Mozart, Concerto for Clarinet and Orchestra, K. 622 (reduction), text pages 116-118. Given as an introduction to Unit 2, Mozart's melody is referred to several times in Chapters 4 and 5. The version on pages 116-118 is a reduction of the orchestral parts to allow performance at the keyboard.

Workbook/Anthology I

Johannes Brahms, "The Sun Shines No More," workbook pages 71.
W. A. Mozart, Variations on "Je suis Lindor," K. 536 (excerpt), workbook pages 73.

Composition

Passage for Flute and Piano. Use the harmony of Mozart's concerto given on page 116 as the basis for a new composition for flute (or oboe or violin) and piano. Do not change the harmony (except in mode), but revise the accompaniment as you see fit. Limit your melody to chord tones with occasional passing or neighboring figures for variety. Before you undertake this assignment, you will need to analyze all 32 measures of the melody as given in the text. The following examples will get you started on your inventive restatement of Mozart's harmonic pattern.

Sample Composition 1 These chords are the same as in the Mozart concerto and also in the same meter. The livelier rhythms and displacement in piano accompaniment, however, create a new effect.

Sample Composition 2   In this version of Mozart's progression, the mode is minor and the meter is now duple. The functional progressions, however, are the same.

Sample Composition 3   The final sample setting has the flute playing an obbligato of chord tones over a static melody in the piano.

For Further Study

Early Western Music.   Medieval Western music has elements in common with the styles of later composers such as Bach, Brahms, and even (Count) Basie, but the theory is quite complex. Accordingly, a study of early music is generally reserved for upper–division and graduate courses. Still, our musical heritage is important in explaining choices made by later composers and audiences; we should not be reluctant to investigate these topics through dictionary or encyclopedia articles. Choose one or more of the topics that follow (or similar subjects) and prepare notes for your own information or for a class presentation (as directed).

Guido of Arezzo.   While chants and early polyphonic music were first learned and taught by rote, a system of notation developed by the year 1000 C. E. that used various shapes for pitches, a clef, and a four–line staff. We credit Guido of Arezzo (ca. 991–1033) with inventing both the staff and a system of sight singing (*solmization*)–still in use today. Consult an article on Guido and summarize his major accomplishments.

The Mass.   The Mass is the most important service of the Catholic church and has played a central role in polyphonic music composition from at least the eleventh century. What are the two major divisions of the mass itself? Which of these divisions is most often set to music? What is a *requiem* mass? How are "high" and "low" masses differentiated? What is a cantor?

Gregorian Chant.   Gregorian chant is the earliest organized form of traditional Western music. These simple, non–metric melodies were written by early Christian church leaders to enhance the Latin texts of the mass and other religious services. Today, we use the term *Gregorian* chant to emphasize the importance of Pope Gregory (590–604 C. E.) who organized the chant liturgy and sent trained singers throughout Europe to teach it. Investigate several topics related to Gregory, chant, and music in the early Christian church.

UNIT 3

Foundations of Tonal Harmony

Joseph Haydn, String Quartet Op. 76, No. 3

Chapter 6
Dissonance

Chapter 7
The Soprano-Bass Framework

Chapter 8
Voice Leading

In the days of Haydn and Mozart, most composers made a living by working for a member of the nobility or for a high official of the church. Mozart, for example, was in the employ of the Archbishop of Salzburg, with whom he had a decidedly strained relationship. Joseph Haydn (1732–1809) was employed as court composer to the benevolent and cultured Prince Nickolaus Esterházy, who ruled a principality near Vienna. Haydn's duties included providing music for concerts, church services, weddings, funerals, and other special occasions, such as the visit of a dignitary or the opening of a new building.

Haydn enjoyed a much better relationship with his employer than Mozart experienced in Salzburg. Yet while revered today, both composers were regarded during their lifetimes as little more than court employees. Haydn needed Esterházy's permission to write music for publication, to travel, or to accept commissions from patrons outside the court.

The *patronage system* reached its height in the late eighteenth century. While the wealthy enjoyed lavish lifestyles, they were socially obliged to support artists. Court composers (*Kapellmeisters*) could count on receiving a basic living wage, at least minimal accommodations, and the protection of the local militia. On the other hand, like other employee-composers, Haydn wore a servant's uniform and was required to perform humbling custodial duties. Even in matters of music, a composer was not always free to realize a work of art as he conceived it. Prince Esterházy, for example, was himself a skilled amateur musician who played an obsolete stringed instrument called a baryton. Haydn would probably have preferred to write for violin or cello, but he dutifully composed over one hundred pieces for the Prince's favorite instrument.

With the rise of the middle class, composers in the early nineteenth century had more numerous employment options than had been available just a generation earlier. Beethoven, for example, was among the first composers to live free of patronage. His revenues came from commissions, royalties, teaching, and concert performances. Yet even Beethoven followed the tradition of dedicating musical works to wealthy patrons or rulers who, in turn, might fund a new composition or facilitate a beneficial social introduction.

Joseph Haydn wrote the song *Gott erhalte Franz den Kaiser* (*God Save the Emperor Franz*) in 1797, in honor of Holy Roman Emperor Francis II. The melody served for a time as the Austrian national anthem. Aware of the song's popularity, Haydn borrowed from himself (a common practice among composers even today) and employed the melody as the basis for a series of variations (String Quartet Op. 76, No. 3). Given here in a reduction for piano, the melody of *God Save the Emperor Franz* and the simple harmony are well suited for a discussion in this unit both of the balances between consonance and dissonance and the importance of a contrapuntal framework.

CD 1, TRACK 66

Joseph Haydn, "God Save the Emperor Franz" from Quartet, Op. 76, No. 3 (II)

You will remember that we discussed folk, art, and popular music in the introduction to Unit 2. Haydn wrote his simple melody so that people could express their devotion to Francis II, their monarch. Today, we would probably consider such a song to be either pop or folk music. At the same time, however, Haydn's theme was later used as the basis of a serious work of art (not to mention one that is still performed two hundred years later). Considering these facts, speculate on whether the melody *God Save the Emperor Franz* is itself art? Or was a work of art created from more humble origins?

In Unit 3, we will explore the three most essential components of the common-practice style: *dissonance* (Chapter 6), the crucial soprano-bass contrapuntal framework (Chapter 7), and, in Chapter 8, a study of *voice leading* sums up the interaction of melodic, harmonic, rhythmic, and textural elements.

CHAPTER 6

Dissonance

From the beginnings of Western music to the present day, composers have been fascinated by the active and stable properties of certain sounds and combinations of sounds. Early "rules" for music composition, in fact, were drafted to emphasize sonorities that contemporary listeners considered stable, while carefully manipulating those that were heard as "dissonant." We use the term CONSONANCE to describe pitches and chords that are stable. DISSONANCE, on the other hand, refers to a pitch or sonority that is active.

Early seventeenth-century composers tentatively employed only one harmonic dissonance—the dominant seventh chord. By the middle of the eighteenth century, however, seventh chords and their resolutions were used liberally both to add color and to define tonality. In the early nineteenth century, composers experimented with exceptional and delayed resolutions for traditional dissonance figures; by the late 1800s, some innovative composers chose not to resolve dissonant chords and pitches *at all*. This latter choice weakened the pillars of tonality, contravened contemporary perceptions of consonance and dissonance, and in the early twentieth century, spawned a music that reveled in its *atonality*.

Consonance and Dissonance in Tonal Music

When we speak of consonance and dissonance in Volume I, we presume a tonal context.[1] Viewed within these limits, definitions are unambiguous. *Consonance* is a position of rest or stasis that we associate with certain diatonic pitches and also with vertical arrangements such as triads and chords. Dissonance on the other hand, is a much more complicated concept. *Dissonance*, which provides the momentum in a musical work, has been described as the "single most important

---

[1] Music that is quasi-tonal and atonal is discussed in this text in Chapters 6–12 of Volume II.

expressive device in the development of tonality."[2] Dissonance creates a musical setting in which resolution is a necessity. We may think of resolution both as the movement from tension to stability and also as the *result* of that movement (the achievement of a stable goal). Dissonance in tonal music is most effective when set in a simple context, uncomplicated by interweaving voices, unexpected rhythmic figures, or harmonic complexities.

Context.   Context is the essence of tonal music. In a series of major or minor thirds and sixths, for example, we will have difficulty hearing any one of them as more important than another without intervening dissonance.

CD 1, TRACK 67-1 CONSONANCE AND DISSONANCE (3 PARTS)
Consonance

TRACK 67-2 CONSONANCE AND DISSONANCE
Dissonance

Likewise, when dissonant intervals occur apart from their defining consonances, no tonal gravity is generated.

But when consonance and dissonance are used *together* (as shown below), the needed points of reference are available, and we hear not only the interplay of tension and stability, but also the hierarchy of relationships that exists in tonal music.

TRACK 67-3 CONSONANCE AND DISSONANCE
Consonance/Dissonance Together

MELODIC DISSONANCE

Dissonance plays two different roles in traditional music. First, a dissonance may be STRUCTURAL if it resolves to a consonance and thus clarifies the tonal center. The regular resolution of a dominant seventh chord is an example of structural dissonance. Other dissonances are EMBELLISHING; they add color, facilitate a smoother line, or otherwise play subordinate roles. The neighboring tone, discussed previously, is an embellishing dissonance. *Chords* that have embellishing roles will be discussed later in this unit.

We also classify dissonance as either *melodic* or *harmonic* (although, as we will discuss, this distinction is not always clear). A MELODIC DISSONANCE is a pitch or group of pitches that occurs in a single voice; the dissonant element is outside the underlying harmony. A HARMONIC DISSONANCE, on the other hand, is an unstable element that occurs as a full-fledged member of the chord.

---

[2]Michael Rogers, *Teaching Approaches in Music Theory* (Edwardsville, IL, Southern Illinois University Press, 1984).

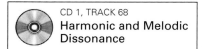

CD 1, TRACK 68
Harmonic and Melodic Dissonance

Again, we can illustrate harmonic and melodic dissonance, respectively, through the dominant seventh chord and the neighboring tone.

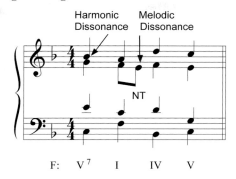

In the last example, the B♭ in the first chord is dissonant both as a minor seventh above the bass and as a member of an E♮–B♭ tritone. Likewise, the melodic dissonance after the second beat (E♮) forms a major seventh above the bass note F_3. The seventh is resolved by step as the alto voice returns the original chord tone (F_4).

NONCHORD TONES are melodic dissonances that occur apart from the harmony; they include neighboring and passing tones (already discussed) as well as other types of melodic figures that occur in predictable formulas. The PREPARATION of a nonchord tone—the consonant pitch that precedes the dissonance—is typically of interest in analysis and original composition. We will order our study of nonchord tones, however, according to their manner *resolution*. Nonchord tones most often resolve by moving stepwise. A few nonchord tones resolve by leap (that is ascending or descending a third or more to the consonant pitch). Finally, when a dissonant pitch is retained and becomes consonant in a new harmony, the resolution is termed OBLIQUE.

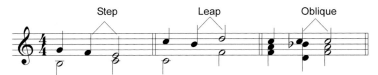

RESOLUTION BY STEP

Several of the most common nonchord tone categories resolve by step. These are summarized in the table below along with the manner in which the dissonant pitch is prepared (approached). Each of these categories will be discussed in the present section.

Nonchord Tones with Resolution by Step

Category	Preparation	Resolution
Neighboring tone	Step	Step
Passing Tone	Step	Step
Appoggiatura	Leap	Step
Neighboring group	Step	Step
Suspension	Oblique	Step

Neighboring and Passing Tones

The passing tone (PT) and the neighboring tone (NT), discussed previously, both resolve by step; likewise, both are prepared by stepwise motion. The passing tone fills in the gap between two chord tones; the neighboring tone embellishes a chord tone by step from above or below. Listen to the passing and neighboring tones in the opening phrase of Bach's chorale "*Verzage nicht, du Häuflein klein*" ("Be Not Dismayed, Thou Little Flock").

CD 1, TRACK 69-1 NEIGHBORING AND PASSING TONES
J. S. Bach, "Be Not Dismayed, Thou Little Flock"
Anonymous Melody, ca. 1530

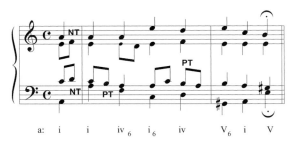

In the last example, upper neighboring tones occur simultaneously in the alto and tenor voices on the first beat. The passing tone in the tenor after the first beat is likewise typical. Notice, however, that the passing tone on the fourth beat is accented (following a chord tone C_4 in the tenor). While nonchord tones occur most often between chord changes, accented passing and neighboring tones are also relatively common.

Chromatic Passing and Neighboring Tones.   Many nonchord tones may be either diatonic or chromatic. In the next example, from *Les Cavaliers* (*The Horsemen*) by French composer Pauline Viardot-Garcia (1821–1910), both chromatic and diatonic neighboring tones occur in the vocal lines over a simple C major piano accompaniment.

TRACK 69-2 NEIGHBORING AND PASSING TONES
Pauline Viardot-Garcia, "Les Cavaliers"

My sister, did you see those two horsemen?
The ones who just passed on their black chargers?
Never did a prince or the son of a queen have such supreme grace!

Neighboring Group. The NEIGHBORING GROUP (NG) is a figure that embellishes a chord tone both from above and below by step. In the neighboring group, two dissonances occur consecutively; the second of these resolves by step.

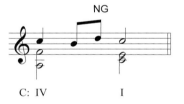

CD 1, TRACK 70

W. A. Mozart, *Die Entführung aus dem Serail*
(*Abduction from the Harem*)
Neighboring Group

In the next passage, from Mozart's 1782 opera *Die Entführung aus dem Serail* (*Abduction from the Harem*), a neighboring group appears in measure 66.

In a structural reduction, neighboring groups are represented with stemless noteheads and connected to the embellished chord tone by a slur.

The Appoggiatura

Prepared by leap, the APPOGGIATURA is an embellishing nonchord tone that occurs on a strong beat and resolves by step. A common appoggiatura (AP) figure involves an ascending leap to the dissonance, followed by descending stepwise motion to the embellished chord tone.

A common type of appoggiatura occurs in Haydn's Sonata in C Major. In measure 7, the chord tone A is preceded by an appoggiatura G♯; a similar appoggiatura E occurs on the next beat. Both appoggiatura are approached by leap and the stepwise resolutions change direction. Finally notice the cadence formula (IV–V⁷–I) that ends the phrase.

CD 1, TRACK 71-1 APPOGGIATURA FIGURES (2 PARTS)
Joseph Haydn, Sonata in C Major
Traditional Approach and Resolution

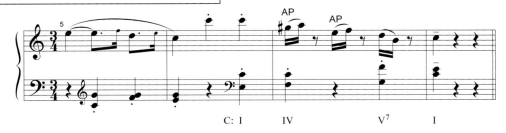

In the Classical era, appoggiaturas are especially common cadential embellishments. Beethoven ends the first phrase of a memorable melody from his Sonata, Op. 13 with a "classic" appoggiatura. The G_5 in measure 8 is approached by leap and resolved by step in the opposite direction. In addition, the $B\flat_4$ at the same point is also an appoggiatura to C_5—a chord tone. We will discuss other aspects of this interesting passage in a later section.

TRACK 71-2 APPOGGIATURAS
Ludwig van Beethoven, Sonata in C Minor, Op. 13 (II)
Simultaneous Appoggiaturas

Sixteenth notes animate the harmony and complement the legato melody. Such a figure, termed ALBERTI BASS, generates more momentum than would be possible with full chords sounded as quarter notes.

Observations about the nature of appoggiatura figures in traditional music include the following:

1. The appoggiatura is approached by leap and resolves by step in the opposite direction.
2. Chromatic appoggiaturas are common.
3. Appoggiaturas occur in strong positions.
4. Unprepared appoggiaturas sometimes occur following a rest or at the beginning of a section.

Nonchord tones are perceived as smoothly and logically associated with a chord tone when the resolution is by step. If the nonchord tone includes a leap (as in the appoggiatura or neighboring group), the resolution effects a subtle, counterbalancing motion in the opposite direction to the preparation. Finally, while some nonchord tones occur in weak metric or harmonic positions, others are accented. Avoid the assumption that pitches on strong beats are chord tones and those that appear between chord changes are nonharmonic. As we will discuss in the next section of this chapter, one of the most important nonchord tone types is characterized by its metric strength.

WORKBOOK/ANTHOLOGY I
I. Resolution by Step, page 75

The Suspension

When one pitch is sustained through a changing harmony (oblique motion), that pitch is said to be *suspended*. A SUSPENSION is a nonchord tone figure in which a chord tone is sustained, becomes dissonant in a new harmony, and then resolves *down by step* to a chord tone. The initial chord tone is termed the PREPARATION; when retained into a new harmony, that pitch becomes the SUSPENSION. Finally, the descending stepwise motion to a chord tone is the RESOLUTION.

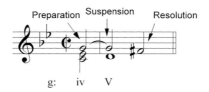

Identification of Suspensions. Suspension figures are differentiated according to the interval formed between the suspended voice and its resolution stated as intervals over the bass. In the last example, the suspended pitch (G_4) is a fourth above the bass and resolves to a third. This is a 4–3 SUSPENSION.

CD 1, TRACK 72-1 SUSPENSIONS
(3 PARTS)
Suspension and Resolution

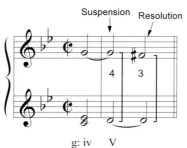

TRACK 72-2 SUSPENSIONS
Octave Placement

The suspension in the last example would be termed "4–3"—even if one or more octaves separate the bass and the suspended voice.

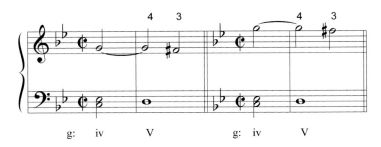

In addition to the 4–3, only three other suspension figures are common in traditional music. The 9–8 SUSPENSION is the second most common figure. Minus one or more octaves between the bass and the suspended pitch, the same effect is created by a 2–1 SUSPENSION. In the second example below (2–1 suspension), notice that a tie between preparation and suspension is unnecessary. When the prepared pitch is rearticulated, the effect is the same.

TRACK 72-3 SUSPENSIONS
9-8 and 2-1 Suspensions

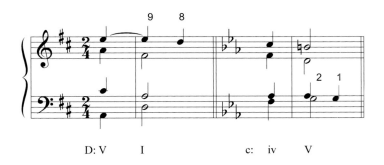

CD 1, TRACK 73-1 SUSPENSIONS, CONTINUED
(3 PARTS)
7-6 Suspensions

A 7–6 SUSPENSION results in an inverted chord of resolution.

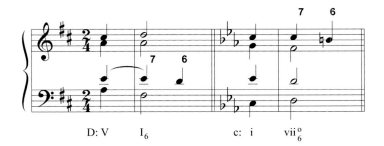

While 4–3, 9–8, and 7–6 suspensions all appear in one of the upper voices, the 2–3 SUSPENSION occurs in the bass.

TRACK 73-2 SUSPENSIONS, CONTINUED
2-3 Suspensions

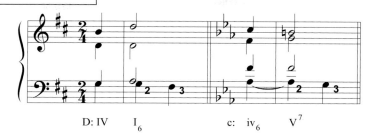

D: IV   I$_6$ c: iv$_6$ V^7

TRACK 73-3 SUSPENSIONS, CONTINUED
Alternate Notation

Be aware that in some meters, suspensions occur as longer note values and not as tied or rearticulated notes.

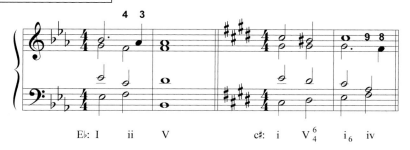

E♭: I   ii   V   c♯: i   V$^6_4$ i$_6$ iv

The Retardation. As a general rule, suspensions resolve through descending stepwise motion. The RETARDATION (RET), however, is a suspended pitch that resolves *upward* by step. The identification is simply "RET" without regard to specific intervals formed above the bass.

C: ii$_6$ V   I

Looking again at a phrase from Beethoven's Sonata, Op. 13, notice that in addition to the appoggiatura (discussed earlier), the cadence is ornamented with a retardation. The passage below is simplified. See page 206 for the complete notation.

CD 1, TRACK 74-1 MORE SUSPENSIONS (2 PARTS)
Ludwig van Beethoven, Sonata, Op. 13 (II)
Retardation

A♭: ii   V   I

Like other suspension figures, the retardation occurs most typically on an accented beat or stronger part of a beat. In the next example, the bass pitch C_3 is retained into a subdominant chord (D–F–A), then resolves upward to double the root.

TRACK 74-2 MORE SUSPENSIONS
J. S. Bach, "Lord, Now Let Thy Servant"
Anonymous Melody, ca. 1700
Various Nonchord-Tone Figures

We can make several observations about the traditional use of suspensions:

1. Suspensions may occur in any voice (including the bass).
2. The dissonance occurs in a relatively stronger metric or harmonic position; the resolution, in a weaker one.
3. The duration of the resolution is equal to or greater than that of the suspension.
4. A retardation is a suspension that resolves by *ascending* step.

A typical 4–3 suspension occurs in the second phrase of Bach's chorale "*O Jesu Christ, mein's Lebens Licht*" ("Lord Jesus Christ, My Life, My Light"). Listen to the example and follow the preparation, suspension, and resolution of a 4–3 figure in the alto voice (measure 7). The pitch G_4 is a chord tone that is suspended to become a dissonance over the dominant. The resolution to F♯ occurs on the third beat. Notice that while the suspension appears on a weak beat, the strength of the chord change accentuates the dissonance.

CD 1, TRACK 75-1 SUSPENSION FIGURES (2 PARTS)
J. S. Bach, "Lord Jesus Christ, My Life, My Light" Anonymous Melody (ca. 1600)
4-3 Suspension

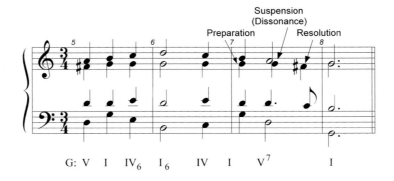

Composers ornament or otherwise obscure the resolution of a suspension in several ways.

1. The embellishment of the resolution with a nonchord tone.

a: i   V

2. The bass may ascend or descend an octave at the point of resolution.

(a:)   C: I   V $_6$

3. The bass pitch may change along with the resolution. In this event, the numeral identification of the resolution coincides with the original bass pitch—not the new one.

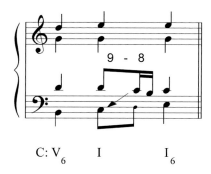

C: V $_6$ I   I $_6$

All three of the previous examples are taken from a Bach chorale harmonization (shown in the next passage). In the three measures shown, there are six different suspension figures with various complexities that sometimes obscure the preparation-suspension-resolution sequence. The passage begins in A minor with the accidental G♯ providing a leading tone. Notice that the cancellation of G♯ in the second half of measure 1 and measure 2 moves the tonality subtly to C major, then back to the original key (as reflected in the analysis). Such brief key changes are called *tonicizations* and will be discussed fully in Chapter 10.

CD 1, TRACK 76
J. S. Bach, "Praise to the Lord, Who with His Love Befriends Thee" Melody by Ludwig Snefl, ca. 1550
Full Phrase with Suspensions

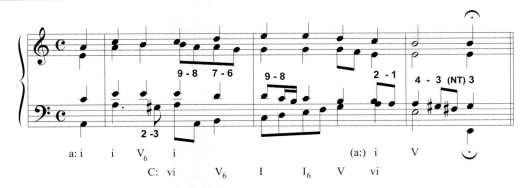

Suspension Chain.   Suspensions may appear in a CHAIN in which the resolution of one suspension becomes the preparation for the one that follows. In the next example, from Haydn's Symphony No. 104, four consecutive 7–6 suspensions occur beginning in measure 5.

CD 1, TRACK 77
Joseph Haydn, Symphony No. 104 in D Major (I)
Suspension Chain

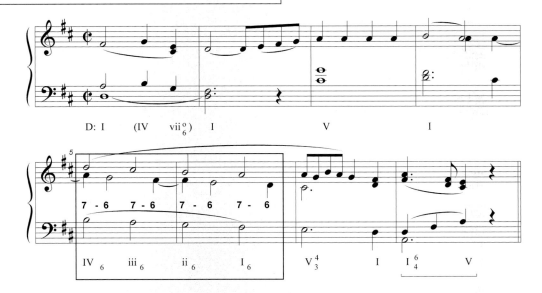

In the last example, as the suspension chain unfolds, harmonic function is suspended (boxed area). While functional progressions are the most common means of focusing the listener's attention on key and mode, other methods are employed for variety. In the last passage, tonality is maintained as the bass descends from $\hat{6}$ down to $\hat{1}$ (harmonized a tenth higher in the soprano). The suspension chain increases momentum as it strengthens tonality (in heightening our expectations of a cadence).

Suspensions constitute a virtual microcosm of traditional tonal tendencies as the listener is guided smoothly across the musical line. The consonant preparation establishes a point of reference; the accented dissonance generates momentum in its need for clarification. The resolution confirms the tonal identity of both chords.

WORKBOOK/ANTHOLOGY I
II. Suspensions, page 77

REVIEW AND APPLICATION 6–1

Nonchord Tones: Resolution by Step

Essential Terms

Alberti bass	harmonic dissonance	retardation
appoggiatura	melodic dissonance	structural dissonance
chromatic passing tone	neighboring group	suspension
consonance	nonchord tone	suspension chain
dissonance	preparation	
embellishing dissonance	resolution	

1. Study the following two-voice fragments and the accompanying analysis. One or more nonchord tone occurs in each segment (circled). In the blank below the nonchord tone, provide a detailed abbreviation to identify the type. For a suspension, write "4–3," "9–8," or "RET," for example, and not simply "SUS."

a.

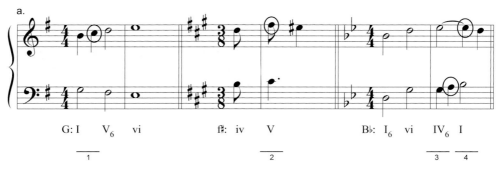

b.

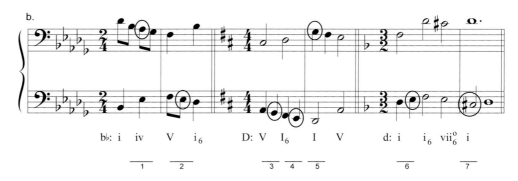

2. Proceed as in the previous lines to identify nonchord tones in these four-part passages.

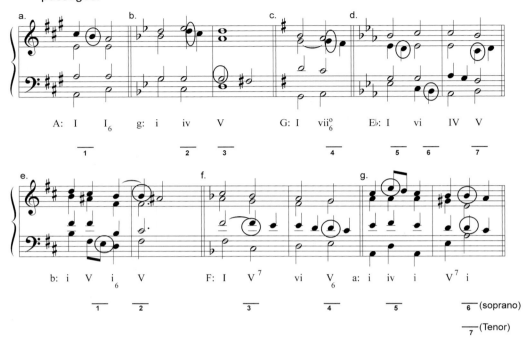

A: I   I$_6$ g: i   iv   V   G: I   vii°$_6$ E♭: I   vi   IV   V

<u> 1 </u>   <u> 2 </u> <u> 3 </u>   <u> 4 </u>   <u> 5 </u> <u> 6 </u>   <u> 7 </u>

b: i   V   i$_6$ V   F: I   V^7 vi   V$_6$ a: i   iv   i   V^7 i

<u> 1 </u>   <u> 2 </u>   <u> 3 </u>   <u> 4 </u>   <u> 5 </u>   <u> 6 </u> (soprano)

                                                       <u> 7 </u> (Tenor)

3. A different type of nonchord tone predominates in each of the two passages below. Identify the type and be prepared to provide an analysis of the harmony.

CD 1, TRACK 78-1 REVIEW AND APPLICATION 6-1 (2 PARTS)
W. A. Mozart, Rondo
Exercise 3-a

TRACK 78-2 REVIEW AND APPLICATION 6-1
Muzio Clementi, Sonata in C Major (III)
Exercise 3-b

SELF-TEST 6–1

Time Limit: 5 Minutes

1. Match one of the terms below to each of the statements by writing the appropriate letter in the blank. In some cases, more than one answer can be considered correct. *Scoring: Subtract 6 points for each incorrect response.*

   A. Neighboring tone   D. Appoggiatura

   B. Retardation   E. Suspension

   C. Passing tone   F. Neighboring group

   _____ a. Prepared by leap and resolves by step in the opposite direction

   _____ b. Includes two consecutive dissonances separated by a third

   _____ c. Fills in the third between two chord tones

   _____ d. Prepared by oblique motion and resolved by step

   _____ e. Embellishes a chord tone above or below by step

   _____ f. A suspension that resolves by ascending step

2. Write a specific abbreviation in the blank to identify each circled nonchord tone. In determining nonchord tone type, consider the analytical symbols as a correct and complete analysis. *Scoring: Subtract 10 points for each error.*

CD 1, TRACK 79
J. S. Bach, "Blessed Jesus, at Thy Word"
Self-Test 6-1, Question 2

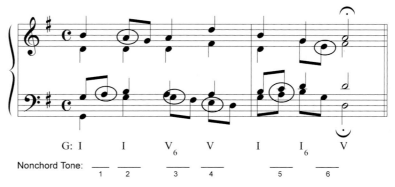

3. Arrange the suspensions in order with the most common first and the least common last. *Scoring: Subtract 4 points for an incorrect order.*

   2–1 (9–8)   2–3   4–3   7–6

   _____   _____   _____   _____
   most   least
   common   common

Total Possible: 100   Your Score _____

OBLIQUE RESOLUTION

Most nonchord tones resolve through stepwise motion, but the *anticipation* and *pedal point* are exceptional dissonances that move to a chord tone through oblique motion.

Nonchord Tones With Resolution by Oblique Motion		
Category	**Preparation**	**Resolution**
Anticipation	Step or Leap	Oblique Motion
Pedal	Oblique Motion	Oblique Motion

The Anticipation

Common at cadences, but also heard elsewhere in traditional works, the AN-TICIPATION (ANT) moves by step *or leap* from a chord tone to a pitch that anticipates the next harmony. In effect, the anticipation moves prematurely to a new harmony while the suspension resolves after the fact.

Anticipations typically conform to the following characteristics:

1. Preparation is by step with resolution through oblique motion.

2. Anticipations occur in weak metric positions.

3. Dotted rhythms often (but not always) accompany an anticipation figure.

Johann Ebeling wrote the melody *Warum sollt' ich mich denn grämen?* ("Why Should Cross and Trial Grieve Me?") in 1666. The final cadence in Bach's harmonization of the melody includes two anticipations, a 4–3 suspension, and numerous passing tones.

CD 1, TRACK 80-1 ANTICIPATION (3 PARTS)
J. S. Bach, "Why Should Cross and Trial Grieve Me?"
Melody by Johann Ebeling (1666)

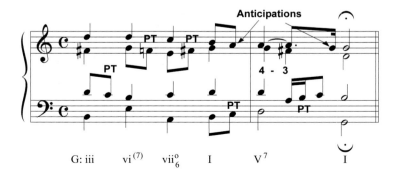

TRACK 80-2 ANTICIPATION
Joseph Haydn, Quartet, Op. 76, No. 3 (II)
Cadence with Anticipation

Numerous anticipations occur in Haydn's variations on *God Save the Emperor Franz.* The passage below occurs at the end of the theme.

The next passage, "*Am Leuchtenden Sommermorgen*" ("On a Bright Summer Morning"), by Robert Schumann, is from a collection of art songs written in 1840 and titled *Dichterliebe* (*Poet's Love*). On an immediate level, the key and mode of this passage change frequently and represent an approach to harmony that will be studied later in both volumes of this text (including the Gr_6^+ in parentheses). Viewed as a whole, however, the dominant-tonic progressions, the anticipation that ends the vocal line, and the half cadence are the same as those employed routinely by Bach and Mozart.

TRACK 80-3 ANTICIPATION
Robert Schumann, "On A Bright Summer Morning" from *Dichterliebe*
Anticipation with Half Cadence

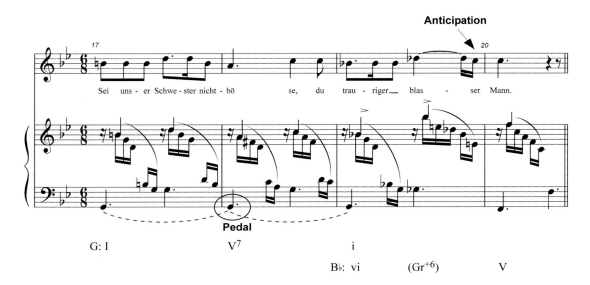

Be not angry with our sister,
You sorrowful, pale man.

Pedal Point

In the Schumann *Dichterliebe* example, notice that the bass pitch (G_2) in measure 18 is circled and identified as "pedal." A PEDAL (or PEDAL POINT) is a dissonant note held through changing harmonies. Pedal point is so-called from the organist's practice of holding down one of the foot pedals throughout a passage. In measure 17 of the last example, the bass G_2 is a chord tone; it becomes a dissonant pedal tone (PED) when held into the dominant seventh in the next measure. The resolution, again by oblique motion, occurs in measure 19 when the harmony changes (to G minor) and the pitch G is again a chord tone.

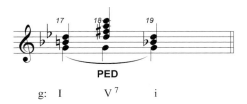

A pedal occurs most often at a tonic or dominant level—as a prolongation of one of these harmonies. Several other characteristics are associated with pedal point:

1. While the pedal tone may occur in any voice, it is often found in the bass.
2. A pedal tone may occur over virtually any number of measures.
3. The notes that form the pedal point may be tied or rearticulated (as in the Schumann example).
4. A pedal tone may be broken between two (or more) different octaves.

Muzio Clementi (1752–1832), a contemporary of Mozart, was an Italian composer, teacher, and pianist. The opening of his Sonata in F Major illustrates again the common Classical-era approach to appoggiaturas as well as passing tones and a bass pedal. While the bass is activated by octave leaps, the tonic pitch is prolonged throughout the four-measure phrase. Notice that when the bass pedal is consonant, it is included in the analysis as the lowest-sounding pitch; when dissonant, the pedal tone is discounted and the next highest pitch constitutes the bass of the chord.

CD 1, TRACK 81
Muzio Clementi, Sonata in F Major (I)
Pedal

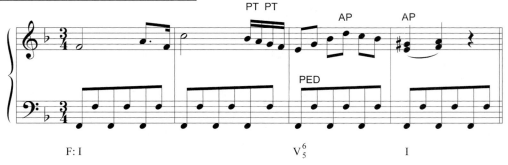

Resolution by Leap

To accentuate the chords they embellish, nonchord tones typically resolve by step. Two categories of nonchord tone, however, resolve by leap: the *escape tone* and the *free tone*.

Nonchord Tones with Resolution by Leap

Category	Preparation	Resolution
Escape Tone	Step	Leap
Free Tone	Leap	Leap

Escape Tone

The ESCAPE TONE (ET) is a figure that is prepared by step, but resolves by leap. The resolution is always in the opposite direction to the initial stepwise motion. The gesture moves first away from the goal pitch (as if attempting to "escape" its natural tendency), then leaps back toward it in compensation.

C: V   I

Several characteristics are common to escape-tone figures:

1. The preparation is by step; the resolution, by leap.
2. An escape tone may occur in any voice.
3. Escape tones occur most often in weak metric positions.

CD 1, TRACK 82-1 ESCAPE TONE FIGURES (2 PARTS)
J. S. Bach, "Draw Us Unto Thee"
Anonymous Melody, ca. 1625

A common escape-tone figure occurs in the second phrase of Bach's chorale *"Zeuch uns nach Dir"* ("Draw Us Unto Thee").

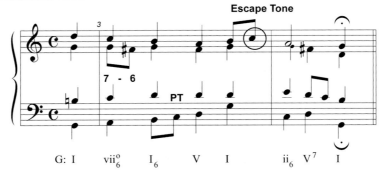

The dissonant escape tone emphasizes the following chord tone despite the resolution by leap. In a melodic reduction, show the escape tone as a stemless notehead connected to the following chord tone by a slur.

Reduction: Bach, "Draw Us Unto Thee"

G: I   vii°   i   V   I   ii   V⁷   I

TRACK 82-2 ESCAPE TONE FIGURES
Joseph Haydn, Sonata in C Major (I)

Escape tones are prominent in the opening theme of Haydn's Sonata in C major.

C: I   V$\frac{4}{2}$ I$_6$ V$\frac{6}{5}$ I   V

The Free Tone

Occasionally, a melodic dissonance is prepared *and* resolved by leap. These FREE TONES (FT) are rare, but may occur either to shape the melodic line, from the force of imitative writing, from a desire to create contrary motion, or other considerations.

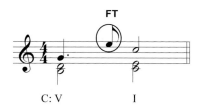

C: V   I

In considering pitches that are approached *and left* by leap, consider first the possibility of consecutive chord tones or the embellishment of another nonchord-tone type. Occasionally, however, a pitch defies other categories and appears because it was necessary to the music. A free tone, for example, is one of several ways to explain the pitch A_2 in the bass (measure 8) of Mozart's Sonata in F Major, K. 332 (first movement). The harmony at this point is dominant, yet the bass, in imitation of the soprano (measures 5–7), includes $\hat{3}$ which is approached and left by leap. Notice also the prolongation of the tonic pitch in measures 1–4.

CD 1, TRACK 83 FREE TONE (2 PARTS)
W. A. Mozart, Sonata in F Major, K. 332 (I)

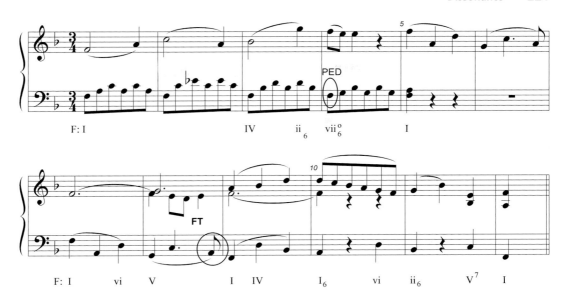

While composers of the Renaissance limited themselves to passing tones, neighboring tones (called auxiliary pitches), and a few other nonchord-tone types, the need both to strengthen tonality and to foster greater emotional affect caused seventeenth-century composers to color the melodic line with a variety of diatonic and chromatic pitches. Even today, traditional composers continue to employ nonchord tones in their stereotypical formulas involving resolution by step, by oblique motion, or by leap.

Traditional Nonchord Tones

Name	Abbreviation	Preparation	Harmonic/Metric Position of Dissonance	Resolution	Comment
Anticipation	ANT	Leap or Step	Weak	Oblique	Common at cadences
Appoggiatura	AP	Leap	Strong	Step	
Escape Tone	ET	Step	Weak	Leap	
Free Tone	FT	Leap	Strong or Weak	Leap	Uncommon
Neighboring Group	NG	Step	Weak	Step	Two consecutive dissonant tones
Neighboring Tone	NT	Step	Weak; less commonly, strong	Step	Returns to original pitch
Passing Tone	PT	Step	Weak; less commonly, strong	Step	Fills in between chord tones
Pedal (Point)	PED	Oblique	Strong	Oblique	Retained through changing harmonies
Retardation	RET	Oblique	Strong	Step (Ascending)	Suspension that resolves upward
Suspension	SUS	Oblique	Strong	Step (Descending)	Resolves by ascending step May appear in "chain"

WORKBOOK/ANTHOLOGY I
III. Resolution by Leap and Oblique Motion, page 79

REVIEW AND APPLICATION 6–2 ━━━━━━━━━━━━━━━

All Nonchord Tone Types

Essential Terms

anticipation   escape tone   free tone   pedal point

1. These lines are similar to the exercises on page 216–217, but *without* given harmonic analysis (the blanks guide you in determining harmonic rhythm). Study the passage and decide on the best roman- and arabic-numeral analysis. Next, circle and label nonchord tones. *Note: If a passing tone creates an implied dominant seventh, analyze that sonority as a seventh chord (and not a nonchord tone).* These exercises include all nonchord-tone types studied in this chapter. Please note that some of the passages have been edited.

 CD 1, TRACK 84-1 REVIEW AND APPLICATION 6-2
Johann Christoph Gluck, Gavotte from *Armide*
Exercise 1-a

 TRACK 84-2 REVIEW AND APPLICATION 6-2
W. A. Mozart, "You Birds, So Every Year"
Exercise 1-b

TRACK 84-3 REVIEW AND APPLICATION 6-2
Joseph Haydn, Sonata in E♭ Major
Exercise 1-c

TRACK 84-4 REVIEW AND APPLICATION 6-2
J. S. Bach, "Deck Thyself in Joy and Gladness"
Exercise 1-d

SELF-TEST 6–2

Time Limit: 5 Minutes

1. In the blank provided, write the nonchord-tone type that fits the description.
Scoring: Subtract 3 points for each error.

_____ a. Rare category in which dissonance is approached and left by leap

_____ b. Prepared by oblique motion, resolves by descending step

_____ c. Resolves by oblique motion; often includes a dotted rhythm

_____ d. Approached by step, resolves by leap in the opposite direction

_____ e. Pitch prolonged through changing harmonies

_____ f. Embellishes a chord tone by step above or below

_____ g. Prepared by oblique motion and resolves by ascending step

_____ h. Prepared by leap, resolves through step

2. Provide a *detailed* analysis for the passage below using the blanks as a guide for harmonic rhythm. Next, circle and identify *six* different nonchord tones.

 CD 1, TRACK 85
Carl Maria von Weber, Theme, Op. 2 (Edited)
Self-Test 6-2, Question 2

Scoring: Subtract 5 points for each incorrect roman numeral; subtract 6 points for each incorrect nonchord-tone identification.

Total Possible: 100   Your Score _____

INTRODUCTION TO HARMONIC DISSONANCE: DOMINANT SEVENTH CHORD

When a dissonant pitch is a chord member, the dissonance is *harmonic* (as opposed to a melodic dissonance such as a passing tone). While tertian harmonic dissonances were used sparingly before about 1680, they have long been a mainstay of the common-practice style, encompassing a wide range of qualities, formulas, and characteristic resolutions.

The dominant seventh chord is by far the most common harmonic dissonance. In fact, authorities sometimes classify seventh chords broadly as either "dominant" or "nondominant." In the present chapter, our survey of the dominant seventh chord will serve as a preparation for the study of counterpoint in Chapter 7. Other harmonic dissonances ("nondominant" seventh chords) will be covered in Chapter 8.

Dominant Sevenths: A Review. In Chapter 3, we discussed the dominant seventh and its inversions as fundamental materials. Before we look more closely at how composers utilize harmonic dissonance to create both variety and a sense of key, review roman-numeral symbols and the arabic-numeral labels that distinguish among root position and the various inversions.

The root-position dominant seventh chord is a major triad with added minor seventh. In major and minor keys, the root is $\hat{5}$. Along with the roman numeral V, an arabic numeral 7 identifies the seventh chord.

Three inversions of the dominant seventh are possible with third, fifth, and seventh in the bass, respectively. Arabic-numeral labels reflect intervals above the bass: $\frac{6}{5}$, $\frac{4}{3}$, and $\frac{4}{2}$.

Preparation and Resolution

Harmonic dissonances are prepared and resolved just as melodic patterns are. The seventh of a seventh chord may have the appearance of a passing tone, a neighboring tone, a suspension, or another nonchord-tone figure. In tonal music, dissonant pitches—whether melodic or harmonic—adhere to the same tonal tendencies. In the dominant seventh chord, $\hat{5}$ is a stable pitch and $\hat{2}$ has only a weak downward disposition. On the other hand, the same chord includes both $\hat{4}$ and $\uparrow\hat{7}$—the two most volatile pitches in the scale.

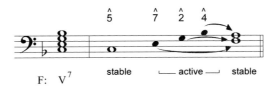

With very few exceptions, the seventh of a dominant seventh chord ($\hat{4}$) resolves down by step to $\hat{3}$. Likewise, $\hat{7}$ ascends to $\hat{8}$—especially in an outer voice. In most instances, the seventh is also *prepared*—either by step or through oblique motion. The oblique preparation-dissonance-resolution figure is similar to a suspension (although harmonically it is quite different).

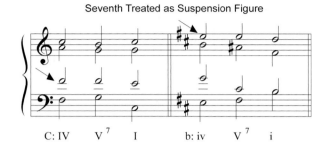

Dominant seventh chords in the next example are prepared and resolved as (descending) passing figures.

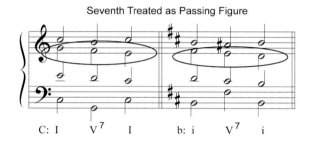

Another common seventh-chord preparation is an upper neighboring figure.

Finally, observe that inversion does not affect the mode of preparation. The seventh itself, of course, resolves down by step.

As we discussed earlier, the fifth may be omitted in a root-position seventh chord to permit a doubling of the root. Just as often, composers score root-position dominant sevenths including all four pitches. If the seventh chord is inverted, however, all four pitches are present in four-voice writing.

Both passing and chordal sevenths occur in the final passage of Haydn's *God Save the Emperor Franz*. In the soprano of measure 19, the eighth note C₅ (circled) is a seventh above the bass. At the same time, however, it has several characteristics that we also associate with a passing tone: weak metric position and a stepwise resolution to a chord tone. Compared with the two dominant seventh chords that occur later in the phrase, however, the soprano figure is better analyzed as a melodic dissonance.

CD 1, TRACK 86-1 INVERTED SEVENTH CHORDS (2 PARTS)
Joseph Haydn, Quartet Op. 76, No. 3

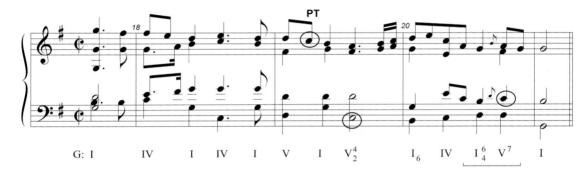

Return to the piano score of Haydn's *God Save the Emperor Franz* and notice that an inverted dominant seventh occurs on the third beat of measure 19 (the seventh is in the bass and resolves down by step to tonic in first inversion). At the cadence (measures 20–21), the tenor C₄ is clearly a full member of the chord; the resolution is again stepwise as we would expect. In the true dominant seventh chord, the dissonant pitch usually has the same length and metric importance as other chord tones. Contrast this with the passing (melodic) seventh in measure 19.

Even in traditional keyboard music, the descending stepwise resolution of a dominant seventh chord is usually clear. In the final movement of his Divertimento in C Major, Joseph Haydn employs numerous dominant seventh chords both in root position and in third inversion. In each case, the seventh (F) resolves to E.

TRACK 86-2 INVERTED SEVENTH CHORDS
Joseph Haydn, Divertimento in C Major

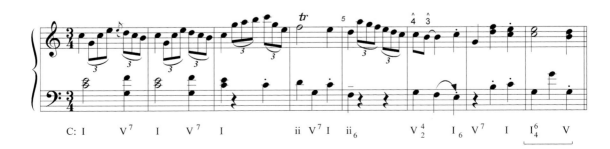

In passages that feature an Alberti bass, one or more pitches may intervene between the seventh of a dominant seventh chord and its resolution.

CD 1, TRACK 87-1 SEVENTH CHORDS IN CONTEXT
(2 PARTS)
Louise Reichardt, "The Flower of Flowers"

Louise Reichardt's simple song *Die Blume der Blumem* (*The Flower of Flowers*) is a model of traditional keyboard accompaniment.

A beautiful flower blooms in a distant land;
It is such a heavenly creation known only to a few.

In the first movement of the Divertimento for Clarinet, Mozart employs dominant sevenths at various points in the first two phrases. Although the first cadence is deceptive, the seventh of the dominant seventh ($\hat{4}$) resolves to $\hat{3}$ in traditional style. In the second phrase, the seventh itself (D_4) is embellished with a neighboring tone.

TRACK 87-2 SEVENTH CHORDS IN CONTEXT
W. A. Mozart, Divertimento for Clarinet, K. 581 (I)

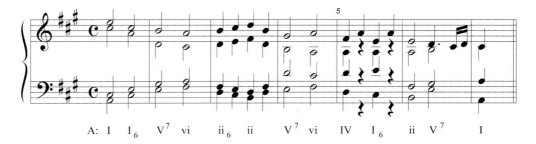

A: I   I$_6$ V^7 vi   ii$_6$ ii   V^7 vi   IV   I$_6$ ii   V^7 I

Embellishing Chords.   In the third measure of the Mozart's Divertimento (above), observe that simultaneous passing tones in all four voices create an *embellishing* C♯-minor triad on the second beat. Created through nonchord-tone movement, EMBELLISHING CHORDS may or may not be logical harmonically. In the Mozart example, a harmonic analysis of the second beat is illogical (ii$_6$ –iii–ii). Accordingly, the second beat is best explained as simultaneous passing tones over the supertonic triad (as in the given analysis).

Embellishing chords are common in chorale literature and are often indicated in analysis with parentheses. In the next example, from Bach's harmonization of "*Nicht so traurig, nicht so sehr*" ("Grieve Not So, Nor Lament"), we might question whether the fourth beat of the first complete measure is III$^+$ with passing iv$_6$ or a iv$_6$ with passing III$^+$?

J. S. Bach, "Grieve Not So, Nor Lament"
Melody attributed to Bach

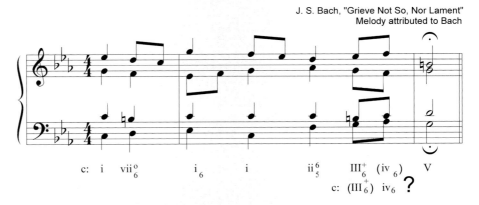

c: i   vii$^o_6$ i$_6$ i   ii$^6_5$ III$^+_6$ (iv$_6$)   V
                                           c: (III$^+_6$)   iv$_6$ **?**

As in the Mozart Divertimento, harmonic logic dictates the better of the two analyses. We have learned that the augmented mediant is extremely rare and would probably not move to the subdominant in any event (as suggested by the first analysis). In addition, the first analysis suggests a change in harmonic rhythm that many would not hear. Finally, note the probability that the unusual harmonic choices were dictated by a tritone leap in the soprano melody.[7]

---

[7]Nondominant seventh chords, like the supertonic six-five in the first complete measure will be discussed in Chapter 8.

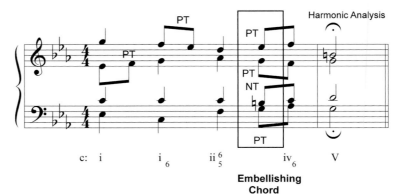

**Embellishing
Chord**

Dissonance is at the same time the most powerful and perhaps the most interesting aspect of traditional tonal music. Used randomly, either melodic or harmonic dissonance can *destroy* a feeling for key. On the other hand, even one or two dissonances have the ability to define the key, form, and melodic contour of a phrase or entire melody.

WORKBOOK/ANTHOLOGY I
IV. Dominant Seventh Chords, page 83

REVIEW AND APPLICATION 6–3

Dominant Seventh Chords

Essential Terms

embellishing chord

1. In the given root-position or inverted dominant seventh chords, use the blank to provide the appropriate roman and arabic numerals. Next, circle the seventh. In the blank measure, provide the pitch to which that seventh would typically resolve. Write only one pitch in the blank measure.

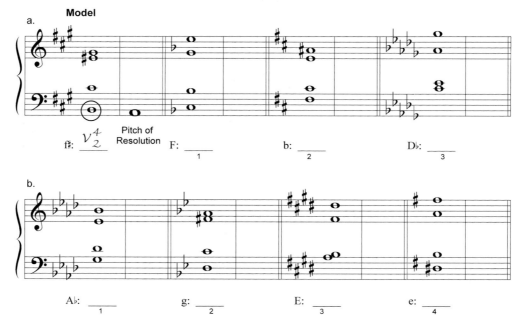

CD 1, TRACK 88-1 REVIEW AND APPLICATION 6-3 (3 PARTS)
G. F. Handel, "Sleepers Awake,"
melody by Philipp Nicolai
Exercise 2-a

2. The following passages include dominant seventh chords in root position and inversion. Provide roman-numeral analysis and identify all nonchord tones.

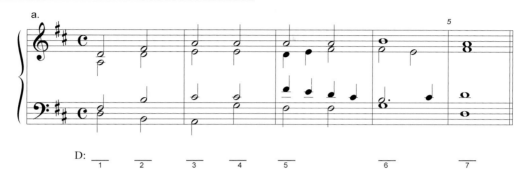

TRACK 88-2 REVIEW AND APPLICATION 6-3
W. A. Mozart, Sonata in B♭ Major, K. 333 (III)
Exercise 2-b

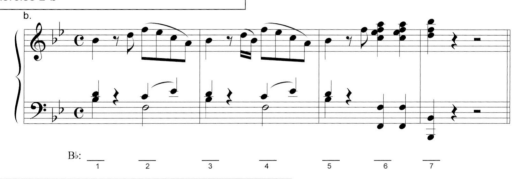

TRACK 88-3 REVIEW AND APPLICATION 6-3
Ludwig van Beethoven, Sonata in G Major, Op. 79 (I)
Exercise 2-c

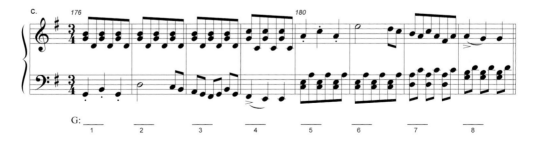

SELF-TEST 6–3

Time Limit: 7 Minutes

1. Begin with a key signature; then construct dominant seventh chords as indicated by the analytical symbols. Add any necessary accidental. *Scoring: Subtract 3* *points for an incorrect signature; subtract 4 points for an incorrect chord (including missing accidental).*

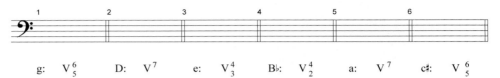

g: V$^6_5$ D: V^7 e: V$^4_3$ B♭: V$^4_2$ a: V^7 c♯: V$^6_5$

2. For each seventh chord given, provide an analytical symbol (including an arabic-numeral label). Circle the seventh of the chord. In the space to the right of the chord, write a pitch that represents a likely resolution of the seventh. *Scoring: Subtract 8 points for an incorrect analytical symbol; subtract 5 points for an incorrect pitch of resolution.*

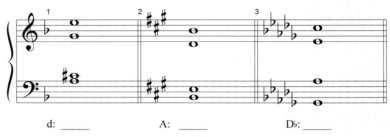

d: _____   A: _____   D♭: _____

(Add a pitch of resolution to the right of the seventh)

3. Some of the following statements are true; others, false. Write "T" or "F" in the blank as appropriate. These problems cover the entire chapter. *Scoring: Subtract 4 points for each incorrect answer.*

_____ a. A chromatic passing tone embellishes a chord tone above or below by half step.

_____ b. A broken octave accompaniment pattern is called Alberti bass.

_____ c. Preparation, suspension, and resolution are the three phases of a suspension figure.

_____ d. The 4–3 suspension is the most common type.

_____ e. The retardation always occurs in the bass voice.

_____ f. A pedal point is a nonchord tone type that imitates the rolling of tympani.

_____ g. Most nonchord tones resolve by step.

_____ h. Dominant seventh chords are often prepared in the manner of a nonchord tone figure.

4. Provide the term that is used to describe a chord formed through simultaneous nonchord tones. *Scoring: Subtract 5 points for an incorrect term.*

_____

Total Possible: 100   Your Score _____

PROJECTS

Analysis

One problem of beginning studies in musical analysis is the fact that traditional works rarely remain in any one key for more than a few measures. To be sure, there is an overall pitch reference for most tonal music, but as we will discuss in Chapters 10, 11, and 12, composers actually strengthen a feeling for this central key by veering away from it. The pieces provided for analysis in this chapter are all excepts to avoid for the present the difficulties associated with deciding when and where to end analysis in one key and begin in another. An exception is the Rameau Gavotte (text page 236) for which keys are identified.

In the given excerpts, you will find most of the nonchord-tone types discussed in the chapter alongside root-position and inverted dominant seventh chords. Center your analysis on these dissonant elements: their preparation, metric position, and resolution. In addition to adding symbols to the score to collect data, write a single, concise paragraph (6-8 sentences) that compares two different excerpts (as directed) in one or more of the following ways:

a. *Harmony.* What is the range of diatonic chords employed? Locate cadences and categorize cadence types. Are the three functions equally represented? Do exceptional progressions occur (dominant to predominant, for example)?

b. *Nonchord Tones.* Comment on the types and frequency of nonchord tones. Are they prepared and resolved as you would expect? Do nonchord tones occur in strong, weak, or a combination of metric positions?

c. *Dominant Seventh Chords.* Locate seventh chords and note their preparation and resolution. Are any resolutions exceptional? Do you find the seventh typically in the highest voice?

Text

Joseph Haydn, Quartet, Op. 76, No. 3 (II), Excerpt, text page 198. Several aspects of this passage are discussed in the text. Complete an analysis as directed. Listen to a recording of the string quartet setting of this melody as you follow the piano score.

Jean-Phillippe Rameau, Gavotte (Edited), text page 236. As noted on the score, this work begins in A minor, moves to C major, then returns to the original key. Complete your roman-numeral analysis in these keys, respectively. Various melodic ornaments have been removed from this version; otherwise, the dance movement itself (which is the subject of a series of variations) is shown complete.

Workbook/Anthology I

Muzio Clementi, Sonatina in G Major (I), Excerpt, Workbook page 85.
Friedrich Kuhlau, Sonatina, Op. 55, No. 4 (II), Excerpt, Workbook page 86.

Composition

Choral Arrangement. The first two phrases of a Bach chorale harmonization are given in the next example. All nonchord tones in Bach's setting have been removed.

J. S. Bach, "Oh, How Blest Are Ye Whose Toils Are Ended"
Melody by Johann Crüger (1647)

Make two different versions of the chorale using Bach's diatonic harmony, but adding nonchord tones. Begin with a harmonic analysis and include this with both arrangements. Remember: It is important that you do not change any of the given chords—add embellishments only. For the first arrangement add nonchord tones sparsely, but try to include five or six different types (including different suspension figures). Your first measure, for example, might look like the next example. Note that this chorale harmonization actually begins more in D minor than F major, but we will not introduce the complexities of key change at this point.

F: vi   vi₆   iii   vi₆

In the second version, add more embellishing tones—as many as three per measure, although you should not use simultaneous nonchord tones unless they are the same type (consecutive passing tones, for example). As in the first arrangement, label nonchord tones and include roman-numeral analysis. Again, the first measure is given below as a sample.

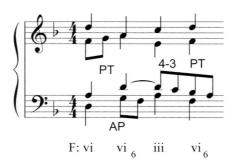

F: vi   vi₆   iii   vi₆

For Further Study

Lutheran Chorale Melodies. While Gregorian chant is the basis of Catholic liturgical music, the chorale melody has been central to the Lutheran service—literally from the time of Martin Luther (1483–1546). Numerous composers wrote chorales to German texts during and after the Reformation, but besides Luther, Johannes Crüger (1598–1662) is among the most important. The settings of chorale melodies in four parts for congregational performance reached their height with the works of J. S. Bach. We often study music theory through chorales because they are brief, but intricate and compact works that bring together many principles of harmony and counterpoint in a homophonic setting.

Prepare an individual presentation or participate in a group project on the Lutheran chorale melody and its importance in Western music. Include some or all of the following topics:

a. A formal definition and examples of chorale melodies.

b. An explanation of how chorale melodies differ from chant melodies.

c. Name and provide biographical sketches of at least two important composers of chorale melodies.

d. Investigate the chorale cantata. Which Baroque composer is considered a master of this *genre?*

In addition to your historical information, locate at least two complete chorale melodies with their original German text, provide copies of these melodies for the class, and lead a performance. In particular, locate the melody *Ein' Feste Berg* which was composed about 1530. We know this tune as "A Mighty Fortress is Our God." Who wrote it? The same melody was used by a major composer as the basis of more than one chorale cantata. Whose settings of this melody do we still value today? Listen to a recording of two or three movements from the cantata *Ein' Feste Berg.* Be prepared to play an excerpt from this recording for the class.

Andantino

Jean Philippe Rameau, Gavotte

a:

C:

C: I　　　　V
　　　a: vii°₆　i

7

The Soprano-Bass Framework

If we limited our listening and performance to the popular styles of today (jazz, various derivations of rock, television themes, and the like), we might conclude that a strong melody with a simple, chordal accompaniment represents the essential texture of Western music. As we have discussed in earlier chapters of this text, however, the original texture of Western music (ca. 600 C.E.) was monophony. Exemplified by Gregorian chant with its gentle contour and text-based rhythm, monophonic music was supplanted around 1000 C.E. by the exciting new possibilities of polyphony that we surveyed in Unit 2. Appearing first as a nonimitative style (with two supporting musical lines), by 1500, the textural ideal was a single melodic fragment that generated a more complex fabric through successive imitation. Homophony—melody and accompaniment to us today—developed only in the seventeenth century.

Punctus Contra Punctum

As was customary in scholarly works, early music theorists, like Philippe de Vitry (1291–1361) and Johannes Tinctoris (*fl.* 1475) wrote their texts in Latin. When they discussed guidelines for *punctus contra punctum* (literally "point against point"), they referred to the composition of two or more equal and complementary melodies that together, created an aesthetically satisfying whole. This texture, of course, is called *counterpoint,* and while the favorite styles and textures of music have changed significantly since the Renaissance, the composition of one musical line against another remains an essential element of virtually all categories of tonal music today. While we could have titled this chapter "Introduction to Counterpoint," our studies at present are more basic and limited largely to a single style. Understand, however, that when you compose a bass to complement a given soprano, you *are* writing counterpoint and these same principles will guide you in later studies.

Importance of Soprano-Bass Framework

The study of counterpoint is an important part of undergraduate music curricula for two main reasons. First, through imitative and nonimitative counterpoint, we encounter some of the essential *genre* of common-practice music: motet, fugue, invention, chorale prelude, and others. This stylistic review permits us to appreciate the structure of major works of the past. At the same time, however, a generic (nonstylistic) study of counterpoint shows how the controlling soprano-bass framework guides the momentum of music in various textures. In Chapter 2 of the second volume, we will examine canon, fugue, and other imitative contrapuntal forms in detail. In the present chapter, our examination of contrapuntal principles will help in understanding how musical lines move through time to create harmony and melody.

In the Baroque style, while the bass is typically subordinate to the melody, it was considered so important to the structure of the composition, that the lowest voice was routinely doubled. As musical tastes changed, this practice was discontinued after about 1750. Still, even in the works of nineteenth-century composers, the framework between the bass and the soprano remains structural. Compare these frameworks as extracted from phrases by J. S. Bach, W. A. Mozart, and Franz Schubert. In each, the melody dominates; yet the bass forms a strong tonal and metric footing that is indispensable to the work as a whole.

CD 1, TRACK 89-1 SOPRANO-BASS FRAMEWORK (3 PARTS)
J. S. Bach, Menuet
Baroque Era

TRACK 89-2 SOPRANO-BASS FRAMEWORK
W. A. Mozart, Concerto for Clarinet, K. 622 (III) (Edited)
Classical Era

TRACK 89-3 SOPRANO-BASS FRAMEWORK
Franz Schubert, Impromptu, Op. 142, No. 2 (Edited)
Romantic Era

Play the bass lines of the last three passages and observe several common traits. First, each has a distinct contour and employs a variety of pitches and rhythms. Next, notice that the key is clarified in the bass voice of each phrase. This is especially obvious in the Bach and Mozart phrases, where an emphasis on $\hat{1}$ and $\hat{5}$ is apparent at a glance (Bach's bass outlines nothing but a tonic triad for the first four measures). Mozart further drives home the key, not only by a reiteration of the tonic pitch, but through a complete descending major scale (measures 4–7). Finally, a reduction of the Schubert bass (which is comprised entirely of chord tones) shows careful attention to melodic tendencies within the scale and a prolongation of the pitch G.

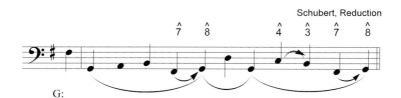

The bass that Haydn composed to complement the melody *God Save the Emperor Franz* makes an effective two-voice composition—even without the alto and tenor. Sing the melody while the bass is performed on an instrument (or sung by a bass vocalist). An interesting and effective two-voice composition provides a framework for the full quartet movement. While the bass part was composed for cello, it is also reasonably singable (the range is G_2–C_4). Although subordinate to the melody, the bass offers an effective musical line that both emphasizes natural melodic tendencies in G major and complements the rhythm of the soprano. Dissonant pitches in the bass and their resolutions (measures 4 and 11, for example) are clearly heard as passing tones. Finally, at strong metric points (across the barline), the two voices either move in opposite directions, or one voice remains stationary while the other ascends or descends. This practice creates a more independent bass melody than would be possible if accented beats were approached in the same direction.

CD 1, TRACK 90
Joseph Haydn, Quartet, Op 76, No. 3
Soprano-Bass Framework

Despite stylistic differences that define music in the Baroque, Classical, and Romantic eras respectively, we can observe numerous categories of similarity in successful soprano-bass frameworks. Some of these characteristics serve to create and maintain tonality; others clarify the independence of the two lines.

Maintaining Tonality and Style

1. Definition of Key and Mode
2. Rhythmic Continuity
3. Consonance and Dissonance

Independence of Lines

4. Contrapuntal Motion
5. Melodic Design

Although we could approach two-voice frameworks in a number of valid ways, in this chapter, we will study five *general principles* (listed above) that are applicable to tonal music in virtually any style.

MAINTAINING TONALITY AND STYLE

Even when a given melody is well crafted and clear in tonality, an ambiguous counterpoint will detract from that musical effect. The bass constitutes a second melody that is complementary to the soprano (and subordinate to it in our present studies); still, both voices must be well designed and explicit in their definition of key. A clear tonal structure, along with characteristic handling of dissonance, helps achieve this goal.

Writing An Effective Bass Voice

Principle 1: Definition of Key and Mode

An effective bass combines with a given melody to produce a clear and consistent harmonic rhythm, a functional harmonic flow, and strong cadences.

Harmonic Implications in the Melody.   While most tonal melodies offer various harmonic interpretations, an inherent tonal logic is usually present in the melody itself. In addition to the resolution of dissonance (discussed in the last chapter), composers use one or more of the following techniques to imply function and harmonic rhythm through a single melodic line.

1. Triad arpeggiation (with or without intervening passing tones).
2. The identification of chord tones through the regular resolution of melodic dissonance.
3. Stronger metric and harmonic positions may be allocated to chord tones; embellishing pitches often (but not always) occur in weaker positions.
4. Especially following a leap, natural tonal tendencies govern the melodic line.

In melody, harmonic rhythm is often apparent through triad outlines, scale passages, and obvious embellishing tones. At the same time, triad and chord outlines limit harmonic choices. Consider the English folk song, *Early One Morning*, for example. Tonic, predominant, and dominant chords are all outlined in the melody itself (and shown on the lower staff); an effective harmonization with different chords would be unlikely.

English Folksong, "Early One Morning"

Chorale Melodies.   While tonal melodies from Bach to Basie have much in common, we will survey principles of bass composition using a chorale tune, *"Nun lasst uns gehn und treten"* "Now Let Us Come Before Him", by sixteenth-century composer Nikolaus Selnecker. Like other liturgical melodies, both the harmonic rhythm and the tonal implications of each phrase are clear.

"Now Let Us Come Before Him"

Now let us come be - fore___ Him, With songs and___ pray'rs a - dore Him, Who

to our life path giv - en All need - ed strength from___ heav - en.

Harmonic Implications in the Bass. The soprano and the bass together are the foundation of tonal harmony. While Bach used the traditional four-voice texture for his harmonization of Selnecker's melody (shown in part in the next example), taken alone, the soprano and bass provide continuity, shape, and harmonic cohesion.

CD 1, TRACK 91
J. S. Bach, "Now Let Us Come Before Him,"
melody by Nikolaus Selnecker (ca. 1590)
Soprano-Bass Framework

Implied Triads. In the first half of the Bach chorale phrase above, observe how the harmony, while somewhat exceptional, is effectively implied by the soprano and bass alone.

Bach, Implied Harmony

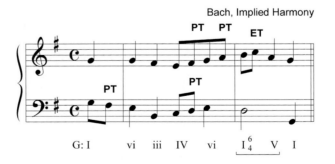

G: I   vi   iii   IV   vi   I$^6_4$ V   I

Strong functional progressions depend not only upon the musical effect of each part individually, but also upon our perception of how the voices combine to imply tertian chords. In two-voice counterpoint, a tertian triad is implied by any of the following:

- doubled root
- root and fifth
- root and third

The third and fifth (without root) will not always imply a triad adequately unless the context for that triad has been established. If our goal is to convey the functional progression I–I₆–IV–V–I, for example, the passage below implies these chords.

In the next soprano-bass framework, however, the root is missing in the first four chords. While we might or might not hear these intervals as the triads identified by roman numerals, a satisfying sense of harmonic function is lacking.

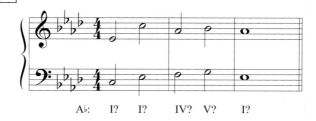

Implied Six-Four Chords.   Another problem with the last passage is the perfect fourth in measure 3. In two-voice counterpoint, two chord tones that form a fourth imply a six-four chord. Because traditional composers employed second-inversion triads only in limited contexts, we can usually imply triads with thirds, fifths, sixths, or octaves, *but not* with fourths. If a fourth is heard as a melodic dissonance or as part of a cadential six-four, however, the implications may be clear.

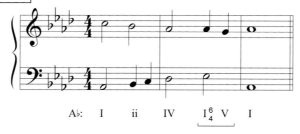

Cadences.   The harmonic rhythm of a Lutheran melody like Selnecker's "Now Let Us Come Before Him" is generally one chord change per beat. Chorales often change key with each new phrase and the scheme of these keys reinforces the primary tonic. In the present chapter, however, we will limit ourselves to the key of G major throughout the melody. Even without key changes, the mixture of authentic and half cadences in the harmonic sketch that follows imparts both a sense of formal design and a clear tonality.

CD 1, TRACK 93-1 CADENTIAL PLANS (2 PARTS)
"Now Let Us Come Before Him"
Effective Cadences

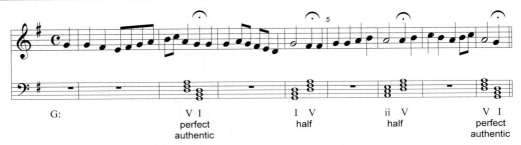

Given the characteristics of the chorale melody and our choice to remain in G major, cadential possibilities are limited. We might use a deceptive, rather than an authentic cadence for the first phrase, for example, or consider weakening the first authentic cadence with an inverted dominant chord (imperfect authentic). Likewise, a IV–V half cadence in the fourth measure (boxed in the next example) is an alternate possibility to ii–V.

TRACK 93-2 CADENTIAL PLANS
Alternate Cadence Plan

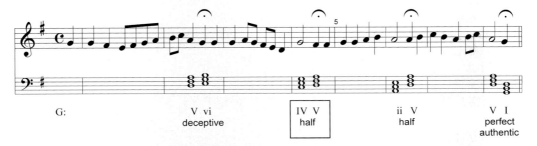

Consistent and logical implied harmonies are important in writing an effective soprano-bass framework. Still, even the best harmonic formulas can be muddled by a lack of continuity in rhythm between the two parts.

Writing An Effective Bass Voice

Principle 2: Rhythmic Continuity

Effective two-voice writing demands parts that are both balanced and complementary in terms of rhythmic momentum.

Rhythmic continuity is most easily conveyed through a consistent pulse of durational values. If the melody moves basically in half and quarter notes, for example, a bass that is composed in eighth and sixteenth notes may detract rather than support. Likewise, if the melody proceeds in eighth notes, a bass in which half notes predominate may be labored.

As we discussed in the last chapter, chorales were intended for solemn congregational performance; the harmonic rhythm usually coincides with the beat pulse. In terms of metric rhythm, however, the basic motion is often the beat *division*. Even before beginning the harmonization, if we create a model rhythmic plan for the soprano-bass framework, our goals will be established even if changes are necessary later. Viewing the rhythmic structure of the melody "Now Let Us Come Before Him" (first and second phrases), the importance of the divided beat is obvious.

Rhythmic Reduction

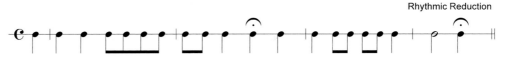

After the opening three pitches, the eighth-note pulse fluctuates only at the two cadences (where harmonic tension is increased). Shown in the next example, the soprano-bass rhythmic flow that Bach employed in his own harmonization of "Now Let Us Come Before Him" is instructive. The bass not only employs exactly the same range of durational values as the melody, but the eighth-note division is clarified in the bass even from the opening anacrusis.

CD 1, TRACK 94-1 RHYTHMIC PLANNING (2 PARTS)
Effective Rhythm

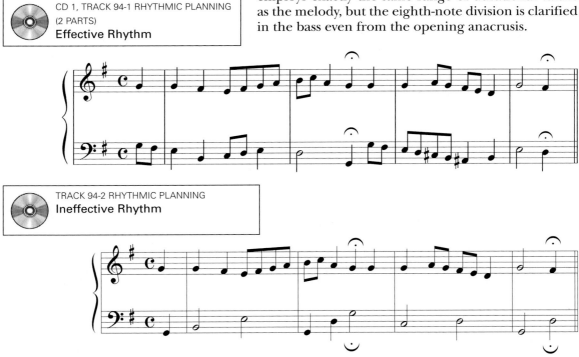

TRACK 94-2 RHYTHMIC PLANNING
Ineffective Rhythm

Composite Rhythm.   The combined effect of multiple voices is termed the COMPOSITE RHYTHM. In most traditional works, the composite rhythm moves at a steady pace with only a few different note values. In Bach's harmonization, the two voices together produce a composite rhythm of eighth notes (slowing only at the cadence). Compare the two-voice reduction with the composite rhythm of the two lines together (lower staff).

Successful composers are also conscious of a natural "give and take" in combining two or more melodic lines. When the motion of one line slows, the other line assumes the momentum to create a consistent composite rhythm. We could probably draft dozens of appropriate rhythmic plans for the bass voice to accompany "Now Let Us Come Before Him." The one shown in the next example, however, is poor on several accounts.

Poor: Too Many Different Values

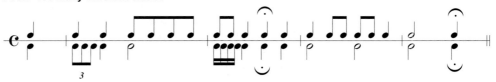

While a skilled composer might write an effective bass using the given plan, notice the inconsistent range of rhythmic values including sixteenth notes, a triplet, quarter, and half notes. The composite eighth-note flow, typical of the chorale style, is missing here and the triplet figure is out of place.

In the next sketch, a bass composed with uniform rhythms will probably sound like an accompaniment—not an independent voice as we want. Rests, especially on strong beats, are rare in the chorale style.

Poor: Bass Has Effect of an Accompaniment

Bach's own soprano-bass rhythmic reduction for "Now Let Us Come Before Him" supports the rhythmic flow of the chorale melody. For our present discussion of the soprano-bass framework, we will use the following rhythmic plan that is quite similar to the one that Bach chose in his harmonization (see page 242).

Effective Rhythmic Plan

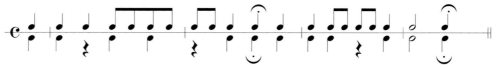

With a workable cadential plan and a consistent rhythmic sketch, we will next plan the harmony in more detail. Assessing the flow of consonance and dissonance will be an ongoing concern in this effort.

A careful analysis of the melody and all potential harmonies is essential—even before the composition of the bass itself. One of the most common errors made by inexperienced composers and arrangers is the choice of harmony that unintentionally creates ambiguous or unresolved nonchord tones and seventh chords in the melody.

Writing An Effective Bass Voice

Principle 3: Consonance and Dissonance

When a pitch in the melody is heard either as a nonchord tone or as the seventh of a seventh chord, the resolution must also be heard as conventional.

We have limited our sample harmonization of "Now Let Us Come Before Him" (shown below) to root-position triads. The melody is almost entirely stepwise, so triad outlines do not mandate any one harmonic plan. In this draft harmonization (shown on the lower staff), passing tones fill in between thirds in measures 1 and 3; an escape tone precedes the first and final cadences.

In another harmonic outline of "Now Let Us Come Before Him" (first phrase only), notice that while the roman numerals suggest an effective harmony, we will not necessarily *perceive* those chords due to the ambiguous nonchord tones. Further, the F♯ on the second beat of measure 1 is ↑$\hat{7}$ in G major and to define this key, we would expect $\hat{8}$ to follow. Instead, ↑$\hat{7}$ moves to $\hat{6}$ which is not a member of the tonic triad. Until the first cadence, the melody itself is oriented more toward E minor than G major.

The next draft harmonization of Selnecker's chorale tune (with vi in place of I) is more effective than the choices in the last example. Again, however, we will not necessarily hear the first beat of measure 2 as a supertonic as suggested by the roman numeral. The pitch B_4 is a nonchord tone, but since the previous pitch is *also* identified as a passing tone, the harmony is ambiguous.

Poor: Remaining Ambiguous Nonchord Tone

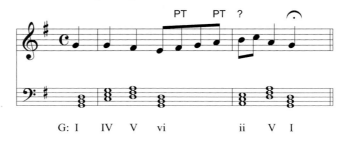

G: I   IV   V   vi   ii   V   I

In J. S. Bach's harmonization of "Now Let Us Come Before Him," numerous chromatic chords (to be studied in later chapters) color the second and third phrases. The first phrase is diatonic in G major, however, and we might note that Bach solves the problem of a melody beginning more in E minor (until the first cadence) by choosing an atypical chord sequence.[1]

J. S. Bach's Harmonization

G: I   vi   iii   IV   vi   I   V   I

The first step in effective contrapuntal writing is planning. An effective harmony—including cadences, the resolution of dissonance, and rate of chord change—should all be established (at least in draft) before the counterpoint is composed. Remember: If the harmonic plan is ambiguous, or if the rhythmic flow is erratic, counterpoint will inherit and accentuate these flaws.

WORKBOOK/ANTHOLOGY I
I. Harmonic Planning, page 87

REVIEW AND APPLICATION 7–1

I. Harmonic Planning

Essential Terms

composite rhythm

1. For each of the three melodies, identify the best single key to harmonize the entire line. Cadential points are identified by fermatas. Choose cadence types

---

[1]Most chorale melodies, including Selnecker's "Now Let Us Come Before Him," were written during the modal period of Western musical history (ca. before 1680) and, therefore, often have characteristics that invite exceptional harmonic choices. Bach's use of the mediant triad in this passage is a case in point.

that fit the given melody. Write roman numerals in the upper blanks and identify the cadence type in the lower blank.

Remember that if $\hat{4}$ in the melody descends to $\hat{3}$, it may be harmonized as the seventh of a dominant seventh chord.

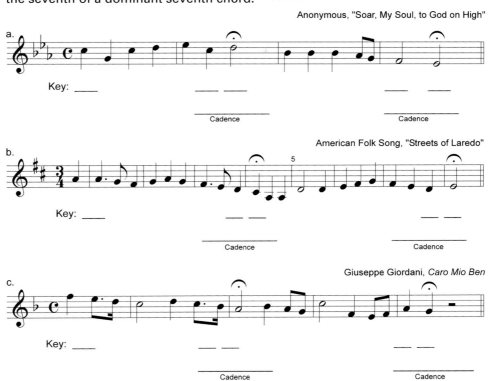

2. Study the melody that follows. Blanks appear to indicate the harmonic rhythm. Choose an appropriate harmony by listing all possible chords for each harmonic change; after you have completed all possibilities for the entire melody, circle a logical harmonic plan, then write the appropriate chords on the staff.

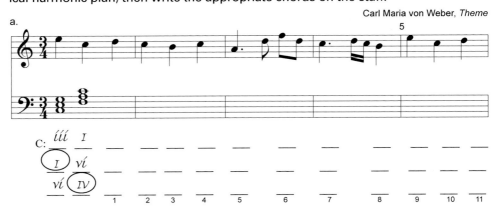

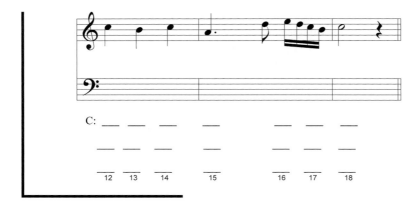

C: __ __ __   __   __ __ __

__   __   __ __ __
12 13 14   15   16 17 18

SELF-TEST 7–1

Time Limit: 7 Minutes

1. Study the three roman numerals below chord changes in *A Gift to be Simple*. In each case, one of the three possibilities listed does not fit the melody. Circle the inappropriate harmonic choice in each group of three. *Scoring: Subtract 8 points for each error.*

Shaker Melody, "The Gift To Be Simple"

	1	2	3	4	5	6	7	8	9
E♭: (1)	I	I	IV	I	I	ii	I	V	I
(2)	IV	V	I	IV	iii	V	IV	IV	ii
(3)	V	vi	vi	V	ii	vi	V	vii°	V

2. The following list of statements concerns an effective bass voice for a given melody. Some of the statements are incorrect. Check "True" or "False" for each statement. *Scoring: Subtract 4 points for each incorrect response.*

True   False

_____   _____ (1) The rhythmic character of the bass should differ substantially from the soprano.

_____   _____ (2) Triads can be implied by root and fifth alone.

_____   _____ (3) Cadences are less important in counterpoint than in homophonic textures.

_____   _____ (4) Implied triads in a melody govern harmonic choices.

_____   _____ (5) The third and fifth alone may not adequately imply a triad.

_____   _____ (6) The composite rhythm of the bass and soprano should have a wide range of durational values.

_____ _____ (7) If a bass voice creates nonchord tones in the given soprano, no resolution is necessary.

_____ _____ (8) Rests are usually ineffective in a bass voice.

3. In addition to root and third, list two other ways of implying a triad in two-voice writing. *Scoring: Subtract 7 points if either answer is incorrect*

_____   _____

Total Possible: 100   Your Score _____

With the harmonic plan completed, we can begin the composition of a bass voice. For instructional clarity, we are limiting our harmonic resources to diatonic triads in root position and first inversion (omitting, for now, seventh chords and all second-inversion chords).

VOICE INDEPENDENCE

Effective counterpoint complements a given melody. In fact, creating voice independence is one of the most important considerations in writing credible counterpoint. Composers create part independence through several means including contrary motion and distinct ranges.

Writing An Effective Bass Voice

Principle 4: Contrapuntal Motion

Contrary contrapuntal motion should predominate.

In polyphonic music, the flow of individual lines from one pitch to another is called the CONTRAPUNTAL MOTION. Two voices can progress horizontally in four different ways. If the movement is CONTRARY, the voices move in *opposite* directions. In OBLIQUE MOTION, one voice moves up or down while the other remains stationary. In the next example, one of many possible harmonizations of "Now Let Us Come Before Him," notice the predominant use of contrary motion in the opening measures.

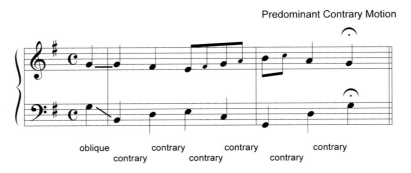

Predominant Contrary Motion

Contrary and oblique motion create the highest degree of voice independence. For variety, and to enhance the melodic line, however, additional categories of contrapuntal motion are available. If the motion is SIMILAR, voices move in the same direction, but by different interval types (a third ascends or descends to a sixth, for example). If contrapuntal motion is PARALLEL, both direction and interval type are the same.

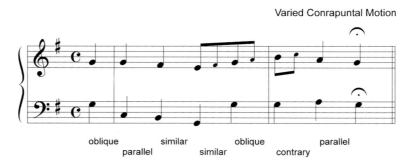

Varied Conrapuntal Motion

oblique   similar   oblique   parallel
    parallel   similar   contrary

Considering the last two examples, the first voices are independent and well delineated through contrapuntal motion. In contrast, the second soprano-bass framework (composed with predominantly similar and parallel motion) sounds arbitrary and is less musical. Not only are the two lines difficult to separate aurally, but the implied harmony is not clear.

Parallel Perfect Intervals.   Parallel perfect octaves, perfect unisons, and perfect fifths do not often appear in traditional harmony.[2] Listen to the parallel perfect fifths in the next example (measure 1 between first and second beats). You will probably hear that voice independence, a cornerstone of effective writing between soprano and bass, falters at this point. Instead, one voice is heard as the accompaniment of the other. Likewise, parallel perfect octaves occur on the last two intervals of the phrase and substantially weaken the cadence.

CD 1, TRACK 95-1 CONSIDERATIONS IN COUNTER POINT (3 PARTS)
Poor: Parallel Perfect Intervals

Parallel Perfect   Parallel Perfect
   Fifths   Octaves

In addition to the parallel perfect fifths and octaves in the last example, the two-voice framework is weak due to the paucity of contrary motion. Still, while contrary and oblique motion are helpful in establishing part indepen-

---

[2]Parallel perfect fourths between two voices are acceptable in some contexts—including four-part homophony. For the present, we will avoid *all* parallel perfect intervals in our two-voice counterpoint.

dence, similar and parallel motion have their place in providing variety. Parallel thirds and sixths between soprano and bass are common, but for no more than

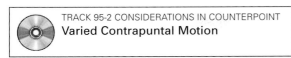

TRACK 95-2 CONSIDERATIONS IN COUNTERPOINT
Varied Contrapuntal Motion

two or three consecutive intervals. Note the mixture of all four types of contrapuntal motion in the initial phrase of "Now Let Us Come Before Him" as J. S. Bach harmonized it (soprano and bass).

J. S. Bach, "Now Let Us Come Before Him"

oblique   contrary   contrary
        similar   parallel   similar

Direct Octaves and Fifths.   When voices move in *similar* (not parallel) directions to form a perfect octave or a perfect fifth (as in the second measure of the previous example), the effect is termed DIRECT OCTAVES (FIFTHS).[3] The consequences of direct perfect octaves or fifths are basically the same problem created by parallel intervals: a weakening of part independence. Except at cadences, traditional composers avoid direct octaves and fifths in soprano-bass

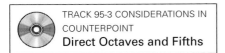

TRACK 95-3 CONSIDERATIONS IN COUNTERPOINT
Direct Octaves and Fifths

counterpoint. A direct octave (or fifth) that includes *stepwise motion in the soprano,* however, is common at a cadence. If the motion occurs within a phrase, or if there is a leap in the soprano, direct octaves and direct fifths should be avoided.[4]

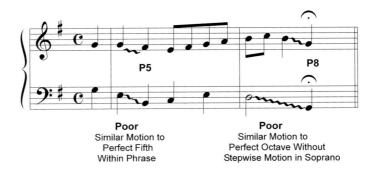

Poor
Similar Motion to
Perfect Fifth
Within Phrase

Poor
Similar Motion to
Perfect Octave Without
Stepwise Motion in Soprano

Few composers adhere to every guideline of "traditional" practice in every composition. Some stylistic considerations, however, like the avoidance of parallel octaves, fifths, and unisons, have very few exceptions. On the other hand, direct octaves and fifths within the phrase are not altogether uncommon—especially outside the four-part vocal style (return to the Haydn example on page 198, for example, and locate direct octaves in the first line). The best

---

[3]Direct intervals are also often termed HIDDEN OCTAVES or FIFTHS.
[4]For purposes of illustration, pitches in Selnecker's melody have been altered in this example.

music is designed intuitively with the composer not so much conscious of "rules" as of creating expressive and graceful lines that combine effectively.

> *Writing An Effective Bass Voice*
>
> **Principle 5: Melodic Design**
> The bass voice should be an effective tonal melody that complements the soprano.

In Volume II of this text, we will discuss imitative and nonimitative counterpoint in a variety of styles. For our current studies of soprano-bass framework, the most important characteristics of melodic design are *range* and *melodic motion.*

Range.   As a general principle, the ranges of the voices should be distinct. The bass voice, for example, should never ascend above the soprano. In Chapter 8, we will discuss part independence in four-voice style—a texture in which one voice may easily intrude into the range of another. In two-voice counterpoint, however, a confusion of the soprano and bass ranges is rarely a problem. Notice that only one pitch (C_4) is common between typical soprano and bass vocal ranges.

Melodic Motion.   In traditional four-voice writing, leaps occur more often in the bass than in other voices. Still, with careful planning, the addition of nonchord tones, and by employing inversions, strive to make your bass voice a melodic, singable line that constitutes a second melody. *Conjunct* melodic motion is preferable in the bass, and leaps between tones in adjacent chords are best considered carefully.

Guidelines for Leaps in Traditional Vocal Style.   While the goal for a melodic line is conjunct motion, well-placed leaps provide variety and energy, and may govern the overall development of a phrase. Leaps of a diatonic third, fifth, or octave are rarely problematic—especially between beats of the same chord or when adjacent chords have identical functions (I–vi or ii–IV, for example). Sometimes, as in the second measure of the next example, composers must choose between successive leaps on the one hand and contrary motion on the other.

Poor: Successive Leaps

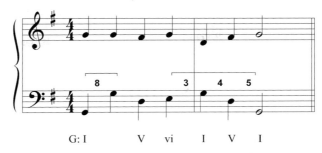

The perfect fourth is another common leap—particularly when the harmonic implications are functional (I–V–I, ii–V–I, and so on).

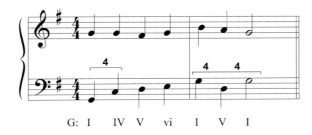

Handle other leaps carefully with stepwise motion in the opposite direction of the leap.

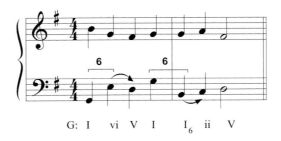

Leaps of a seventh or a ninth (shown in the following example) are rare in traditional vocal style and should be avoided for now. As we discussed earlier, resist a leap involving $\hat{7}$ or $\hat{4}$ unless an appropriate resolution is possible.

Poor: Awkward Leaps

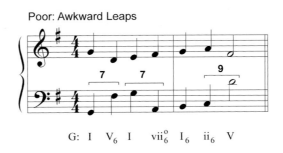

In two-voice writing, independence is as important as effective tonal design. To this end, contrary motion is paramount in separating voices. Remember, however, that each voice in contrapuntal writing is itself a melody. In chorale style, the soprano dominates; yet the bass must be a viable line of music that exhibits the characteristics of traditional melodic writing.

WORKBOOK/ANTHOLOGY I
II. Voice Independence, page 89

REVIEW AND APPLICATION 7–2

Voice Independence

Essential Terms

contrapuntal motion	direct octave	oblique motion
contrary motion	fifths	similar motion
direct fifth	hidden octaves	parallel motion

1. Classify the contrapuntal motion between beats in the following soprano-bass counterpoints (ignore the cue-size notes). Label the motion as contrary (**C**), oblique (**O**), parallel (**P**), or similar (**S**). Use the table below each example to report the data from your analysis.

G. F. Handel, "Oh Lord, My God, How Great the Load"
Melody ca. 1625

Contrapuntal Motion

	Contrary	Oblique	Parallel	Similar
Number of Occurrences				

J. S. Bach, Menuet

Contrapuntal Motion

	Contrary	Oblique	Parallel	Similar
Number of Occurrences				

2. Locate and circle parallel fifths, octaves, or unions in the two-voice counterpoint below. The bass has been edited to include various errors of parallel motion.

Felix Mendelssohn, "Sleepers Wake"

3. Study the given pitches, then complete the bass with the *closest* chord tone (root or third) that constitutes the specified contrapuntal motion with the given soprano note. Most given chords are in root position, but both first and second inversions will be necessary to complete the bass as directed (these possibilities are not reflected in the roman-numeral symbols).

SELF-TEST 7–2

Time Limit: 5 Minutes

1. Choose a term from the list to match each definition listed. Write the letter of the term in the blank. *Scoring: Subtract 5 points for each incorrect answer.*

A. Contrary motion   E. Oblique motion
B. Direct octaves   F. Conjunct motion
C. Parallel octaves   G. Disjunct motion
D. Contrapuntal motion

_____ (1) Melodic motion that is stepwise
_____ (2) An octave between a pair of voices that moves in parallel motion to another octave
_____ (3) The directional motion between a pair of voices
_____ (4) Motion between soprano and bass that arrives at an octave in similar motion (without stepwise motion in the soprano)
_____ (5) Melodic motion that is primarily by leap
_____ (6) Contrapuntal motion in which one voice remains stationary while another ascends or descends
_____ (7) Contrapuntal motion in which voices move in opposite directions

2. Choose a letter from the list that identifies the error in contrapuntal writing in each frame below. Frames contain only one error each. Consider harmonic implications to be correct. You many use some letters from the list more than once; others, not at all. *Scoring: Subtract 15 points for each error.*

A. Parallel octaves   E. Unresolved leap
B. Parallel fifths   F. indistinct vocal range
C. Direct fifths   G. Improper Implied six-four chord
D. Direct octaves

F: I   vi   V   b: i   iv   i   ii°₆   G: vi   IV₆   I   vii°₆   A♭: I   IV   V   I

Answer: _____   _____   _____   _____
            1   2   3   4

3. Direct octaves and fifths concern one of the following types of contrapuntal motion. Make a check mark in the appropriate blank. *Scoring: Subtract 5 points for an error.*

   Direct octaves and fifths concern

_____ (1) contrary motion
_____ (2) oblique motion

_____ (3) parallel motion

_____ (4) similar motion

Total Possible: 100   Your Score _____

Composing the Bass

With the five general principles of soprano-bass composition in mind, we can compose a bass voice to complement the melody "Now Let Us Come Before

 CD 1, TRACK 96-1 COMPOSING THE BASS (3 PARTS)
Using Root Position

Him." A good starting point is a draft note-against-note framework, implying root-position triads and based on the harmonic plan devised earlier.

Sing the bass voice of the last example and assess it both musically and as a complement to the soprano melody. You will probably agree that the line is disjunct and relatively difficult to sing. In addition, the bass lacks a rhythmic identity to separate it convincingly from the soprano.

Using Inversions. Due to the special handling that traditional composers have reserved for second-inversion chords, we will not employ them for the present. However, notice that with two *first-inversion* triads substituted for the ones scored originally in root position, the bass is smoother. Inverted chords not only

 TRACK 96-2 COMPOSING THE BASS
With Inversion

create a better melodic line, but they generate momentum; we hear inverted triads as midpoints in a phrase. In contrast, root-position sonorities more often signal an arrival.

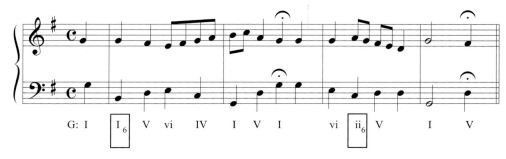

Nonchord Tones. While inversions in the last example smooth the bass, they add no supplementary rhythmic interest. We can use a variety of nonchord tones, however, to further improve the line. These supplementary pitches create rhythmic interest and generate intensity. The bass may still sound like a bass at this point, but the new version is considerably improved with the inversions and several nonchord tones.

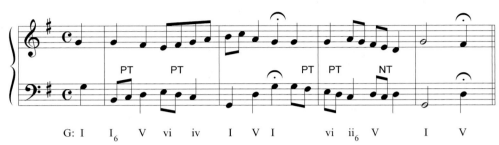

Octaves in Contrary Motion.   Earlier in this chapter, you learned that parallel octaves are among the *least* effective contrapuntal possibilities. In the passage above, notice the contrary motion across the barline between measures 3 and 4. While contrary motion is preferable, *successive octaves*—even in contrary motion—are generally avoided, due to the listener's perception of diminished part independence.

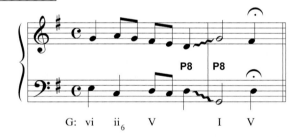

We can eliminate the octaves by inverting the tonic chord (measure 4 in the next example). This change creates a I_6–V half cadence. At an interior point, the loss of harmonic strength is insignificant. The line is further improved by another (optional) passing tone. Finally, assess the added color of a *chromatic* neighboring tone (C♯) to embellish the pitch D_3 and followed by a diatonic passing tone (C♮).

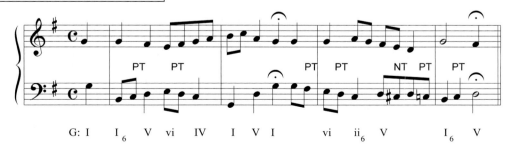

Contour.   Especially outside the four-part style, we could criticize the bass line (and the soprano as well) as lacking a dynamic contour. Independent lines are most effectively delineated when melodic contours differ. In our bass, G_3

serves not only as the first pitch, but also as the first cadential point. An effective contrapuntal line usually has a stronger sense of ascending or descending direction than our bass offers.

Melodic Contour

If we begin the line on G_2 rather than G_3, the two phrases convey a more convincing sense of direction.

Improved Melodic Contour

Final improvements to our bass voice are included in the next example. The additional passing tone (circled) is not essential, but it lends an immediate sense of rhythmic and melodic identity to the passage that, as a whole, is dominated by eighth notes in conjunct motion.

CD 1, TRACK 98-1 COMPLETED SOPRANO-BASS FRAMEWORK (2 PARTS)
Final Version

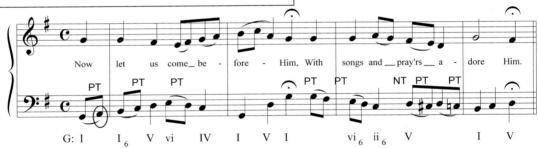

Bach changed keys during the second phrase of his harmonization of Selnecker's chorale melody (as shown below). Accordingly, a comparison with our bass counterpoint in G major is less instructive than it might be otherwise. Nevertheless, despite a wider range of harmonic choices in Bach's version, notice several similarities between the two harmonizations of "Now Let Us Come Before Him." These include a similar balance of ascending and descending motion, equivalent contrapuntal movement between voices, similar cadential plans, and a traditional use of nonchord tones.

TRACK 98-2 COMPLETED SOPRANO-BASS FRAMEWORK
Bach's Counterpoint

Naturally, we might continue to tinker with the bass to eliminate leaps or to make other improvements. But as the basis of a chorale harmonization, the last version will suffice. We should stress that most successful tonal composers would not progress through the various stages of two-voice composition as we have done in this chapter. Rather, the process for experienced composers is intuitive, based on an ingrained knowledge of tonal music.

WORKBOOK/ANTHOLOGY I
III. Composing A Bass Voice, page 91

REVIEW AND APPLICATION 7–3

Composing A Bass Voice

Essential Terms

octaves (fifths) in contrary motion

1. Compose a bass counterpoint to complement the melody *Good King Wenceslaus.* Many harmonizations are possible, but follow the harmonic rhythm outlined by blanks. Each blank is a chord change. You may change bass notes, however, during the same chord. Follow the process outlined in this chapter for deciding on a key and cadence scheme, revising with inversions, assessing nonchord tones in the melody, and so on. Provide roman numerals in the blanks. When a phrase repeats, you may use the same or a different harmonization.

Use another sheet of paper to sketch your counterpoint; then recopy on this page.

Traditional, "Good King Wenceslaus"

2. Compose a bass counterpoint for the melody *Born to Lose*, which was popular during World War II and is still sometimes heard today. The original harmonic rhythm moves in quarter and half notes, but longer values are possible as well. You need not duplicate the original harmony if you know it. Follow the procedure described above for problem #1. The rate of harmonic flow, however, is entirely up to you. Provide roman numerals below the bass line. Plan cadences and other aspects of the counterpoint carefully.

Ted Daffan, "Born to Lose"

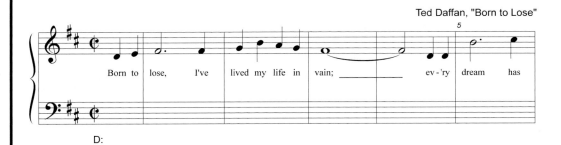

3. Two chorale melodies are given for analysis, harmonization, and the composition of a bass voice.

Heinrich Albert, "God Who Madest Earth and Heaven"

a.

God,- who mad - est earth and heav - en, Fa - ther, Son, and Ho - ly Ghost;
Who the night and day hast giv - en, Sun and Moon and star - ry host;

Whose al - might - y hand sus - tains__ Earth and all that it __ con - tains. __

Anonymous Melody, "O Lamb of God Most Holy"

b.

O Lamb of God most ho - ly, Up - on the cur - sed tree_____ slain;
E'er pa - tient, meek, and low - ly, Tho' heap'd with hate and dis - dain.

All sins Thou bor - est for_____ us, Else had des - pair reigned

o'er_____ us. Have mer - cy on us O_____ Je - sus!

SELF-TEST 7–3

Time Limit: 5 Minutes

1. Study the two-voice framework and locate one serious error in each measure where a blank appears. Circle the error; then choose from the list below and write the appropriate letter in the blank. Look for errors involving parallel motion, unresolved dissonance in the soprano or bass, a perfect fourth between chord tones, and the like. Be sure to check motion into and out of the measure as well as the measure itself. *Scoring: Subtract 8 points for each incorrect answer.*

   A. Parallel octaves, fifths, or unisons

   B. Perfect fourth between chord tones

   C. Direct octaves or fifths

   D. Root missing

   E. Unresolved melodic dissonance

   F. Implied (noncadential) six-four

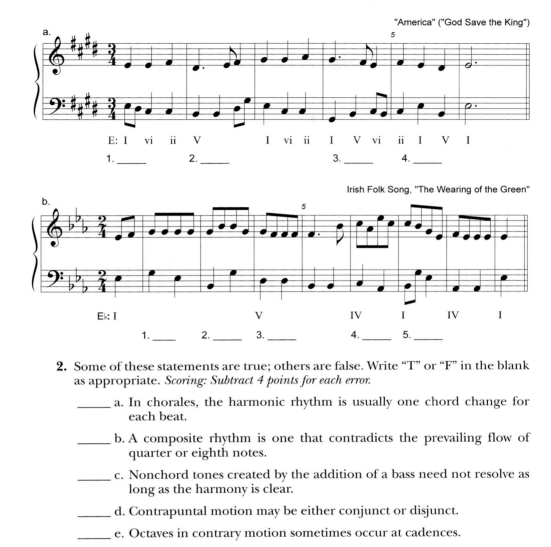

"America" ("God Save the King")

E: I vi ii V   I vi ii I V vi ii I V I

1. _____   2. _____   3. _____   4. _____

Irish Folk Song, "The Wearing of the Green"

E♭: I   V   IV   I   IV   I

1. ____   2. _____   3. _____   4. ____   5. _____

2. Some of these statements are true; others are false. Write "T" or "F" in the blank as appropriate. *Scoring: Subtract 4 points for each error.*

_____ a. In chorales, the harmonic rhythm is usually one chord change for each beat.

_____ b. A composite rhythm is one that contradicts the prevailing flow of quarter or eighth notes.

_____ c. Nonchord tones created by the addition of a bass need not resolve as long as the harmony is clear.

_____ d. Contrapuntal motion may be either conjunct or disjunct.

_____ e. Octaves in contrary motion sometimes occur at cadences.

_____ f. Chord inversions are useful in smoothing the bass line.

_____ g. The bass often remains unchanged across the barline.

Total Possible: 100   Your Score _____

PROJECTS

Analysis

In effect, we analyze counterpoint any time we use roman-numeral analysis because the arabic labels show clearly when the bass has the root, the third, the fifth, and so on. Less obvious is the contrapuntal motion between bass and soprano. While we may not be aware of it, contrary motion usually predominates—especially over the barline. Another way of saying this is that we usually *do* notice when the bass moves ineffectively: if the bass remains stationary across the barline, for example, or moves too often in parallel or similar motion with the soprano.

The analysis projects in this chapter will reinforce concepts of effective contrapuntal writing, but it is more in the experience of *composing* that your mastery of this material will be demonstrated. Effective contrapuntal writing is not acquired overnight; you must work and rework a bass voice for any given soprano. The process of analyzing your own efforts is on-going.

Text

Joseph Haydn, Quartet, Op. 76, No. 3 (II), Excerpt, text page 198. This setting was conceived for instruments and does not conform precisely to the guidelines for vocal writing (as discussed in Chapter 7). Study the soprano-bass counterpoint (the first violin and cello) and locate any points that are exceptional. Evaluate Haydn's bass as a melody. Even as conceived for cello, is it singable? Determine the instance of parallel, similar, and oblique motion as compared to contrary motion. How often does similar or parallel motion occur over the barline?

Workbook/Anthology I

J. S. Bach, "Beside Thy Manger Here I Stand," chorale harmonization, soprano-bass framework, workbook page 93.
J. S. Bach, "Jesus, My Treasure," chorale harmonization, soprano-bass framework, workbook page 94.

Composition

Duet in Instrumental Style.   Compose a contrapuntal duet for instruments as directed by your instructor. While our present text studies of counterpoint will center on a vocal style, you may have fun writing for instruments that are both capable of performing wide leaps. As always, begin with a harmonic progression or series of progressions. Consider composing four four-measure phrases with a variety of cadences (ending with perfect authentic). Avoid six-four chords for now. The first two phrases of the duet might be based on progressions like these:

Sample Harmonic Plan

A: I   V   vi   IV   I   IV   V   IV   V   I   vi   ii   V   I

Half   Authentic

Next, compose a soprano melody (taking into account the capabilities of the instruments you have chosen). Consult Appendix A on page 477 for information on ranges and transposition. Two sample melodies are shown in the next examples; both conform to the first four measures of the given progression (note that your instructor may want you to use a completely different progression for your own duet). Both of the sample melodies are conceived for flute and both include leaps that we would not associate with vocal music. The first is relatively more simple in style and rhythm. Either melody is appropriate as a model.

With the melody complete, write a complementary bass voice. The bass in these samples was written with bassoon in mind, although other instruments (as well as keyboard) are alternate possibilities. Adhere to the harmonic plan, however, and make sure that any nonchord tones in the soprano or bass adhere to traditional types. Likewise, resolve the seventh of any implied dominant seventh chord as you have practiced through text and other exercises. Your use of leaps, however, may reflect the instrumental medium. Continue one of these samples or compose a new one along lines suggested by your instructor.

First Sample

Second Sample

For Further Study

Parallel Motion. In Chapters 7 we have stressed the importance of contrary motion as a means of separating voices in a contrapuntal composition. In world music, however, and in Western music outside the common-practice era, parallel motion is the cornerstone of the compositional process. A type of polyphonic music called organum began in the West about 850 C.E. with the duplication of a chant melody by another voice singing a perfect fifth above or below. The passage below is from the *Musica enchiriadis* —some of the earliest known examples of Western polyphonic music.

From the *Musica enchiriadia*
ca. 850

Sit - glo - ri - a Do - mi - ni, in sae - cu - la - lae - ta - bi - tur Do - mi - nus in o - pe - ri - bus su - is.

In the Middle Ages, English composers wrote gymel—a type of music based on parallel thirds. An entire system of improvised harmony, *fauxbourdon* (false bass), developed in the late Middle Ages and Renaissance. By "sighting" a given interval above or below the ever-present chant melody, a tertian texture of parallel first-inversion triads emerged.

Undertake research on one or more aspects of parallel harmony (organum, gymel, or *fauxbourdon*) and prepare a brief presentation. Include basic definitions and historical facts, but center your presentation on recorded examples. You might provide the class with a brief cantus firmus, explain the system of parallel chords you have researched, and actually improvise a harmony.

Systems of improvised triadic harmony appear in the music of several African peoples and in other parts of the world as well. As an alternate project, obtain a recording and listen to music of the Zulu or another African people. Compare this effect with recorded examples of French *fauxbourdon*.

CHAPTER 8

Voice Leading

Traditional Western music—whether a trio sonata by Handel or the chorus of an Andrew Lloyd Webber musical—is grounded in principles of tension and stability, motion and stasis, proportion and balance. We might think of tonal principles as *laws*; that is, essential governing doctrines that create and maintain order. Problems of proportion and balance, on the other hand, are often solved through the use of traditional *structures* such as duple-compound meter, the G minor scale, or binary form. Finally, the *conventions* of Western music include the orchestra, the 88-key span of the piano, the instrumentation of a rock combo, and our traditional concepts of tone production (the use of vibrato, for example). Western conventions make our music sound familiar even as they permit composers a great deal of latitude to exercise creative talents.

One of the most important conventions of traditional Western music, applicable to both vocal and instrumental styles, is VOICE LEADING—the movement of individual parts (voices) from one chord to another. Central to voice leading is the choice of an appropriate *contrapuntal motion*—both for individual parts and for the separation of the bass line from the soprano, alto, and tenor. Earlier, you studied contrapuntal motion in a two-voice context. Now, we will expand our studies to center on the four-voice texture.

CONTRAPUNTAL MOTION

As we discussed in Chapter 7, four different types of contrapuntal motion are recognized: *contrary, oblique, similar,* and *parallel.*

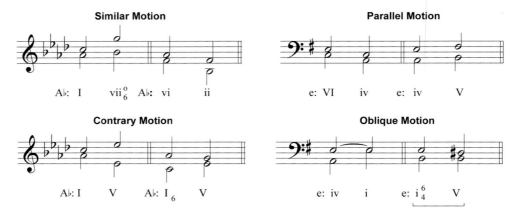

Contrapuntal Motion in the Four-Voice Style

Successful compositions in the four-voice style feature a variety of contrapuntal motion. Two areas, however, are particularly important for smooth voice leading:

1. The motion between any two *individual voices*.

2. Contrapuntal motion between the *bass* and *the upper three voices* (soprano, alto, and tenor).

   Motion Between Individual Voices.   A major consideration in judging contrapuntal motion is whether the voices involved are *inner, outer*, or a combination. OUTER VOICES are the soprano and bass. As the most prominent, the outer voices define contrapuntal motion in four-voice writing. Voice leading principles in the INNER VOICES (the alto and tenor) are generally more flexible, since they are less exposed.

   Any of the four contrapuntal motions may form appropriate voice leading between a pair of voices, but contrary and oblique motion are preferable. Reserve similar motion for instances in which contrary or oblique motion is impractical (reasons of doubling, range, or creative choice, for example). Parallel intervals such as thirds, fourths, or sixths, while less common, supply variety. However, as we discussed in Chapter 7, parallel motion by *perfect unison, perfect fifth,* or *perfect octave* should be avoided. These intervals decrease the effect of voice independence and result in a structurally weakened composition.

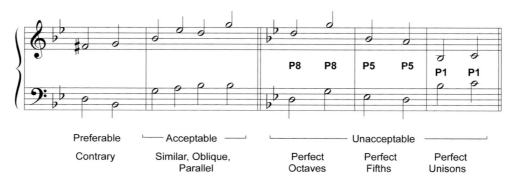

Even between voices that are not adjacent (as in the first two progressions in next example), parallel unisons, fifths, and octaves still have an inelegant effect that is best avoided.

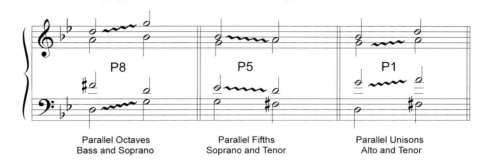

Parallel Octaves   Parallel Fifths   Parallel Unisons
Bass and Soprano   Soprano and Tenor   Alto and Tenor

Parallel Perfect Intervals: Exceptions.   Parallel perfect unisons, octaves, and fifths are acceptable when a chord is repeated. The perfect fifths between the soprano and alto voices in Bach's *"Freu dich sehr, o meine Seele"* ("O Be Glad, My Soul, Be Cheerful") do not diminish the four-voice texture because the entire measure is heard as a tonic chord (with passing tones in the tenor and bass).

J. S. Bach, "O Be Glad, My Soul, Be Cheerful"
Anonymous 15th-Century Melody

Notice the series of *parallel fourths* in another passage from the same chorale. While contrary contrapuntal motion is preferable, composers routinely employ parallel fourths (as well as sixths and thirds) in four-voice writing.

"O Be Glad, My Soul, Be Cheerful"

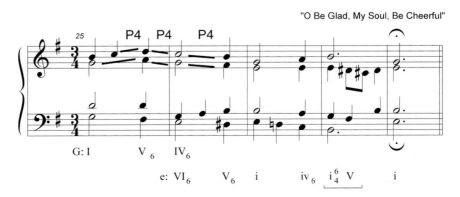

Motion Between the Bass and the Upper Voices.   In the traditional vocal style, composers treat the bass separately from the soprano, alto, and tenor—the UPPER VOICES.

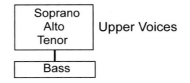

The contrapuntal motion between any two voices is important, but that between the bass and the upper voices is crucial. To facilitate independence, composers most often move the bass in *contrary motion* with the upper voices. This is especially important across the barline and at cadences. As shown in the next example, if the bass descends, the upper voices should ascend; where the bass ascends, the soprano, alto, and tenor most often descend.

 CD 2, TRACK 02-1 CONTRARY MOTION
(3 PARTS)
Block Chords

a: i   i₆   V   i   VI   iv   V⁷   i

In Bach's harmonization of *"Du Friedensfürst, Herr Jesu Christ"* ("Lord Jesus Christ, Prince of Peace"), we see predominantly contrary contrapuntal motion between the bass and the soprano. Likewise, movement between the bass and alto, and between the bass and tenor is also largely contrary (although instances of oblique and similar motion occur as well). Observe that the subdominant chord in measure 2 is analyzed as embellishing.

TRACK 02-2 CONTRARY MOTION
J. S. Bach, "Lord Jesus Christ, Thou Prince of Peace"
melody attributed to Bartholomäus Gesius (ca. 1600)

A: I   IV   vii°₆ I   V₆   (IV₆) V⁶₅   I   I₆   IV₆   I   ii₆   V   I
                           Embellishing
                              Chord

Even in instrumental music, composers typically adhere to the conventions of voice leading. Various contrapuntal motions are employed in Haydn's

God Save the Emperor Franz, but discounting the off-beat soprano pitches, the contrapuntal motion from one accented point to another is most often contrary between the bass and upper voices (although oblique and similar motion occur frequently).

G; I   IV   I   IV   I   V   I   V$^4_2$ I$_6$ ii$_6$ I$^6_4$ V^7 I

Contrapuntal motion is among the most important aspects of voice leading. Contrary motion should predominate—especially between the bass and the upper voices. In creating effective tonal music, however, following "rules" is no substitute for a combination of technical skill and musical intuition. Successful composers achieve a balance between adherence to traditional guidelines on the one hand, and the necessity for variety and creative expression on the other.

MELODIC STYLE

The conventions of Western musical style foster both a vocally conceived musical line and enhanced tonal implications. In four-voice writing, these stylistic traits include the following:

1. Careful treatment (or avoidance) of awkward melodic intervals such as the tritone.
2. Attention to a tonal resolution of the leading tone.
3. The regular resolution of pitches heard as harmonic dissonances.

The Leading Tone in Inner and Outer Voices.   If the leading tone appears in an outer voice, our tonal conditioning makes us expect that the tonic will follow. A "frustrated" leading tone (as in the first example below), weakens tonality. In the second example, ↑$\hat{7}$ ascends to $\hat{8}$ and thus clarifies the key. The direct octaves at the cadence (soprano-bass) are considered acceptable when the soprano moves by step.

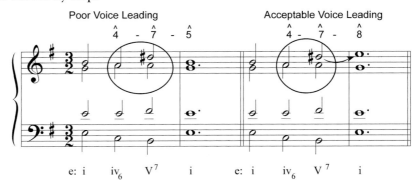

Poor Voice Leading   Acceptable Voice Leading

$\hat{4}$ - $\hat{7}$ - $\hat{5}$ $\hat{4}$ - $\hat{7}$ - $\hat{8}$

e: i   iv$_6$ V^7 i   e: i   iv$_6$ V^7 i

Leading tones with traditional resolutions appear in the bass, tenor, and alto voices in Bach's *"Aus meines Herzens Grunde"* ("My Inmost Heart Now Raises").

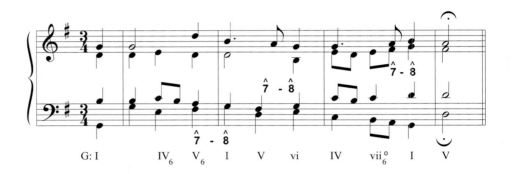

In an inner voice, the tendency of the leading tone is less pronounced; $\uparrow\hat{7}$ ascends to $\hat{8}$ *or* it may take another course. Both possibilities occur in the first phrases of Bach's *"Nun danket alle Gott"* ("Now Thank We All Our God"). While a descending $\uparrow\hat{7}$ to $\hat{5}$ melodic movement, seen in the alto (measure 4), would constitute poor voice leading in the soprano or bass, this exception is common in an *inner voice* and it is customary at a cadence.

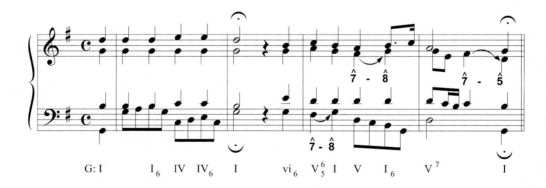

In "Come, Holy Ghost, God and Lord," the descending tetrachord ($\hat{8}$–$\uparrow\hat{7}$–$\hat{6}$–$\hat{5}$) in the alto highlights another possible treatment of the leading tone. As we have discussed, when $\hat{5}$ is the goal of a melodic line, $\uparrow\hat{7}$ often descends to $\hat{6}$, then continues to $\hat{5}$. This same melodic pattern might also occur in the soprano or bass. At the cadence, observe that $\uparrow\hat{7}$ ascends above $\hat{8}$ to $\hat{3}$. Bach could have let the alto descend to B to provide the third of the triad with tripled root (a common practice at cadences). The unusual melodic motion (best avoided in our studies for the present) effects a change from open to close structure and was probably chosen for its sonority.

G: I   IV I₆   V   IV₆   I   V   I

The Augmented Second.   Especially in vocal writing, traditional composers usually avoid the augmented second. In minor keys, progressions involving iv–V and ii°–V are among those with the potential for a melodic augmented second between ↓$\hat{6}$ and ↑$\hat{7}$.

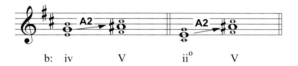

b: iv   V   ii°   V

Except for providing special effects (reminding us, for example, of the Middle East), composers avoid the augmented second either by arranging ↓$\hat{6}$ and ↑$\hat{7}$ in different voices or by employing melodic minor (↑$\hat{6}$–↑$\hat{7}$) in a single line. In the chorale below, Bach's harmonization complements Johann Crüger's melody (a complete ascending melodic minor scale).

d: i   V₆   i   III   vi°₆   vii°₆   i₆   i⁶₄   V   I
          F: V₆   I

In later chapters, we will encounter chromatic harmonies that offer the potential for various awkward melodic intervals. Avoid the augmented second altogether, and in addition, adhere to natural melodic tendencies in any voice—especially following a leap. Remember that while a keyboard performance may reveal your success in crafting a tonal work, the ultimate appraisal of four-part composition is in vocal performance.

WORKBOOK/ANTHOLOGY I
I. Contrapuntal Motion, page 95

GUIDELINES FOR CHORD CONNECTION

As we have discussed, important considerations in voice leading include the use of contrary motion; the avoidance of parallel perfect fifths, octaves, and unisons; the resolution of awkward intervals; and so on. In addition, several general guidelines, detailed here, will help ensure lines that are smooth and tonally distinct.

Open and Close Structure.   Two spatial positions are possible in four-part writing. In *close position*, the tenor and soprano are separated by less than an octave; the tenor and soprano are an octave or more apart in *open position*.

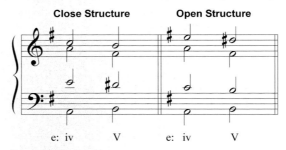

Composers use either open or close structure for the first chord in a passage and then typically maintain that arrangement for several chords. Changes of spatial position, however, are appropriate alternative voice-leading choices. When contrary motion between the bass and the upper voices is not practical, for example, avoid parallel perfect intervals by changing from open to close structure or the reverse.

In the first progression that follows, notice how the upper voices move against the bass. In the second progression, however, different melody notes necessitate an alternate approach to avoid parallel octaves between tenor and bass. The change from close to open position, while not as smooth as the more conventional approach, provides acceptable voice leading.

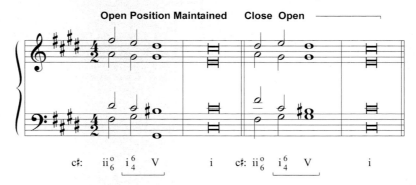

Common Tones.   When a pitch is present in two consecutive chords (C–E–G and A–C–E, for example), that pitch is termed COMMON. In root movement by fifth (ascending or descending), one tone will always be common; when root movement is by third, there will be *two* common tones. No common tones are produced when root movement is by second.

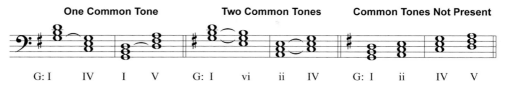

One Common Tone	Two Common Tones	Common Tones Not Present
G: I IV I V	G: I vi ii IV	G: I ii IV V

When possible, retain common tones in the same voice or voices (they may be either tied or rearticulated). If this choice is impractical (because of the preference for certain notes in the melody, perhaps), move the upper voices in contrary motion to the bass to the closest chord tones above or below. Both progressions in the next example exhibit appropriate voice leading.

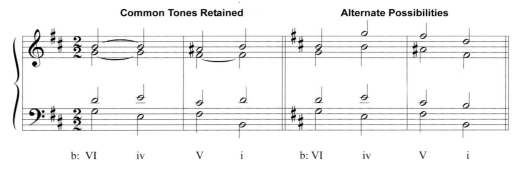

Common Tones Retained	Alternate Possibilities
b: VI iv V i	b: VI iv V i

Melodic Motion.   The Austrian composer Arnold Schoenberg (1874–1951) summed up voice-leading procedure by admonishing students to "Obey the law of the shortest way." In the four-part vocal style, individual melodic lines move predominantly by step and to the closest chord tone. When leaps occur (that is, when stepwise motion is impossible or impractical), consider the following guidelines for a smooth line.

1. Adhere to melodic tendencies following a leap. If pitches in an individual voice ascend from $\hat{1}$ to $\hat{4}$, for example, the next pitch should be $\hat{3}$. If this is impossible, consider alternate choices carefully.

2. Follow a leap with stepwise motion in the opposite direction.

3. Leaps of a seventh are rare in the four-part style.

4. An octave leap is generally permissible—especially if followed by stepwise motion in the opposite direction.

5. Avoid awkward intervals (unresolved tritone, augmented second, and so on).

Doubling.   Composers may choose an alternate doubling to avoid voice-leading problems. The conventional choices for doubling major and minor triads were introduced in Chapter 3 (pages 103–104):

• In root position, double the root.

• In first inversion, double the soprano.

• In second inversion, double the bass (the fifth).

Diminished Triads.   Composers almost always use diminished triads (vii°₆ in major keys; vii°₆ and ii°₆ in minor) in first inversion and with doubled bass in four-part style. Exceptions are rare.

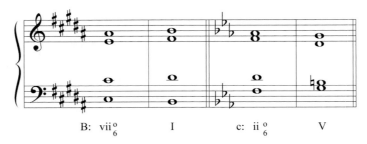

B: vii°₆   I   c: ii°₆   V

Second Inversion.   As we will discuss in detail later in this chapter, major and minor triads in second inversion appear almost invariably with doubled bass.

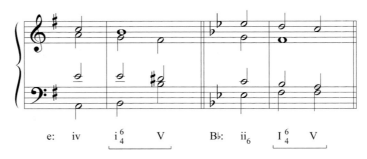

e: iv   i⁶₄ V   B♭: ii₆   I⁶₄ V

Composers occasionally vary the doubling of root-position and first-inversion major and minor triads. Chords in root position sometimes appear with doubled fifth, doubled third, or with a tripled root (and third). The last of these possibilities is especially common at cadences.

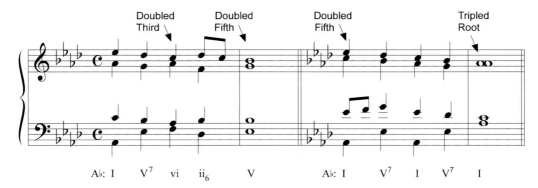

Doubled Third   Doubled Fifth   Doubled Fifth   Tripled Root

A♭: I   V⁷ vi ii₆   V   A♭: I   V⁷ I   V⁷   I

Voice Crossing and Voice Overlap.   As we have discussed, the four-part style centers on voice independence. Traditional composers usually avoid choices in which one part intrudes into the range of another. VOICE CROSS-ING occurs when one line (the alto, for example) is written higher than the ad-jacent part above it (the soprano). The same situation exists when one part moves lower than the notes of the line below. In the next example, stem place-ment shows that the soprano crosses below the alto several times. While voice

crossing is common in early Western music (as in the anonymous composition that follows), it is *not* traditional in the four-part vocal style.

Se - duc - tum hos - tis ma - li ti - a Re - de - mit mor - te pi - a.

He redeemed [mankind], misled by the enemy's wickedness.

J. S. Bach harmonized nearly four hundred chorale melodies, so among the thousands of melodic phrases and chord connections, we should not be surprised to find exceptional procedures occasionally. These are not "mistakes"; most often, digressions occur to preserve the independence of a melodic line, to resolve a dissonance, or for purely musical reasons.

In the final two phrases of the chorale "*Mit Fried und Freud ich fahr dahin*" ("In Peace and Joy I Now Depart"), Bach crosses the bass and tenor voices twice

(measures 10–11) and the alto and soprano voices cross in measure 12. The interesting harmonies will be discussed in later chapters.

VOICE OVERLAP, which decreases part independence, occurs when one voice (the tenor, for instance) moves to a position that is higher than the previous pitch of the adjacent upper voice (the alto). Likewise, if an upper voice moves below the previous pitch of the adjacent lower voice, overlap occurs as well. In the following passage, observe that the fourth soprano pitch (D_4) is lower than the previous alto pitch (F_4).

Poor: Voice Overlap

$$\text{B}\flat\text{:}\quad \text{I}\qquad \text{V}\qquad \text{I}_6\qquad \text{I}\qquad \text{IV}_6\qquad \text{V}\qquad \text{I}$$

Common (Musical) Sense.   One of the goals of music theory is to strengthen both notated and aural perception of musical patterns. Knowledgeable students who are experienced performers often rightly rely on musical instincts for solutions to voice-leading questions in exercises and original compositions. Sing through each line of a composition and trust your own judgment.

> WORKBOOK/ANTHOLOGY I
> II. Guidelines for Chord Connection, page 97

REVIEW AND APPLICATION 8–1

Voice Leading

Essential Terms

common tone	outer voices	voice leading
inner voices	voice crossing	voice overlap

1. The chorales below have been edited to include errors including parallel unisons, octaves, or fifths as well as other problems such as an augmented second or an unresolved tritone. Circle and identify the error. Provide a complete roman- and arabic-numeral analysis.

 CD 2, TRACK 07-1 REVIEW AND APPLICATION 8-1 (3 PARTS)
Felix Mendelssohn, *Sleepers Awake*
Exercise 1-a

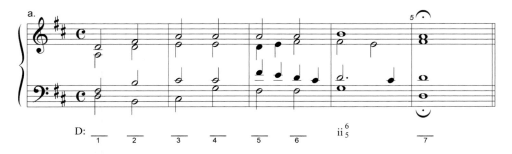

 TRACK 07-2 REVIEW AND APPLICATION 8-1
J. S. Bach, "My Inmost Heart Now Raises"
Exercise 1-b

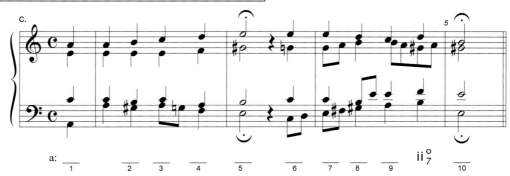

2. In four-part style, fill in the inner voices of the cadences suggested. Use conventional doublings, but choose the spacing yourself. Remember that you may need to add an accidental in minor. In the lower blank, identify the cadence (half, authentic, Phrygian, and so on).

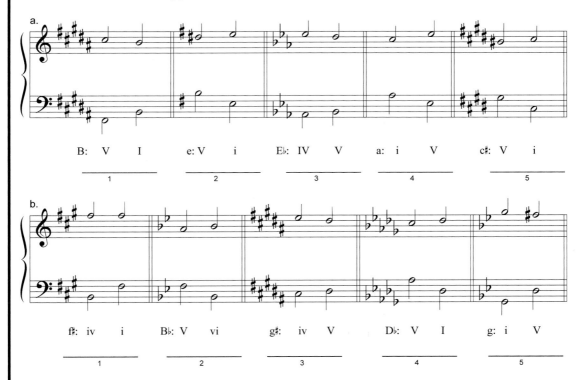

3. The following three- and four-chord progressions include root movement by second, by fifth, and by third. Supply the inner voices; retain common tones where appropriate. Use conventional doublings and spacings for root-position sonorities. Be sure to add accidentals if necessary.

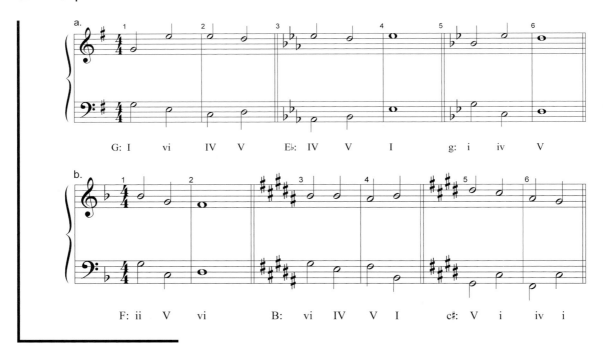

G: I   vi   IV   V   E♭: IV   V   I   g: i   iv   V

F: ii   V   vi   B: vi   IV   V   I   c♯: V   i   iv   i

SELF-TEST 8–1

Time Limit: 5 Minutes

1. Each line below includes one or more augmented seconds; there are four such intervals in the three lines together. Locate and circle each augmented second. In addition, use the blank to name an appropriate cadence for each phrase (AC, HC, PC, DC, and so on). *Scoring: Subtract 5 points for each augmented second not located; subtract 5 points for each incorrect cadence.*

2. Each frame below includes one significant error in voice leading. Write the appropriate letter in the blank to identify the error. *Scoring: Subtract 12 points for each incorrect response.*

A. Unequal fifths   D. Octaves in contrary motion

B. Parallel fifths/octaves   E. Melodic augmented second

C. Direct fifths/octaves   F. Melodic tritone

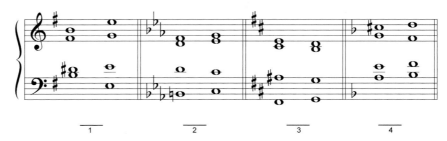

    1   2   3   4

3. Provide the most common pitch doubled in each triad bass position. Consider the problem right or wrong. *Scoring: Subtract 7 points for an incorrect list.*

Triads in root position: Double _____

Triads in first inversion: Double _____

Triads in second inversion: Double _____

Total Possible: 100   Your Score _____

SIX-FOUR CHORDS

We have considered the deliberate ways in which traditional composers handle melodic and harmonic dissonance, volatile scale degrees, and spatial position. Especially in vocal music, the same concern is applied to scoring *six-four chords*—triads in second inversion. A root-position major or minor triad is inherently stable due to the perfect fifth present. Inverted, however, the fifth becomes a much less stable fourth. In first inversion, the two pitches comprising the fourth are above the bass. When the fifth of a triad serves also as the bass, however, the fourth exists between the *bass* and the *root* (which is one of the upper voices). In second inversion, a major or minor triad is relatively unstable and, accordingly, requires resolution.[1]

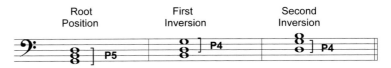

---

[1] Diminished triads are inherently unstable even in root position. As we discussed in Chapter 4 and elsewhere, diminished triads are most often used in first inversion with the tritone in the upper voices and away from the bass. Both root-position and second-inversion diminished triads are rare.

To avoid the tonal ambiguities of a fourth between the bass and the root, composers have traditionally employed six-four chords either as arpeggiations of a single triad or in one of three stereotypical nonchord-tone categories:

- appoggiatura
- passing tone
- neighboring tone

Only four types of six-four chords are utilized consistently in traditional literature; these categories are known, respectively, as *cadential, passing, neighboring,* and *arpeggiated.*

Cadential Six-four

By far the most common type of second-inversion triad, the cadential six-four has an effect like the appoggiatura or suspension. We discussed the CADENTIAL SIX-FOUR in Chapter 5 in conjunction with harmonic function (see pages 174–175). In the tonic six-four, the root and third above the bass resolve down by step to the third and fifth of the dominant. You will remember that because the tonic six-four is a dominant embellishment, we employ a special analytical symbol $I_4^6 \quad V$.

Cadential Six-Four

The cadential six-four is commonly preceded by a chord of predominant function (although other possibilities exist). Both progressions shown in the next example are common patterns involving the cadential six-four.

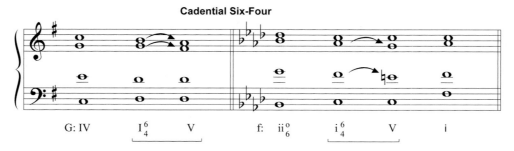

Cadential Six-Four

Voice Leading in the Cadential Six-Four. In four-part style, voice leading in six-four chords follows the descending stepwise motion discussed earlier. Heinrich Isaac (ca. 1450–1517), for example, was a Flemish composer of the late Renaissance who wrote both sacred and secular works. Bach harmonized Isaac's chorale melody "*O Welt, ich muss dich lassen*" ("O World, I Must Depart Thee") and included the setting in his *St. Matthew Passion.* The final cadence of the chorale includes a cadential six-four (the bass is embellished with a neighboring tone). Note also the voice crossing between tenor and alto in measure 11.

CD 2, TRACK 08-1 VOICE LEADING IN CADENTIAL SIX-FOUR (3 PARTS)
J. S. Bach, "O World, I Must Depart Thee"
melody by Heinrich Isaac, ca. 1500

Bach's use of the cadential six-four in the last passage is typical in many respects:

1. The bass of the six-four is doubled and retained to become the root of the dominant that follows.
2. The root and third of the tonic six-four resolve down by step to the third and fifth of the dominant.
3. The cadential six-four occurs most often in a strong metric or harmonic position.
4. The cadential six-four often begins a three-chord cadence formula that culminates with an authentic cadence.
5. The 4–3 suspension that occurs along with the resolution to dominant is common.

In the final phrase of "Grieve Not So, Nor Lament," Bach drops the bass of a cadential six-four an octave and adds simultaneous anticipations. Observe that the bass is doubled in this instance in the alto; the tenor and soprano resolve stepwise from the I_4^6 to V^7.

TRACK 08-2 VOICE LEADING IN CADENTIAL SIX-FOUR
J. S. Bach, "Grieve Not So, Nor Lament"
melody by J. S. Bach, ca. 1735

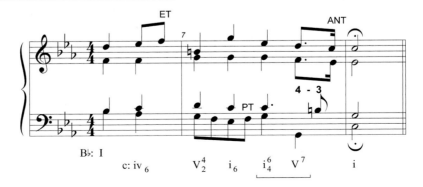

In instrumental music, composers use the cadential six-four in a similar way. Especially in keyboard scoring, however, the voice leading may be less obvious as parts come and go, moving from one register to another. Still, as shown in the conclusion of Franz Schubert's *Originaltänz* (*Original Dance*) Op. 9, No. 23, the stepwise resolution of the I$_4^6$ to V is usually maintained. On the other hand, note the parallelisms on the second and third beats of each measure that are common piano sonorities, but avoided in vocal scoring.

TRACK 08-3 VOICE LEADING IN CADENTIAL SIX-FOUR
Franz Schubert, Originaltänz, Op. 9, No. 23

The Passing Six-four

THE PASSING SIX-FOUR, the second most common second-inversion type, occurs as the bass ascends or descends by step. Often, the soprano moves against the bass in contrary motion. Unlike the cadential six-four (a tonic chord with dominant function), the passing six-four occurs in various functions. Among the most common formulas are I–V$_4^6$–I$_6$ (ascending) or I$_6$–V$_4^6$–I (descending). No special symbol is necessary for passing and other noncadential six-fours.

Passing Six-Four

In a harmonization of Martin Luther's "*Ein' feste Burg ist unser Gott*" ("A Mighty Fortress Is Our God"), Bach connects tonic chords in first inversion and root position with a dominant six-four.

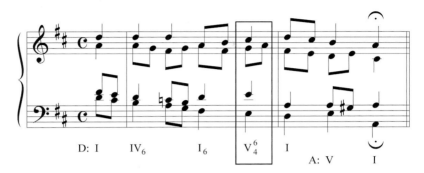

The Four-Three Chord. Josephine Lang (1815–1880) was a German composer who achieved a degree of popularity with her *lieder*. In the work quoted below, a passing four-three (a seventh chord in second inversion) spans the major third between bass pitches in measure 85. In measure 87, the keyboard texture and resolution to V_2^4 partially obscure a cadential six-four that takes a surprising turn to D minor.

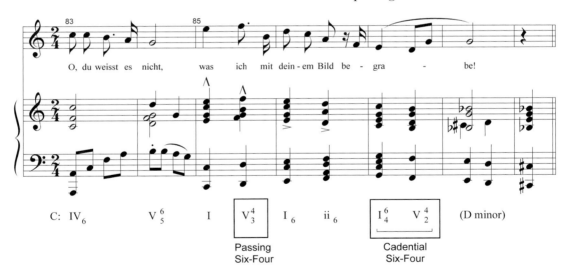

O, you don't know what I bury with your portrait!

Composers employ the passing six-four stereotypically:

1. The chord may occur on a strong or a weak beat (as a passing tone does).
2. The bass ascends or descends by step. All three pitches are chord tones.
3. The soprano or other voice often moves stepwise in contrary motion with the bass.
4. The bass of the six-four is doubled.

The Neighboring Six-Four

A third category of second-inversion chord (known, variously, as PEDAL, STATIONARY, or NEIGHBORING SIX-FOUR) combines the effects of a neighboring figure with a bass pedal. The bass (doubled in another voice) remains stationary to form a pedal while two upper voices ascend to form a six-four, then descend to the original pitches (as a neighboring tone does). In the neighboring six-four, we see the prolongation of the bass pitch (which is usually $\hat{1}$ or $\hat{5}$, as in the passage below).

Neighboring Six-Four

The neighboring six-four is heard as the embellishment of a single triad, so it is not especially common in chorale literature (where harmonic rhythm typically changes on every beat). A characteristic passage employing a neighboring six-four occurs in Beethoven's Sonata, Op. 53. Arpeggiations in the bass support a figural passage in the upper line.

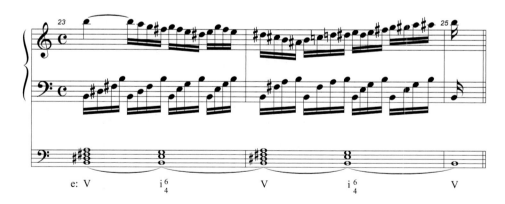

While the passage in the last example may appear complex, reduction reveals a simple embellishment of V^7 in E minor.

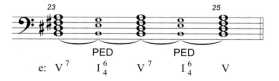

Traditional use of the neighboring six-four includes these characteristics:

1. The bass remains stationary (or ascends or descends an octave).

2. In four voices, the bass is doubled.

3. Upper voices ascend by step to the six-four, then descend to the original pitches.

4. The neighboring six-four occurs most often in a weak metric or harmonic position.

In instrumental music, the approach to voice leading may obscure famil-iar harmonic clichés. In the string quartet version of Haydn's *God Save the Em-peror Franz,* for example, the second-inversion chord in measure 8 conforms neatly to a classic neighboring six-four model. In the next measure, the six-four is ca-dential because it concludes the phrase.

TRACK 10-2 NEIGHBORING SIX-FOUR
Joseph Haydn, Quartet, Op. 76, No. 3 (II)

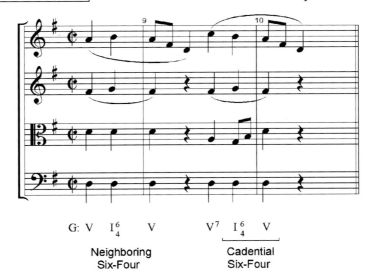

The Arpeggiated Six-Four

The fourth category of traditional six-four chord is also the least common. When the same triad or chord is reiterated with different bass positions, any second-inversion arrangement is termed an ARPEGGIATED SIX-FOUR.

Arpeggiated Six-Four

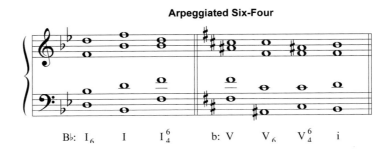

An arpeggiated six-four appears in the opening phrase of Bach's chorale "*Puer Natus in Bethlehem*" ("A Child Is Born In Bethlehem"). The third chord in the arpeggiated series is an inverted dominant seventh. Notice also the use of a plagal cadence.[2]

Typical arpeggiated six-four figures are summarized as follows:

1. The chord occurs in a series of sonorities with an identical function.
2. The bass of an arpeggiated six-four is doubled in four-part style.
3. Upper voices in the arpeggiated six-four follow conventional voice-leading guidelines.

We are so accustomed to hearing tonal music that we instantly recognize an exceptional six-four type. The cadential six-four is heard as a cliché and part of a cadence formula; passing and neighboring six-fours lead us toward melodic and harmonic goals through stepwise motion. Finally, in the rare instances where it appears, the arpeggiated six-four effects a subtle adjustment to a more stable sonority. Six-four chords other than these are disorienting and, for this reason, are extremely rare in traditional literature. Use atypical second-inversion sonorities judiciously.

WORKBOOK/ANTHOLOGY I
III. Six-Four Chords, page 101

REVIEW AND APPLICATION 8–2

Six-Four Chords

Essential Terms

arpeggiated six-four   cadential six-four   neighboring six-four
passing six-four

---

[2]The secondary dominant (V_6/V) will be discussed in Chapter 10.

1. Provide roman- and arabic-numeral analysis for the fragments below. In the lower blank, identify the type of six-four present (write "cadential," "passing," and so on). If a six-four chord does not conform to one of the four types, write "none."

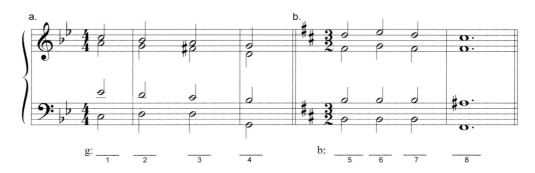

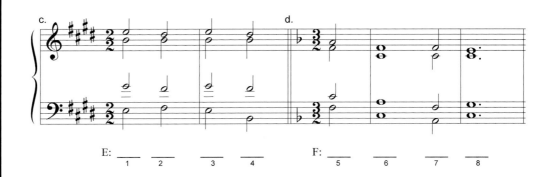

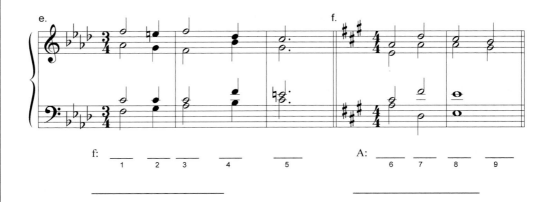

2. Continue as in the previous exercise. Provide roman-numeral analysis and identify the type of any six-four (or four-three) chord present.

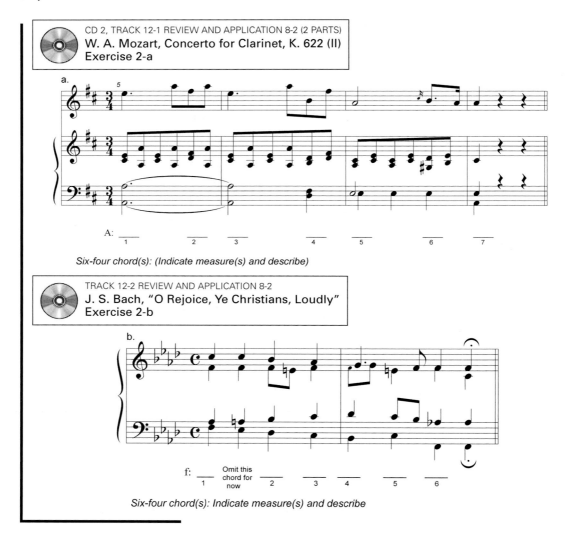

CD 2, TRACK 12-1 REVIEW AND APPLICATION 8-2 (2 PARTS)
W. A. Mozart, Concerto for Clarinet, K. 622 (II)
Exercise 2-a

A: ___ ___ ___ ___ ___ ___ ___
     1   2   3   4   5   6   7

Six-four chord(s): (Indicate measure(s) and describe)

TRACK 12-2 REVIEW AND APPLICATION 8-2
J. S. Bach, "O Rejoice, Ye Christians, Loudly"
Exercise 2-b

f: ___ Omit this chord for now ___ ___ ___ ___
    1   2   3   4   5   6

Six-four chord(s): Indicate measure(s) and describe

SELF-TEST 8–2

Time Limit: 5 Minutes

1. Match the characteristic of the six-four chord with its type from the list. Write the appropriate letter *or letters* in the blank. *Scoring: Subtract 5 points for each error.*

   A. Arpeggiated   B. Cadential

   C. Neighboring   D. Passing

   _____ a. bass remains stationary

   _____ b. upper voices move by step to the next chord

   _____ c. tonic chord, but dominant in function

   _____ d. least common six-four type

   _____ e. bass ascends or descends by step

_____ f. involves a progression of three chords

_____ g. most common type

_____ h. commonly tonic-subdominant-tonic

2. Identify the type of six-four chord in each of the frames below. Choose an appropriate letter from the list. If a six-four chord conforms to none of the categories, choose "none of the above." *Scoring: Subtract 20 points for each incorrect answer.*

   A. Arpeggiated   D. Passing
   B. Cadential   E. None of the above
   C. Neighboring

Total Possible: 100   Your Score _____

NONDOMINANT SEVENTH CHORDS

In Chapter 3, we discussed the construction of a triad upon each degree of a major or minor scale. We also explored voice leading and other aspects of the dominant seventh chord in Chapter 6 as summarized below:

1. The dominant seventh is major-minor in quality (major triad with minor seventh).
2. The seventh is usually prepared by step or oblique motion.
3. The seventh of a dominant seventh resolves down by step.
4. A root-position dominant seventh may occur with fifth omitted and root doubled (frame c, below).

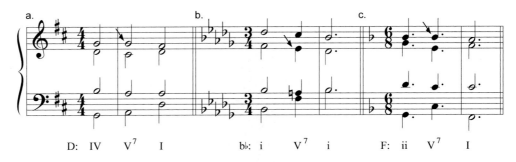

When the dominant seventh is inverted, the preparation and resolution are identical. However, inverted dominant sevenths should have all four pitches present.

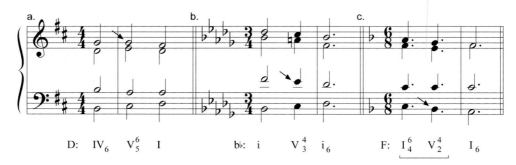

Having reviewed the dominant seventh, we will center our present discussion on seventh chords *other* than the dominant; these are termed NONDOMINANT SEVENTHS.

Diatonic Seventh Chords as Fundamental Materials

Theoretically, we can add a seventh above the root of any diatonic triad.[3] Shown in the next example, diatonic seventh chords on each scale degree represent fundamental (possible) musical materials.

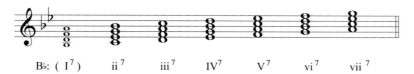

Seventh Chord Quality.   Several different qualities of seventh chords are available in a major scale. We classify seventh chords according to two criteria:

1. The quality of the triad
2. The quality of the seventh

In addition to the major-minor seventh, three other qualities of diatonic seventh chord occur in major keys (shown in the next example). Just as we often refer to the major-minor seventh as "dominant," so are other seventh-chord qualities known by abbreviated references. Remember that a tonic seventh chord is all but nonexistent in traditional harmony.

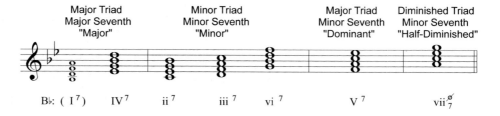

---

[3]A major seventh added to the tonic chord is extremely rare in traditional literature. With the addition of a dissonant seventh, the chord may no longer have tonic function.

Half-Diminished Seventh. The considerable instability of the "HALF-DIMINISHED" (diminished-minor) SEVENTH CHORD is identified in analysis with a slashed circle symbol (ϕ). In major keys, only the leading-tone seventh is half diminished.

Fully Diminished Seventh. Considering all three forms of minor, only one additional quality of seventh chord emerges: the leading-tone seventh (vii$^{o}_{7}$) in minor is a diminished triad with a superimposed diminished seventh. We call this quality FULLY DIMINISHED (or just DIMINISHED). With two tritones, the diminished seventh is among the most volatile and useful chords in the common-practice inventory.

Diminished Triad
Diminished Seventh
"Fully-Diminished" ("Diminished")

Observe that there are two different meanings in analysis for the circle symbol. With a root-position or inverted *triad*, the circle calls our attention to the diminished quality. With a seventh chord, the circle (without slash) denotes a diminished triad with *diminished seventh* (that is, a fully-diminished seventh chord). The slashed circle is used only with a half-diminished (diminished-minor) seventh chord.

The circle and circle/slash symbols, used in conjunction with roman and arabic numerals, give us an effective graphic representation of the sound with a single analytical figure:

- diatonic position relative to the tonic
- quality
- bass position
- relative stability

All possibilities for seventh-chord quality in minor keys are shown in the next example. However, those in parentheses (and appearing as cue-sized notes) are not often used in traditional music. The major-minor subdominant and subtonic sevenths (IV^7, VII^7) are also uncommon. We are so familiar with the major-minor sonority in a dominant role that we tend to hear *any* seventh of this quality as dominant in function.

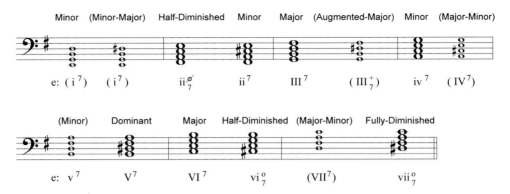

Dominant and nondominant seventh chords provide basic color to the common-practice vocabulary while creating the tension that defines key. Many different seventh chords are possible as fundamental materials, but some are more useful in tonal composition than others.

VOICE LEADING IN SEVENTH CHORDS

Earlier, we discussed function in harmony and the classification of chords as predominant, dominant, or tonic. If a chord includes a seventh, that chord must *still* be heard clearly in one of the traditional functional roles. There are no significant differences in function between diatonic seventh chords in major keys and their counterparts in the minor mode. Note, however, that the major-minor seventh will be heard as dominant and that a tonic seventh will almost certainly *not* be heard as having tonic function.

In the four-part style, several general guidelines regarding seventh chords are applicable:

1. In root position, major, minor, and dominant seventh chords appear with all four pitches present *or* they may be scored with the root doubled and the fifth omitted. Whether in root position or inverted, half-diminished and diminished seventh chords should include all four pitches.

2. Regardless of quality, all four pitches should be present if a seventh chord is inverted.

3. The seventh of a seventh chord is most typically approached by step or through oblique motion.

4. Seventh chords resolve through descending stepwise motion of the dissonance.

5. When a seventh chord contains a tritone (that is, dominant, half-diminished, and diminished qualities), the first choice is to resolve the tritone according to natural tonal tendencies.

The Supertonic Seventh

The dominant seventh chord is by far the most common harmonic dissonance. Next in frequency of occurrence, however, is the SUPERTONIC SEVENTH. In major keys, the supertonic seventh is minor in quality. Either a minor ($\uparrow\hat{6}$) or a half-diminished ($\downarrow\hat{6}$) quality is diatonic in minor, although the latter is more common.

D: ii^7 d: ii$^{\o}_7$ ii^7

(common)   (common)   (less common)

Composers use the supertonic seventh in a predominant role, often in cadence formulas, and commonly (although not always) in first inversion. As with any seventh chord, the dissonant seventh is prepared by step or by oblique motion and it resolves by descending step.

To conclude the second phrase of "*Nun lob, mein 'Seel', den Herren*" ("My Soul, Now Bless Thy Maker"), Bach uses a cadence formula that includes ii^7 in first inversion; the classic resolution is to dominant.

CD 2, TRACK 13-1 SUPERTONIC SEVENTH (3 PARTS)
J. S. Bach, "My Soul, Now Bless Thy Maker"
anonymous 15th-Century Melody

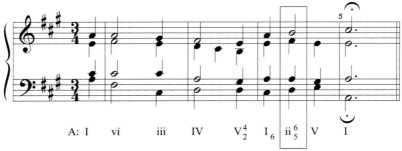

A: I   vi   iii   IV   V$^4_2$ I$_6$ ii$^6_5$ V   I

Franz Schubert employs almost exactly the same cadential progression in the opening of his song, *Der Alpenjäger* (*The Alpine Hunter*). With or without a seventh, the supertonic in cadential formulas often appears in first inversion. This structure permits the $\hat{4}$–$\hat{5}$–$\hat{1}$ bass line that we associate with subdominant, dominant, and tonic chords. Notice that in this instrumental setting, the seventh itself (F) is unprepared (measure 3).

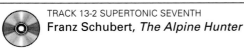
TRACK 13-2 SUPERTONIC SEVENTH
Franz Schubert, *The Alpine Hunter*

Auf ho- hem Ber- ges- rü - chen, wo fri- scher al - les grünt,

F: I   ii$^6_5$ V   I

In the high mountains
Where all is green.

Johann Fischer (1662–1716) was a German composer who lived nearly a generation before Bach and Handel. Fischer was known for his keyboard music, such as the *Rondeau* in the next example. Because the practice of listing all accidentals in a key signature was not yet fully established in the late seventeenth century, composers like Fischer sometimes used one fewer flat in minor keys than we do today.

TRACK 13-3 SUPERTONIC SEVENTH
Johann Fischer, Rondeau

Notice, however, that E♭ is written in as an accidental in all instances. Fischer's *Rondeau* shows a typical use of ii⁷ in minor. Because the chord is half-diminished, the circle/slash accompanies the analytical symbol.

The Leading-Tone Seventh

The leading-tone seventh is common as a dominant substitute. In major, the leading-tone seventh chord is half-diminished; in minor, the chord is fully diminished.

An effective resolution of the (half-diminished) leading-tone seventh in major centers upon both the tritone (between root and fifth) and the seventh above the root. In chorales, J. S. Bach rarely used the half-diminished seventh in a dominant role. Instead, he preferred the dominant seventh chord in major keys, and in minor, the fully diminished seventh.

The fragment below, from a character piece by Frédéric Chopin, illustrates a Romantic-era use of vii°⁷ in major. Note especially the parallel octaves in the treble and bass staves (measures 51 and 53). While this practice was acceptable in keyboard music—especially by Chopin's time—parallel octaves constitute a serious error in the traditional vocal style. The pitch D_4 in the alto (measures 2 and 4) is an anticipation.

**Frédéric Chopin, Prelude in B♭ Major, Op. 28, No. 21
Half-Diminished**

In four parts, composers resolve diminished triads in either of two ways. One possibility is to resolve the two tritones according to natural tendencies (an augmented fourth expands; a diminished fifth contracts). This resolution results in a major or minor triad with a doubled third.

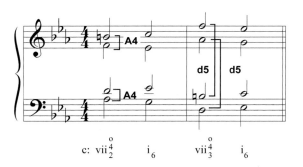

Instead of the tritone resolution (shown in the last example), Bach often prefers to double the root; this results in either unequal fifths or parallel fourths (below, boxed). Either outcome produces acceptable voice leading in a diminished-seventh resolution.

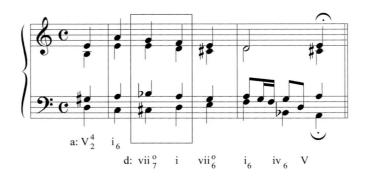

a: V_2^4 i_6

d: vii_7^o i vii_6^o i_6 iv_6 V

Bach's harmonization of another Crüger melody, *"Jesu meine Freude"* ("Jesus, Priceless Treasure") includes six different seventh chords—two of them fully diminished—within the first two phrases. The leading-tone sevenths are boxed.

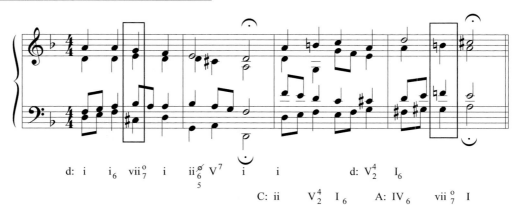

d: i i_6 vii_7^o i $ii_{6\ 5}^{\o}$ V^7 i i d: V_2^4 I_6

C: ii V_2^4 I_6 A: IV_6 vii_7^o I

Other Diatonic Seventh Chords

Although the dominant, supertonic, and leading-tone sevenths are the most common, sevenths may add color to other diatonic triads as well. Voice leading centers first upon the resolution of the seventh and second, upon any active intervals present. Especially in major, the subdominant seventh (in root position or inversion) may be included in a cadence formula. The passage below, from Bach's harmonization of *"O Herre Gott, Dein göttliches Wort"* ("Lord God, Thy Divine Word"), is embellished by numerous nonchord tones and exhibits the regular resolution of a subdominant seventh (measure 4).

CD 2, TRACK 15-1 OTHER SEVENTH CHORDS (2 PARTS)
J. S. Bach, "Lord God, Thy Divine Word"
anonymous 16th-Century melody
Subdominant Seventh

A rare, half-diminished submediant seventh occurs in the sixth phrase of *"Schwing dich auf zu deinem Gott"* ("Soar, My Soul, to God on High"). The augmented fourth in the outer voices resolves by expanding to a sixth; in the alto,

TRACK 15-2 OTHER SEVENTH CHORDS
J. S. Bach, "Soar, My Soul to God on High"
anonymous 17th-Century Melody
Submediant Seventh

the seventh resolves down by step. The cadence is deceptive with doubled third to avoid parallel fifths between bass and tenor.

Finally, remember that harmonic and melodic dissonance are not always separable in tonal music. In the next passage, from the first movement of Mozart's Sonata in A Minor, K. 310, we might disagree about whether the sevenths in measures 6 and 7 are chord tones or appoggiaturas.[4] Both choices fully explain how tonality is established and maintained; both are logical; both reflect Mozart's individual compositional procedure. Note the tonic pedal through the first four measures.

---

[4]Notice that the chords in measures 6–8 constitute a harmonic sequence, descending by step. Where melodic factors generate a harmony, we should not be surprised that the progressions themselves are nonfunctional.

CD 2, TRACK 16
W. A. Mozart, Sonata in A Minor, K. 310 (I)
Interpreting Harmonic Movement

a: i V^7 i V^7

i $ii(^6_5)$ V $III(^6_5)$ VI ii^o_6 i^6_4 V^7 i

Since they began to be regularly employed in the mid-seventeenth century, seventh chords have provided an essential source of color, variety, and individual expression in tonal music. At the same time, dissonant harmonies strengthen tonality by allowing us to identify chords as either stable or active. With regular resolutions, seventh chords outline the hierarchy of tonal relationships. With *atypical* resolutions, however, harmonic dissonances obscure the tonality. As we will discuss fully in Volume II, the ambiguity of irregular resolution became an interesting possibility to some composers in the mid-nineteenth century. By 1880, tonal obscurity was an integral element of many composer's styles. And by 1900, the dissonances that Bach so carefully prepared and resolved had become just another sonority—with no more significance than the triad, the interval, or an individual pitch.

WORKBOOK/ANTHOLOGY I
IV. Nondominant Seventh Chords, page 103

REVIEW AND APPLICATION 8–3

Seventh chords

Essential Terms

diminished seventh chord   fully diminished
half-diminished seventh chord   nondominant seventh

1. Construct seventh chords of the quality specified using the given pitch as the root.

| 1 | 2 | 3 | 4 | 5 | 6 | 7 | 8 |
| Major | Diminished | Major | Minor | Half-Diminished | Minor | Dominant | Major |

2. Continue as in the previous exercise, but use the given pitch as the *third*, *fifth*, or *seventh* as specified.

Given Pitch:	Third	Fifth	Third	Seventh	Fifth	Third	Seventh	Third
Quality:	Diminished	Major	Dominant	Major	Half-Diminished	Minor	Major-Minor	Minor

3. Use roman and arabic numerals (plus any additional symbols necessary) to identify the given chords in the keys indicated.

e: _____ _____   Eb: _____ _____   c#: _____ _____   F: _____ _____
     1   2   3   4   5   6   7   8

4. Identify the first chord given in each measure. Next, resolve that chord in traditional four-part style.

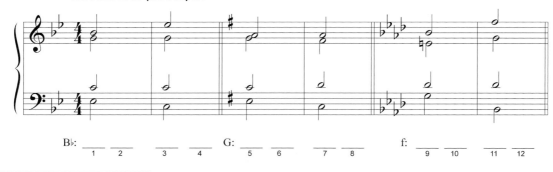

Bb: _____ _____ _____ _____   G: _____ _____ _____ _____   f: _____ _____ _____ _____
       1   2   3   4   5   6   7   8   9   10   11   12

SELF-TEST 8–3

Time Limit: 5 Minutes

1. Provide a complete analysis of each chord below (including arabic-numeral designations and other appropriate symbols). *Scoring: Subtract 10 points for each error (an incorrect or omitted numeral or symbol should be considered an error).*

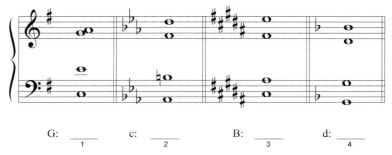

G: _____   c: _____   B: _____   d: _____
      1   2   3   4

2. Construct the chords specified by the analytical symbols. Begin with a key signature and provide any necessary accidental. *Scoring: Subtract 16 points for an incorrect chord spelling (including missing or incorrect accidental); subtract 4 points for an incorrect or missing key signature.*

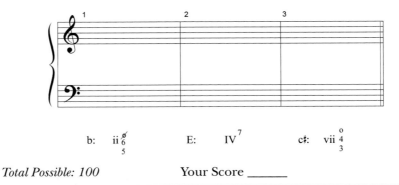

$$b:\quad ii^{\substack{\o \\ 6 \\ 5}}\qquad\qquad E:\quad IV^{7}\qquad\qquad c\#:\quad vii^{\substack{o \\ 4 \\ 3}}$$

Total Possible: 100   Your Score _____

PROJECTS

Analysis

Students are often surprised at how often the principles of four-part vocal writing can be seen in keyboard and other instrumental music. This is largely because the principles of voice leading govern not only vocal music, but *tonal* music. If melodic tendencies are ignored, if seventh chords resolve atypically, when unusual six-four chord categories are employed, we hear not a dilution of the vocal style, but of the tonal system of music. Through chorales (included in the workbook/anthology), we have a compact example of tonal harmony. Harmonic rhythm is fast; rhythmic activity is minimal; and metric and melodic irregularities are relatively rare. In other works (as provided in this project section), you will find a more varied harmonic approach and a more varied texture. Still, the musical concept is the same and you will be able to synthesize all of your studies to this point with investigations like these:

1. Provide a roman-numeral analysis. Classify cadences and explain how they have varied strengths. Be prepared to comment on the rate of harmonic rhythm. Are there exceptional harmonic progressions?

2. How is dissonance handled in the given work? Locate and classify nonchord tones. What is the range of harmonic sevenths. Which chords have added sevenths; where are they more frequent? Are resolutions typical? How are harmonic sevenths prepared?

3. Comment on the use of root-position and inverted triads and chords. What percentage of chords are in root position? Where, metrically, do these occur most often? Classify any six-four chords present. How many are cadential? Passing?

4. Study the soprano-bass counterpoint and draw conclusions about contrapuntal motion in general and across the barline in particular.

Text

Giuseppe Giordani, "Caro Mio," text page 308. This aria is generally attributed to Giuseppe Giordani (1744–1798) who was known for his operas as well as sacred music. The opera from which this work may have been taken is unfortunately lost and we are left only with the beautiful melody and varied accompaniment. As we will discuss in later chapters, few works remain in the same key throughout. Giordani's aria begins in D major, moves to the dominant (A major), then returns to the original key. The key in which you should conduct your analysis is clearly marked on the score. Finally, note that the chords marked on the score "vii$^{o}_{7}$/V" are secondary dominants and will be discussed fully in Chapter 10.

Workbook/Anthology I

J. S. Bach, "Rejoice Ye Christians Loudly": (melody by Andreas Hammerschmidt, 1646), workbook page 105.

J. S. Bach, "Eternity, Tremendous Word" (Melody by Johann Crüger, 1653), workbook page 106.

Composition

Four-Part Chorale Composition. Compose a chorale melody and create a harmonization in vocal style. Set the one or more stanzas of text below (or another as directed by your instructor) in the style of a Lutheran congregational chorale. The text punctuation will guide you in planning the strength of cadences.

> Friend, would you have me going
> a mile or two with you?
> Then up! Let us be walking
> for I have much to do.
>
> Land, would you have me doing
> some patriotic deed?
> Then tell my mission quickly
> while I am here to heed.
>
> Love, would you have my kisses?
> Then hasten, let me know
> that rapture in my passing
> for shortly I must go.

Begin by devising a rhythmic and metric plan.

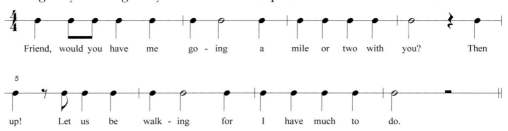

As we have discussed in other chapters, your next step is to plan cadences, then the full harmonic scheme. Use a harmonic rhythm typical of chorale style where chords change basically every beat or two. Once you have the harmonic plan in place, compose a melody using the given text. Notice in the next example that the setting is basically syllabic—one note of melody for each syllable.

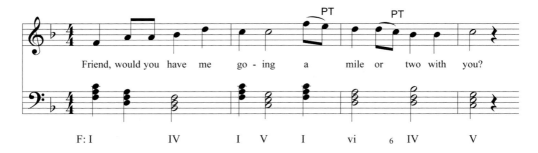

CD 2, TRACK 17-1 (2 PARTS)
Chorale Project
Soprano-Bass Framework

The next step is the creation of a strong, soprano-bass counterpoint. Notice that the bass in the next example complements the melody the while the lowest voice of the previous harmonic sketch was more static and less interesting.

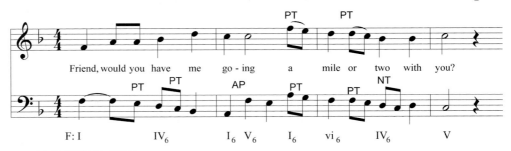

TRACK 17-2
Chorale Project
Four Part Setting

Finally, add alto and tenor voices in four-part style. The result should be a chorale composition that can be performed by the class.

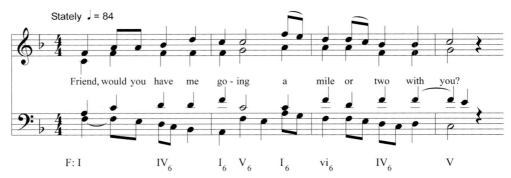

Notice that a full vocal score allows the clarification of text placement in a work such as this chorale.

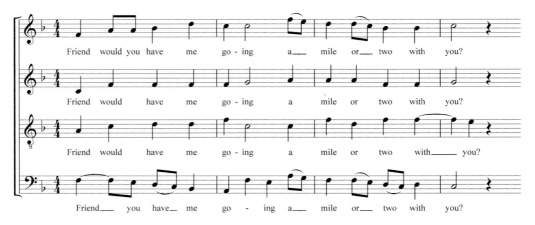

For Further Study

Investigating Music Theory Pedagogy. The theory of tonal music has changed little since the late nineteenth century, but the way we discuss and teach it undergoes constant revision. There are several current views of music theory pedagogy and we can sum these up as having an approach centered on (1) comprehensive musicianship (like this text), (2) one that stresses linear (Schenkerian) analysis, or (3) a book that organizes topics according to harmonic materials. All of these methods are valid, of course, and excellent books have been written embracing each point of view (as well as a number of hybrid methods). Harmony and linear analysis texts are often published in a single volume while the comprehensive musicianship direction usually requires two volumes. Differences among texts in the same category usually concern the extent of written information, the numbers of examples, the type and number of exercises, and available supplements (workbook, audio or CD-ROM, and so on).

Choose three or four topics (cadential six-four, appoggiatura, perfect internal and so on) and investigate different approaches and explanations in theory texts as are available in your library or from your instructor. Compare the topic as presented in this text with one of the other books listed as comprehensive musicianship. Compare the topic also with one book from each of the other two categories (linear analysis and harmony). Comparatively speaking, how concise are definitions? Is the index easy to use? Did you find your topic on the first try? How long is the explanation? Are there musical examples? Are they recorded? Is the material shown in two or more contexts? Are there exercises (perhaps elsewhere) in the text. Summarize your reactions to the presentations in terms of strengths and weaknesses.

Comprehensive Musicianship Texts

Ralph Turek, *The Elements of Music: Concepts and Applications*, Two Volumes, McGraw-Hill.
Bruce Benward and Gary White, *Music in Theory and Practice*, Two Volumes, William C. Brown.

Linear Analysis Texts

Carl Schachter and Edward Aldwell, *Harmony and Voice Leading*, One Volume, Wadsworth Publishing.
Robert Gauldin, *Harmonic Practice in Tonal Music*, One Volume, W. W. Norton and Company.
Miguel A. Roig-Francoli, *Harmony in Context*, One Volume, McGraw-Hill.

Harmony Texts

Stefan Kostka and Dorothy Payne, *Tonal Harmony*, One Volume, McGraw-Hill.
Robert Ottman, *Elementary Harmony: Theory and Practice* and *Advanced Harmony: Theory and Practice* (Two-volume set), Prentice Hall.

Guiseppe Giordani, "Caro mio ben"

UNIT *4*

Symmetry and Embellishment

George Gershwin, "Oh, Lady Be Good"

Chapter 9
Melody Forms

Chapter 10
Secondary Dominants

P opular music is *not* a phenomenon of the twentieth century. If we rely on the definitions of art, folk, and pop presented in Unit 2, music that is primarily for entertainment or for commercial purposes may be defined as "popular." By this standard, Western popular music probably originated from merchants' songs and minstrels' ballads during the Middle Ages.

Although Western society has traditionally maintained separable folk, art, and pop *genre*, in the last few decades, with the unparalleled influence of the recording and marketing industries, many Westerners have grown up recognizing only two categories of music: "song" and "other." Routinely, we hear members of the media—even knowledgeable musicians—refer to instrumental works as "songs." Indeed, the traditional distinction between instrumental and vocal *genre*—not to mention the basic understanding of aesthetic enrichment on the one hand and simple diversion on the other—is becoming increasingly blurred.

Still, we must not minimize the historical importance of the popular song. Typically published with piano accompaniment, pieces like *Tenting Tonight On the Old Camp Ground* and *Over There* expressed both the despair and the courage of a nation at war. In their respective eras, *'S Wonderful* and *Top of the World* detailed the emotions of a new love relationship; Al Jolson's *California Here I Come,* Leonard Bernstein's *New York, New York,* and *MacArthur Park* (Jimmy Webb) extolled the virtues of favorite states, cities, and places. That some of these songs may be unfamiliar is not surprising. By definition, popular music is acclaimed for a time, then, with few exceptions, consigned quickly to obscurity.

One song writer who is not likely to be forgotten any time soon is **George Gershwin** (1898–1937)—one of America's most distinctive composers. He was born in Brooklyn at the turn of the century and, like many popular composers of his era, he had minimal formal training in music. Innate talent allowed Gershwin to master the style and content of musical comedy, however, and by the age of twenty-two, he had written the first of numerous Broadway shows, including *Lady, Be Good* (1924), *Strike Up the Band* (1927), *Funny Face* (1927), and others.

Gershwin is one of the few composers to achieve acclaim in both popular and "classical" *genre.* As we will discuss further in this unit, popular music is most often comprised of one or more periodic, tonal melodies (often with syncopated or otherwise memorable rhythms), syllabic texts, homophonic textures, and verse and refrain structures. Popular songs are rarely more than three or four minutes in duration. By contrast, many traditional "classical" *genre* are lengthy and intricate; melodies are not only stated, but developed in contrasting keys and with varying textures. That Gershwin was able to create lasting popular tunes like *Oh, Lady Be Good* as well as concertos (*Rhapsody in Blue,* 1924), tone poems (*An American in Paris,* 1928), and an opera (*Porgy and Bess,* 1935) evidences the range of his prodigious gift.

With lyrics with his brother Ira, Gershwin composed the song *Oh, Lady Be Good,* in 1924. The harmonic spectrum of this homophonic work is entirely functional, although jazz and popular colorations enrich the palette. The "verse and refrain" form, dating from Medieval times in Western music, has a sectional structure expressed as **A B**. The verse (the "A" section) in Gershwin's song begins in E minor and is heard with two different sets of lyrics. Emphasizing the relative major, the "B" material (the refrain) is sung both times to the *same* text. As is the case with many popular songs, the refrain melody of *Oh, Lady Be Good* is more memorable than the verse.

In Unit 4, we will discuss the formal strategies by which traditional composers (folk, art, and pop alike) have enabled the listener to perceive symmetry and contrast in melodic and rhythmic ideas over increasingly greater spans of time. In addition, we will survey the application of functional progressions at secondary levels. Occurring frequently in *Oh, Lady Be Good* (and in most other tonal works as well), these embellishing tonal excursions decorate the harmony and at the same time, reinforce a central tonality.

Verse

Lis- ten to my tale of woe, it's
Au -burn and bru - nette and blonde, I

ter - ri - bly sad, but   true.   All dressed up, no   place to go, Each ev'- ning I'm aw - fl'y   blue.
love 'em all, tall   or   small.   But some - how they   don't grow fond, They stag-ger but ne - ver   fall.

I   must win some   win-some miss!   Can't go on like   this.   I could blos- som   out I know, With
Win -ter's gone, and   now it's Spring!   Love where is   thy   sting?   If some - bo - dy   won't re-spond I'm

CHAPTER *9*

Melody Forms

Like writers, successful composers shape musical works by defining both the long- and the short-term goals. In a novel, a succession of chapters defines plot—the largest component element. Groups of related paragraphs within each chapter shape and define associated and contrasting elements of the overall story line. Finally, every paragraph is constructed of several complete sentences—each of these with its own design as simple or complex. Should the reader take any one sentence, paragraph, or chapter out of order, the relative completeness of that one element would not be affected; however, without defining context, the meaning would be obscured. The same principles exist with more condensed structures such as limericks, sonnets, or ballads. Meaning is conveyed from writer to reader through series of cumulative and related events.

PERIODIC DESIGN

PERIOD STRUCTURE (or PERIODICITY) is the musical equivalent of paragraph structure in prose. We have discussed how phrases are defined through cadences (either *terminal* or *progressive*); likewise, two phrases can be heard as one longer event termed a PERIOD. The first phrase of the period, called the ANTECEDENT PHRASE, is typically progressive in effect; an answering CONSEQUENT PHRASE completes the period.

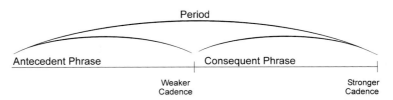

315

We use this same type of structure every day in constructing sentences. Notice that in the sentence below, the first clause ends with a comma, telling the reader to expect more information; another clause follows to complete the sentence. The period punctuation signals the culmination of the complete thought.

While the performers arrived at the concert hall on time, the inclement weather delayed the conductor for nearly a half hour.

Both clauses in the previous sentence provide information; each has a subject, a verb, and other parts of speech. Yet without the other, neither clause projects the image of an orchestra awaiting the arrival of its conductor. Identical patterns control periodic melodies so that they hold our attention as events unfold. Cadences delineate the internal divisions of melodies just as punctuation marks divide sentences. Most typically (certainly not always), the first cadence of a period is progressive; the second, terminal.

While there any many different clause types in sentence construction, composers combine and extend phrases in one of two ways:

1. By joining two phrases that are *similar,* but not identical
2. *Contrasting* one melodic idea with another

Parallel Period

In many melodies, the consequent (answering) phrase is simply a repetition of the antecedent phrase, but with a cadential adjustment that creates a more final effect. An antecedent phrase often ends with a progressive melodic cadence; the consequent, with a terminal effect. This structure, termed a PARALLEL PERIOD, is seen in Robert Schumann's "Wild Rider" from *Album for the Young.* Cadences (measures 4 and 8) delineate the two phrases that are constructed from identical melodic material. Observe, however, that the antecedent phrase ends with a progressive melodic cadence ($\hat{2}$) while the consequent phrase concludes with a terminal cadence ($\hat{1}$). Harmonically, the first phrase ends on the dominant; the second, with the tonic. This small, but crucial difference in the second phrase allows the listener to connect the two phrases—not merely as repetition, but as musical *growth.*

CD 2, TRACK 19-1 PARALLEL PERIOD (2 PARTS)
Robert Schumann, "Wild Rider"
from *Album for the Young*

The parallel period is especially common in folk music (or commercial music composed to impart a folk flavor). Stephen Foster (1826–1864) composed nearly two hundred songs in his short life. *Oh, Susanna!*, which sold 40,000 copies in 1851, begins with a parallel period that is very similar to the one in the last passage. Notice that Foster's melody is pentatonic.[1]

TRACK 19-2 PARALLEL PERIOD
Stephen Foster, *Oh Susannah!*

Repeated Phrase.   The mere repetition of a phrase (without progressive cadential weight) may be equivalent to a period in length, but the growth associated with antecedent/consequent design is missing. Repetition adds length; the antecedent/consequent structure of a parallel period, on the other hand, creates momentum. Where the Schumann and Foster parallel periods include contrasting cadences (progressive/terminal), the traditional melody *Good King Wenceslaus* is comprised of two identical phrases. This construction is known as a REPEATED PHRASE and we would not employ the terms "antecedent" or "consequent" to describe either of them.

CD 2, TRACK 20-1 REPEATED PHRASE
(3 PARTS)
Traditional, *Good King Wenceslaus*

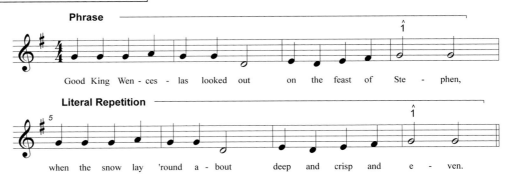

Phrase Length.   Traditional composers have written phrases of virtually every conceivable length—from a few beats to several measures. Moreover, the number of measures in a phrase is dependent on the tempo and meter (a phrase may be eight measures in length at a fast tempo or a duple meter). For composers in the eighteenth and nineteenth centuries, however, phrases are often symmetrical arrangements of four measures. While this model is typical, exceptions (not "irregularities") abound. Phrases in Foster's *Oh, Susanna,* for

---

[1]While we have provided text with this example, the notation is beamed in an instrumental style to avoid the complications of a flagged note on each new syllable of text (shown below).

Vocal Notation

example, are four measures, but only eight beats in length as compared to the more typical sixteen beats in *Good King Wenceslaus.*

TRACK 20-2 REPEATED PHRASE
George Gershwin, *Oh, Lady Be Good*

The refrain of Gershwin's *Oh, Lady Be Good* begins with a repeated phrase. With a half-note beat, the two phrases are eight measures in length and end with terminal melodic cadences.

Good King Wenceslaus and *Oh, Lady Be Good* are repeated *phrases* and lack the musical growth associated with periodic forms. Compare a parallel period like the one that Beethoven composed for his "Ode to Joy" with the two repeated phrases just given. Instead of mere repetition, Beethoven employs the antecedent/consequent design to join two phrases into one longer formal division.

CD TRACK 20-3 REPEATED PHRASE
Ludwig van Beethoven, "Ode to Joy" Compared with Parallel Period

Time-Line Analysis. Among many helpful graphic tools that aid in understanding traditional music is *time-line analysis.* A graphic representation of formal events is called a TIME LINE—a flexible analytical graph that can be tailored to delineate a passage of any length and virtually any complexity. The same line, for example, might represent a few measures or several hundred. Measure numbers delineate the scope of the analysis.

In the analysis of forms, we often designate phrases on a time line with lowercase letters.[2] The melodic material of the first phrase is represented with the letter "a." If the melody and cadence of a second phrase are the same as the

---

[2]We reserve uppercase letters for larger formal events called *parts.* The analysis of small forms will be discussed in Chapters 11 and 12.

first, the letter "a" is again appropriate The time line below, which includes measure numbers and melodic cadences, details the phrase structure of any eight-measure repeated phrase such as *Good King Wenceslaus.*

If measure numbers are not needed on the time line, an alternate representation of the repeated phrase might employ repeat signs.

The same time line illustrates the repeated phrase that begins the refrain of *Oh, Lady Be Good* (page 318). A time line often includes an indication of the key.

Good King Wenceslaus and *Oh, Lady, Be Good* are repeated phrases; *Oh, Susanna!,* Schumann's *Wild Rider,* and Beethoven's "Ode to Joy" (see page 324), however, are parallel *periods.* Despite the repetition of melodic material, periodic structure occurs due to the antecedent/consequent construction. All three melodies would be diagramed identically on a time line.

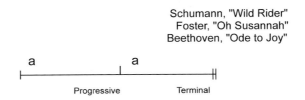

A parallel period with cadential progression has been common in Western popular music since the turn of the twentieth century. *Ring of Fire,* popularized by Johnny Cash's 1969 recording, includes mixed meter—a device common in pop music of the 1970s. The first phrase ends with an imperfect authentic cadence; the consequent phrase has a perfect authentic cadence.

CD 2, TRACK 21
Merle Kilgore and June Carter, *Ring of Fire*
Parallel Period

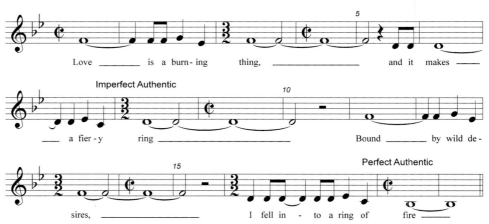

In the following time line, observe that abbreviations for harmonic cadences are used.

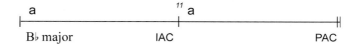

Repetition is central to both melodic and harmonic construction. As we have seen, the simplest functional progressions are also the most effective. Likewise, the repetition of a memorable melodic phrase facilitates the listener's grasp of tonality, proportion, and style.

Variation

If the second phrase of a period begins like the first, but incorporates substantial differences after the first few notes, the periodic structure is still known as parallel. The construction is also parallel if the consequent phrase is a transposition of the antecedent phrase. In either case, we use the same letter on a time line to designate the consequent phrase. The variation is indicated by a superscript numeral (a^1). Different variations of the same material in subsequent phrases (if any) are indicated with sequential numerals (a^2, a^3, and so on).

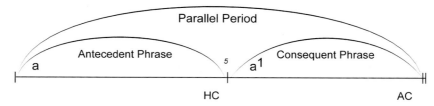

The American folk song *Down in the Valley* begins with a tonic triad outline in the first phrase and continues with an arpeggiation of the dominant seventh

CD 2, TRACK 22-1 VARIATION (2 PARTS)
American Traditional, *Down in the Valley*

in the second phrase. The period is parallel—not only because the two phrases begin with the same material, but because we hear the second phrase as a variation of the first.

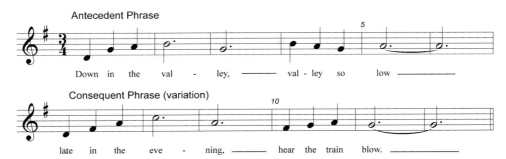

Antecedent Phrase

Down in the val - ley, ——— val - ley so low ———

Consequent Phrase (variation)

late in the eve - ning, ——— hear the train blow. ———

A similar parallel-period structure occurs in the first movement of Haydn's Quartet, Op. 54, No. 2. The first phrase ends with a half cadence; the second is authentic. The "G. P." in measures 6 and 12 means "general pause" and indicates a lengthy fermata.

TRACK 22-2, VARIATION
Joseph Haydn, Quartet, Op. 54, No. 2 (I)
Sequential Parallel Period

Sequential Parallel Period.   When the second phrase of a parallel period begins higher or lower than the first, yet duplicates the basic contour and intervallic structure, the type is distinguished as SEQUENTIAL PARALLEL. The previous Haydn example illustrates sequential parallel period structure. While the second phrase ends differently than the first (with an authentic cadence rather than the weaker half cadence that ends the first phrase), the second phrase begins a second lower and basically duplicates both the initial intervals and rhythms of the first phrase. The periodic structure occurs because we hear the second phrase as a sequential variation of the first. The general pauses do not affect the formal structure, but they might be included on a time line to show how the phrases are elongated.

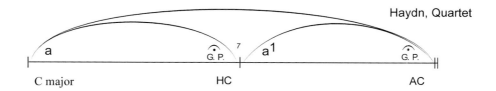

Remember that any analytical system has limitations and must be employed according to individual needs. While we could use or devise an analytical method to account more dramatically for the differences between any two melodies, such an approach would be overly detailed for most purposes.

> WORKBOOK/ANTHOLOGY I
> I. Repeated Phrases and Parallel Periods, page 107

Contrasting Period

When two phrases are heard as complementary, yet are based on different melodic materials (a and b), the periodic structure is CONTRASTING. As always, periodic structure is based on a weaker cadence followed by a stronger one.

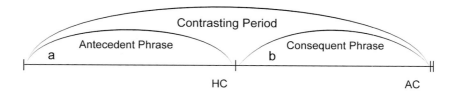

A renewed interest in folk styles was among important traits of Western music in the mid-nineteenth century. Johannes Brahms made arrangements of many folk songs from his native Germany. *Die Sonne scheint nicht mehr* (*The Sun Shines No More*) begins with an eight-measure contrasting period. Both cadences are in E major. The first is plagal; the second, perfect authentic.

CD 2, TRACK 23-1 CONSTRASTING PERIOD (3 PARTS)
Johannes Brahms (arr.), *The Sun Shines No More*

The sun shines no more; so beautiful, but as before,
The day is not so bright, not so full of love anymore.

TRACK 23-2 CONSTRASTING PERIOD
Joseph Haydn, Symphony No. 104 in D Major (IV)

Haydn uses a contrasting period for the third and fourth phrases of his Symphony No. 104 (fourth movement). We will discuss the first half of this melody in the next section.

The second half of Beethoven's "Ode to Joy" is also a contrasting period. The first period is parallel. Taken together, the structure of the two periods enables us to hear the sixteen-measure theme as beginning from a single motive (measure 1), then evolving into a phrase (measures 1–4); a period (measures 1–8); and finally (with the addition of the second period) into a complete melody.

TRACK 23-3 CONSTRASTING PERIOD
Ludwig van Beethoven, "Ode to Joy"
Parallel and Constrasting Periods

Parallel periods may be based on repetition, transposition, or another form of variation. If a period is contrasting, the melody of the second phrase is substantially different from the first. In all cases, the first phrase ends with a weaker cadence than the second one, giving us the familiar antecedent/ consequent effect. We will discuss other possibilities for melodic design in the next section.

WORKBOOK/ANTHOLOGY I
II. Contrasting Periods, page 111

REVIEW AND APPLICATION 9–1

Periodic Structure

Essential Terms

antecedent phrase	parallel period	repeated phrase
sequential parallel	consequent phrase	period
time line	contrasting period	periodicity

1. Using the list below, identify the forms of the following periods by writing the appropriate letters in the blanks.

A. Parallel Period

B. Contrasting Period

C. Repeated Phrase

CD 2, TRACK 24-1 REVIEW AND APPLICATION 9-1 (3 PARTS)
Welsh Folk Song, *The Ash Grove*
Exercise 1-a

a.

Melodic form: _____

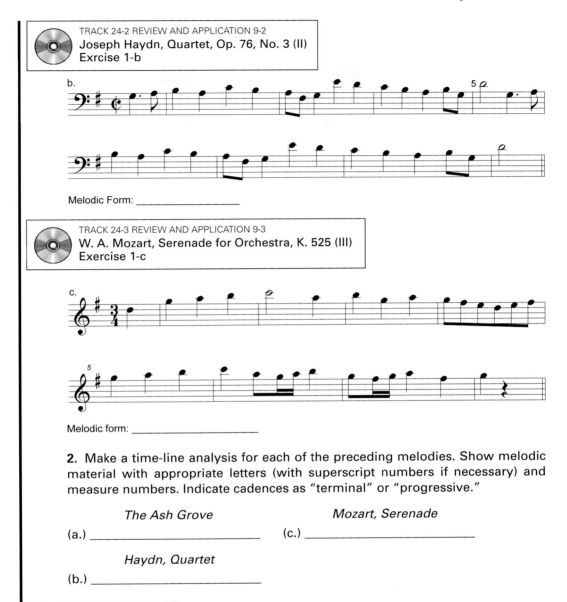

TRACK 24-2 REVIEW AND APPLICATION 9-2
Joseph Haydn, Quartet, Op. 76, No. 3 (II)
Exrcise 1-b

Melodic Form: _____

TRACK 24-3 REVIEW AND APPLICATION 9-3
W. A. Mozart, Serenade for Orchestra, K. 525 (III)
Exercise 1-c

Melodic form: _____

2. Make a time-line analysis for each of the preceding melodies. Show melodic material with appropriate letters (with superscript numbers if necessary) and measure numbers. Indicate cadences as "terminal" or "progressive."

The Ash Grove

(a.) _____

Haydn, Quartet

(b.) _____

Mozart, Serenade

(c.) _____

SELF-TEST 9–1

Time Limit: 5 Minutes

1. Viewing the time-line analyses below, choose an appropriate letter from the right column to represent the form. Write the letter in the blank to the left of the time line. *Scoring: Subtract 15 points for each error.*

A. Parallel period

B. Contrasting period

C. Repeated phrase

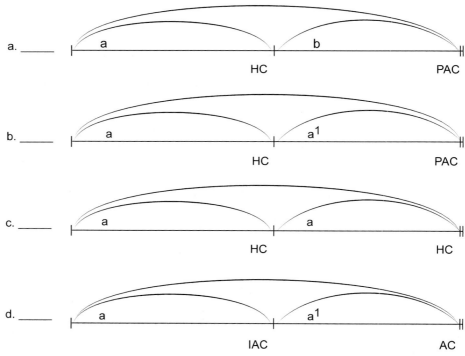

a. _____

a   b

HC   PAC

b. _____

a   a¹

HC   PAC

c. _____

a   a

HC   HC

d. _____

a   a¹

IAC   AC

CD 2, TRACK 25-1 SELF TEST 9-1 (2 PARTS)
J. S. Bach, *Peasant Cantata*
Question 2-a

2. Identify the two melodies below as (1) parallel period, (2) contrasting period, or (3) repeated phrase. Write your answer on the blank. *Scoring: Subtract 20 points for each incorrect answer.*

a.

Melodic form:_____

TRACK 25-2 SELF TEST 9-1
Bob Hilliard and Mort Garson, *Our Day Will Come*
Question 2-b

b.

Our   day   will   come, ———   and   we'll   have   ev - 'ry thing.

We'll   share   the   joy ———   fall - ing   in   love   can   bring.

Melodic form:_____

Total Possible: 100   Your Score _____

Phrase Group

Composers use repetition, variation, and contrast to create periodic forms from antecedent and consequent phrases. A similar sense of musical growth is possible by joining phrases that do not have the antecedent/consequent relationship. While a period has the weak-strong cadential design, some works are structured so that two *or more* weaker cadences precede the stronger one.

In a PHRASE GROUP, phrases end with relatively weaker cadences (half, imperfect authentic, deceptive, or plagal). When composers employ a phrase group, the listener expects additional material to follow. Two different phrase-group plans are illustrated in the next diagram; many others are possible.

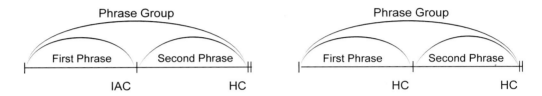

A phrase group of three phrases is not uncommon. Again, as long as the cadences are relatively weak, a variety of possibilities exists.

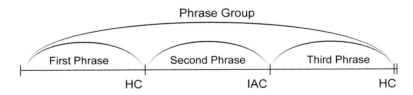

We can categorize the structure of a phrase group as "parallel" or "contrasting" just as we do with periods. By using the term "phrase group," however, we suggest a less definitive construction. The terms "antecedent" and "consequent" are reserved for periodic structure. For a phrase group, we speak of the "first phrase" or the "second phrase" of a phrase group.

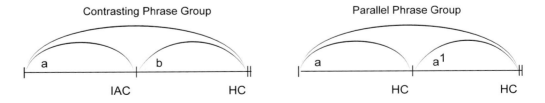

The first two phrases of William Boyce's *Ode for His Majesty's Birthday, 1772* comprise a contrasting phrase group (an imperfect authentic followed by a half cadence). Brackets emphasize the same organization identified by slurs in the previous examples.

CD 2, TRACK 26-1 CONSTRASTING PHRASE GROUP (3 PARTS)
Wiliam Boyce,
Ode for His Majesty's Birthday, 1772

TRACK 26-2 CONTRASTING PHRASE GROUP
J. S. Bach, Menuet

A similar contrasting phrase-group structure occurs in Bach's Menuet in G Minor.[3]

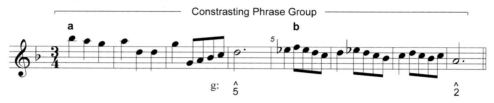

A phrase group in which the second phrase modulates to a related key is especially common. The second phrase may end with an authentic cadence, but because the key is not tonic at this point, we *do not* refer to this organization as a period.

In the parallel phrase group below, from Mozart's Sonata in D Major, K. 284 (third movement), the first phrase ends on $\hat{2}$ in D major; the second phrase

TRACK 26-3 CONTRASTING PHRASE GROUP
W. A. Mozart, Sonata in D Major, K. 284 (III)

modulates to the dominant and ends on the new tonic (the equivalent of a "weak" cadence since the cadence is not strong in D major).

In the last example, the first three pitches of the second phrase are identical to those of the first phrase. Accordingly, we hear a parallel construction even though there are substantial differences otherwise. The identification of keys shows the phrase-group structure on the time line; were these designations omitted, the diagram would represent a parallel *period*.

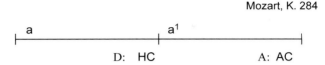

Mozart, K. 284

Robert Schumann's *Träumerei* (Dream) from *Scenes from Childhood* begins with a parallel phrase group. Neither of the two phrases ends with an authentic cadence in the tonic key, yet one phrase leads smoothly to the other through the repetition of the opening motive. Notice that Schumann expands the range of the melody in the second phrase.

CD 2, TRACK 27-1 PARALLEL PHRASE GROUP (2 PARTS)
Robert Schumann, "Träumerei"
from *Scenes from Childhood*

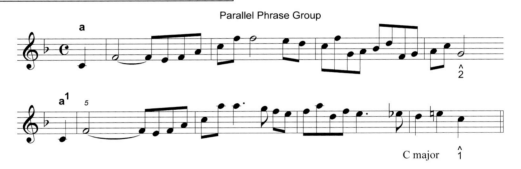

Parallel Phrase Group

In Bach's Sarabande from the *French Suite No. 6*, the second phrase of a parallel phrase group begins with a transposition of the original melodic material a third higher. Popular throughout Europe by 1700, a sarabande is an instrumental dance cast in a slow, triple meter and featuring an agogic accent on the second beat of each measure.

TRACK 27-2 PARALLEL PHRASE GROUP
J. S. Bach, Sarabande from *French Suite No. 6 in E Minor*

The Irish-American Victor Herbert (1859–1924) was one of the earliest film composers, and was a founder of the American Society of Composers, Authors, and Publishers (ASCAP). He also wrote operettas that are still enjoyed today. The title song from his *Babes in Toyland* (1903) begins with a contrasting phrase group.

CD 2, TRACK 28-1 CONTRASTING PHRASE GROUP
(2 PARTS)
Victor Herbert, "Toyland"

Contrasting Phrase Group

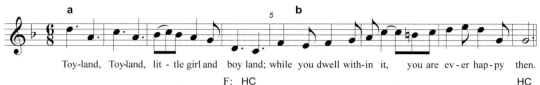

Toy-land, Toy-land, lit - tle girl and boy land; while you dwell with-in it, you are ev - er hap-py then.

F: HC   HC

TRACK 28-2 CONTRASTING PHRASE GROUP
"Toyland," Third and Fourth Phrases
Contrasting Period

While the first two phrases of Toyland make a phrase group, the third and fourth phrases comprise a true contrasting period. The third and fourth phrases are both in F major: The third ends with a half cadence; the final cadence is authentic.

Contrasting Period

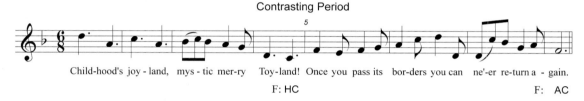

Child-hood's joy - land, mys - tic mer-ry Toy-land! Once you pass its bor-ders you can ne'-er re-turn a - gain.

F: HC   F: AC

Taken together, the weak-weak-weak-strong cadential structure of Herbert's melody ties all four phrases together into a larger melody form known as a *Double Period*. As we will discuss in the next section, the reference to *double period* denotes length more than form. In fact, there may be no periods at all in a "double period."

WORKBOOK/ANTHOLOGY I
III. Phrase Groups, page 113

THE DOUBLE PERIOD

Although the term "double period" is in common use today, it is one of many terms whose meaning has changed over time. By definition, the first and second phrases of a double period do not comprise a period, but a phrase group. Moreover, the third and fourth phrases may also comprise a phrase group. Still, the term is in common use and we should understand DOUBLE PERIOD to mean four phrases that follow the cadential pattern weak-weak-weak-strong.

Double Period

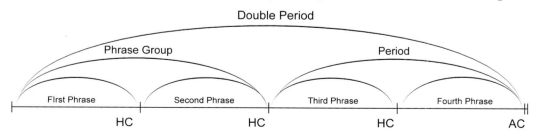

Phrase Group   Period

First Phrase   Second Phrase   Third Phrase   Fourth Phrase

HC   HC   HC   AC

Remember that in terms of form, an authentic cadence in a key *other* than tonic, is defined as "weak." We may extend our identification of double periods according to the melodic material that begins each of the two component parts: parallel or contrasting. Victor Herbert's "Toyland", for example, is a PARALLEL DOUBLE PERIOD. Both the initial phrase group and the following period are contrasting, but since the first and third phrases begin with the same material, the double period is heard as parallel. A time-line analysis reveals the makeup of the phrase group and the period (contrasting) as well as the parallel structure of the double period. Observe that in discussing double-period structure, the melodic content of the second and fourth phrases is not a consideration.

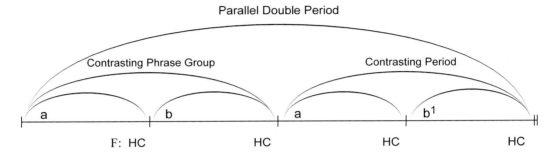

A similar parallel double period opens Joseph Haydn's Symphony No. 104 (fourth movement). All four cadences are in D major. The first, second, and third are weak; the fourth, strong.

CD 2, TRACK 29
Joseph Haydn, Symphony No. 104 in D Major (IV)
Double Period

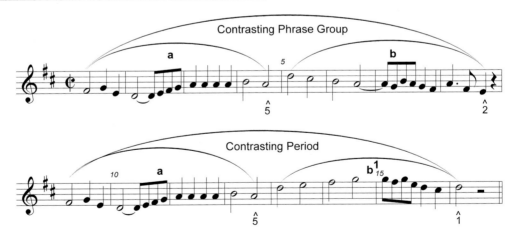

The fourth phrase of Haydn's melody (b^1) begins as an inversion of the second phrase (b). MIRROR INVERSION, in which pitches duplicate the intervals of an original pattern, but in the opposite directions, is common in traditional music and presents an additional opportunity for variation. The second and third measures of each phrase are different, but the power of a motive to attract and hold our attention should not be minimized.

Mirror Inversion

Less elaborate time lines (omitting the slurs and key indications, for example) convey useful information to knowledgeable musicians.

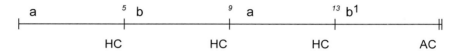

A phrase group followed by a period forms a double period even when the fourth phrase consists of entirely new melodic material (designated "c" in the next example). William Boyce used this construction in his *Ode* for King George. The double period is parallel since the first and third phrases consist of identical material.

CD 2, TRACK 30
William Boyce, *Ode for His Majesty's Birthday, 1772*
Double Period

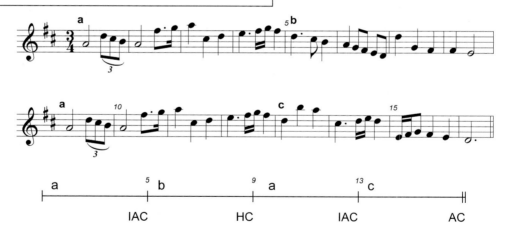

Sectional Double Period

Some common melody forms combine features of periods and phrase groups. A SECTIONAL DOUBLE PERIOD, for example, is one that includes two periods or phrase groups that do not conform to the weak-weak-weak-strong double period model. Beethoven's "Ode to Joy", for example, is a sectional double period that is comprised of parallel and contrasting periods, respectively. Because the cadential structure is weak-strong, weak-strong, we would not use the term "double period" without qualification. Notice that the fourth phrase is identified on the score (as well as on the time line below) as a variation of the first (a^1).

CD 2, TRACK 31
Ludwig van Beethoven, "Ode to Joy"
Sectional Double Period

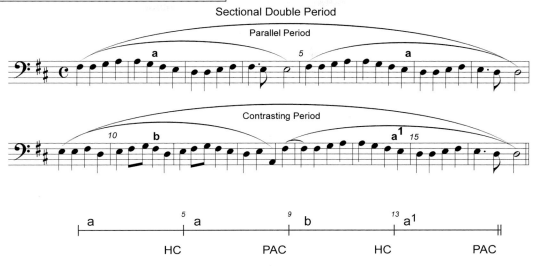

Others might place less emphasis on the metric displacement in measures 12–13 (where the final phrase actually begins a beat early—on the fourth beat of the measure) and view the first, second, and fourth phrases as identical in melodic content. With this view, we could omit the superscript numeral (a^1) from an analytical representation of the final phrase.

Earlier, we identified the first two phrases of Foster's *Oh Susanna!* as a parallel period. Combined with the second (contrasting) period, the entire song is a sectional double period.

CD 2, TRACK 32
Stephan Foster, *Oh, Susanna!*
Sectional Double Period

Unlike the contrasting double period that organizes Beethoven's "Ode to Joy," the fourth phrase of *Oh, Susanna!* is identical to the second.

A double period is a form that permits melodic material to be stated, varied, and contrasted while focusing the listener's attention on the ultimate musical goal. In addition, key and cadential effect—as well as texture and orchestration—may serve to connect ideas while they also facilitate variety at the same time. While in later chapters of the text we will discuss more intricate

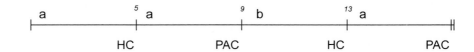

WORKBOOK/ANTHOLOGY I
IV. Double Periods, page 115

forms, we should remember that successful composers have employed rather simple structures for memorable melodies and even complete works.

REVIEW AND APPLICATION 9–2

Double and Repeated Periods

Essential Terms

double period	phrase group
sectional double period	mirror inversion

1. Construct a time-line analysis of the two melodies below. Provide letters to represent phrases as well as measure numbers. Use the first blank to identify the form. The longer line below is for your time line.

Scottish Folk Song, "Ye Banks and Braes O' Bonnie Doon"

*Form:*_____

Analysis: _____

W. A. Mozart, Serenade for Orchestra, K. 525 (III)

Form: _____

Analysis: _____

SELF-TEST 9–2

Time Limit: 7 Minutes

1. Use the list below to choose the most appropriate description for each time line shown. Letters represent the melodic material and cadences. *Scoring: Subtract 10 points for each error.*

A. phrase   E. phrase group

B. repeated phrase   F. sectional double period

C. contrasting period   G. parallel period

D. double period   H. none of these

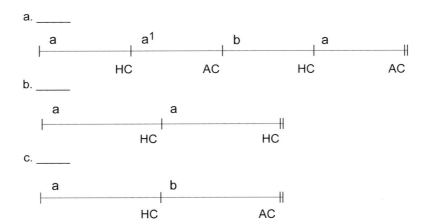

d. _____

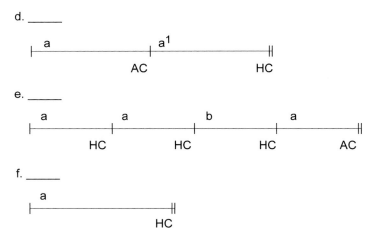

e. _____

f. _____

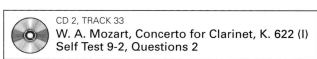

2. Study the melody that begins Mozart's Concerto for Clarinet. Each of the four phrases is marked, and the cadences are indicated with abbreviations. Place a check mark on the blank beside each statement that is true about the melody. If a statement is not true, leave the blank unmarked. *Scoring: subtract 8 points for each incorrect answer.*

_____ a. Measures 1–8 constitute a parallel period.

_____ b. The form of the complete melody is a double period.

_____ c. Measures 9–16 are a contrasting period.

_____ d. Measures 1–8 comprise a phrase group.

_____ e. The melodic material of the first and second phrases is contrasting.

CD 2, TRACK 33
W. A. Mozart, Concerto for Clarinet, K. 622 (I)
Self Test 9-2, Questions 2

Total Possible: 100   Your Score _____

ALTERNATE MELODY FORMS

We would be remiss if we failed to acknowledge that while the four-measure phrase and the eight-measure period are convenient models of formal melodic structure, composers have routinely adapted these models to serve less symmetrical melodies. Such structures are not "irregular" or "atypical"; rather, they show that in the hands of a skilled composer, musical expression is not confined by a certain number of measures or an anticipated sequence of phrases.

Phrase Structure

Traditional music literature abounds with phrases that are three, five, six, and seven measures in length. Edward MacDowell (1862–1908), among the first American composers to achieve an international reputation, employs a six-measure phrase in his Concerto for Piano No. 2 in D Minor. The phrase shown below begins with an ascending scale; these clear tendencies, however, are interrupted in measures 3–4 by augmented seconds that delay the cadence. The phrase terminates with a half cadence.

CD 2, TRACK 34-1 ALTERNATE PHRASE STRUCTURE (3 PARTS)
Edward MacDowell, Concerto for Piano No. 2
in D Major (III)
Six-Measure Phrase

Harry T. Burleigh (1866–1949) was a Black American who achieved wide recognition as a vocalist, music editor, and composer. The fifth movement of his suite *From the Southland* (1907) begins with a phrase of six measures that, like the MacDowell phrase in the last example, concludes with a half cadence.

TRACK 34-2 ALTERNATE PHRASE STRUCTURE
Harry T. Burleigh, "On Bended Knees,"
from *The Southland*
Six-Measure Phrase

Antonin Dvořák, who is said to have been introduced to spirituals by Harry Burleigh, employs a five-measure phrase in the second movement of his "New World" Symphony. While the arch-like ascent in C♯ minor (from $\hat{1}$ to $\hat{5}$ and back down) is ordinary enough, the composer maintains interest through three different levels of syncopation (beat, beat division, and beat subdivision).

TRACK 34-3 ALTERNATE PHRASE STRUCTURE
Antonin Dvořák, Symphony No. 9 in E Minor
("From the New World") (II)
Five-Measure Phrase

Asymmetrical Period and Phrase-Group Structure

We are accustomed to the antecedent/consequent structure discussed earlier in this chapter where phrases of equal length combine to form a period or phrase group. In some melodies, however, these are of unequal length.

Cole Porter (1891–1964), for example, creates an asymmetrical parallel period for his song, *Why Shouldn't I?* The form is generated by a text (written by Porter himself) that has unequal numbers of syllables in the two lines:

Why shouldn't I take a chance when romance passes by,
Why shouldn't I know of love?

 CD 2, TRACK 35-1 ASYMMETRICAL STRUCTURE (2 PARTS)
Cole Porter, "Why Shouldn't I?"
Parallel Period

Porter's musical setting combines phrases of four and three measures, respectively.

No special significance is attached to the asymmetrical period structure of Porter's song on a time-line analysis.

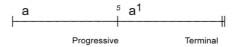

The influence of text setting on melodic construction is seen in the song, *Sommerabend* ("Summer Evening") by Johannes Brahms. Notice that the composer matches phrase structure with the punctuation of the three lines of poetry. The result is a ten-measure phrase group that is divided into three phrases.

 TRACK 35-2 ASYMMETRICAL STRUCTURE
Johannes Brahms, "Summer Evening"
Phrase Group

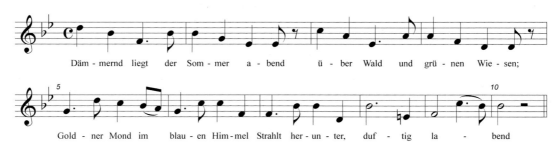

At twilight the summer
Over green fields and forest;
Golden moon in the blue sky
Shines down, hazy, fragrantly refreshing.

On a time line, the three phrases are identified as having three contrasting melodic ideas.

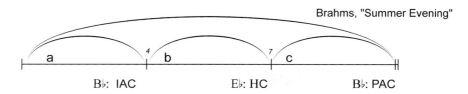

Brahms, "Summer Evening"

Bb: IAC   Eb: HC   Bb: PAC

Less Common Double-Period Structure

The double period is basic to melody; accordingly, text setting, style, or the need to extend and develop ideas within the phrase may result in various asymmetrical designs. As we have discussed, cadences, the repetition and variation of melodic material, and metric considerations are helpful in differentiating among phrases, periods, phrase groups, and double periods.

Phrase Extension.   Composers often build momentum by elongating one or more phrases in a period or phrase group through PHRASE EXTENSION. A melody from the second movement of Tchaikovsky's Symphony No. 4 is a conventional double period except that the final phrase is eight, rather than four measures. After three consecutive weak cadences, Tchaikovsky delays the final cadence for an additional four measures.

CD 2, TRACK 36 PHRASE EXTENSION (3 PARTS)
Peter Illyich Tchaikovsky, Symphony No. 4
in F Minor (II)
Double Period

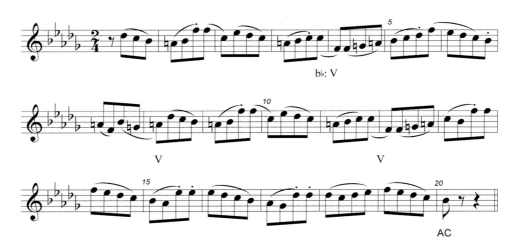

Elision.   A common explanation for asymmetrical period or phrase-group structure is ELISION—the simultaneous occurrence of the end of one phrase and the beginning of another. In the first-movement theme of the Sonata in C Major, K. 309, Mozart elides the second and third phrases in a four-phrase group. Mozart's melody also illustrates a MOTTO—a memorable motive that recurs as an introduction to periodic or phrase-group structure.

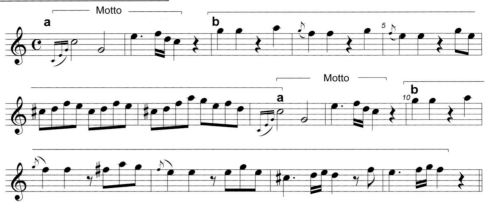

SHAPING COMPLETE MUSICAL WORKS

In Chapter 12 of this volume, we will discuss *small forms* in which sectional divisions are determined largely by the key scheme. In closing the present chapter, we will survey several important shaping principles in which key is less significant. *Bar form* and *verse and refrain* combine phrases, periods, phrase-groups, and double periods into a complete work, but *without* specific key implications. While not really forms, *strophic* and *through-composed* are two creative choices through which the shape of a composition may be defined.

To this point, we have identified phrases and periods with lowercase letters. This is because uppercase letters (**A**, **B**, **C**, and so on) are reserved to identify larger divisions of a composition called PARTS. In turn, each part may comprise one or more phrase groups or double periods. On a time line, we may choose between a detailed analysis (by using both uppercase and lowercase letters as in the upper line below) or only the most significant *parts* of a composition (with uppercase letters as shown on the lower line).

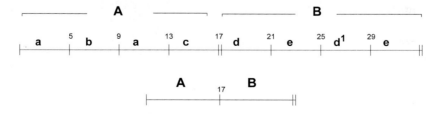

Bar Form

From Medieval times, composers have often structured their works in two parts with the first of those parts repeated. The direct repetition of material does not normally constitute formal growth, but as used by composers from at least the thirteenth century, BAR FORM, designated **A A B**, has had a special attraction. In most cases, the second **A** section is indicated with repeat signs and not written out in full. In our study of traditional Western music, we include bar form mainly because many Lutheran chorale melodies (and, accordingly, the harmonizations of these tunes) are in bar form.

The chorale melody "*Wachet auf, ruft uns die Stimme*" (shown following) is in bar form. Composed by Phillipp Nicolai in 1599, the melody was later harmonized by J. S. Bach and others. The two principal sections of Nicolai's melody are identified in the following time line. Especially when illustrating large-scale divisions, key references at the beginning and ending points are helpful.

Philipp Nicolai, "Wake, Awake, for Night is Flying"

Now let all the heavens adore Thee,
And men and angels sing before Thee.
With harp and cymbals clearest tone;
Nor eye hath seen, nor ear hath yet attain'd to hear
What there is ours, but we rejoice and sing to Thee
Our hymn of joy eternally.

Composers gradually lost their enthusiasm for bar form during the eighteenth century. While we might not describe an AAB design today as "bar form," the formal plan is frequently encountered in Renaissance and Baroque music. In addition, it is helpful to remember that, especially in terms of formal structures, little heard in the music of today is new.

Verse and Refrain

Like bar form, *verse and refrain* structure in Western music dates back in concept to the Middle Ages. VERSE AND REFRAIN FORM contrasts one melody that is repeated to different texts (the verse) with another that has the *same* text each time it occurs (the refrain—also termed the "chorus"). Verse and refrain form was employed throughout the common-practice period and is especially familiar to us today through folk and popular tunes.

Lucie Campbell (1885–1963) was a Black gospel singer and composer who recorded and published numerous works in the first part of the twentieth century. Her setting of the *Twenty-third Psalm* (1919) illustrates verse and refrain in its most essential form. Observe that three verses are sung to the same music (a double period in form). Following each verse, a sixteen-measure sectional double period constitutes the refrain.

Lucie Campbell, "The Lord is My Shepherd"

peace; We will walk thro' the val - ley with Je - sus a - lone; On His

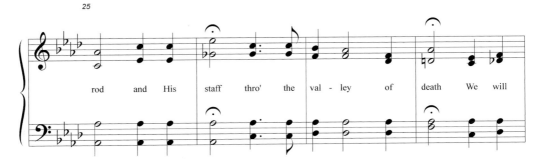

rod and His staff thro' the val - ley of death We will

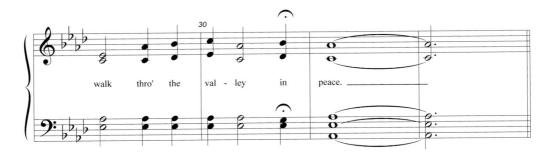

walk thro' the val - ley in peace. _____

Musical Comedy Style.   The verse and refrain in *Campbell's Twenty-third Psalm* are nearly identical in key, melodic material, rhythm, and form. In other songs, the two sections are substantially different. In traditional American musical comedy, the verse of a song may serve as a bridge between spoken dialogue and a memorable song melody. The verse may revolve around one pitch—almost like an operatic recitative. When the refrain begins, the true "tune" associated with that number is recognizable immediately.

   This musical-comedy structure is seen in Gershwin's *Someone to Watch Over Me.* The verse begins with a single pitch (C_5) reiterated and embellished. When the refrain begins, however, the melody ascends dramatically, then descends gradually to the title lyrics. The verse sets the mood, key, and meter; the refrain catches and holds our attention. Notice the descending sequence in the refrain. In addition, measure 33 offers the motive in doubled rhythmic values.

George Gershwin, "Someone To Watch Over Me"
Lyrics with Ira Gershwin

Thirty-Two Bar-Song Form.   A combination of repeated phrase and contrasting period in duple meter have been so common in popular music that we term that structure THIRTY-TWO-BAR SONG FORM. The refrain of *Oh, Lady Be Good* (page 312) is in this form which we would illustrate on a time line as **a a b a**. Likewise, Hank Williams' classic *Your Cheatin' Heart* (shown in the next example) is also complete with statement, contrast, and restatement.

Hank Williams, "Your Cheatin' Heart"

Strophic Design

When a song has multiple stanzas (*strophes*), composers may choose to employ the same music—without refrain— for each of them. If a work is STROPHIC, each different stanza of text is sung to the same music. A strophic setting is common in simple songs, although composers such as Schubert and Schumann chose strophic settings for some of their *lieder*. In addition to setting the song text, composers may provide instrumental introductory and ending sections, as seen in the complete *lied Morgengruss* ("Morning Greeting") from the cycle *Die Schöne Müllerin* (*The Beautiful Miller Woman*).

Franz Schubert, "Morning Greeting" from
The Beautiful Miller Woman

stört dich denn mein Blick so sehr? So muss ich wie - der ge - hen, so muss ich wie - der
vor aus eu - rem run - den Tor, ihr blau - en Mor - gen ster - ne ihr blau - en Mor - gen-

ge hen, wie - der ge - hen.
ster - ne, ihr Mor - gen- ster - ne!

Good morning, lovely millermaid!
Why do you hide your head as if something would happen to you?
Does my greeting trouble you so?
Does my look disturb you so?
Then I must be gone.

O let me stay only in the distance,
And at your dear window gaze from afar, from very far.
Fair head, come out!
Open your round doors, you blue morning stars,
You morning stars!

Through Composition

If a composition has *no* literal or transposed restatement of sections, musical growth may occur by a process termed THROUGH COMPOSITION. Especially common in German *lieder* of the nineteenth century, through composition is most effective in relatively brief works. Music that is through-composed often relies not on restatement, but upon the subtle variation and transformation of melodic material.

Antonio Caldara (1670–1736) was a celebrated composer of the late Baroque era. Born in Venice, his many works were written at a time when *opera seria* was popular all over Europe. Caldara worked at various courts and ended his impressive career as *Kapellmeister* in Vienna. The aria "Come raggio di sol" ("As on the Swelling Wave") is typical of songs written for both amateur and professional performers. The work is through-composed. Although motives may be traced throughout the brief song, there are neither repeated sections (as in bar form) nor contrasting sections (as in verse and refrain form).

mentre del mare, men - tre del mare nel pro - fon - do

se - no sta la tem - pe - - sta a

sco - - sa: _____ co - sì ri - so ta - lor ga - io e pa

ca - to di con - ten - to, di gio-ia un lab-bro in - fio - ra, men - tre nel suo se-

gre - to il cor pia - ga - to _____ s'an-gio-scia_e si mar - to -

ra - e. _____

As on the swelling wave in idle motion,
Wanton sunbeams at play are gaily riding,
While in the bosom, while in the bosom of the unfathomed ocean
There lies tempest in hiding:
So manly that wear a mein contented, many a visage whereon
a smile e'er hovers,
While, deep within, the bosom a heart tormented in secret anguish covers.

As we have seen, traditional composers construct their works so that the listener perceives clear relationships within each parameter. In harmony, this means functional progressions; likewise, melodies exhibit a gravitational pull toward the tonic; rhythms are metric and typically include motivic repetition and variation. In form, composers shape phrases from a single principal motive; in turn, phrases grow into periods; periods, into double-periods. Whether these internal divisions are symmetrical ("four-square") or more uneven patterns is less important than the listeners' constant awareness of the interplay of new, contrasting, and restated material.

 WORKBOOK/ANTHOLOGY I
V. Alternate Melody Forms, page 117

REVIEW AND APPLICATION 9–3

Summary of Melody Forms

Essential Terms

bar form	refrain	verse	phrase extension
elision	strophic design	through composition	thirty-two-bar song form

1. The following song can be analyzed in detail (phrase by phrase) and in overall form. Make a time line that shows each phrase and the melodic content, as we have done in this chapter. Be sure to provide measure numbers at the beginning of each internal division. In addition, identify the overall form of the complete song and the terms used for each of the major sections.

Hugh Martin and Ralph Blane,
"Have Yourself A Merry Little Christmas"

2. Choose a letter from the list that corresponds to the statement. Use each description only once.

A. repeated phrase   F. phrase

B. verse and refrain   G. contrasting period

C. parallel period   H. strophic

D. double period   I. through-composed

E. bar form   J. sectional double period

_____ (1) a phrase that is repeated without change

_____ (2) a work without direct sectional repetition or contrast

_____ (3) a melody in which three weaker cadences are followed by a single stronger one

_____ (4) the smallest complete musical statement

_____ (5) two periods, each having a weaker/stronger cadence plan

_____ (6) a song in which all stanzas are sung to the same music

_____ (7) sections with varied text contrasted with a melody always sung to the same text

_____ (8) two phrases, culminating in weaker and stronger cadences, respectively, that contain different melodic materials

_____ (9) A form found in many chorale melodies

_____ (10) phrases based on the same melodic material, but with a weaker cadence followed by a stronger one

SELF-TEST 9–3

Time Limit: 5 Minutes

1. Some of the following statements are true; others, false. Write "T" in the blank for true statements; "F" if false. These problems include material from throughout the chapter. *Scoring: Subtract 10 points for each error.*

_____ a. The thirty-two-bar song form can be represented **A A B**.

_____ b. The terms "antecedent" and "consequent" are applicable only to double period structure.

_____ c. A phrase group may include three phrases.

_____ d. A sectional double period has the cadential structure weak-weak-weak-strong.

_____ e. If each verse of a song is sung to the same music, the form is known as through-composed.

_____ f. In musical comedy verse and refrain structure, the verse is more interesting musically than the refrain.

_____ g. A repeated phrase is equivalent to a period in length, but not form.

_____ h. If one of the phrases modulates to another key, the form of the melody cannot be a double period.

_____ i. A parallel period may contain some varied material in the second phrase.

_____ j. An examination of cadences is a more reliable tool for understanding melody forms than tracing melodic material.

Total Possible: 100   Your Score _____

PROJECTS

Analysis

There is an important difference between accumulating data and reaching useful conclusions about a piece of music. While time-line diagrams are useful both in accumulating data and sharing conclusions with others, they do not constitute analysis in themselves. As you draw together your studies of melody forms by completing one or more of the projects, use a time-line as a beginning point in your analysis. Remember that while there are both knowledgeable and somewhat less helpful ways of understanding a given melody, musicians sometimes differ on the identification of phrases, cadences, and larger divisions.

Consider some or all of these points in an analysis of the works provided in the text and workbook:

1. Identify cadences, phrases, and periods (phrase groups).
2. Provide information about principal motives and their development.
3. Locate and classify the use of sequence (if any).
4. Study and report on elements of tonal construction (melodic tendencies and step progressions, for example) as well as range, tessitura, style, and so on.

Text

Thomas Arne, "When Daisies Pied," Text, page 355. Thomas Arne (1710–1778) was one of the most popular and influential English composers of his day. He wrote many popular opera, oratorios, and songs. This song is a setting of a text from Shakespeare's *Love's Labor Lost*. "When Daisies Pied" is in a form common in brief songs. Begin your analysis in G major, but note a change of key to D major as marked on the score. Identify the overall form of this song. Next, address the melody of each phrase. Identify principal motives and their treatment; instances of sequence, and so on. The imitation of a cuckoo appears at several points; more important, the text painting affects the formal development of the song. Be prepared to comment on this and other aspects of formal design.

Workbook/Anthology I

Alexander Hume, "Flow Gently Sweet Afton," workbook page 119.
Christoph Gluck, Gavotte from Amide, workbook page 120.

Johann Crüger, "Now Thank We All Our God," workbook page 121.
Frankie Lymon and Morris Levy, "Why Do Fools Fall in Love?" workbook page 122.

Composition

Verse and Refrain in Musical Comedy Style. Use Gershwin's *Oh, Lady Be Good* (page 311.) as a model and compose a brief verse and refrain in musical comedy style. Make a lead sheet (as shown in the example) for voice and an improvised piano accompaniment on chords you specify. As in the Gershwin song, make your verse less tuneful than the refrain.

Your first job will be to write a set of lyrics (one verse will be sufficient unless your instructor specifies otherwise). The lyrics that follow were composed by a freshman music major who developed the idea simply by flipping through a news magazine. An article on vegetarians caught her eye and, armed with a cookbook, she put together this humorous text.

VERSE

> (*Character is pensive, somewhat unsure with halting rhythms*)
> At times I just crave something wild,
> A meal with substance, served with style.
> > (*with more confidence*)
> But then I'll never walk that mile:
> For I'm a vegetarian!
>
> > (*again brooding*)
> Brussel sprouts with mushrooms plain,
> Carrots, peas, and whole-wheat grain;
> The only thing I roast is toast!
>
> > (*with confidence*)
> But far and wide, I still can boast:
> For I'm a vegetarian!
>
> A *committed* vegetarian!
> ... Well ... actually,
> Not a very-an, because ...

REFRAIN

> (*Character comes to life and sings in strict meter, much faster in the manner of a "patter" aria*)
> I love meat!
> But I don't eat it any more—not even for a treat.
> I love meat!
> Fried chicken, garlic shrimp and bacon simply can't be beat.
> I love meat!
> I'm sick of eggplant casserole and peppers stuffed with leek.
> Give me brisket, give me turkey
> Leg of lamb or beef in jerky,
> I love, really love meat!

A lead sheet gives the melody and outlines the chords that support it in a jazz or musical theatre style. Accompanists learn stock patterns and are expected to add improvised ornamentation including runs, trills, humorous embellishments, and so on. If a skilled accompanist is available for class performance, the lead sheet fragments that follow (and a little consultation among pianist, singer, and composer) are all that will be necessary for a polished reading.

CD 2, TRACK 38
Verse and Refrain
Sample Project

A simple verse and refrain can be quite interesting—even without the more colorful harmony (to be studied in later chapters of Volume I and throughout Volume II) that is typical of musical theatre style.

For Further Study

American Popular Song. Westerners, like the members of most world cultures, are singers. We sing when we are happy; we sing when we are sad. Our folk songs fall into several categories, but the most common are patriotism and societal bonding, religion, education, and the simple expression of feelings—whatever they are. British and American folk songs are usually brief and relatively simple because they are typically taught by rote. Since the mid-nineteenth century, however, music for commercial purposes (composed specifically with a modest level of musical knowledge in mind) has flourished in America. In the late nineteenth and early twentieth centuries, several developments created an immense demand for pop music—one that continues to the present day. First, stage works from Vaudeville to sophisticated musical comedies achieved increasing respectability and popularity. In addition, the advent of radio and sound recording created new media that made popular music both cheaper and more accessible.

Prepare the materials for a presentation or paper on American popular music from about 1900 through the origin of rock and roll in the 1950s. Use the Internet and other sources to research three or more of the following topics:

1. Composers and styles of "Tin Pan Alley"
2. Show tunes of the 1920s and 1930s
3. Blues
4. Country and Western
5. The Swing Era
6. Early Rock

Provide a listening list for each movement you choose and be prepared to play examples for a class presentation. In addition to basic historical and biographical information, study one or more scores for each topic and include technical information about the structure of the music.

Thomas Arne, "When Daisies Pied"

G Major:

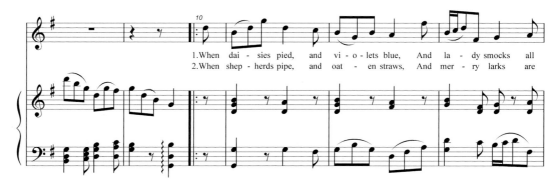

CHAPTER 10
Secondary Function

Function in tonal music is defined as the systematic progression of chords from active to stable roles. As we have discussed, traditional music is energized by persistent dominant-tonic progressions. The function is termed PRIMARY when these progressions reinforce the tonic. In D major, for example, a dominant-tonic progression channels our attention to the pitch D through the strong tendency of ↑$\hat{7}$ combined with a descending-fifth root movement. A triad or chord of dominant function provides the impetus necessary to emphasize the primary tonic.[1]

Primary Function

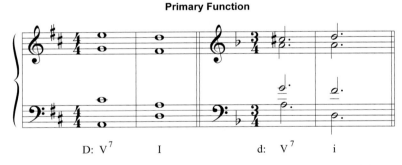

Composers define the primary tonal area through repetition, relative length, and association with an important theme. Still, all but the shortest compositions require more variety than is available within any one major or minor scale. Even when we consider the possibilities presented by chromatic embellishments (a chromatic neighboring tone, for example) and alterations in minor, additional resources are absolutely necessary to provide vitality. In most traditional works, variety is achieved through *secondary function*.

---

[1]In addition to the dominant and dominant-seventh chords, other sonorities, to be discussed later in this chapter, have the potential to be heard in a dominant role.

SECONDARY FUNCTION

The process that establishes a key center *other* than the primary tonic is termed SECONDARY FUNCTION. Secondary progressions not only provide harmonic and melodic color, but they fortify the principal tonality as well. In the last example, primary function is represented by the two-chord progression that establishes D as a pitch reference. In a key other than D, the same progression still establishes D as a pitch reference. If the primary tonality is not D, however, the function occurs at a secondary level.

Study the harmonic sketch in the next example. The tonic key, G major, is established not only by an opening dominant-tonic progression, but also through the cadential formula (IV–V–I) at the end of the line. The boxed chords, however, focus on D major and represent secondary function in the key of the dominant.

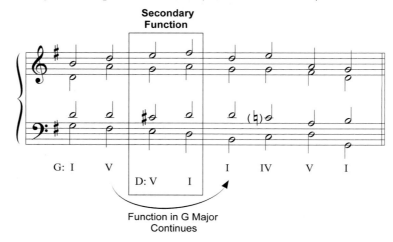

The harmony in the last example occurs in the *Chaconne in G Major* by George Frideric Handel. The primary tonic is G major, but with the C♯, we hear

CD 2, TRACK 39
G. F. Handel, Chaconne in G Minor
Secondary Function

secondary function in measures 2–3. Inversions smooth the bass line and the 7–6 suspension in measure 3 (as well as other nonchord tones) provide additional melodic interest.[2]

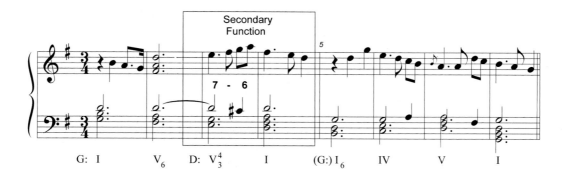

---

[2]A chaconne is a type of variation form that was popular during the Baroque era.

A passage from Bach's setting of the chorale tune "*Freu dich sehr, o meine Seele*" ("O Be Glad, My Soul, Be Cheerful") is nearly identical to the Handel phrase in the last example. The key is again G major; in this series, however, two dominant-tonic progressions create the secondary area of D major.

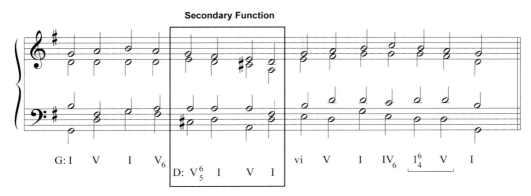

Compare the four-part arrangement below with the previous harmonic reduction. While several chords are inverted in order to provide a smoother bass line, there are relatively few nonchord tones in this passage (see measures 6 and 7).

CD 2, TRACK 40
J. S. Bach, "O Be Glad, My Soul, Be Cheerful"
Anonymous 15th-century Melody
Secondary Function

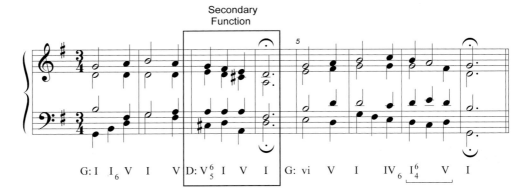

The key of Bach's chorale is G major, but accidentals disrupt the natural melodic tendencies in the primary tonic and introduce a new, *local* area of emphasis on the dominant (D major). In effect, D has been made a tonic *within* G major—a procedure called *tonicization*.

Tonicization

A temporary tonic is created within a prevailing tonality through a process called TONICIZATION. In Bach's setting of "O Be Glad, My Soul, Be Cheerful" (in the last passage), we would not term the brief excursion from G major a modulation (that is, a change of key) because the sensation of G as the tonic is never really lost. Indeed, G major returns immediately after the tonicization and is reconfirmed by a I_4^6–V–I cadence formula (measures 7–8). Moreover, the tonicization of D major (the dominant key) actually enhances our perception of G major as the primary tonal area.

Tonicizations occur in minor keys just as they do in major. Whether the mode is major or minor, composers use the same chords to tonicize the dominant. Max Bruch (1838–1920) was a German composer of Jewish heritage who was known in his time as a composer of orchestral, keyboard, and vocal works—

CD 2, TRACK 41

Max Bruch, Andante Con Moto from *Three Piano Pieces*, Op. 12, No. 2 Tonicization

often employing Jewish folk tunes. The next passage, from Bruch's *Piano Pieces*, Op. 12, begins in G minor, tonicizes the dominant in measures 7–8, then returns to the primary tonic.

Notice in the following reduction of the Bruch excerpt that the fully diminished leading-tone seventh (vii°₇) is central in establishing the primary tonality of G minor; the dominant seventh, on the other hand, tonicizes the secondary area—D major.

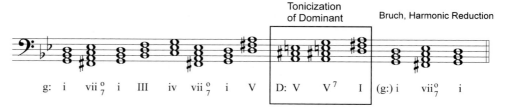

In the three previous musical excerpts (works by Handel, Bach, and Bruch), the tonicized area is the dominant. Next to the tonic, the dominant is the most important triad in the diatonic inventory. Thus, a tonicization of the dominant actually *strengthens* the tonic key. Likewise, the subdominant is a frequent area for tonicization (as will be discussed presently) because it increases our anticipation of the dominant. Finally, the submediant key (the relative minor in a major key), having the same pitch inventory as the tonic key, is also frequently tonicized.

Tonic Key

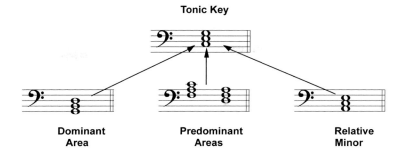

| Dominant | Predominant | Relative |
| Area | Areas | Minor |

Secondary Dominants and Tonics

The primary dominant facilitates the establishment of primary function. A SECONDARY DOMINANT, however, moves the tonality toward a new, "local" tonic. In analysis, we usually underscore secondary dominant-tonic relationships in order to clarify the overall dominance of the tonic key. In addition to reinforcing the primary tonality, the secondary dominant chord typically contains one or more accidentals that briefly tonicize the key. In its supplementary role, a secondary dominant chord is defined by the resolution that follows.

   Tonicization in Major.   The tonic represents primary function. With one important exception, any other diatonic scale degree can be tonicized. We may make the major or minor triads built upon $\hat{2}$, $\hat{3}$, $\hat{4}$, $\hat{5}$, or $\hat{6}$ sound like temporary tonics by preceding them with the appropriate dominant. But by definition, the tonic triad is a position of stability. The leading-tone triad, therefore, is *not* tonicized because it is diminished in quality and cannot be heard as a tonic.

Potential Areas for Secondary Function

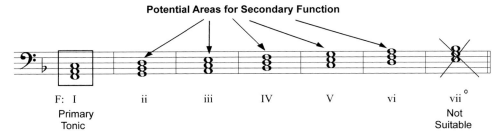

   Tonicization in Minor.   In minor keys, the dominant and subdominant triads are the most frequently tonicized. While the mediant rarely occurs as a secondary area in major keys, it is frequently tonicized in minor keys (the relative major). In addition, the *subtonic triad* in minor (and unavailable in major) is also often tonicized. The diminished supertonic and leading-tone triads are unsuitable for tonicization.

Potential Areas for Secondary Function
Minor

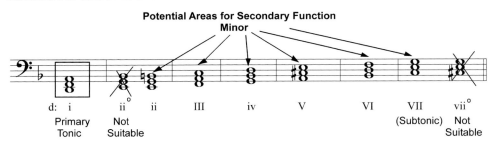

Secondary dominants are perceived through a *retroactive* association. In any given major or minor key, a chromatic chord tone creates instability by re-aligning the context. In F major, for example, if C♯ is introduced and subsequently resolves to D, we hear the former pitch *retroactively* as a new ↑7̂. Combined with the powerful descending fifth root movement, the C♯ diverts our orientation briefly from F major to D minor (the relative minor).

While the harmonic sketch in the last passage provides variety within the key of F major, we might *further* embellish (and strengthen) the primary tonic with a tonicization of the supertonic (G minor).

Tonicization of vi and ii

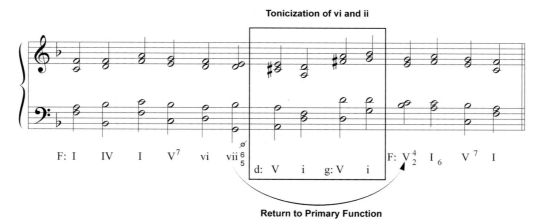

Return to Primary Function

The chords in the last example are extracted from Bach's harmonization of the sixteenth-century tune "*Herr Christ, der einig Gotts Sohn*" ("The Only Son from Heaven"). The primary key is F major. However, within the first three measures, both the submediant and the supertonic areas are tonicized.

CD 2, TRACK 42

J. S. Bach, "The Only Son From Heaven"
Anonymous 16th-century Melody
Tonicizations

F: I   IV   I   V^7 vi   vii$^{\o6}_5$ F: V$^4_2$ I$_6$ V^7 I

d: V^7 i

g: V   i

Although analysis in the last passage correctly identifies, D major, and G minor as temporary tonalities, no distinction is made between areas of primary and secondary function. Depending on our needs, we may use either (or both) of two different methods to analyze secondary functional progressions and to display them as ancillary to the primary tonic.

Analyzing Secondary Dominants

Since about 1960, theorists have employed two different methods to identify secondary dominants and their resolutions. We will term these approaches "basic" and "dual-level," respectively. The analysis of basic tonicizations is discussed in the following section.

Basic Tonicizations. A BASIC TONICIZATION usually includes two chords: one dominant in function and one tonic. In analysis, use a slash to separate the dominant sonority (V, V^7, or V$^6_5$, for example) from the diatonic area tonicized (such as ii, iii, or IV). Observe the analytical symbols in the next line:

F: V/ii   ii   V$^6_5$/V   V   V^7/vi   vi

In a spoken reference, we would describe the first progression above as "five of two to two." The second progression is "five six-five of five to five"; the third, "five-seven of six to six."

F: V/ii   ii   V$^6_5$/V   V   V^7/vi   vi

"five of two to two"   "five six-five of five to five"   "five-seven of six to six"

In Bach's harmonization of "The Only Son from Heaven" (the previous example), a dominant seventh chord tonicizes the submediant in F major. Instead of suggesting through our analysis that we are reoriented to a new tonic for the span of only two chords, the basic symbols clarify the secondary relationships. Likewise, because G minor is the supertonic area, the symbols V/ii–ii identify the second tonicization.

Bach, "Only Son from Heaven"
Basic Tonicization

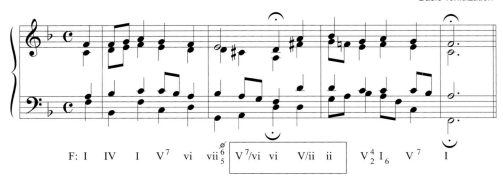

F: I   IV   I   V^7 vi   vii$^{\o6}_5$ $\boxed{\text{V}^7\text{/vi}\ \text{vi}\ \text{V/ii}\ \text{ii}}$ V$^4_2$ I$_6$ V^7 I

Dual-Level Analysis. DUAL-LEVEL analysis of secondary function is based on a symbol that specifies local function on one level and primary function on another. The two levels are often separated by a bracket.

F: $\underbrace{\text{V}^7\qquad\text{i}}_{\text{vi}}$ $\underbrace{\text{V}\qquad\text{i}}_{\text{ii}}$

In the previous Bach passage, notice that the D minor triad in the second measure is analyzed as a submediant even though it *sounds* like tonic in D minor. Likewise, the G minor chord in measure 3 has a tonic—not a predominant function. The dual-level analysis provides a clearer explanation of how tonality is being maintained at both secondary and primary levels.[3]

Bach, "Only Son from Heaven"
Dual-Level Analysis

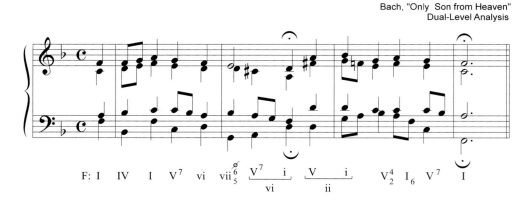

F: I   IV   I   V^7 vi   vii$^{\o6}_5$ $\underbrace{\text{V}^7\quad\text{i}}_{\text{vi}}$ $\underbrace{\text{V}\quad\text{i}}_{\text{ii}}$ V$^4_2$ I$_6$ V^7 I

In addition to a tonicization of the submediant and supertonic seen in the last example, secondary function within the mediant (with *two* accidentals), subdominant, and dominant as temporary tonics are analyzed as shown in the line below. In each case, the secondary dominant includes a seventh. In most cases, the dominant triad alone is sufficient to fulfill the dominant role

---

[3]Dual-level analysis is used primarily for passages of *extended tonicization* as discussed on page 378.

(although later in this chapter, we will discuss several other chords that have the same function).

F: V^7/III   III   F: V^7/IV   IV   F: V^7/V   V

Constructing Secondary-Dominant Progressions

Sketching secondary dominant-tonic relationships will strengthen your analytical skills by emphasizing the concepts involved. For the present, we will confine our examples to block chords. Voice leading in triads and chords with chromatic alterations will be discussed in a later section of this chapter.

Construct V/V in any major or minor key by following the three steps detailed below. Do your work on scratch paper at first if necessary, but the eventual goal is to perform the steps mentally.

1. Determine the root of the temporary tonic.
2. Build the dominant triad (or the dominant-seventh chord) in that *major* key.
3. Add accidentals as necessary (reflecting differences between the primary and secondary key signatures).

Asked to construct a V^7/V in E major, begin by identifying the root of the dominant triad in the primary tonic key (in this case, B). Next, in this key, build a dominant triad within this latter key signature. Within the primary key, construct the same chord and add one or more accidentals as necessary (an A♯ is needed in this case because E major has only four sharps).

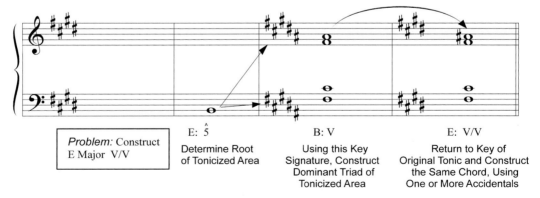

Problem: Construct E Major V/V	E: $\hat{5}$	B: V	E: V/V
	Determine Root of Tonicized Area	Using this Key Signature, Construct Dominant Triad of Tonicized Area	Return to Key of Original Tonic and Construct the Same Chord, Using One or More Accidentals

The process outlined in the last example may appear tedious, but it is learned quickly. Use an identical route to construct V^7/vi in E♭ major. The sixth scale degree is C; the dominant seventh of C (major or minor) is G–B–D–F. When we construct this chord in E♭ major, a B♮ is necessary.

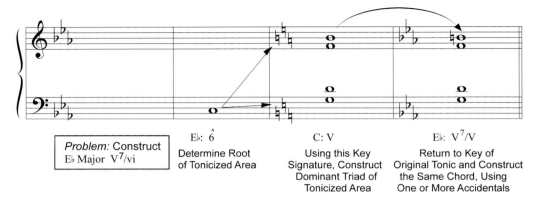

| *Problem:* Construct Eb Major V^7/vi | Eb: $\hat{6}$ Determine Root of Tonicized Area | C: V Using this Key Signature, Construct Dominant Triad of Tonicized Area | Eb: V^7/V Return to Key of Original Tonic and Construct the Same Chord, Using One or More Accidentals |

In a later section of this chapter, we will discuss the construction of other secondary dominant sonorities. For now, remember that to be heard as a dominant, a triad must be *major*. Use this fact as a way of double-checking your work to ensure that you have added any necessary accidental(s). If a secondary dominant seventh chord is needed, the quality must be major-minor.

WORKBOOK/ANTHOLOGY IV
I. Introduction to Secondary Function
page 123

REVIEW AND APPLICATION 10–1

Tonicization

Essential Terms

| dual-level analysis | secondary dominant | tonicization |
| primary function | secondary function | |

1. The progressions below are analyzed as modulations (complete changes of key). A better approach would be identification as a secondary dominant-tonic series. Use the blanks to revise the analysis using simple symbols (V/V–V, for example). Include arabic-numeral labels and other symbols as indicated in the original analysis.

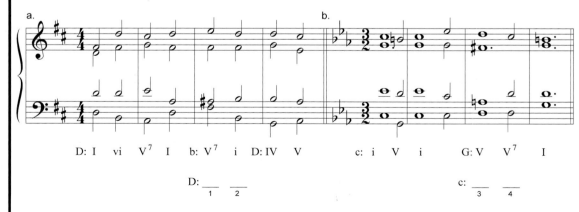

a.

D: I   vi   V^7 I   b: V^7 i   D: IV   V

b.

c: i   V   i   G: V   V^7 I

D: ___   ___
   1   2

c: ___   ___
   3   4

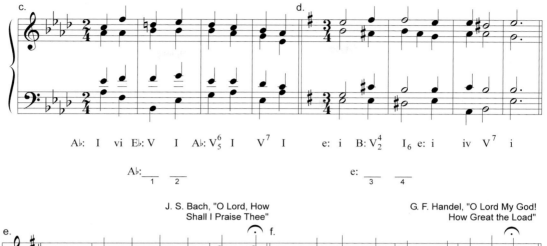

Ab: I vi Eb: V I Ab: V$_5^6$ I V^7 I   e: i B: V$_2^4$ I$_6$ e: i iv V^7 i

Ab: ___ ___
    1   2

e: ___ ___
   3   4

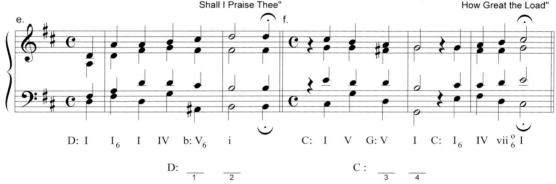

J. S. Bach, "O Lord, How
Shall I Praise Thee"

G. F. Handel, "O Lord My God!
How Great the Load"

D: I I$_6$ I IV b: V$_6$ i   C: I V G: V I C: I$_6$ IV vii$_6^o$ I

D: ___ ___
   1   2

C: ___ ___
   3   4

2. Using block chords (without voice-leading implications), write progressions that involve secondary dominants as indicated. Provide any needed accidental(s).

Bb: V I V/V V   e: i iv V^7/V V   D: V I v/vi vi

3. Provide roman-numeral analysis for these passages.

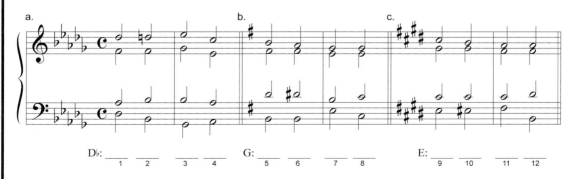

Db: ___ ___ ___ ___   G: ___ ___ ___ ___   E: ___ ___ ___ ___
    1   2   3   4   5   6   7   8   9 10 11 12

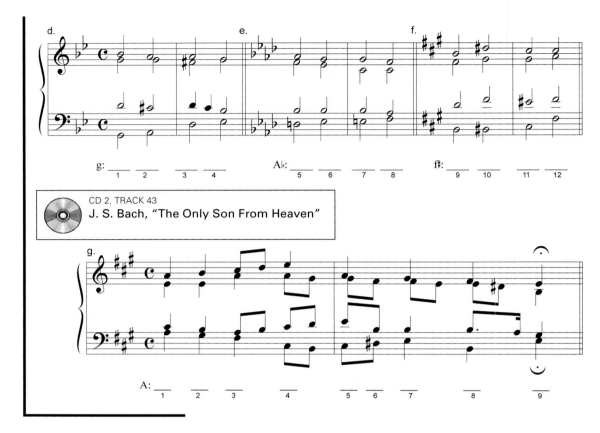

CD 2, TRACK 43
J. S. Bach, "The Only Son From Heaven"

SELF-TEST 10–1

Time Limit: 5 Minutes

1. Match each statement with a term from the list. More than one answer is correct in some cases. *Scoring: Subtract 4 for each error.*

   A. Primary function   E. Secondary dominant
   B. Secondary function   F. Simple tonicization
   C. Local key   G. Secondary tonic
   D. Tonicization

   _____ a. The creation of tonic function at a secondary level

   _____ b. The process of creating an area of secondary function

   _____ c. Chord that creates tonic function at a local level

   _____ d. Harmonic function in the tonic key

   _____ e. Term for an area of secondary function

_____ f. Chord that realigns tendency tones

_____ g. Use of symbols such as V/ii, V/V, and so on

2. Write the chord that would facilitate a dominant/tonic progression at the secondary level suggested. Provide any necessary accidental. *Scoring: Subtract 9 points for an incorrect notation (including missing or extra accidentals).*

       F: V / ii   A: V / vi   g: V / V

3. Provide roman-numeral analysis (including arabic-numeral labels) for chords where blanks appear. *Scoring: Subtract 7 points for an error.*

CD 2, TRACK 44

J. S. Bach, "In Thee, Lord, Have I Put My Trust" (Edited)
Self Test 10-1, Question 3

F: ___ ___ ___   ___ ___ ___
    1 2 3   4 5 6

4. What is the term that designates function at a secondary level? *Scoring: Subtract 3 points for an incorrect answer.*

_____

Total Possible: 100   Your Score _____

FUNCTION IN CHROMATIC PROGRESSIONS

Successful tonal composers do not employ chromatic pitches randomly. Moreover, the accidentals themselves hold the key to function. Used in secondary dominant chords, accidentals fall into three broad categories that facilitate our recognition of their functional roles. We will study each of these categories in turn in the present section.

1. The accidental is a new leading tone.

2. The accidental is a new fourth-scale degree.

3. The *absence* of an accidental creates an area of secondary function.

Tonicization With New Leading Tone

Tonicizations are often effected through the introduction of an accidental that is heard retroactively as a new leading tone. Remember that the cancellation of a flat has the same effect as a sharp and may likewise function as ↑$\hat{7}$ in a temporary area. In addition, if a key has five, six, or seven sharps, a new ↑$\hat{7}$ may be a *double sharp*. Each of the chords below, for example, includes an accidental that may be heard as a new ↑$\hat{7}$. For the present, we will limit our discussion to chords in which a new ↑$\hat{7}$ appears in major triads and major-minor seventh chords.

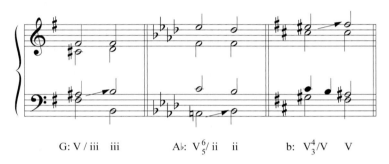

$$\text{G: V / iii \quad iii} \qquad \text{A}\flat\text{: V}^6_5\text{/ ii \quad ii} \qquad \text{b: V}^4_3\text{/V \quad V}$$

In major keys, a tonicization of the mediant always involves *two* accidentals—both of them "sharps" (including, of course, the possibility of canceled flats and double sharps). When a chord has two "new" sharps, the last of them (in the order of sharps) usually functions as the new ↑$\hat{7}$.

New Leading Tones

$$\text{G: \quad V}^7\text{/V} \qquad \text{E}\flat\text{: \quad V}^7\text{/V} \qquad \text{C}\sharp\text{: \quad V/V}$$

As we have discussed, both harmonic and melodic factors must coincide to facilitate an effective secondary dominant-tonic relationship:

1. The new ↑$\hat{7}$ ascends to $\hat{8}$ in an outer voice. In inner voices, however, new ↑$\hat{7}$ may descend or effect another resolution.

2. The chord following the new ↑$\hat{7}$ should permit a dominant-tonic progression in the secondary area. That is, if a pitch is to be heard as a new ↑$\hat{7}$, a new $\hat{8}$ must be available as a chord tone in the following harmony.

As we can see in Bach's harmonization of "The Only Son from Heaven" (page 371), the C$\sharp$ in measure 2 is a new ↑$\hat{7}$ that emphasizes D, the submediant in F major. Without the accidental, the chord would be simply a diatonic mediant (A–C–E)—the triad with the most ambiguous functional tendencies. With the C♯, however, the triad A–C♯–E is *major* in quality, can no longer be heard as diatonic in F major, and functions instead as a secondary dominant to tonicize the submediant. The new ↑7̂ appears in an inner voice, so Bach chose an alternate resolution down to 5̂. The passing seventh is analyzed here as the seventh of a secondary-dominant seventh (A–C♯–E–G). Just as correctly, the pitch G could be heard as a passing (nonchord) tone.

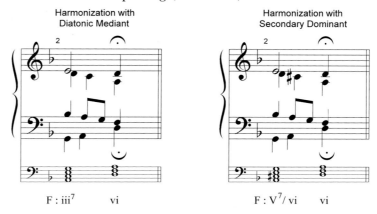

Likewise, the triad on the last beat of measure 2 in the Bach harmonization is not a submediant (a minor triad), but another secondary dominant. This time, F♯ creates a major triad and provides a leading tone to G—the supertonic.

Tonicization is common in popular music. In Gershwin's *Oh, Lady Be Good,* for example, the verse ends with a tonicization of the dominant (V⁷/V–V⁷–I). In this case, the A♯ that empowers the dominant effect descends a chromatic half step to become the seventh of a dominant seventh at the primary level—a common alternate resolution.

Alongside the secondary progression, a number of nonchord tones create an interesting passage that builds momentum prior to the beginning of the refrain (not shown).

CD 2, TRACK 45
George Gershwin, *Oh, Lady Be Good*
Tonicization with New Leading Tone

Although *Oh, Lady Be Good* begins in E minor, the verse ends in the major mode (with the additional three sharps provided as accidentals).[4] Notice that without the A♯ in measure 19, the progression would be a common predominant-dominant-tonic series (ii⁷–V⁷–I). The secondary dominant fulfills the predominant role and, at the same time, adds color and strength to the dominant.

Recognizing Secondary Relationships.   When you encounter an accidental in traditional music, remember that it has a stereotypical role at either the primary or the secondary level. Assuming that there is not a key change (indicated, perhaps, by a new key signature), bear in mind two possibilities before considering secondary function:

1. *Is the accidental nonchordal?* Many accidentals in tonal music can be accounted for as chromatic passing tones, neighboring tones, appoggiaturas, and so on.

2. *Is the key minor?* If so, the accidental may be the result of ↑$\hat{6}$ or (↑)$\hat{7}$.

In some compositions, accidentals result entirely from altered $\hat{6}$ or $\hat{7}$. If a work (or section) is in minor, numerous accidentals may be generated through ↑$\hat{6}$ or ↑$\hat{7}$ (and also from the cancellation of these accidentals, of course). At the same time, chromatic nonchord tones provide colorful additions to the diatonic vocabulary. Although other explanations are possible, all of the accidentals in the next passage can be viewed either as alterations in minor or as chromatic nonchord tones.

CD 2, TRACK 46-1 RECOGNIZING SECONDARY DOMINANTS (2 PARTS)
Jean-Philippe Rameau, Menuet
Nonchord Tones

---

[4]Popular composers and arrangers traditionally provide harmonic explanations for pitches that actually have simpler nonchordal underpinnings. The V⁷ in measure 19, for example, is described in the published score as B¹³ (with the G♯ as a thirteenth above the root). Because improvisation is so important in jazz and commercial music, however, the extended tertian harmonization provides a wide range of pitches that "work" with the given bass and melody.

g: V   V

g: V₆   i   (v)   iv₆   V

If a chromatic pitch cannot be explained as a nonchord tone or an alteration in minor, the next logical possibility is a secondary dominant; that is, the accidental may be a new *leading tone*. Test the theory by asking whether a new *tonic pitch* appears in the following chord. Remember, in an inner voice, ↑$\hat{7}$ may not resolve directly to $\hat{8}$. Study the resolutions of secondary dominants in Bach's harmonization of "*Valet will ich dir geben*" (in the next example). Two different areas are tonicized within the first three phrases.

TRACK 46-2 RECOGNIZING SECONDARY DOMINANTS
J. S. Bach, "Valet, Would I Now Thee Give"
melody by Valerius Herberger

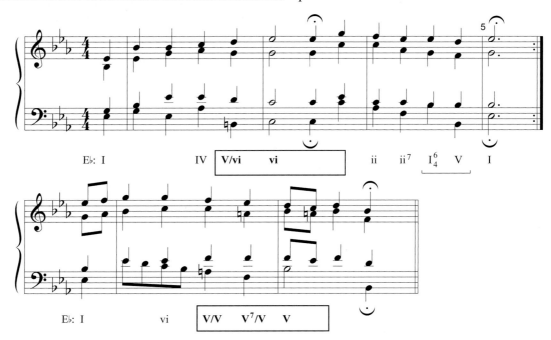

Eb: I   IV   **V/vi vi**   ii   ii⁷ I⁶₄ V   I

Eb: I   vi   **V/V V⁷/V V**

When accidentals are clearly chord tones, an added sharp (or a flat that is made natural) may be a new $\uparrow\hat{7}$ creating the instability necessary to define a new, temporary tonality. As we have learned, either a major triad or a major-minor seventh chord may define the new key. Remember, however, that a secondary dominant chord by itself is not proof of a new relationship. Both the temporary dominant *and the new tonic* are necessary to establish a tonicization.

Tonicization with the Fourth Scale Degree

Next to the leading tone, $\hat{4}$ has the strongest tonal tendency. In a V^7–I progression, for example, $\hat{4}$, the seventh of the dominant seventh, resolves down by step to $\hat{3}$. We have discussed tonicizations in which an accidental—a new $\uparrow\hat{7}$—generates the secondary dominant. In some tonicizations, however, the secondary dominant chord comprises only diatonic pitches. Consider a tonicization of the subdominant in F major, for example. The dominant of B♭ is F–A–C; the new (temporary) $\uparrow\hat{7}$ is A.

F: V/IV   IV

Although a skilled composer could cause the listener to perceive a tonicization of the subdominant with the chords in the last example, there is no accidental to more clearly differentiate between a tonicization and a simple I–IV progression. Accordingly, composers often employ the *dominant seventh* in a tonicization of the subdominant. The seventh is an accidental—a new flat—and is heard, retroactively, as $\hat{4}$ in the area tonicized.[5] Just as the new $\uparrow\hat{7}$ resolves to $\hat{8}$ in other tonicizations already discussed, the new $\hat{4}$ almost invariably descends to $\hat{3}$ to clarify the secondary area. In the second example below, the E♭ guides the listener away from the primary tonic (F major) and toward the subdominant.

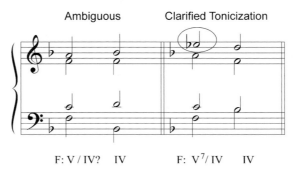

F: V / IV?   IV   F: V⁷/ IV   IV

Bach begins the Sarabande from the fourth *English Suite* with a tonicization of the subdominant. Without the E♭, we would hear the second chord in the passage that follows as the tonic in F major. The new flat, however, clarifies the secondary area (as $\hat{4}$ descends to $\hat{3}$). In the third and fourth measures, F

---

[5]A sharp that is canceled may also be a "new flat." Likewise, a tonicization of the subdominant in the key of C♭ major would typically include B♭♭.

major is confirmed through a series of tonic-dominant progressions. Bach wrote his Sarabande for performance on the harpsichord. The detailed notation of individual lines, however, is an imitation of the lute—a popular instrument of Bach's day.

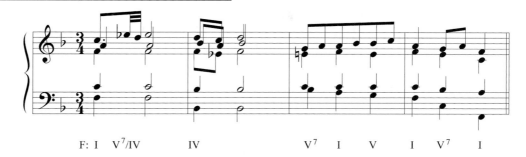

Mozart employs a similar tonicization of the subdominant in his Sonata in F Major. Notice the bass pedal heard throughout the phrase on the first beat of each measure.

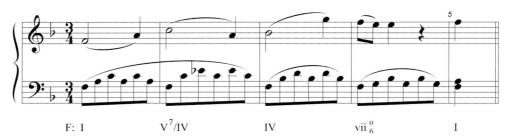

Tonicization of the Subdominant in Minor. In minor keys, the subdominant triad is minor in quality. A minor triad cannot function as a dominant, so in minor keys, we are not likely to confuse the tonic with V/iv. Because a new ↑$\hat{7}$ is present in the secondary dominant triad, the seventh is optional.

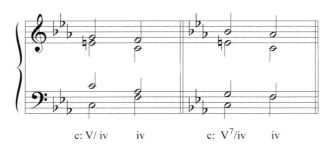

Bach's harmonization of "*Vater unser im Himmelreich*" ("Our Father, Thou in Heaven Above"), a sixteenth-century German melody, illustrates the first of the two progressions in the last example. The key of the chorale is C minor. Beginning the last phrase, however, we hear the E♮ as a new ↑$\hat{7}$ even without a

CD 2, TRACK 48-1 TONICIZATION OF THE MEDIANT (2 PARTS)
J. S. Bach, "Our Father, Thou in Heaven Above"
Anonymous 16th-century Melody

harmonic seventh (as we would need in C major). Note also the cadence formula that includes both a cadential six-four and a picardy third.

c: V_6/iv   iv   V   VI   iv i_4^6 V^7 I

(picardy third)

WORKBOOK/ANTHOLOGY I
II. Secondary Function, Continued page 127

Tonicization of the Submediant in Minor.   A new flat also facilitates a tonicization of the submediant area in minor keys. As is the case with the subdominant in major, V/VI in minor includes no accidental to define the new area. Accordingly, the dominant seventh is often employed. The accidental is a new $\hat{4}$, becomes the seventh of the secondary dominant seventh, and resolves to $\hat{3}$ in the new key.

f♯: III   VI   f♯: V^7/VI   VI

As the German composer Paul Hindemith (1895–1963) admonished his composition students, "There are only twelve tones; you must use them carefully." Knowledgeable tonal composers usually heed Hindemith's advice. Accidentals are especially volatile and are not employed arbitrarily in traditional music.

Tonicization of the Mediant in Minor.   The leading tone has long been central to our Western system of musical organization. As we have discussed, before the advent of tonality in the late sixteenth century, composers routinely raised the seventh degree of a minor scale or mode to provide a leading tone. We are so conditioned to ↑$\hat{7}$–$\hat{8}$ in ascending passages that except in stereotypical patterns, a loss of the leading tone may quickly result in tonal ambiguity.

Composers exploit this effect in tonicizations of the mediant in minor (the relative major). Minor and relative major keys have a common pitch inventory. In A minor, for example, G♯ (an accidental) centers our attention on the tonic.

If the accidental is omitted, appropriate melodic and harmonic choices quickly establish C major. This effect is illustrated in Bach's harmonization of the melody "O How Cheating, O How Fleeting." The first measure establishes A minor; the second, with cautionary G♮, is a tonicization of the mediant.

J. S. Bach, "Oh How Cheating, O How Fleeting"
Melody by Michael Franck, 1562

a: i   V   i   i   V⁷/III III

Gershwin used an identical relationship in his song *Oh, Lady Be Good*. The first phrase of the verse is in E minor. Beginning with measure 5, however, the D♯ disappears and the tonic gravitates toward the relative major. The first phrase of the melody descends from $\hat{5}$-$\hat{1}$ in E minor; the second mirrors this structure a third higher. Likewise, the harmony of the second phrase is a transposition of the first.

TRACK 48-2 TONICIZATION OF THE MEDIANT
George Gershwin, *Oh, Lady Be Good*
Popular Style

Extended Tonicization

While most tonicizations, by definition, are brief, some are more extensive and may include not only dominant and tonic, but secondary *predominant* chords as well. An effective analysis of such passages often depends on maintaining a consistent approach. Earlier in this chapter, we discussed an analytical procedure for basic (brief) secondary function. If the tonicization is more extended, dual-level analysis (page 364) may be more helpful.

The basic analysis of secondary function given on page 377 for Gershwin's song is correct, but we may lose track of the inherent function in the tonic key. Compare the basic and dual-level analyses in the next example. On a local level, functional progressions occur in G major, and are shown above the line. The numeral "III" (below the line) designates the mediant in the primary key. The extended (dual-level) approach tells us that the function has shifted to the relative major, but specifies that the primary tonic remains E minor.

George Gershwin, "Oh, Lady Be Good"

A phrase from Haydn's *God Save the Emperor Franz,* is more logically explained when analyzed as an extended tonicization of the dominant (including a secondary *predominant* chord). Compare the extended analysis below with the one on page 395. Again, both analyses are helpful, but the version here makes clear the predominant, dominant, and tonic roles of each chord.

CD 2, TRACK 49
Joseph Haydn, Quartet, Op. 76, No. 3 (II)
Tonicization of the Dominant

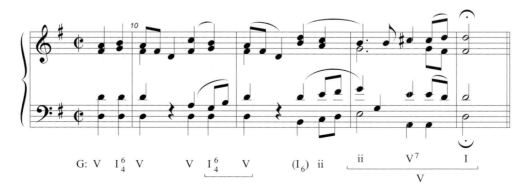

Dual-level analysis is valuable in highlighting substitute functions at a secondary level—passages that may otherwise appear harmonically ambiguous. The reduction that follows is in B minor; V/III progresses not to the mediant, however, but to an apparently nonfunctional F♯ minor triad. The first analysis of the passage is dubious, but in the second, the dual-level method pinpoints a tonic substitute (V–vi) in A major (the subtonic key).

We study harmony and voice leading through four-part chorale settings because within the space of a few beats, tonal areas and harmonic implications may vary significantly. The progression in the final example in this section occurs in Bach's harmonization of *"Es wolle Gott uns gnädig sein"* ("May God Bestow on Us His Grace"). In addition to the use of a dominant-tonic substitute pro-

CD 2, TRACK 50
J. S. Bach, "May God Bestow on Us His Grace"
melody by Matthias Greitter, ca. 1525

gression at a secondary level (measure 17), notice the V_5^6/V in the extended analysis (this constitutes *tertiary function* in B minor).

Most common-practice harmonies do not appear as complex as those in the last passage. Still, viewed at the functional (upper) level, notice that the progressions could hardly be *simpler*. As we have discussed, dominant-tonic chains predominate in tonal music; the predominant function provides variety and prepares the dominant-tonic progression. Composers use tonicization (through a new ↑$\hat{7}$, a new $\hat{4}$, or the cancellation of an accidental) not only to strengthen the tonic key, but also to maintain the listener's interest.

Constructing Secondary Progressions With Subdominant and Submediant

Earlier in this chapter, we studied the construction of secondary dominant-tonic relationships through a new ↑$\hat{7}$. For tonicizations of the subdominant in major or of the submediant in minor, the process is only slightly different:

1. Determine the root of the temporary tonic.

2. Build the dominant seventh chord in that *major* key.

3. Add accidentals as necessary (reflecting differences between the primary and secondary key signatures).

Create a harmonic sketch that includes a tonicization of the subdominant in B♭ major beginning with the root of the secondary area (E♭); next, build a dominant seventh in that key (B♭–D–F–A♭). Finally, add the accidental (A♭), which is necessary in the primary tonic (B♭ major).

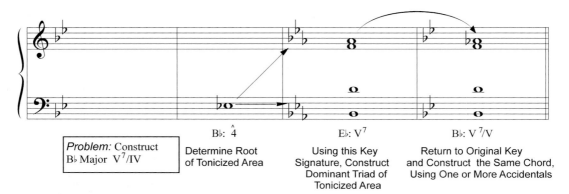

In D♯ minor, use an identical process to tonicize the submediant with a dominant seventh chord. The sixth scale degree is B. In the "local" key, the dominant seventh is F♯–A♯–C♯–E♮ with the E♮ functioning as a new $\hat{4}$ and resolving to $\hat{3}$.

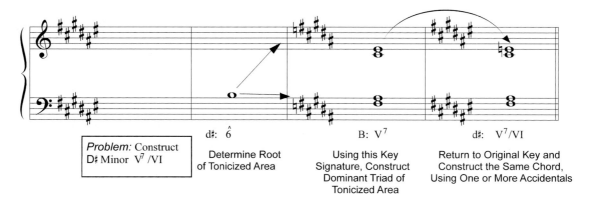

Finally, remember that some tonicizations (such as V/III in minor) occur *without* an accidental. To construct V₆/III in G♯ minor, for example, the mere absence of an F✗ creates the potential for a shift to the relative major.

g♯: V   i   g♯: V⁷/III   III

WORKBOOK/ANTHOLOGY I
III. Other Aspects of Secondary
Function, page 129

REVIEW AND APPLICATION 10–2

Tonicizing the Subdominant and Other Areas

Essential Terms

no new terms

CD 2, TRACK 51-1 REVIEW AND APPLICATION 10-2 (2 PARTS)
Exercise 1-a and 1-b

1. The following fragments are from Bach's chorale harmonizations. Provide roman numerals (including the analysis of secondary function as necessary).

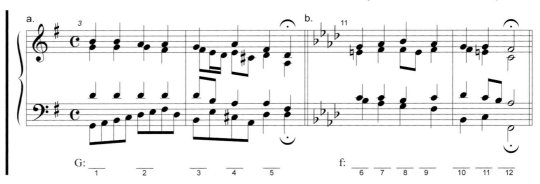

TRACK 51-2 REVIEW AND APPLICATION 10-2
Exercise 1-c and 1-d

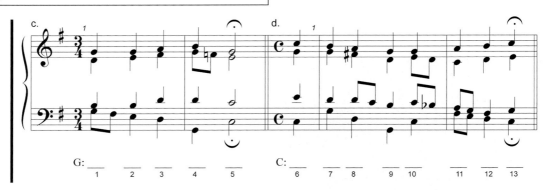

2. Use block chords to construct the secondary dominants and tonics. Add accidentals as necessary.

3. Each of the chords below has the potential to function as a diatonic triad, a primary dominant, or a secondary dominant in a number of different keys. For each key listed, provide an appropriate analytical symbol (IV, V^7, V$^6_5$/IV, and so on). These examples are notated entirely with accidentals.

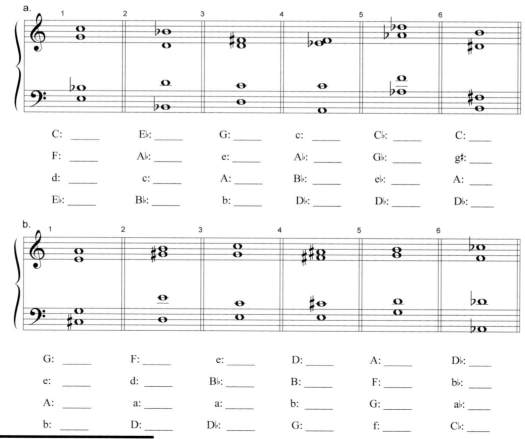

C: _____	E♭: _____	G: _____	c: _____	C♭: _____	C: _____
F: _____	A♭: _____	e: _____	A♭: _____	G♭: _____	g♯: _____
d: _____	c: _____	A: _____	B♭: _____	e♭: _____	A: _____
E♭: _____	B♭: _____	b: _____	D♭: _____	D♭: _____	D♭: _____

G: _____	F: _____	e: _____	D: _____	A: _____	D♭: _____
e: _____	d: _____	B♭: _____	B: _____	F: _____	b♭: _____
A: _____	a: _____	a: _____	b: _____	G: _____	a♭: _____
b: _____	D: _____	D♭: _____	G: _____	f: _____	C♭: _____

SELF-TEST 10–2

Time Limit: 5 Minutes

1. Make a check mark by all correct statements concerning each topic. In some cases, only one statement is correct; in others, all may be correct. Consider each problem entirely right or entirely wrong. *Scoring: Subtract 7 points for an incorrect answer.*

   a. In major keys,

   _____ (1) the leading-tone triad is not tonicized.

   _____ (2) the dominant is often tonicized.

   _____ (3) a tonicization of the submediant requires two accidentals.

   _____ (4) a tonicization of the subdominant is ineffective without the dominant seventh.

   b. A dominant seventh chord

   _____ (1) is often employed in a tonicization.

   _____ (2) is necessary in a tonicization of the supertonic in major keys.

   _____ (3) can be used to tonicize the subtonic in minor keys.

   _____ (4) can be used to tonicize the leading-tone triad in major keys.

   c. In analysis,

   _____ (1) a new flat may be a new leading tone.

   _____ (2) the basic method of charting secondary function is better than a dual-level approach.

   _____ (3) a new sharp is a chromatic nonchord tone.

   _____ (4) an extended tonicization may be analyzed with the dual-level method.

   d. In determining the role of a new accidental, the following are logical steps:

   _____ (1) Consider the accidental as nonchordal.

   _____ (2) View the accidental as a new leading tone.

   _____ (3) Evaluate the accidental as a lowered second scale degree.

   _____ (4) All of the above are appropriate.

2. Using block chords, construct the three chords suggested. Add accidentals as necessary. *Scoring: Subtract 10 for each incorrect notation.*

F: V^7/IV f#: V^6_5/VI Db: V^4_2/vi

3. Provide a detailed analysis of the six chords where blanks appear. Expect secondary function. Exclude nonchord tones from your analysis. *Scoring: Subtract 7 points for an incorrect analytical symbol (consider each problem entirely right or entirely wrong).*

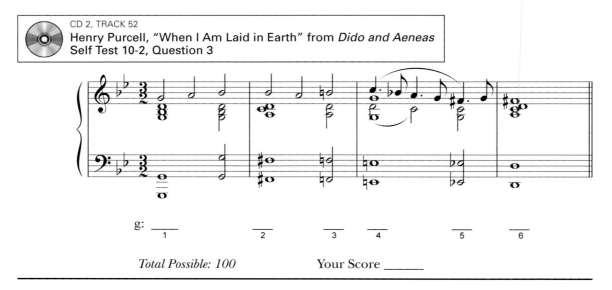

CD 2, TRACK 52
Henry Purcell, "When I Am Laid in Earth" from *Dido and Aeneas*
Self Test 10-2, Question 3

Total Possible: 100   Your Score _____

SECONDARY LEADING-TONE CHORDS

While the dominant and dominant-seventh chords are convenient sonorities for establishing a temporary tonic, other chords fulfill this role as well. You will remember that two different diatonic triads have dominant function: V and vii°. Accordingly, we may tonicize a secondary area with either the leading-tone triad or with the leading-tone seventh. Moreover, the leading-tone seventh may be either half- or fully diminished. In short, any of the chords below has the power to define the pitch F as the tonic.

Chords of Dominant Function

F: V   I   V⁷   I   vii°   I   vii°⁷   I   vii°⁷   i

Composers use the leading-tone triad in secondary progressions as they would the dominant-seventh chord. In the next passage, for example, vii°/V creates an emphasis on the dominant.

D: I   V⁷   I   IV   vii°₆/V   V

Voice leading in a secondary leading-tone chord follows expected guidelines: $\hat{4}$ descends to $\hat{3}$; ↑$\hat{7}$ ascends to $\hat{8}$ in an outer voice. This same resolution occurs typically in both major and minor. As is the case with diminished triads generally, the chord appears in first inversion with the bass doubled.

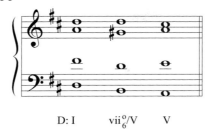

$$D:\ I \qquad vii^{o}_{6}/V \qquad V$$

The progression in the last example is extracted from Bach's harmonization of "*Gott den Vater wohn' uns bei*" ("God the Father, Be Our Stay"). Notice that the voice leading in both the primary (measure 5) and the secondary (measure 6) leading-tone triads is identical.

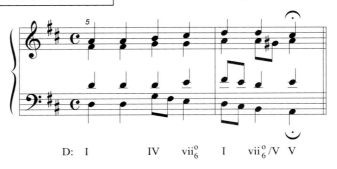

$$D:\ I \qquad\qquad IV \quad vii^{o}_{6} \quad I \quad vii^{o}_{6}/V \ \ V$$

Secondary Leading-Tone Sevenths. While traditional composers relied upon the half-diminished leading-tone seventh chord to initiate a tonicization, the fully diminished leading-tone seventh is more common. In the next passage, from Bach's harmonization of "*Hinunter ist der Sonnenschein*" ("The Happy Sunshine Now Is Gone"), notice the tonicization of the supertonic that employs both vii°7/ii and V/ii (ending in a half cadence with a 4–3 suspension at the secondary level). The dual-level (extended) analysis clarifies the harmonic function of Bach's phrase.

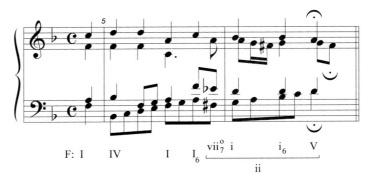

$$F:\ I \qquad IV \qquad I \quad I_6 \quad \underbrace{vii^{o}_{7}\ i \qquad i_6 \quad V}_{ii}$$

In the third movement of his Sonata in E Major, Beethoven employs the fully diminished seventh to tonicize both the subdominant and the dominant areas in the course of a passage in the final movement. The key is E minor. Triplets (unmarked after the first beat) create an animated texture that is punctuated by quarter notes in the bass. Despite three tonicizations, a basic analytical approach is sufficient here.

Ludwig van Beethoven, Sonata in E Major, Op. 14, No. 1 (III)

Even in major keys, composers often use the fully diminished seventh as a chord of dominant function in a secondary progression. Bach's chorale "*Lobe den Herren, den mächtigen König der Ehren*" ("Praise to the Lord, the Almighty") is in A major, but the composer embellishes the final phrase with a tonicization of the submediant including a fully diminished seventh. Note the occurrence of a secondary *predominant* (measure 16).

J. S. Bach, "Praise to the Lord, the Almighty"
Anonymous 17th century Melody
Submediant Seventh

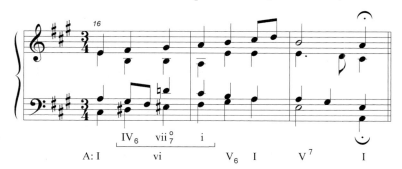

Ornamented and Atypical Resolutions

Just as functional progressions are often colored by nonchord tones and exceptional resolutions, so, too, are tonicizations enriched and even obscured by atypical resolutions. Secondary dominant chords, for example, may occur as embellishing sonorities—the result of converging nonchord tones. Likewise, progressions at secondary levels may involve a tonic substitute (V–vi, for example). Both of these possibilities appear in Bach's harmonization of *"Jesus, meine Zuversucht"* ("Jesus Christ, My Sure Defense") by Johann Crüger. The chord analyzed as vii$^{\varnothing}_7$/V (measure 8) is actually formed through passing tones in the bass and tenor, and suggests a change in harmonic rhythm that is not support-

CD 2, TRACK 55
J. S. Bach, "Jesus Christ, My Sure Defense"
melody by Johann Crüger, ca. 1650
Embellishing Chord

able. While such an analytical approach may not constitute a significant error, remember that the half-diminished seventh is not often employed in a tonicization.

In the last example, the progression in measures 9 and 10 might be analyzed in a number of ways. Following the cadence in measure 8 (D major), we will hear the first two chords in measure 9 as V/ii and V/V, respectively. Beginning with the third beat, however, the function shifts to B minor through a deceptive cadence. Note also the irregular resolution of the V$^4_2$/vi in measure 9. Normally, the seventh, E$_3$, would descend to the third of the tonic triad. Bach, however, adds an escape tone (D$_3$) that emphasizes the root of the following tonic substitute. The remainder of the phrase maintains B minor.[7] Alternately, we might analyze the

---

[7]Note the tritone leap in the tenor (measure 10); in this context (approached and concluded by step), the melodic movement ↑7̂–4̂–3̂ is not overly difficult to sing.

entire phrase in B minor (although our perception of the first few chords in this key would be retroactive).

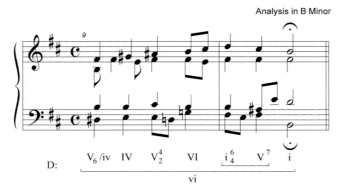

Analysis in B Minor

D: V_6/iv IV V_2^4 VI i_4^6 V^7 i

vi

Voice Leading in Secondary Progressions

The principles of voice leading are cumulative: The guidelines for spacing, doubling, tendency tones, and contrapuntal motion that were discussed previously also apply to secondary progressions.

Active Tones. Most secondary dominant chords include an accidental. Accidentals are active tones and, accordingly, should not be doubled. In addition, scrutinize the approach to any altered tone. Avoid cross relationships (see below) and awkward intervals. Finally, follow the conventions of seventh chord use:

- A root-position dominant seventh may appear with all four tones present or with the root doubled and the fifth omitted.

- In inverted dominant seventh chords and all leading-tone sevenths, use all four pitches.

The four-part passage below contains several voice-leading errors.

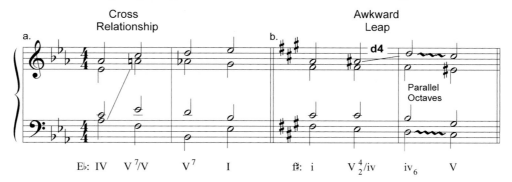

Eb: IV V^7/V V^7 I   f♯: i V_2^4/iv iv_6 V

In the first progression, a pitch and its chromatic alteration (a CROSS RELATIONSHIP) exists between the A♭ in the bass and the A♮ in the alto. While composers sometimes maintain a musical flow with relatively more difficult lines, they are best avoided for now. In the second progression, several problems result from the A♯–D leap in the soprano. First, the A♯ is a new ↑$\hat{7}$ and should resolve to $\hat{8}$ (B). In addition, however, the diminished fourth is difficult—regardless of the scale degrees involved. Finally, parallel octaves occur between soprano and bass in the last measure.

Observe the improved voice leading in the revisions that follow.

Corrected Voice Leading

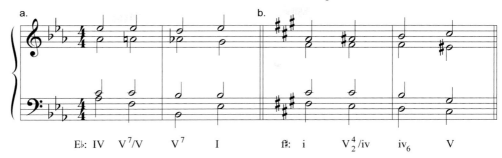

Eᵇ: IV   V⁷/V   V⁷   I   f♯: i   V⁴₂/iv   iv₆   V

As is always the case with voice leading in four parts, contrary motion helps to ensure part independence (and at the same time, avoids parallel unisons, octaves, and fifths). Adhere to tendency tones (especially in secondary tonal areas), avoid unnecessary or awkward leaps, and employ conventional resolutions, doublings, and spacings.

WORKBOOK/ANTHOLOGY I
IV. Secondary Leading-Tone Chords, page 131

REVIEW AND APPLICATION 10–3

Secondary Function

Essential Terms

cross relationship

1. Use traditional four-part procedures to construct the progressions in the keys indicated. Furnish all necessary accidentals.

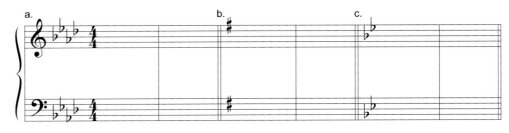

Aᵇ: I   vii°₆/ii   ii   V⁷   e: i   VI   V⁷/III   III   g: iv   V⁷/V   V   i

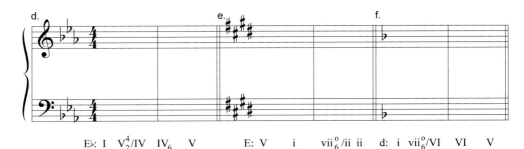

Eᵇ: I   V⁴₂/IV   IV₆   V   E: V   i   vii°₆/ii   ii   d: i   vii°₆/VI   VI   V

2. Identify the given chords in the keys suggested. Look not only for secondary dominants, but diatonic chords as well. Write the appropriate analytical symbols in the blanks.

a.

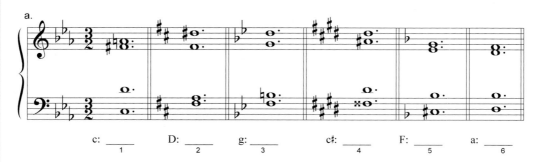

c: _____   D: _____   g: _____   c#: _____   F: _____   a: _____
     1   2   3   4   5   6

b.

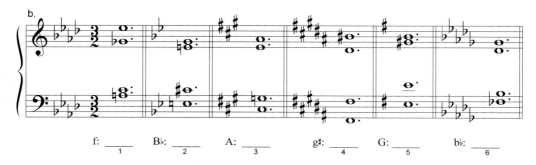

f: _____   B♭: _____   A: _____   g#: _____   G: _____   b♭: _____
    1   2   3   4   5   6

3. Provide harmonic analyses of the following passages. Write roman and arabic numerals in the blanks.

CD 2, TRACK 56-1 REVIEW AND APPLICATION 10-3 (2 PARTS)
J. S. Bach, "Our Father, Thou in Heaven Above"
Exercise 3-a

a.

E♭: _____ _____ _____ _____ _____ _____ _____ _____ f: _____
      1   2   3   4   5   6   7   8   9

(f:) _____ _____ _____ _____ _____ _____ _____
      10   11   12   13   14   15   16

TRACK 56-2 REVIEW AND APPLICATION 10-3
Mortimer Wilson, Sonatina, Op. 45, No. 1 (III)
Exercise 3-b

F: ___ ___ ___   ___ ___ ___ ___ ___ ___ ___ ___   ___ ___ ___
   1   2   3   4   5   6   7   8   9   10 11   12 13 14

SELF-TEST 10–3

Time Limit: 5 Minutes

1. Consider the same chord in each of the several keys suggested. Use the blank to provide a roman-numeral symbol. If the chord cannot function in one or more of the keys (a secondary dominant for the leading-tone triad, for example), write "none" in the blank. *Scoring: Subtract 8 points for each error.*

Eb: ____   g: ____   F#: ____   d: ____   e: ____
    1   2   3   4   5

2. Construct the chords specified in four parts. Add any necessary accidentals. *Scoring: Subtract 12 for each incorrect chord.*

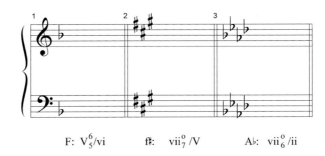

F: V_5^6/vi   f#: vii$_7^o$/V   Ab: vii$_6^o$/ii

3. Some of the following statements are true; others, false. Write "T" for a true statement; "F," if false. *Scoring: Subtract 3 points for each error.*

_____ a. The fully diminished seventh is common in the dominant role of a tonicization.

_____ b. Secondary predominants may occur in extended tonicizations.

      _____ c. Passages with unclear function in the tonic key may actually be clear-
      ly functional at a secondary level.

      _____ d. In the table of chord classification, V/vi is a fourth-class chord.

      _____ e. An accidental that is a new flat is often a new subtonic.

      _____ f. Cross relationships are acceptable in secondary progressions.

      _____ g. Active tones may be doubled in secondary dominant-tonic
      progressions.

Total Possible: 100   Your Score _____

PROJECTS

Analysis

As we will discuss in Chapter 11, a change of key can be temporary—with a reasonably quick return to the original tonic (a tonicization)—or a complete redefinition of functional and melodic tendencies (a modulation). The text and
workbook pieces for analysis fall into the former category. One of the most interesting characteristics of traditional music is the frequency with which these
secondary tonal areas occur and how composers guide the listener smoothly
from one area to the next. Moreover, these local tonal centers are not random,
but planned specifically to reinforce the primary key. Other important areas for
the analysis of secondary function include the following:

1. Define the overall tonality and understand how it is established and
   maintained.

2. Locate areas of secondary function and define their relationship to the tonic
   key. Are there extended tonicizations?

3. Study the secondary dominant chords themselves and determine the frequency of categories (dominant, dominant seventh, leading-tone, and so on).

4. Comment on any exceptional progressions, cross relationships, awkward intervals, and the like.

5. Determine how often the chromatic embellishment occurs in the melody as
   opposed to the accompaniment.

6. Are multiple interpretations possible for secondary dominants (that is, can
   they be seen alternately as nonchord tones?).

Text

Antonio Caldara "As on the Swelling Wave," text page (Chapter 9), page 347. This song
begins and ends in G minor, but between these tonal pillars, you will find a number of significant areas of secondary function. Locate each of these tonicizations
and determine their relationship to the principal tonic.

J. S. Bach, Prelude in C Major (Well-Tempered Clavier I), text page 395. Bach wrote the first
volume of his *Well-Tempered Clavier* in 1722. The work includes one prelude and
one fugue (a work featuring strict imitative counterpoint) in each of the major
and minor keys. The Prelude in C Major is written in a simple lute style (called
style brisé). Many of the dissonances can be interpreted as either melodic or harmonic. In your analysis, decide which approach you think is better and remain
consistent within that choice.

Workbook/Anthology I

J. S. Bach, Prelude in D Major (*Well-Tempered Clavier I*), workbook page 145.
George Frideric Handel, Adagio from Suite in F Major, workbook page 147.

Composition

Keyboard Prelude in the Style of Bach. Bach's Prelude in C Major (page 395) is a skillfully articulated chord progression. Complete a detailed harmonic analysis of Bach's prelude, then compose a prelude of your own with a similar broken-chord effect. Begin by devising interesting harmonic progressions, then set them in motion with arpeggiations (not necessarily *style brisé*). Avoid duplicating Bach's rhythmic placements exactly; many similar patterns are appropriate. Note that you must employ traditional voice leading to resolve seventh chords and melodic dissonance just as Bach did in the C Major Prelude.

Begin your composition with a chord progression of 6–10 measures that establishes the tonic key. Use relatively simple progressions and a uniform harmonic rhythm (one or two chord changes per measure). The sample introductory progression in the next example is in D minor with a tonicization of the subdominant.

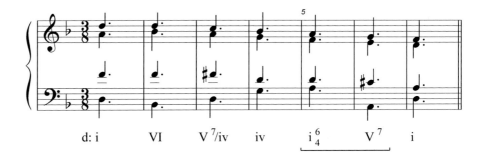

Next, apply two or three different arpeggiated patterns to the progression, then decide which one you like best. Use both left and right hands in an ascending, descending, or in combined patterns according to divisions of the meter you choose. This first sample (the first four measure of the sample progression) has no nonchord tones, although a stepwise bass adds interest.

CD 2, TRACK 57-1 CHAPTER PROJECT
(2 PARTS)
First Sample Phrase

First Sample

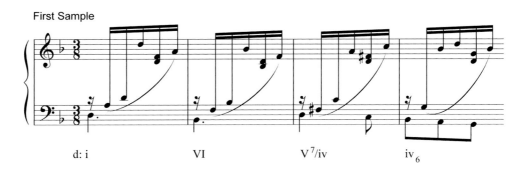

TRACK 57-2 CHAPTER PROJECTS
Second Sample Phrase

The second pattern is based on the same progression (and includes neighboring tones), but is less like Bach's Prelude in C Major in its arpeggiated bass.

Second Sample

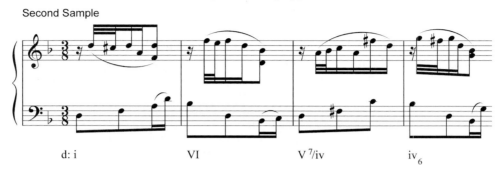

Plan the work in three parts and 30–40 measures in length (20 measures or so if you choose a quadruple meter). In the first section (as in the examples shown), establish the tonic key with diatonic progressions and a tonicization of the dominant or subdominant. Follow the same process to write a progression for the second section. Make this the longest and with two or three different tonicizations (one of these might be extended over three or four measures). Use a variety of secondary dominant chords in the middle section (remembering that properly voiced diminished sevenths are the most colorful and have the strongest tendencies to resolve). In the final section, return to diatonic progressions with a tonicization of dominant or subdominant. Your goal is to employ a uniform arpeggiation (with appropriate variations) from beginning to the end of the prelude (although you might end with a flourish as Bach does).

For Further Study

Equal Temperament. Bach composed his two volumes of the *Well-Tempered Clavier* at least partly to show the advantages of a new system of tuning keyboard instruments that we call twelve-tone equal temperament. Equal temperament remains the approach by which pianos are tuned today (nearly 300 years later). Before equal temperament, several other tuning systems had been in use; these include Pythagorean Tuning and Mean-Tone Temperament.

Tuning and temperament is an interesting topic that will be explored in an appendix to Volume II of this series. Instrument builders needed a way to divide the octave into smaller steps, but in such a way that the use of enharmonic equivalents was not disrupted. This problem has interested scholars from Pythagoras to the present day.

In twelve-tone equal temperament (equal temperament), the keyboard is actually tuned out of tune when compared to the sizes of intervals as they occur naturally. Over three hundred years, we have become accustomed to this slight discrepancy and most musicians accept it as "correct."

Center a class presentation on the differences between mean-tone tuning (in use before Bach's day) and twelve-tone equal temperament (which became the norm by the time of Mozart and Haydn). You need not be lengthy or especially technical, but help the class understand the problems encountered by instrument builders. You will find numerous Internet sites that not only discuss these temperaments but also offer downloadable audio clips of scales, intervals, and excerpts to clarify the small, but crucial differences between them.

J. S. Bach, Prelude in C Major
from *Well-Tempered Clavier,* Volume I

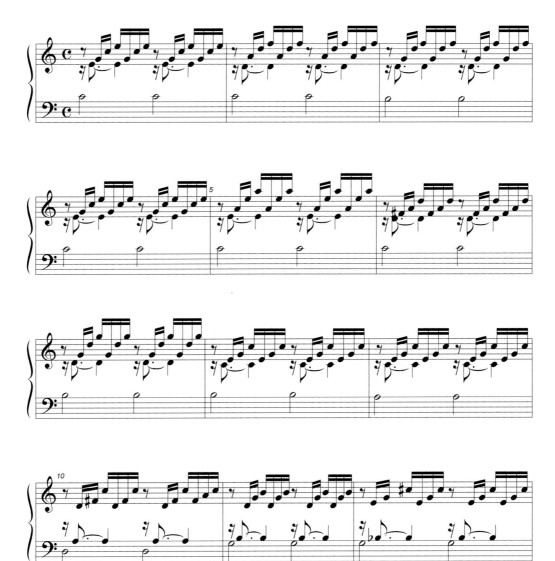

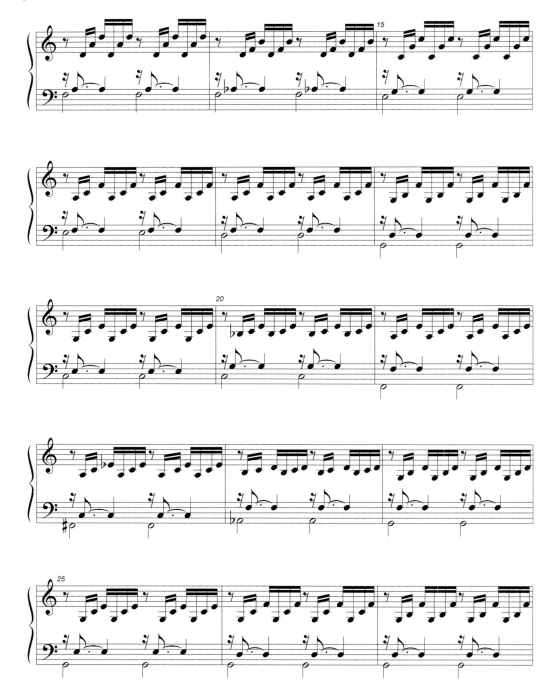

Musical Shape and Growth

Muzio Clementi, Sonatina

Chapter 11
Modulation

Chapter 12
Binary and Ternary Designs

I n many world societies, including parts of Africa, some Native American cultures, and much of Asia, the direct repetition of rhythmic and melodic ideas (often with slight variations in text or music) is the cornerstone of composition. The basic musical fragment is both easy to learn and to pass along from one generation to the next. Variations are often accomplished through improvisation. In the West, some of the earliest secular music involved epic poems, stories, and dialogues that might constitute hundreds of lines—all but the last of them sung to the same brief musical phrase. At a time when music was not notated, repetition was a facile solution to the creation of a cohesive musical whole.

Contrast.   The *contrast* of one musical idea with another is also an ancient way of lengthening a single work, while at the same time separating and defining the most important internal divisions. In early Western music, contrast is often followed by restatement. In vocal music, sectional division may derive from the poetic structure of the text. The *Kyrie*, for example, is the first movement of the Ordinary of the Roman Catholic mass. Divisions of the simple Latin text often led composers to a statement–contrast–restatement formal scheme. Each phrase of the *Kyrie* is repeated three times; the middle phrase ("*Christe eleison*") contrasts in text, forming a natural opportunity for the composer to employ new melodic ideas as well.

statement	*Kyrie eleison*[1]
contrast	*Christe eleison*
restatement	*Kyrie eleison*

The facsimile below is a kyrie from the *Liber Usualis,* a collection of Roman Catholic liturgical music. The melody is shown in unmeasured Gregorian notation (ca. 1300). The letters "iij" that follow the first two lines of text tell the performer to sing the phrase three times.

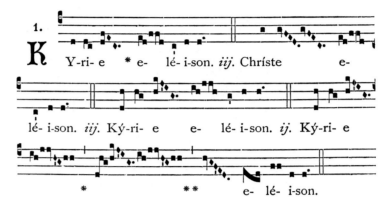

As Western music became more complex, notation was indispensable to the development of our musical system. We continue to rely on repetition, variation, and contrast, but on a grander scale than was imagined by the Medieval *Jongleur* who sang the same brief melodic formula dozens of times in recounting a noble deed or the news of the day. Even in the sacred and secular music of the Renaissance, entire sections of a composition are rarely manipulated as is characteristic in Mozart and Beethoven, for example. Except for jazz and commercial music, improvisation, so important in other world cultures, is virtually unknown in the West today.

In addition to the musical forms discussed in Chapter 9 (*e.g.,* bar, strophic, and verse/refrain forms), composers since about 1680 have organized many of their works through statement–contrast (binary) or statement–contrast–restatement (ternary) sectional divisions. These sections are delineated through contrasting melodic materials. In other works, however, it is not melodic material that is contrasted, but two principal *keys*. In Chapter 11, we will study modulation: the process by which composers effect a convincing change of key. Chapter 12 centers on modulation as a defining formal principle.

Muzio Clementi was born in Rome in 1752. He lived and worked during the time of Mozart, Haydn, and Beethoven—composers who have been identified historically as far more significant figures. Yet, as is true of many composers today, Clementi pursued a path that combined artistic achievement, composing, teaching, and entrepreneurship. Highly celebrated in his day, Clementi was, like Mozart, a child prodigy who traveled widely among the great cities of Europe as a concert artist. Like Haydn and Handel before him, Clementi found London to be a fertile climate for his activities; he died there in 1832.

Today, we remember Clementi not as a towering historical figure, but as an ac-

---

[1] The text translates "Lord have mercy. Christ have mercy. Lord have mercy."

complished composer who, in his day, wrote successfully for amateur and professional alike. His keyboard works, like the Sonatina in C Major, employ the same important key relationships that define the weightier sonatas of Mozart and Haydn. We will study sonata form fully in the second volume of this text, but in the Clementi Sonatina ("little sonata"), we see in miniature many of the important elements of the sonata principle. There are two important themes, for example, and not only is there tonicization of various diatonic areas, but also complete reorientations of key. These *modulations* have the capacity to govern formal structure in works from simple two-part compositions to lengthy symphonic movements. In addition, as we will discuss in Chapter 12, Clementi's Sonatina includes major formal principles that remain useful today in the unification of a longer work.

CD 2, TRACK 58
Muzio Clementi, Sonatina in C Major, Op. 36, No. 1 (I)

Muzio Clementi, Sonatina in C Major, Op. 36, No. 1
First Movement

CHAPTER *11*

Modulation

One of several major differences between Renaissance and mature Baroque styles centers on the concept of key and mode. Where common-practice composers limited themselves to either major or minor, their predecessors before about 1680 employed various modes (Dorian, Phrygian, Lydian, and so on). In addition, while fifteenth- and sixteenth-century composers clearly organized sections of their music around a single pitch, they did not view key as an organizing principle for an entire work. Especially in complex Renaissance polyphony, composers structured their music in a series of related, but self-contained segments.

MODULATION

In the last chapter, we discussed tonicization—a temporary tonal fluctuation within a given key. In G major, a tonicization of the dominant (or of any other appropriate diatonic area) not only provides new color, but also strengthens the psychological sensation that G is the most important pitch. If a change of key is substantial, however, if the old key center is supplanted by another through relative length, emphasis, association with a major theme, or for another reason, then a *modulation* has occurred. MODULATION is a key change that reorients the listener's expectations to a new set of melodic tendencies and functional progressions. Tonicization is important in coloring the tonal palette, but contrasting keys also have the capacity to shape the overall structure of a composition.

In Gershwin's *Oh, Lady Be Good* (see page 311), in addition to contrasting melodic material, a key change delineates the verse from the refrain. In the verse, the listener perceives E as the tonal center; in the refrain, the pitch reference is G. As a whole, the work unfolds in two major sections—each oriented around a different key.

Despite the repetition of both verse and refrain, the last diagram adequately illustrates the form. The direct repetition of complete musical sections does not typically affect formal development. Accordingly, although a time-line analysis of Gershwin's song (below) stipulates a repetition of the second part, there are few significant differences between this more detailed analysis and the boxed illustration.

Earlier, we studied a passage from a minuet by J. S. Bach. The entire composition, like Gershwin's song, is in two parts. These divisions are identified graphically in the score itself with double bars. Even without the score reference, however, the first section of Bach's work clearly modulates from G minor to B♭ major; the second part opens in B♭ major and returns to G minor. Remember that Bach omitted the second flat from the key signature as was the custom in some Baroque music.

B♭: I   V/V   V   IV   V   I

g: V/iv   iv   i V i V   iv V i

The entire Menuet is only 32 measures long; beginning and ending in G minor, we hear this key as the principal tonal center. The modulation to the relative major (B♭), however, helps us to perceive the work in two parts. The key of B♭ major emerges from a tonicization of its supertonic (C minor) in measure 13, and the cadence formula (including all three functions) in measures 15–16 establishes the modulation. The second part of the Menuet begins with new melodic material (measure 17). At the same time, B♭ major is already fixed in our minds as the new tonality.

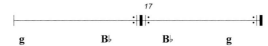

g   B♭   B♭   g

Open and Closed Sections.   Compare the time lines of Gershwin's song (page 404) with the graphic representation of the Bach Menuet. Both works are in two sections and in both instances, the two-part form is defined through a change of key. As we will discuss in Chapter 12, however, the implications of CLOSED SECTIONS (ending in the *same* key in which they begin) are quite different from *open sections*. An OPEN SECTION begins in one key and then roams *away* from that key. The two sections of the Gershwin song are both closed; by contrast, the Bach's Menuet begins with an open section.

Modulation and Tonicization

We have defined modulation as the process by which a key change both delineates sections of a composition and establishes new long-term tonal relationships. Tonicization is a temporary excursion into the pitches of a new scale. We should keep in mind, however, that any successful change of key—whether modulation or tonicization—hinges on three elements:

1. The establishment of the first key (the "old" key)
2. The introduction of one or more accidentals[1]
3. The establishment of the new key through functional progressions

_____

[1] In the case of modulations to the relative major, of course, the *loss* of an accidental is the reorienting factor.

Whether the music actually modulates, or merely touches on a new key, a sequence of three events—the *process* of key change—is the same. Relative length and other factors enable us to distinguish between modulation and tonicization, but since the moment at which the new key first appears is the same in both cases, our studies in this chapter center primarily on a series of events.

We can consider the equivalence of temporary and permanent key change through the first phrase group of Clementi's Sonatina. The movement opens in C major; the passage shown in the next example illustrates a modulation to the

CD 2, TRACK 59-1 MODULATION AND TONICIZATION (2 PARTS)
Clementi, Sonatina with Modulation to Dominant (as written)

dominant. Note the establishment of the old key, the appearance of an accidental ($\uparrow\hat{7}$ in the new key), and the subsequent reinforcement of the new tonality through a cadence.

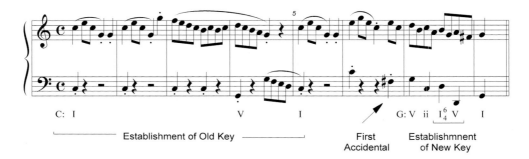

Clementi continues in G major for eight more measures after the establishment of the new key (the work was given in full beginning on page 401). Moreover, as we will discuss fully in Chapter 12, the change of key defines the form of the movement as binary. For these reasons, we can categorize the change of key from C major to G major as a true modulation. Study the next passage, however, as Clementi *might* have composed it had he decided to remain in C major and merely tonicize the dominant.

TRACK 59-2 MODULATION AND TONICIZATION
Clementi, Sonatina with Tonicization of Dominant (Edited)

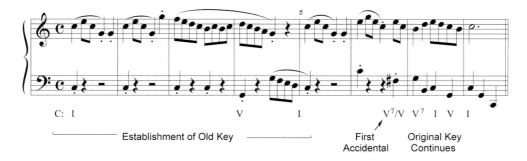

The last two examples provide models of modulation and tonicization, respectively. Yet observe that both the point at which the first accidental appears and the chord that follows that accidental (clarifying function in G major and C major, respectively) is basically the same.

Tonicization	C: I		V /V⁷	V	C major	→
Modulation	C I		G: V⁷	I	G major	→

In assessing the importance of a fluctuation in key, relative length is an excellent guide. Returning to the Bach Menuet (page 404–405), notice that the modulation to B♭ major is ten measures long. Since the entire movement is only 32 measures, the key change is consequential in a relative sense. In addition, not only is the new key affirmed by a cadence formula (measures 15–16), but within the B♭ major passage, the dominant is tonicized. Finally, some modulations are employed to define shape more often than others. If the key is major, we might expect the dominant or submediant areas to be emphasized. A modulation to the relative major is common if the tonic key is minor. In Clementi's Sonatina, each of these facts points to a true modulation from G minor to B♭ major rather than a transient (or local) digression.

In our present studies, the goal is an understanding of how keys may be heard as distinct, yet related. Especially before about 1820, composers most often conveyed the listener smoothly from one tonal area to another by choosing keys that were within a sharp or flat of one another (as seen in the Bach and Clementi examples). By 1820, composers became more adventurous in selecting key relationships. These techniques and tonal couplings, employed by traditional composers as early as 1680, are still valid in tonal music today.

Closely Related and Distant Keys

When the signatures (and the corresponding scales) of two keys differ by no more than one flat or one sharp, they are CLOSELY RELATED. When keys are closely related, six of the seven pitches are identical. If two keys differ by *more* than one sharp or flat, the key relationship is known as DISTANT.

For any major or minor key, five other keys are closely related. Given the key of C major, for example, in addition to the relative minor (which has exactly the same key signature), the keys of F major (one flat) and G major (one sharp), together with *their* relative minors (D minor and E minor, respectively), constitute the five closely related keys.

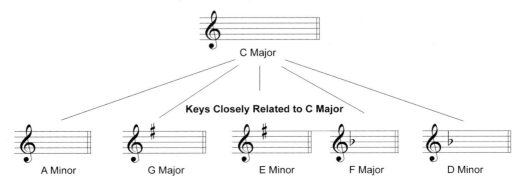

The relationships among the closely related keys are further illustrated by a comparison of the respective scales (excluding ↑$\hat{6}$ and ↑$\hat{7}$ in minor keys).

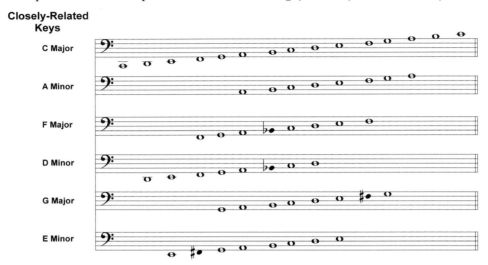

If keys are distant, they are, by definition, *not* closely related, but the degree of distance is relative. The keys of C major and B minor are distant, yet they have five pitches in common.

The keys of C major and D♭ major are also distant, but with only two pitches in common (F and C), the degree of remoteness is greater than with the keys of C major and B minor.[2]

Excluding altered pitches in minor, any pair of closely related keys has six pitches in common; accordingly, any tonal digression (whether modulation or tonicization) is potentially more facile and convincing than a key change between distant keys. However, while eighteenth-century composers relied primarily on

---

[2]The keys of C♯ major and A♯ minor have *no* pitches in common with C major and are farther distant than C major–D♭ major.

closely related keys for modulations, by the early nineteenth century, composers like Beethoven and Schubert had devised harmonic links that permitted rapid and convincing modulation between even remote keys.

WORKBOOK/ANTHOLOGY I
I. Closely Related and Distant Keys, page 141

REVIEW AND APPLICATION 11–1

Closely Related and Distant Keys

Essential Terms

closely related key	distant key	open section
closed section	modulation	

1. For each key specified, write the appropriate sharps or flats in the first frame. Next, name the five keys that are closely related to the one given. Provide those key signatures as well. The closely related keys may be listed in any order.

Given Key ———————— **Closely-Related Keys** ————————

a.

D Major _____ _____ _____ _____ _____

b.

F Minor _____ _____ _____ _____ _____

c.

B Major _____ _____ _____ _____ _____

d.

G Minor _____ _____ _____ _____ _____

e.

A Major _____ _____ _____ _____ _____

2. Complete the table that includes examples of closely related and distant keys. The specified key is in the leftmost column. In the second column, list any one of the five closely related keys. In the third and fourth colums, provide the names of two different keys that are distant in increasing order of remoteness (that is, list the most distant key in the right-hand column).

Given Key	Closely Related	Distant I	Distant II
a. E minor	_____	_____	_____
b. C♯ major	_____	_____	_____
c. D minor	_____	_____	_____
d. B♭ major	_____	_____	_____
e. F♯ minor	_____	_____	_____
f. A♭ major	_____	_____	_____

SELF-TEST 11–1

Time Limit: 5 Minutes

1. Choose a term from the list to match each statement. Write the appropriate letter in the blank. *Scoring: Subtract 5 points for each error.*

   A. Modulation   D. Closely related keys
   B. Open formal section   E. Distant keys
   C. Closed formal section   F. Tonicization

   _____ a. the relationship between D major and B major

   _____ b. section of a composition that begins and ends in the same key

   _____ c. a redefinition of melodic tendencies

   _____ d. the relationship between D major and B minor

   _____ e. a temporary change in tonal emphasis

   _____ f. section of a composition that begins in one key and ends in another

2. Some of the following statements are true; others are false. Write "T" or "F" in the blank as appropriate. *Scoring: Subtract 5 for each incorrect answer.*

   _____ a. A true modulation lasts at least fifty measures.

   _____ b. Modulations and tonicizations both begin with the introduction of an accidental (or the absence of one in minor).

   _____ c. If a change of tonal focus is a true modulation, there may be tonicizations of diatonic areas in the new key.

   _____ d. A tonicization must include one chord from each function: predominant, dominant, and tonic.

   _____ e. In terms of relative length of the key change, tonicizations and modulations are about the same.

   _____ f. Modulations may help to define sections of a longer work.

3. Consider the given key; then arrange the other keys in order from closely related to most distant. If two of the keys are closely related, they can be listed in any order before distant keys. If there are no closely related keys, list the distant keys according to the number of pitches in common (if any) with the given key. *Scoring: Subtract 10 points for an incorrect problem.*

Given Key	Additional Keys
a. B Major	(D minor, B♭ major, F♯ major, G major, E major)

____1____ ____2____ ____3____ ____4____ ____5____

b. A Minor	(E major, C major, C minor, D major, B♭ major)

____1____ ____2____ ____3____ ____4____ ____5____

c. E♭ Major	(C minor, F major, B major, G major, A♭ major)

____1____ ____2____ ____3____ ____4____ ____5____

d. D♯ Minor	(E minor, B major, F♯ major, A minor, C♯ minor)

____1____ ____2____ ____3____ ____4____ ____5____

Total Possible: 100   Your Score _____

COMMON-CHORD MODULATION

The establishment of a new pitch focus (whether tonicization or modulation) depends on a *retroactive* association. Once we become accustomed to the functional relationships and melodic tendencies within one key, an accidental (heard as a chord tone) upsets our equilibrium. In a tonicization, the primary tonality quickly reasserts itself and the original functional relationships return. If the key change is a modulation, however, a new tonal hierarchy unfolds, causing the listener to perceive a different pitch as the tonal center.

In the melody below by Antonio Caldara, the key of D minor is carefully designed through adherence to tonal tendencies in the melody itself. In measure 7, however, accidentals (C♯ and F♯) disrupt the effect of D minor; measure

CD 2, TRACK 60
Antonio Caldara, *Come Raggio di Sol*
Retroactive Association

8 brings a reorientation to G as a new, temporary tonic. *Retroactively*, we associate the C and F♯ with the new key.

In the Caldara example, we hear the pitch A (measure 6) as $\hat{5}$ in D minor. Retroactively, however, we perceive the same pitch as having been $\hat{2}$ in G minor.

One pitch—heard as functional in two different keys—serves as a PIVOT TONE (pivot pitch) in a modulation.

The Common Chord. The phenomenon illustrated in the Caldara melody occurs also in tonal harmony. Once a key is established, any nondiatonic chord creates tension; the tension is resolved through logical progressions in a new key. One chord however, the COMMON CHORD, may serve both as the last element in the old key and, retroactively, as the first chord in a new key.

In the next example, G major is established through the first four chords. The C♯ temporarily upsets our perception of function in G major, but subsequent progressions introduce C♯ as a new $\uparrow\hat{7}$; by the end of the line, we accept the tonal reorientation to D major.

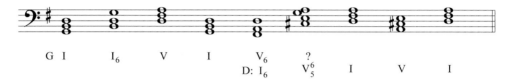

The progression just discussed was extracted from Bach's harmonization of the chorale melody *"Freu dich sehr, o meine Seele"* ("O Be Glad, My Soul, Be Cheerful"). The change of key from G major to the dominant key is effected smoothly through a common chord (boxed). We first hear the D major chord as V₆ in G major; as the passage continues, however, we reinterpret the sonority as the new tonic.

CD 2, TRACK 61-1 COMMON-CHORD MODULATION (3 PARTS)
J. S. Bach, "O Be Glad, My Soul, Be Cheerful"

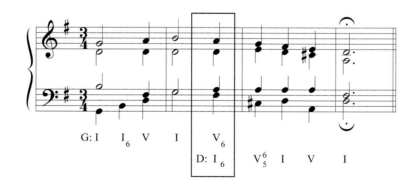

Modulation by COMMON CHORD, in which one sonority is diatonic in both old and new keys, is the most common type of key change in traditional music.[3] In the passage below, from Bach's harmonization of *"Alles ist an Gottes Segen"* ("All Depends On Our Possessing"), the second phrase begins in the tonic key (G major), then modulates to the dominant through common chord. Initially, we hear the E minor sonority (on the first beat of measure 4) as a subme-

---

[3] The term "Pivot Chord" is often used in other sources to refer to the common chord. Modulation by common chord is also known as "pivot-chord modulation" and "direct modulation."

diant in G major. But when the next chord (an A major triad) disrupts our perception of G major, and as the phrase continues and cadences in D major, we reinterpret the E minor triad as having been the supertonic in the new key.

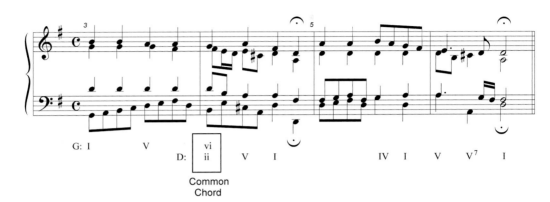

G: I   V | vi / ii | V   I   IV   I   V   V⁷   I

D:

Common
Chord

Study the next passage from Haydn's Sonata in E Minor. The tonic key is established over the first twelve measures, but through a common chord in measure 12 (e: iv = G: ii), a modulation to the relative major is persuasive. In this example, the new tonic continues for over thirty measures (not shown) and constitutes a true modulation.

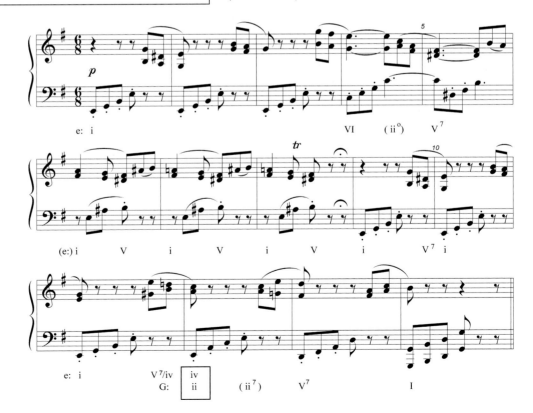

e: i   VI   (ii°)   V⁷

(e:) i   V   i   V   i   V   i   V⁷   i

e: i   V⁷/iv | iv / ii | (ii⁷)   V⁷   I

G:

When old and new keys are closely related (as in the two previous Bach chorales as well as Haydn's sonata passage), *several* chords are common between them. In many cases, composers choose a common chord that represents *predominant* function in the new area. With this pivot, the first chord to be heard entirely in the new key has dominant function and progresses, in turn, to the new tonic. We see this structure in measures 11–14 of Haydn's sonata.

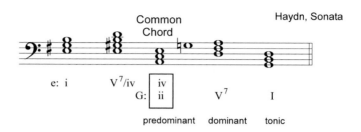

Nearly the same plan occurs in the chorale, "All Depends on Our Possessing" (page 413). The common chord has predominant function in the new key and is followed by dominant and tonic chords, respectively.

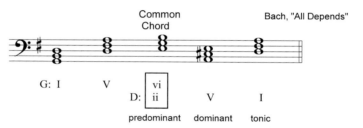

In the Bach setting of "O Be Glad, My Soul, Be Cheerful" (page 412), where a common-chord modulation occurs from G major to D major, there are no predominant chords in either the old or new keys (measures 1–4). The new tonic serves as the pivot chord. Dominant–tonic progressions in D major (the new key) follow.

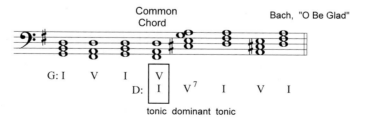

Students may find Bach's choice of common chord in the last passage less effective in their own compositions, but a skilled composer utilizes *any* common chord to create a smooth transition between keys. Especially when $\uparrow\hat{6}$ and $\uparrow\hat{7}$ in minor are considered, a given key has at least one chord in common with many different additional keys. The chart that follows displays diatonic triads in

F major together with triads that are common in closely related (above the line) and distant keys (below the line). Notice that in each vertical column, the quality of the triads is the same. In major keys, a supertonic triad is invariably minor in quality. Accordingly, we will not hear a *major triad* built upon $\hat{2}$ as a supertonic. Likewise, a minor triad cannot be heard as having dominant function; a diminished triad cannot be heard as a tonic, and so on.

		I	ii	iii	IV	V	vi	vii°
	F:	**I**	**ii**	**iii**	**IV**	**V**	**vi**	**vii°**
Closely-Related Keys	d:	III	iv		VI		i	ii°
	C:	IV		vi		I	ii	
	a:	VI		i		III	iv	
	B♭:	V	vi		I		iii	
	g:		i	ii	III	IV		vi°
Distant Keys	G:			ii		IV		
	e:			iv		VI		
	E♭:		iii		V			
	c:	IV					ii	
	f:		ii		IV	V		vii°

Modal Shift

You probably observed in the last line of the previous table, that F major and F minor have four triads in common—including the pivotal dominant and leading-tone chords. However, a change of key from F major to F minor is *not* a modulation in the sense that the listener perceives a new set of melodic and harmonic tendencies. Rather, the tonic in both instances is the same. A MODAL SHIFT (see also page 65–66) is a better way of describing changes of mode from major to minor (or the reverse). Beginning with a major key and shifting to the parallel minor, for example, three flats are added to the key signature *without* an accompanying loss of tonal orientation.

As early as 1680, tonal composers exploited the harmonic and melodic interest available from modal shifts between major and parallel minor keys. Likewise, although less common, a modal shift from minor to the parallel major introduces three new sharps while the tonic pitch itself remains constant.

In the next passage, Carl Phillip Emanuel Bach shifts abruptly from F major to the parallel minor (measure 68) and remains in the minor mode for five measures. Listen to the excerpt and notice that beginning in measure 68, although we experience a new harmonic and melodic palette, functional progressions occur at the same level. In fact, the progressions in F major (measures 59–64) are mirrored in measures 68–72.

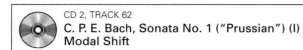

CD 2, TRACK 62
C. P. E. Bach, Sonata No. 1 ("Prussian") (I)
Modal Shift

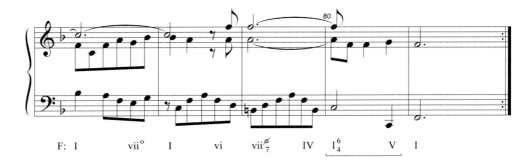

F: I   vii°   I   vi   vii⌀₇   IV   I⁶₄   V   I

Planning Common-Chord Modulations

The techniques of common-chord modulation discussed in this section are all available for use in your own composition and arranging projects. Begin by considering the two keys involved and the common chords available between them. If the tonic is B♭ major and the new key is C major, two good possibilities exist.

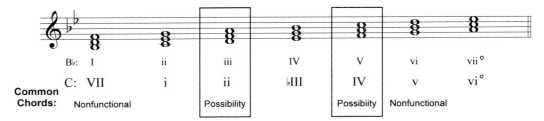

B♭: I   ii   iii   IV   V   vi   vii°

C: VII   i   ii   ♭III   IV   v   vi°

Common Chords: Nonfunctional   Possibility   Possibiity   Nonfunctional

Five triads in B♭ major are *not* common with C major: VII, ii, IV, v, and vii°. But the two chords that are common, iii and V, are both acceptable as common chords in a modulation to C major. Begin by planning the harmonic link between keys.

B♭: I   IV V I   iii   B♭: I   IV V I   V
         C: ii V I   C: IV V I

Next, listen to both modulations and decide which is smoother and more convincing (remember that inversions as well as melodic and rhythmic factors will enhance either choice).

Modulation from B♭ Major to C Major

B♭: I   IV   V   I   iii   B♭: I   IV   V   I   V
          C: ii   V⁷ I   C: IV   V⁷ I

Both choices have about the same musical effect. We hear the mediant in B♭ as an extension of the tonic; the dominant in B♭ creates the customary momentum that will be frustrated by a progression in C major. But either modulation "works" since the common chord is predominant in the new key.

In scoring either chord progression, we would make certain that the melody complements the harmony, that melodic tendencies in the new key are strictly adhered to, and that voice-leading principles are taken into account. In the chorale phrase that follows, observe how the initial harmonic connection is obscured slightly by the 4–3 suspension. Although the modulation itself has begun at that point, it is the second progression in the new key that is most forceful and convincing. In the melody, B♮ (new ↑$\hat{7}$) reinforces C major in its resolution to $\hat{8}$. At the cadence, the soprano line $\hat{4}$–$\hat{3}$–$\hat{2}$–$\hat{1}$ draws our attention further into the new key.

CD 2, TRACK 63-1 MODULATION (2 PARTS)
Phrase with Modulation to Supertonic

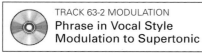

TRACK 63-2 MODULATION
Phrase in Vocal Style
Modulation to Supertonic

In another style, the same basic modulation is equally effective.

Modulation by common chord is effective not only when keys are closely related, but between pairs of distant keys that share at least one diatonic triad. In Volume II, we will discuss ways in which even nondiatonic chords may be heard as common through modal borrowing and enharmonic reinterpretations. Moreover, while common-chord modulation is a convenient means of changing keys in traditional music, in the next section of this chapter, we will discuss other ways of effecting a convincing transition between tonal planes.

WORKBOOK/ANTHOLOGY I
II. Common-Chord Modulation, page 143

REVIEW AND APPLICATION 11–2

Common-Chord Modulation

Essential Terms

common chord   modal shift   pivot chord

1. For each pair of keys specified, indicate all common chords by writing in the appropriate roman numeral in the lower line of blanks. If a triad in the upper line *cannot* be heard as common in the second key, leave the blank empty.

a.

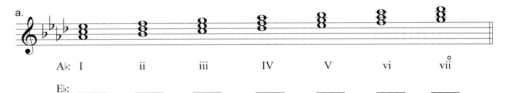

A♭: I   ii   iii   IV   V   vi   vii°

E♭: ____   ____   ____   ____   ____   ____   ____

b.

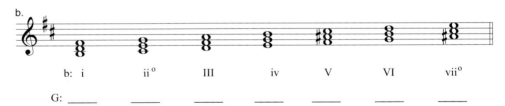

b: i   ii°   III   iv   V   VI   vii°

G: ____   ____   ____   ____   ____   ____   ____

c.

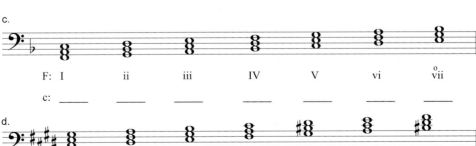

F: I   ii   iii   IV   V   vi   vii°

c: ____   ____   ____   ____   ____   ____   ____

d.

c♯: i   ii°   III   iv   V   VI   vii°

A: ____   ____   ____   ____   ____   ____   ____

2. For each given triad, besides the interpretation furnished, list *up to four* additional keys in which the sonority can be heard as diatonic. Write the name of the key in the first blank, the roman numeral, in the second. In some cases, many different keys are possible. In others, however, only one or two keys would include the given chord as a diatonic possibility. Consider alterations in minor, but remember that the triad *as given* constitutes the pivot chord. The same triad with the same quality must be diatonic in another key or keys to be included in your list.

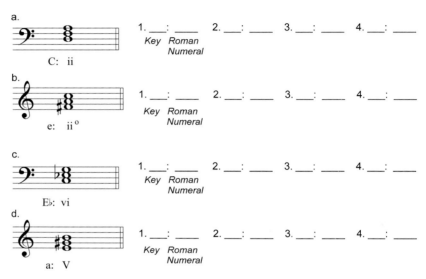

a.

C: ii

1. ___ : ____   2. ___ : ____   3. ___ : ____   4. ___ : ____
   Key Roman
        Numeral

b.

e: ii°

1. ___ : ____   2. ___ : ____   3. ___ : ____   4. ___ : ____
   Key Roman
        Numeral

c.

E♭: vi

1. ___ : ____   2. ___ : ____   3. ___ : ____   4. ___ : ____
   Key Roman
        Numeral

d.

a: V

1. ___ : ____   2. ___ : ____   3. ___ : ____   4. ___ : ____
   Key Roman
        Numeral

3. For each modulation suggested, choose a common chord that will present *predominant function in the new key*. Write this chord on the staff, then add dominant and tonic triads in the new key. Provide accidentals as necessary. Several chords may be common between the two keys, but limit your choice of pivot chord to one that is a predominant.

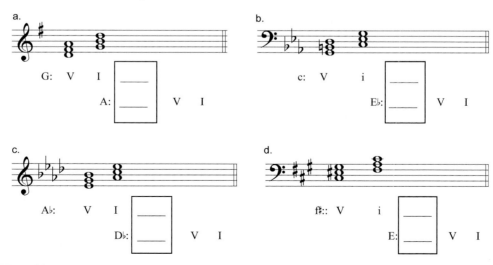

a.

G: V   I
A: [____]   V   I

b.

c: V   i
E♭: [____]   V   I

c.

A♭: V   I
D♭: [____]   V   I

d.

f♯:: V   i
E: [____]   V   I

SELF-TEST 11–2

Time Limit: 10 Minutes

1. Choose the best answer for each question and make a check in the appropriate blank. *Scoring: Subtract 8 points for an error.*

a. A modulation may be recognized by

____ (1)   the use of a tonic substitute.

____ (2)   tonicization within the new area.

____ (3)   tonicization within the old key.

____ (4)   an accidental that disrupts the melodic tendencies.

b. Modulation by common chord includes

____ (1)   a chord that has the same function in old and new keys.

____ (2)   a new leading tone.

____ (3)   a chord that is diatonic in old and new keys.

____ (4)   a chord that has predominant function.

c. When planning a common-chord modulation, the best choice for pivot chord is one with

____ (1)   tonic function in the new key.

____ (2)   dominant function in the new key.

____ (3)   dominant function in the old key.

____ (4)   predominant function in the new key.

d. A modal shift

____ (1)   is not a modulation.

____ (2)   is a modulation to the relative minor.

____ (3)   is a modulation to the parallel major.

____ (4)   is a modulation to the dominant.

e. The keys of E♭ major and F major have

____ (1)   no triads in common.

____ (2)   one triad in common.

____ (3)   two triads in common.

____ (4)   three triads in common.

2. For the pairs of keys given, choose an appropriate common chord (if any). Notate this chord and provide roman numerals to indicate the chord's function in old and new keys. If there are no suitable common chords, write "none." *Scoring: Subtract 10 points for an incorrect answer.*

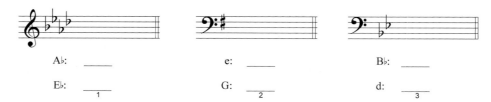

A♭: _____   e: _____   B♭: _____

E♭: _____   G: _____   d: _____
         1   2   3

3. For each chord given, choose two keys in which it might form a pivot. The chord is given with accidentals and without a key signature. Use the blanks to identify the two keys (there may be other choices in some cases) with roman numerals and additional symbols as necessary. *Scoring: Subtract 10 points for an error.*

Old Key: _____   Old Key: _____   Old Key: _____

New Key: _____   New Key: _____   New Key: _____
         1   2   3

Total Possible: 100   Your Score _____

CHROMATIC MODULATION

In the Western diatonic scale, half steps do not occur consecutively; as a consequence, successive half steps create a strong sense of expectation. Composers exploit this instability to link two keys—either because no common chord exists or simply as an alternate method, even when keys are closely related.

Nineteenth-century composers often wrote "incidental" music to plays. Audiences enjoyed short orchestral or chamber works before the dramatic production and also between acts. Schubert's "*Entr'acte*" from the popular drama *Rosamunde* is such a composition. The passage below is in B♭ major. The tonicization of the supertonic (C minor) in measures 6–7 is convincing, not because of a common chord, but through the ascending chromatic bass line that begins in measure 5 and carries the listener forcefully to the new tonic. The return to B♭ major (measure 8) is by common chord (boxed).

CD 2, TRACK 64
Franz Schubert, *Entr'acte* from *Rosamunde*
Chromatic Modulation

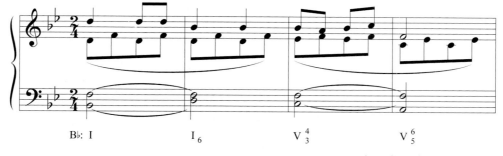

B♭: I   I₆   V⁴₃   V⁶₅

(continued on next page)

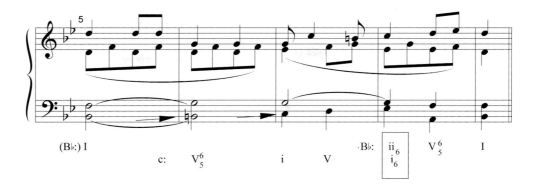

A CHROMATIC MODULATION, seen in the Schubert *"Entr'acte,"* is a change of key that occurs through an ascending or descending series of half steps. A common chord is *not* employed and the chromatic line (all chord tones) occurs typically in one voice.

The Schubert example illustrates several common elements in chromatic modulation:

1. The first of the three pitches is diatonic in the *old key* and harmonized from that vocabulary.

2. The second of the ascending pitches is ↑$\hat{7}$ in the new key, lies a *chromatic* half step above the first, and is harmonized with a chord of dominant function in the new tonal area.

3. The third pitch is $\hat{8}$ in the new key and is harmonized with a chord of tonic function.

Observe the elements of a successful chromatic modulation as extracted from the Schubert passage. The composer employs dominant seventh and tonic chords to establish the new key. Just as effectively, other chords of dominant function (vii$^{o}_{6}$ or vii$^{o}_{7}$, for example) would have been alternate possibilities.

Schubert, *Entr'acte*

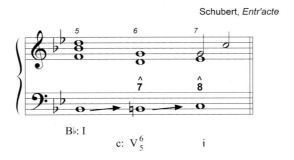

A modulation virtually identical to Schubert's occurs in Bach's Menuet (given in full on pages 404–405). The crucial chromatic line appears here among strong beats over three successive measures (with two intervening quarter notes in measure 24). The octave displacement in the chromatic line (B$\flat_2$–B$\natural_3$) is a common variation of stepwise motion—especially in instrumental music.

CD 2, TRACK 65-1 CHROMATIC MODULATION (3 PARTS)
J. S. Bach, Menuet

In his harmonization of the chorale, "*Gott der Vater wohn' uns bei*" ("God the Father Be Our Stay"), Bach employs a chromatic modulation to link two keys through an ascending line. The phrase begins in D major, then modulates to E minor, culminating with a half cadence. Again, the three chromatic pitches (D♮–D♯–E) appear in the bass.

TRACK 65-2 CHROMATIC MODULATION
J. S. Bach, "God the Father, Be Our Stay"
Anonymous 15th-century Melody

While the chromatic link occurs most often in the bass, it may appear in other voices as well. In setting Hassler's melody, "*O Haupt voll Blut und Wunden*" ("O Sacred Head Now Wounded"), for example, Bach utilizes an ascending line in the tenor. The keys of D major and B minor are closely related, but Bach chooses a chromatic modulation that is convincing despite the absence of a common chord.

TRACK 65-3 CHROMATIC MODULATION
J. S. Bach, "O Sacred Head, Now Wounded"
Melody by Hans Leo Hassler, ca. 1600

Descending Chromatic Line

Chromatic modulation in some keys cannot be effected convincingly by an ascending line. In major keys, if we modulate to the subdominant (from C major to F major, for example), the new ↑$\hat{7}$ (E) is not an accidental at all, but a diatonic pitch in the old key ($\hat{3}$). This is the same problem that we discussed earlier regarding a tonicization of the subdominant in major.

Composers often modulate to the subdominant using a line that *descends* chromatically and culminates in the new fourth and third scale degrees, respectively. As with other chromatic modulations, there is no common chord. As shown in the next example, the first of the three pitches is harmonized in the old key and is a chromatic half step above new $\hat{4}$; the second and third pitches belong to the new key and represent dominant and tonic functions.

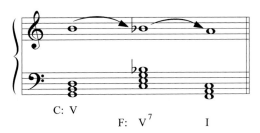

A passage in Beethoven's Sonatina in D Major illustrates a change of key through the descending chromatic line. While the composer returns to the original key immediately, as we have discussed, the same point of tonal reorientation would link two keys in a modulation.

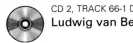

CD 2, TRACK 66-1 DESCENDING LINE (2 PARTS)
Ludwig van Beethoven, Sonatina in D Major (I)

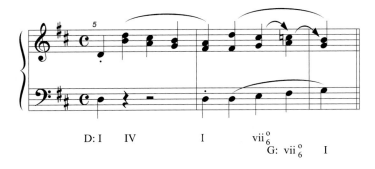

Bach's harmonization of "Why Should Cross and Trial Grieve Me?" includes several brief phrases that touch on the keys of C major, D minor, F major, and G major. The first two modulations are by common chord (boxed). In measure 10, notice the descending chromatic line in the tenor (ornamented with a neighboring tone) that establishes F major without the aid of a common chord.

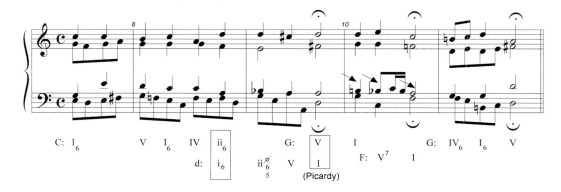

Although chromatic modulation and tonal shift have the power to link distant keys quite easily, most traditional composers employ other relationships (to be studied in Volume II) for this purpose. As we have seen, however, the ascending or descending chromatic line—together with appropriate harmonic choices—provides an interesting and compelling modulation between closely related keys.

WORKBOOK/ANTHOLOGY I
III. Chromatic Modulation, page 147

PHRASE MODULATION

In Bach's harmonization of a melody by Bartolomäus Gesius, *"Befiehl du deine Wege"* ("Commit Thou All That Grieves Thee"), the third phrase begins in D major (the primary tonality) and modulates immediately to E minor through a common chord (D: IV = e: III). After a half cadence in E minor, the next phrase begins abruptly in A major. There is no common chord.

PHRASE MODULATION describes that process by which a formal division ends in one key and the next section begins in another. This approach is seen in measures 7–8 of the Bach chorale. Still, others would suggest that the modulation is chromatic, with the three half steps (D♯–D♮–C♯) divided between alto and soprano voices.

$$e: \quad V$$
$$A: \quad V^6_5 \quad I$$

In the final movement of Mozart's Quartet in D Minor, K. 421, the composer employs an unexpected modal shift from the primary tonic to the parallel major (measure 97).

TRACK 67-2 PHRASE MODULATION
W. A. Mozart, Quartet in D Minor, 421 (IV)

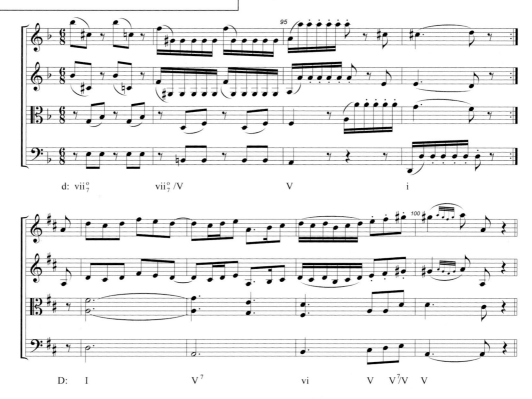

We might discuss the modal shift in the last passage as a common-chord process (d: V = D: V). More important, however, is Mozart's choice to end one section in the key of D minor and initiate the next one in the major mode. A modal shift presents the probability of a smooth connection in any event, but when the listener perceives that one section has ended, the beginning of a new phrase is accepted virtually regardless of the tonal relationships involved. In the Mozart Quartet, the two modes (D minor and D major) are linked through different formal divisions.

The Pivot (Common) Pitch.   In the Mozart quartet excerpt the composer signals the end of a section with a convincing cadence bolstered by reiterated sixteenth notes on the tonic pitch. Although the style is different, Bach creates the same separation of formal divisions with a pause (fermata). In still other works, a single pitch (diatonic in both old and new keys) connects phrases that differ in tonality. The PIVOT (COMMON) PITCH often combines the features of common-chord and phrase modulation.

Heinrich Lichner was a German composer who is remembered today principally for a few keyboard pieces such as "Tulips" (from a collection entitled *Bright Flowers*). While the primary tonality is G major, a transitional passage in E minor (measure 25) concludes with a tonicization of the subtonic (measures 31–32). Reiterated in measure 34, we hear the pitch D_5 as $\hat{1}$ in D major, the temporary tonic key. Lichner then reinterprets D as $\hat{3}$ in B♭ major. There is no diatonic common chord between the distant keys of D major and B♭ major.[4] We may hear D as a common *pitch*, but the phrase ending in D major, followed by a new phrase (and new melodic material) in B♭ major allows us to connect the two tonalities through a phrase modulation. Notice that the excerpt from "Tulips" shown in the next passage consists solely of tonic and dominant harmonies.

CD 2, TRACK 68
Heinrich Lichner "Tulip" from *Bright Flowers*
Pivot Pitch

Especially in a lengthy work, composers establish tonal hierarchies. We might term the primary tonality the *background*. Other keys may come and go

---

[4]In Volume II, we will discuss modal borrowing in which a B♭ major triad might be heard as related to D major through the parallel minor (D minor).

on a temporary or local level, but the primary tonality is always present—either literally, or through an emphasis on one of its allied keys. Western composers have favored smooth transitions that are most convenient when keys are closely related. To connect the two keys, composers use a common chord, a chromatic line, or the perception of a discrete formal division. In the next chapter, we will explore the ways in which traditional composers use modulation as a defining *principle* to create forms that govern works of virtually any length.

WORKBOOK/ANTHOLOGY I
IV. Summary of Modulation
Techniques, page 149

REVIEW AND APPLICATION 11–3

Identifying Modulation

Essential Terms

phrase modulation   chromatic modulation   pivot (common) pitch

1. View each key change in the passages below as a modulation (even though some are obviously tonicizations). Provide roman-numeral analysis, *changing key identification as necessary* (blanks are provided for keys). Below each key change, identify the type of modulation (common-chord, chromatic, or phrase).

CD 2, TRACK 69 REVIEW AND APPLICATION 11-3
J. S. Bach, "O Sinner, Come Thy Sin to Mourn"
Exercise 1-a

2. In the space provided, choose a chord that is common to both keys, but one that will have predominant function in the new key. Write this chord in the first measure. In the second measure, provide dominant and tonic chords. Include any necessary accidentals.

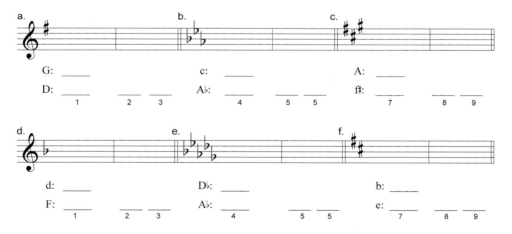

3. For the modulations suggested, use the upper staff to provide a melodic link of three pitches that would connect the two keys in a chromatic modulation. On the lower staff, enter roman numerals and block chords to indicate the harmony that would accompany the change of key. The first example is completed as a model. Refer to pages 422–426 for a review of the techniques involved.

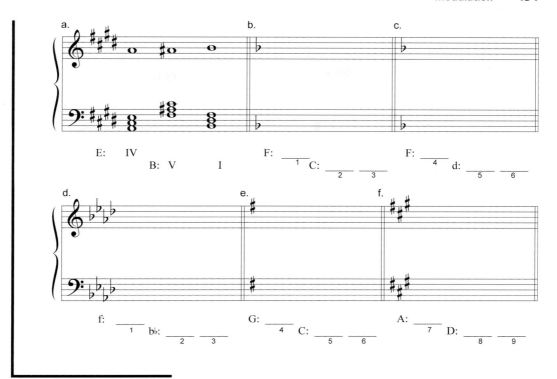

E: IV

B: V   I

F: ___
   1   C: ___ ___
           2   3

F: ___
   4   d: ___ ___
           5   6

f: ___
   1   b♭: ___ ___
            2   3

G: ___
   4   C: ___ ___
           5   6

A: ___
   7   D: ___ ___
           8   9

SELF-TEST 11–3

Time Limit: 5 Minutes

1. Some of these statements are true; others are false. Write "T" or "F" in the blank as appropriate. Note that these questions concern the entire chapter. *Scoring: Subtract 5 points for each error.*

    ____ a. In a chromatic modulation, there is no common chord.

    ____ b. In a modulation to the dominant by chromatic link, the line descends through new $\hat{4}$ and $\hat{3}$.

    ____ c. A phrase modulation includes a common chord.

    ____ d. The triad A–C–E would be a good choice for common chord in a modulation from A minor to E minor.

    ____ e. A pivot pitch sometimes joins two keys in a phrase modulation.

    ____ f. The keys of A♭ major and F minor represent modal shift.

    ____ g. Chromatic modulation is the most frequently used method of key change.

    ____ h. In a chromatic modulation to the supertonic, the first two pitches in the line are new $\uparrow\hat{7}$ and $\hat{8}$.

    ____ i. An open section is one that begins in one key and ends in another.

    ____ j. Relative length is one of several measures of a modulation.

2. These questions concern the Bach Gavotte in the next example. *Scoring: Subtract 10 points for each wrong answer.* Consider the problem entirely right or entirely wrong.

CD 2, TRACK 71

J. S. Bach, Gavotte from Suite No. 5
Self Test 11-3, Question 2

In each set of choices that follow, check *all* that apply.

a. This passage illustrates modulation through

    ___ (1) common chord

    ___ (2) phrase link

    ___ (3) chromatic link

    ___ (4) modal shift

b. The following characteristics of modulation are present:

    ___ (1) relative length of new area

    ___ (2) cadence in new area

    ___ (3) tonicization of areas within the new key

c. The section shown in the last example is

    ___ (1) open

    ___ (2) closed

    ___ (3) connected

d. The chord immediately before the first chord in the new key

    ___ (1) has tonic function (in the new key)

    ___ (2) has predominant function (in the new key)

    ___ (3) has dominant function (in the new key)

    ___ (4) is nonfunctional in the new key

e. Provide a detailed roman-numeral analysis for the final cadence (measures 7–8).

Key _____: _____ _____ _____ _____ | _____ |
             1   2   3   4   5

Total Possible: 100   Your Score _____

PROJECTS

Analysis

The analysis of key change is only one area for study, but we would anticipate a completely different practice from one era of Western music to the next. In the Renaissance, for example, there is rarely an overall key center; sections are clear in tonality, but the relationship among them is not rigid. In the Baroque and Classical eras, the establishment of a central tonality (and predictable excursions from it) are reflected not only in practice, but also through the titles of works ("Sonata in D Major," for example). In the mid- and late nineteenth century, composers were often more flexible in choosing distant contrasting keys, but they usually remained faithful to a central pitch center. All of this changed at the end of the nineteenth century as the principles of tonality were eroded. In addition to constantly shifting keys, some composers employed two of more keys alternately and even simultaneously.

As we will discuss further in Chapter 12, modulation often defines the overall shape of a work. Successful composers lead listeners through a kaleidoscope of local tonalities, but they also identify the key of major sections and of the work as a whole. In an analysis of the key scheme of a traditional work, consider some or all of the following:

a. Determine the overall key scheme. If modulations occur, are they closely related or distant?

b. Discuss both modulation and tonicization in the work. If a change of key occurs, does the original key return? Is there one or more modulation?

c. Are areas tonicized? How do these local tonalities support any modulation?

d. Identify the method of modulation (chromatic, common-chord, and so on). Undertake a roman-numeral analysis of relevant passages.

Text

W. A. Mozart, Theme from Sonata for Piano in D Major, K. 284 (III), text page 462. Mozart used this brief theme for a series of variations in his sonata, K. 284. In addition to modulation, there are also areas of tonicization. How are these differentiated? Formulate a rationale for the point at which analysis in one key ends and an understanding through the next tonality begins.

George Gershwin, *Oh, Lady Be Good*, Unit III, text page 323. "Oh, Lady Be Good" was discussed in Chapter 6 as well as in the present chapter. The two major sections of the work are defined by key as well as melodic style. Provide a complete analysis, taking into account both modulation and tonicization.

Workbook/Anthology I

Johannes Brahms, Waltz, Op. 30, No. 3, workbook page 155.
Melchior Vulpius, "The Newborn Child" (Harmonization by J. S. Bach), workbook page 156.
W. A. Mozart, Minuet, workbook page 157.
Henry Purcell, "Turn Then Thine Eyes," workbook page 158.

Composition

A Cappella Choral Arrangement. Make a four-part choral arrangement of the Italian folk song, "Maid of Sorrento" (given here) or another work as specified by your instructor.

Italian Folk Song, "The Maid of Sorrento"

Set the single (given) verse twice for an SATB choir. Begin and end the first verse in C major as shown in the lead sheet. There are many viable approaches to this arrangement assignment and your version may vary in texture and style. However, you should adhere to traditional voice-leading considerations. Your first verse might begin with the melody in the soprano and a few passing and neighboring tones in the accompaniment. Notice in the example that chord symbols have been replaced with roman-numeral analysis. Continue this practice in your own arrangement.

> CD 2, TRACK 72 CHAPTER PROJECTS (2 PARTS)
> "Maid of Sorrento," Four-Part Setting

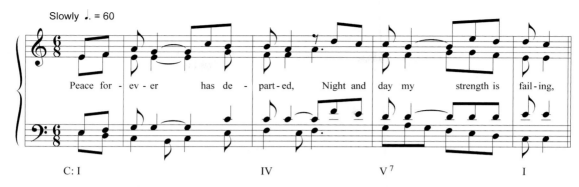

When you have completed the first verse, write a brief modulating transition to prepare for a second statement of the text—this time in G major. In the sample arrangement shown, the characteristic short-long pattern of the melody becomes a motive that connects the C major and G major settings. The transition employs fragments of text and melody, centering on the supertonic in C major which, with a change of mode, becomes the dominant in G major. The

 TRACK 73 CHAPTER PROJECTS
"Maid of Sorrento," Modulating Transition

actual modulation is by common chord. The second setting of the verse begins with basses on the melody, accompanied in long notes in sopranos and altos.

For Further Study

Music of Black Americans. We regularly hear spirituals on vocal and choral concerts and the contributions of Black jazz musicians is documented and well appreciated, but in a profession dominated by white males for centuries, we pay special attention today to the art music of Black Americans. Although their training was usually informal, slaves and free Blacks were often revered in the eighteenth and nineteenth centuries for their musical skills. In the late nineteenth century, the end of slavery and the establishment of colleges such as Tuskegee and Howard University brought increased (although still limited) opportunities for Black Americans to receive formal training in Western music. As American art music emerged in the early twentieth century, the mannerisms of ragtime, jazz, spirituals, and folk songs found their way into the music of many composers. One of the first Black American composers to achieve a wide reputation was Scott Joplin (1868–1917), who is known for his ragtime pieces but he also wrote three complete operas.

Investigate the life and work of three different Black American composers (excluding jazz and pop composers for the present) as the basis of a class presentation or paper. Choose from the list below as well as composers recommended by your instructor and your personal favorites. In addition to a biographical summary, investigate the range of works by each composer, compile a list of suggested listening, and present details about the composers' education and professional careers.

Harry T. Burleigh (1866–1949)

Scott Joplin (1868–1917)

Nathaniel Dett (1882–1943)

Florence Price (1887–1953)

William Grant Still (1895–1978)

William Levi Dawson (1899–1990)

Howard Swanson (1907–1978)

Ulysses Kay (1917–1995)

George Theophlius Walker (b. 1922)

Coleridge-Taylor Perkinson (1932–2004)

Leslie Adams (b. 1935)

Alolphus Hailstork (b. 1941)

Anthony Davis (b. 1951)

Julius Penson Williams (b. 1954)

TRACK 74
W. A. Mozart, Sonata in D Major, K. 284 (II) Theme
Classical Era

CHAPTER *12*

Binary and Ternary Designs

From monophonic chant melodies, Western music evolved into contrapuntal polyphony in the Middle Ages and Renaissance. Because contrapuntal compositions are relatively intense (from the constant flow of interweaving lines), works in this texture are typically only a few minutes in length. As textures became less complex, however, composers sought ways of presenting a longer movement that could still be perceived as a unified whole. Even in the Renaissance, the contrast of two or more themes was recognized as one way of attaining both contrast and continuity. During the early eighteenth century, many composers realized that *key*—another, even more powerful defining element—was also at their disposal.

Small Forms. In Chapter 9, we discussed periodic forms that serve as models for common-practice melody. SMALL FORMS, on the other hand, structural divisions like *binary* and *ternary*, are under study in the present chapter. These two- and three-part forms are defined by key and usually comprise two or more double periods or phrase groups of similar length. Composers use small forms to structure piano, vocal, and orchestral works of moderate proportions. In Volume II, we will discuss LARGE or GRAND FORMS (sonata form, rondo, and others) that shape longer movements in major keyboard, chamber, and symphonic works.

The Classical Style

Noted musicologist Charles Rosen published *The Classical Style: Haydn, Mozart, and Beethoven* in 1971.[1] The volume, which won a National Book Award (1972), has been so influential that Rosen's ideas about the importance of key

---

[1] Charles Rosen, *The Classical Style: Haydn, Mozart, and Beethoven* (W. W. Norton and Company, 1971, New York).

relationships continue to color the way we teach, study, and perform traditional music today. Rosen stresses that, while different themes may clearly separate sections of a movement, the contrast of two different keys is even more important. The argument is especially compelling when we understand that many traditional multi-part compositions have only one principal theme.

Formal Principles

For every model of Western musical structure, there are many exceptions—especially in terms of form. We may talk about the conventions of tonality, meter, and melodic structure with some clarity, but the creative formal process generates inevitable deviations. Even in music from the Classical era, a melody may appear straightforward in form until an extension, omission, or elision suddenly curtails conformity with any model (as composers vent their individual artistic expression). Unless we have dozens of models, our awareness of formal structure must be basic indeed. Here, Rosen and others who espouse an understanding based on formal *principles* (as opposed to forms) enable us to begin with the most essential outlines of shape; within that shape, we are free to explore and draw conclusions about the ways in which an individual composer defines the details.

THE BINARY PRINCIPLE

While the term "binary" may designate a composition in two parts, the BINARY PRINCIPLE unfolds within a sequence of three "events" that are wholly dependent on key: (1) The statement of a tonic key, (2) a digression from that key, and (3) a return to the tonic.

This statement–digression–return sequence of events has the power to define a movement of any length—from dozens to hundreds of measures. Length is not typically a consideration in identifying a binary work, but neither is thematic content. A monothematic movement may convey a binary structure just as well as a work that includes several different themes.

Key is central to defining the binary principle. A binary work is in two sections: The first part opens in the tonic key and digresses to a related key; the second part begins in the same related key and returns to the tonic.

Part I   Part II

Tonic Key   Related Key   Related Key   Tonic Key

Simple Binary

A binary movement typically comprises a double period (or similar phrase groups) in form. Accordingly, we use uppercase letters to represent parts (as we discussed in Chapter 9). If the two parts begin with the same melodic material, the movement is MONOTHEMATIC and the parts are designated **A** and **A**[1]. If the second part begins with a contrasting theme, the movement is POLYTHEMATIC and the parts are identified as **A** and **B**.[2]

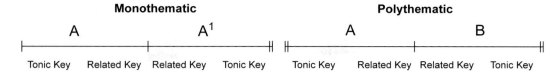

Monothematic				**Polythematic**			
A		A¹		A		B	
Tonic Key	Related Key	Related Key	Tonic Key	Tonic Key	Related Key	Related Key	Tonic Key

Because we are accustomed to defining melodic material sequentially as "A" and "B," extra care is warranted to avoid a common error. In a polythematic work, the first part is designated "A" and the second, "B." If the work is *monothematic,* however, any reference to "B" material is incorrect. Instead, describe "A" material in the second part as "the transposed A theme," the "restatement of A," and so on.

Baroque Binary

In the seventeenth and eighteenth centuries, dancing was an important entertainment, and court composers were expected to provide music suitable to any dance style. Bach wrote several dance suites for keyboard. The music of each movement has a rhythmic identity that reflects the formal dance steps. The allemande, a German dance, is usually in duple meter with a short anacrusis; the sarabande, Latin American (Spanish) in origin, is cast in a slow triple meter with an agogic accent on the second of the three beats.

Dance movements that found their way into the Baroque suite were often cast in binary form with both of the two parts repeated. This interpretation of the binary principle, with repeat signs typically indicated in the score, is known as BAROQUE BINARY. Shown below in its entirety, the Sarabande from Bach's *French Suite No. 6 in E Major* is a monothematic baroque binary. The texture may appear more complex than it actually is due to Bach's delineation of voices with individual stems.

CD 2, TRACK 75
J. S. Bach, Sarabande from French Suite No. 6 in E Major
Baroque Binary Form

---

[2]If a monothematic movement does not feature a *transposition* of the opening material (A¹) in the second part, it does not conform to the binary principle.

On a time line (see next example), both the binary principle and the monothematic structure of the work are clear. The tonic key is E major; a digression to the dominant occurs early in the first part (measure 6). The second part begins with a transposition of the original theme and, after an exploration of F♯ minor (measures 12–14), the tonic key is restated in the final two measures.

Bach, Sarabande

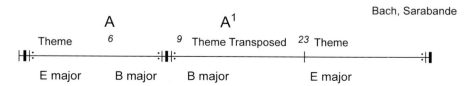

Thematic Contrast.   While many binary movements are monothematic, composers often underscore the tonal digression with a new, contrasting theme. Jacques Champion Chambonnières (ca. 1601–1672) was a French composer of the early Baroque era who taught, performed, and composed exclusively for the harpsichord. His Sarabande (shown in the next example), like the one that Bach composed for his *French Suite No. 6,* is "baroque" binary in form, with the second part twice as long as the first. While Bach's dance movement is monothematic, however, Chambonnières' version contrasts two different themes. One theme (**A**) is associated with the tonic key; the second (**B**), with the digression. In addition, Bach's Sarabande is thicker in texture than that of Chambonnières and has a more pronounced emphasis on the second beat.

Study the time line below and notice that the related key is defined before the contrasting theme begins. Likewise, the return to G major (measure 17) is dramatized by a tonicization of the supertonic. The two themes of Chambonnières' Sarabande are similar in style and rhythm, but differ both in interval content and in melodic contour. Accordingly, our time line designates the first part as **A** and the second as **B**.

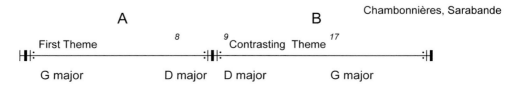

Chambonnières, Sarabande

For a more detailed time line, trace phrase and period structure as you did in Chapter 9. The "A" material of the Chambonnières Sarabande is a two-phrase group; the "B" material is a sectional double period. The use of continually new and transposed melodic material in the Baroque era contrasts with Classical- and Romantic-era composer's preference for recycling phrases and periods more or less unchanged.

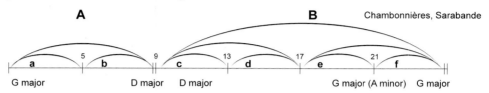

Binary Movements in Minor. If a work begins in minor, the related key is often the *relative major*. In Chapter 11, we studied Bach's Menuet in G Minor (see pages 404–405). The work is a baroque binary that opens in the tonic key, then modulates to the relative major at the end of the first part. The second part begins with new melodic material and returns to G minor.

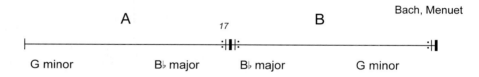

Bach composed numerous minuets and other unpretentious dance movements for his children and less experienced harpsichord students. Proportions are modest in these works, and the technical demands minimal. Still, pieces like the D Minor Menuet (shown below) exhibit all of the features that we associate with the binary principle. The form is a polythematic baroque binary with the relative major as the related key.

CD 2, TRACK 77
J. S. Bach, Menuet in D Minor
Binary Movement in Minor

Although the D minor Menuet is shorter than the one in G minor on page 404, the two pieces are illustrated similarly on a time line.

Bach, Menuet in D Minor

Especially in keyboard music of the early and mid-Baroque, binary forms that begin in minor keys may modulate to the minor dominant in the first part. Arcangelo Corelli lived in the first half of the seventeenth century; his works were decisive in the development of the mature common-practice style. Corelli's *Sonata da Camera* (chamber sonata) is really a four-movement dance suite consisting of a Prelude (shown below), Allemande, Sarabande, and Gigue. The prelude is a polythematic baroque binary that begins in E minor, modulates to B minor, then returns to the original key. Within this framework, various diatonic areas are tonicized.

CD 2, TRACK 78
Archangelo Corelli, *Sonata da Camera* **Op. V, No. 8**

Rounded Binary

An important variation of binary form includes a return not only of the opening key in the second part, but of the opening *melodic material* as well. In ROUNDED BINARY form, the thematic material associated with the tonal digression returns with the tonic key. The form is binary, but the effect of the movement is a three-part division.

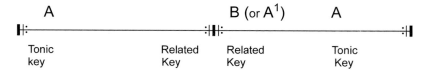

Rounded binary is a hybrid pattern that often combines elements of both two- and three-part forms. Bach's Menuet in G Major, for example, is rounded-binary in form. Notice, however, that a modulation to the related key does not really occur in the first part (ending with a half cadence in the tonic). Instead, Bach takes care in the second part to establish D major fully, with four measures (11–14) devoted to a dominant seventh chord. As soon as the related key is established, we begin moving back toward G major both in tonality and theme.

The second phrase of the G major theme (measures 18–21) now serves as a transition to a return of the **A** material (measure 22).

[Not Recorded]

J. S. Bach, Menuet in G Major

In no other area of musical analysis is there more spirited disagreement among authorities than form. This is especially true of rounded binary. Some would disdain the term "binary" used to discuss a movement, like Bach's menuet, that fails to modulate in the first part. To others, the relative length and importance of the two sections (especially with repeats) outweigh concerns about tonality. Performed with repeats as written, we probably will hear the menuet as binary. On the other hand, should we play the movement from beginning to end without repeats, a three-part form would emerge. In addition, we should consider the significance of the "rounding" itself (the return of the opening thematic material). Where the rounding is minimal, it may be heard as little more than a coda or ending formula to the second part, nothing more than a reminder of material previously heard. But if the return of the tonic key and opening thematic material are carefully prepared and planned to attract our attention, then the movement is more properly discussed as being in three parts. While composers continue to cast works in binary form today, *rounded* binary has a more elegant legacy. Tonal and thematic recurrence, combined with unlimited possibilities of contrast in the second section, spawned *sonata form*—perhaps the most influential formal design of the common-practice era.[3]

In traditional binary movements, we expect modulation to the dominant if the tonic is major, or to the dominant or relative major in minor keys. In actuality, however, other keys may articulate the tonal digression. This is especially true in the Romantic era (ca. 1825–1900) when experiments with tonal relationships attracted composers like Chopin and Brahms. Less well-known, Gustave Merkel was a German whose music for young pianists continues to be useful today. His *The Jolly Huntsman* is rounded binary in form. First, while the piece begins in F major, the first part ends in A minor (a mediant, rather than a dominant relationship as expected). In addition, the second section touches upon the keys of D minor and C major before returning to F major.

CD 2 TRACK 79
Gustave Merkel, *The Jolly Hunstman*, Op. 31, No. 2

---

[3]Sonata form is treated in detail in Chapter 5 of Volume II.

Coda.   Another interesting feature of Merkel's short work is the inclusion of a *coda*. A CODA (Latin, "tail") is a section designed to effect a definitive close. The coda of *The Jolly Huntsman* (beginning with the final beat of measure 34) consists largely of tonic and dominant arpeggios. Some traditional works have codas; others do not. In this binary piece, we recognize the beginning of the coda when the melodic interest shifts suddenly to the left hand (with arpeggiated accompaniment in the right-hand part).[4] Codas are usually proportional in length to the works they conclude. The coda in Merkel's composition spans eight measures—the same length as the initial **A** section (although it has substantially less melodic and rhythmic interest). In a sonata or other lengthy work,

---

[4]The left-hand in measures 35–38 is an effect termed "horn fifths" and imitates a characteristic pattern played on a pair of natural (valveless) French horns. The "horn" is not only a common orchestral instrument, but was also used as a hunting signal—hence the use of horn fifths in Merkel's *The Jolly Huntsman*. See also measure 1 of Haydn's Quartet, Op. 76, No 3 on page 198.

a coda may be as long or longer than Merkel's entire composition. On a time line, designate a coda as shown below.

Merkel, *Jolly Huntsman*

A   7   10   B   22   A   35   Coda

F major   A minor   A minor   F major   F major

As we have discussed, the binary principle rests upon the establishment of a primary key, a modulation away from that key, and an eventual return. Binary movements may be simple ("baroque") or rounded, monothematic or polythematic, with or without a coda. In the next section, we will discuss ternary form which has many of the same elements of binary, but with several important differences.

WORKBOOK/ANTHOLOGY I
I. Binary Forms, page 159 Analysis, page 161

REVIEW AND APPLICATION 12–1

The Binary Principle

Essential Terms

baroque binary	dance suite	polythematic	simple binary
binary principle	grand forms	rounded binary	small forms
coda	monothematic		

1. Study the brief work that follows. Provide a time line that includes part and key designations. In a paragraph of prose, explain why the given composition does or does not conform to the binary principle. Is the structure monothematic? polythematic?

[Not Recorded]   J. S. Bach, March

Time Line _____

SELF-TEST 12–1

Time Limit: 5 Minutes

1. Consider an answer set (a., b., etc.) all right or all wrong. Some of the statements below are correct; others are incorrect. For each group, check *all* that are true (this means that you will check from one to all four of the items). *Scoring: Subtract 11 points for an error.*

a. The binary principle rests upon

_____ (1) a modulation to the dominant or another related key.

_____ (2) contrast of themes.

_____ (3) a digression from the tonic key.

_____ (4) a return to the tonic key.

b. A simple binary form

_____ (1) need not conform to the binary principle.

_____ (2) may be polythematic.

_____ (3) is never monothematic.

_____ (4) is diagramed **A B** or **A A**[1]

c. Baroque binary

_____ (1) differs from simple binary only in key scheme.

_____ (2) is typically monothematic.

_____ (3) includes repetition of both parts.

_____ (4) is common in eighteenth-century dance movements.

     d. If a binary form is rounded,

        _____ (1) there is a digression from the tonic key and an eventual return.

        _____ (2) the theme associated with the first part returns at the end of the second part.

        _____ (3) the second part is in a related key.

        _____ (4) there may be a coda.

     e. The related key in a binary movement

        _____ (1) may be the dominant.

        _____ (2) may be the relative major (if the tonic is minor).

        _____ (3) may be the same as the tonic key.

        _____ (4) is less important than the contrast of themes.

2. Three time lines are given below. Choose a term from the list that best describes each. *Scoring: Subtract 15 points for an incorrect choice.*

    A. Baroque binary

    B. Simple binary

    C. Rounded binary

    D. None of these

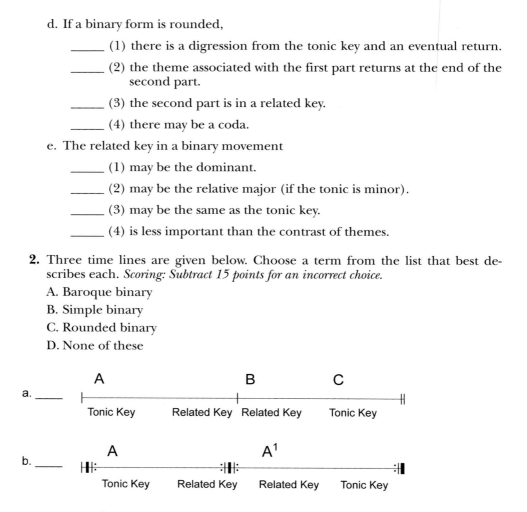

Total Possible: 100   Your Score _____

THE TERNARY PRINCIPLE

The binary principle includes a two-part form—most typically with a full-blown modulation to a related key before the end of the first part. In contrast, the TERNARY PRINCIPLE rests upon three *closed sections.* The first part ends in the tonic key; a second part begins and ends in a related key; and the third part is a restatement of the opening material. Like binary forms, ternary movements may be monothematic or polythematic.

Monothematic Ternary

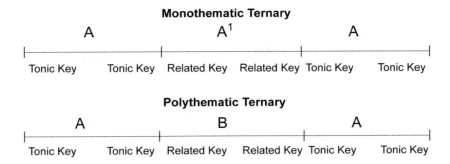

A		A^1		A	
Tonic Key	Tonic Key	Related Key	Related Key	Tonic Key	Tonic Key

Polythematic Ternary

A		B		A	
Tonic Key	Tonic Key	Related Key	Related Key	Tonic Key	Tonic Key

Key schemes in ternary form are more varied than in binary. If the work is in major, the second part may begin and end in the dominant, subdominant, relative minor, *parallel* minor, or another key. If the tonic key is minor, the relative and parallel major keys are the most common digressions (again, many other possibilities exist).

Simple Ternary

The two previous time lines represent SIMPLE TERNARY FORM (as distinguished from other ternary forms that will be discussed presently). The next example, by Robert Schumann, is a polythematic ternary with the second part in the relative minor. Like many other composers of the nineteenth century, Schumann earned a living not only through teaching and performing, but by composing for publication as well. As is true today, music publishers of Schumann's day furnished music for amateur and professional performers alike. The *Drei Clavier-Sonaten für die Jugend*, Op. 118a ("Three Children's Sonatas") are interesting and musical pieces that are within the technical grasp of less experienced pianists.

CD 2, TRACK 80
Robert Schumann, Sonata No. 1 from *Three Children's Sonatas*

(continued on next page)

Schumann's ternary movement is typical in many ways. First, the themes contrast in tonality (with a diversion to the relative minor in the second part). Notice also the legato markings that accompany the **A** material; the middle section lacks such instructions and includes rests that emphasize beats 1 and 3. In addition, the two sections differ in texture: The opening theme is accompanied by an inconsistent number of voices (as shown through stem placement) while the **B** material is more clearly homophonic. On the other hand, the two melodies are similar in rhythmic variety, meter, range, and melodic motion.

Illustrated on the time line in the next example, Schumann's sonata movement includes a brief coda (measures 47–50).

Schumann, Sonata

| A | 15 | B | 36 | A | 47 | Coda |

| G | | G e | | e G | | G |

A final example of simple ternary form, Mazurka in G Minor by Frédéric Chopin, is similar in length to the Schumann sonata, yet the work is intended for more sophisticated performers. Chopin wrote numerous mazurkas—a Polish dance in triple meter that was popular throughout Europe in the nineteenth century. The key scheme here is typical for a ternary movement (minor–relative major key relationships). As we see in the Mazurka, Op. 67, No. 2, composers often link the second and third parts with a transition. In Chopin's work, the transition (measures 33–40) is monophonic. Fashioned from theme material, the transition has the effect of dramatizing both old melodic material and the tonic key.

[Not Recorded]

Frédéric Chopin, Mazurka Op. 67, No. 2

Da Capo Aria Form

Composers sometimes follow the contrasting section of a ternary form with a literal repeat of the first section. In *DA CAPO* ARIA FORM, the third part of the work is not notated; rather, the phrase *da capo* (It. "the head") instructs the performer to return to the beginning and conclude the work at a point marked with the word *fine* (It. "end"). This point is usually at the end of the first section. Although not common today, *da capo* aria form occurs in traditional vocal and keyboard works throughout the common-practice period. The *da capo* (or *dal segno*) *aria* is a cornerstone of Baroque opera and oratorio.[5]

Within a generation after the birth of opera, composers began to adapt the same principles to fit a religious setting. Giacomo Carissimi (1605–1674) is among the pioneers of ORATORIO—a major work for chorus, orchestra, and soloists, but without costumes or staging. The story of an oratorio is usually (but not always) biblical, and a narrator may tie together elements of the basic plot. Oratorios follow the same "number" concept identified with early *opera seria*: a series of self-contained recitatives, arias, ensemble numbers, and choral pieces.

George Frideric Handel was a prolific composer of both opera and oratorio. Few today are unfamiliar with the Christmas portion of his *Messiah* (1742). Another popular work is *Judas Maccabeus* (1746). The aria "Wise Men Flatt'ring" from this oratorio is a typical example of the *da capo* ternary form and is given here with a piano reduction of the orchestral score. Following a lengthy orchestral introduction (24 measures), the soprano begins in F major with a simple theme that Handel "borrowed" from his opera *Agrippina* and inserted into *Judas Maccabeus* at some time after the first performance.[6] Excluding the orchestral introduction and repeats, the second part is shorter than the first (32 measures as opposed to 54 measures), but based on exactly the same melodic material transposed to D minor. Note that in some *da capo* arias, the second part is *substantially* shorter than the first

---

[5] Instead of simply restating the first part, eighteenth-century singers were expected to add ornamentation to the original notes of the melody.

[6] The reuse of original material—including entire sections of a composition—is still common among composers today. Likewise, the practice of adding numbers while reducing or deleting others was a regular feature of early opera and oratorio. Today, we see the same principle in Broadway musicals that may go through a year or more of "tinkering" before settling on a satisfactory sequence of numbers.

section, and may be more transitional than thematic. Likewise, the "closed" structure of the second part may be relatively less rigid to better prepare for the return of the tonic. In Handel's aria, a *da capo* indication at the end of the second part would have suggested a repetition of the entire first section; the use of *dal segno* (%), however, returns the performers to the point at which the soprano enters (skipping the orchestral introduction).

The *da capo* aria form is so common that a time line such as the one below provides most relevant information. Notice that this ternary form is monothematic.

Handel, "Wise Men Flatt'ring"

[Not Recorded]

G. F. Handel, "Wise Men, Flatt'ring"
from *Judas Maccabaeus*

(continued on next page)

But __ true ____ wis - dom can __ re - lieve us, god - like __ wis - dom from a - bove, god - like wis - dom from a - bove; ___

(continued on next page)

Dal Segno

Compound Ternary Form

A form is classified as COMPOUND if one or more of its component sections is in either two or three parts. The most typical of these complex forms is COMPOUND TERNARY—a three-part movement, closed in tonality, in which the first and second parts are themselves two-part forms (often rounded).

Minuet and Trio. In the Classical and Romantic eras, minuets are usually cast in a stereotyped compound ternary called MINUET AND TRIO FORM. The first (**A**) division is *itself* in two parts—either **a b**, or rounded— **a ba**. The middle part (**B**) is called the TRIO and has a similar structure with contrasting melodies (**cd** or **c dc**).[7] The entire A part (without repeats) ends the movement.

---

[7] The "trio" is not the third part of a work, but was originally a section for three instruments (two oboes and bassoon). While most Classical composers scored the section for a full ensemble, notice that Haydn retained the "trio" tradition in his Quartet in F Major (page 464).

In most Classical-era minuets, the internal divisions are simple or rounded binary forms. The internal binary divisions support the overall three-part construction of the minuet and trio as a whole. Moreover, we can see why certain formal designs remained in favor for hundreds of years while others were soon discarded: Forms like minuet and trio permit organization and control from motive to phrase, phrase to period, the growth into internal small forms, and finally into a complex compound ternary design.

On the time line below, notice that the first part (**A**) ends in the tonic key; the first part of a binary form, on the other hand, would conclude in the related key. Thus, the minuet and trio as a whole conforms to the closed tonal sections of the ternary principle.

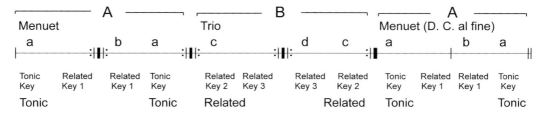

Haydn and Mozart are generally credited with having originated the string quartet—a four-movement "symphony" for two violins, viola, and cello.[8] Typically, the third movement of a string quartet is a minuet and trio. The movement below, for example, from Haydn's Quartet in F Major, is illustrative in numerous respects:

1. The **A** and **B** parts are both rounded binary forms.
2. The second part is in the subdominant key.
3. The time signature is repeated for the second part and the word "trio" appears.
4. The two parts are equivalent in length and style.

CD 2 TRACK 81
Joseph Haydn, Quartet in F Major (III)
Compound Ternary

---

[8]Haydn wrote eighty-two string quartets; Mozart composed twenty-six.

Menuetto D. C.

Classical-era composers included minuets in many multi-movement orchestral and chamber works (such as quartets, symphonies, serenades, and divertimentos), but composers of the nineteenth century used the same form to create different stylistic effects. Like the minuet, the scherzo (fast and dramatic) and waltz (a heavier, legato style) are in triple meter; in duple meters, the march, among others, employs minuet and trio form.

Two- and Three-part Forms

If we accept the binary and ternary principles as resting primarily upon key relationships, then what should we make of works that lack these tonal relationships? As a general rule of thumb, they should be considered on a case-by-case basis. As we have seen, the first part of a rounded binary is not always open tonally. Yet, the most important aspect of the binary principle (a return to the tonic key after a digression) is fulfilled in the second part. Likewise, characteristic of minuet and trio form is a binary or rounded binary within each major part.

For other purposes, we can simply use the terms "two-part form" or "three-part form" without the implications of the binary or ternary tonal principles when the need arises. The following dance by Franz Schubert for example, is not really binary (the two sections begin and end in the same key), but we may identify the form instead as "two-part."

CD 2, TRACK 82
Franz Schubert, Dance
Two-Part Form

(continued on next page)

Binary and ternary forms, as discussed in this chapter, define the shape of many smaller common-practice works. Moreover, the binary principle of tonal and thematic contrast evolved to produce sonata form—perhaps the most dramatic and flexible means of shaping growth in traditional music. Likewise, the ternary principle and its variants continue to be attractive designs for composers today.

Workbook/Anthology I
III. Ternary Forms, page 167. Analysis, page 169

REVIEW AND APPLICATION 12–2

Essential Terms

compound ternary	*da capo ternary form*	*three-part form*
ternary principle	*minuet and trio*	*two-part form*

1. Use the blanks to add key schemes (use the words "tonic" and "related" as appropriate) to make the time lines conform to their descriptions. In which cases might two answers be correct?

a. Rounded Binary

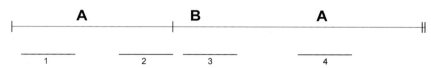

b. Minuet and Trio

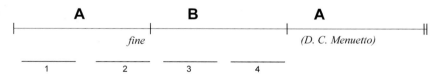

2. Study the following composition and discuss the form as a specific type of binary or ternary form. How does the work conform to the binary or ternary principle? Make a time-line analysis that shows key scheme (use specific key names) and thematic material. Thomas Arne (1710–1778) was an English composer in the generation after Bach. What is a gavotte?

CD 2, TRACK 83
Thomas Arne, Gavotte
Review and Application 12-2

Allegro moderato

(continued on next page)

Time Line _____

SELF-TEST 12–2

Time Limit: 5 Minutes

1. Some of these statements are true; others, false. Write "T" or "F" in the blank as appropriate. Note that these questions concern the entire chapter. *Scoring: Subtract 5 points for each error.*

    _____ a. To be classified as binary, the first section must include a clear modulation to a related key.

    _____ b. If a binary form is in minor, the most common related area is the subdominant.

    _____ c. The minuet and trio form is a compound ternary design.

    _____ d. The *da capo* aria form is often found in Baroque opera and oratorio.

    _____ e. Ternary could be classified as a "small" form.

    _____ f. Baroque binary forms may be monothematic.

    _____ g. If a simple ternary form begins in D major, the first part will usually end in A major.

    _____ h. A coda is an introductory passage that may be found in either binary or ternary movements.

    _____ i. Key scheme in ternary forms is usually more rigid than in binary forms.

    _____ j. *Da capo* aria form is binary.

2. Fill in the blanks a.–f. that follow the score of Schumann's "Humming Song." *Scoring: Subtract 7 points for each error.*

_____ a. Overall form of the movement

_____ b. Key scheme for the component parts

_____ c. Representation of the form with letters (A, B, and so on)

_____ d. Term for relationship of themes between/among parts

_____ e. Is this form simple or compound?

_____ f. Does this movement have a coda?

3. Provide the English translation for the Italian words *da capo. Scoring: Subtract 8 points for an incorrect answer.*

_____

Total Possible: 100   Your Score _____

PROJECTS

Analysis

The analysis of small forms permits a synthesis of many facets of Western music as we have presented them in this volume. Among the areas that might be addressed are an understanding of how tonality is achieved, strengthened, and varied (on both primary and secondary levels); a knowledge of scale systems and how they support tonality; an awareness of rhythm and meter—how these govern the flow not only of melodic patterns, but of consonance and dissonance; and the recognition of how musical figures grow from motive and phrase to periods, double periods, and open or closed sections. Formal analysis also allows us to develop the way we communicate with other knowledgeable musicians; we make time lines, melodic and harmonic reductions, and share our conclusions in organized presentations and papers.

All aspects of a work need not be analyzed at any one time, of course, but to test your achievement in mastering the materials of traditional Western music that we have studied over these twelve chapters, strive for a comprehensive analysis of at least one work provided in the text or workbook.

Text

Ludwig van Beethoven, Sonatina in G Major (III), text page 474. Composers in the eighteenth and nineteenth centuries often chose a compound meter for the last of a multi-movement work as seen in this sonatina. Beethoven is known for his thirty-two *sonatas*—some of which are lengthy and difficult works. But even composers of great stature usually write at least occasionally for young pianists, and Beethoven was no exception. Locate major key areas, identify themes, and make an assessment of the overall form of this work.

Workbook/Anthology I

Robert Schumann, Romance for Oboe and Piano, workbook page 173.
Domenico Scarlatti, Sonata in G Major, workbook page 175.
Joseph Haydn, String Quartet in F Major, Op. 3, No. 5 (II), workbook page 177.

Composition

Sonatina for Piano. Any number of complete movements in Chapter 12 will serve as a model for the composition of a binary sonatina, but in particular, you might consider Clementi's Sonatina on page 401–402. Begin by composing a double period (or structure of similar length) that ends in the dominant (or relative major if your work begins in minor). Adhere to a simple, classical style and employ basic harmonies. The first two phrases of the following sample correspond to measures 1-8 in the Clementi Sonatina. Use more variety if you choose, but the goal of the project is to employ a strong, functional harmony that exploits binary structure.

Create an uncomplicated Alberti bass or other stereotypical accompaniment. In the sample, the bass is relatively slow moving due to the eighth-note movement in the melody.

g: i   V   i   V

g: i
Bb: vi   V⁷   I   V⁷   I   V⁷   I V⁷   I

The next part of the sonatina might be a phrase group that continues in the relative key. After a contrasting phrase, the sample here restates the original material in the relative key.

Bb: IV   I   IV   I   IV   ii   V⁷/ii   ii   V⁷

I   V⁷   I   V⁷   I   V⁷   I   V⁷   I

At this point, half of your sonatina is finished and you may follow the same process to compose a second part. Begin the second part in the related key and return to the tonic. While a monothematic movement is a possibility, we might agree that the eighth-note motive of the sample is becoming stale. For this reason, we might employ a polythematic structure and compose at least a period or phrase group of new material. Return to the opening material for a rounded binary if you choose and consider ending with a brief coda. Be prepared to submit a complete melodic, harmonic, and formal analysis of your composition if asked to do so.

For Further Study

The Baroque Suite of Dances. Dancing was always a popular court entertainment and many of the musicians on the payroll were expected to compose them. Each dance had its own unique pattern of steps and these were supported in the music by definite metric and rhythmic effects. In the early seventeenth century, a few composers began to compose a group of dances for concert performance; the trend grew throughout the century and, by about 1700, the dance suite was a favorite form of musical entertainment. Although many of the dances themselves had fallen out of fashion, the unique musical patterns remained familiar to the nobility; moreover, by grouping several different dances as a single composition, the mood and musical affect were constantly varied. By Bach's day, the dance suite consisted of five or more movements—many of which were in baroque binary form. We use the anagram ACSOG to remember the most common suite structure. The letters stand for:

Allemande   a dance with German characteristics; duple meter
Courante   a faster movement of Italian origin—usually a fast triple meter.
Sarabande   a dance in triple meter—often with an accent on the second beat
Optional   while several dances were expected in virtually any suite, composers might add one or two movements of their choice in the "optional" group. The minuet was popular at this point, as were other dances like the pavane or gavotte.
Gigue   The final movement of the suite was often a lively gigue (jig) in compound meter.

Continue a study of the dance suite by choosing three complete works that are available in your library. Choose scores by three different composers, then note the movements included. Copy the first three or four measures of each movement as a thematic index. In this way, you can easily compare varying rhythms of three different allemandes, three different sarabandes, and so on. Are all of the dances binary? Do the keys of the individual movements support an overall tonality for the suite? Which dance or dances appear in the optional group? Are there exceptions to our expected "ACSOG" structure? Compare textures among the movements. Which movements tend to be homophonic? contrapuntal? Finally, with the score, listen to one or more recorded performances and document your reactions.

CD 2, TRACK 85 PROJECTS (2 PARTS)
Ludwig van Beethoven, Sonatina

[Not Recorded]

Ludwig van Beethoven, Sonatina in G Major (III)

APPENDIX *A*

Ranges and Instrumentation

The process of choosing instruments to create a desired orchestral effect is called INSTRUMENTATION (ORCHESTRATION). The Western orchestra reached its present size and diversity by about 1850. By this time, valves had been invented that greatly improved the flexibility of brass instruments; an advanced system of keys and rings on woodwind instruments was devised by Theobald Boehm (1794–1881); and the idea of constructing many instruments in *families* (several different sizes and ranges) provided the spectrum of orchestral color that we take for granted today. In this appendix, we will survey standard orchestral and band instruments, their ranges, and appropriate notational practices.

Range and Transposition

The RANGE of an instrument is the span between the highest and lowest pitches. The lowest pitch is defined by the size of the vibrating source. On instruments like the flute, clarinet, trumpet, and saxophone, this is a column of air; the length of the vibrating string determines fundamental pitch on stringed instruments. Pitches at the highest end of an instrument's range depend typically on the skill of the performer. In the upper register of wind and stringed instruments, harmonics permit experienced performers to produce extremely high notes. The highest pitch on the piccolo, violin, and tuba, for example, depends on the highest harmonic that a given performer can produce with sufficient stability. The lowest pitch, however, is defined by the length of the vibrating string or air column.

The instrumental ranges given on pages 483–484 specify the lowest pitch for each instrument and also suggest a practical upper limit for performers of moderate abilities (high school musicians, for example).

Written and Concert Pitch. The sounding tone that results when an instrumentalist plays a given note is termed CONCERT PITCH. Written and concert (sounding) pitches are not always the same. TRANSPOSITION—a notation that is higher or lower than concert pitch—was introduced earlier in Chapter 1 with the octave sign and an alternate tenor clef (𝄞). The lines below sound an octave higher and lower, respectively, than notated.

Sounds Octave Higher   Sounds Octave Lower

The INTERVAL OF TRANSPOSITION is the distance between the written and sounding pitches. Octave transposition, seen in the next example, is a common way to avoid ledger lines in some instrumental parts. The double bass sounds an octave lower than notated; the piccolo, an octave higher. These instruments are *transposing* because the notated (written) and sounding pitches are different. To score a passage for the double bass, write the part an octave higher than you want it to sound. Likewise, the notes on the piccolo part will sound an octave higher than those you write. In the lines below, the interval of transposition is an octave; in a later section of this appendix, we will discuss other common transpositions.

ORCHESTRAL AND BAND INSTRUMENTS

Modern orchestral instruments fall into one of four categories: strings, brass, woodwinds, or percussion. Strings constitute the backbone of the orchestra. While winds and percussion are employed for color, effect, and contrast, at least some members of the string section play most of the time.

Strings

The violin, viola, violoncello ('cello), and double bass are the primary stringed instruments. Each member of the string family has four strings, but the OPEN (tuned) strings are different for each instrument. The open strings of the violin, viola, and cello are tuned in fifths; the bass, in fourths. Notice that the viola reads its part in the alto clef.

Stringed instruments are extremely flexible and can be either bowed or plucked (a special effect termed *pizzicato*). The ranges of stringed instruments are given on page 484.

Wind Instruments

If an instrument is pitched in the key of C, the concert and written pitches are the same (although some, the piccolo for example, sound that pitch in a different octave). The flute and oboe are concert-pitch instruments that are notated in the treble clef. The bassoon is a bass-clef instrument pitched in C (although it reads orchestral parts occasionally in the tenor clef). Modern composers and arrangers usually write tuba parts at concert pitch, although by using different fingerings, performers may substitute an instrument in any one of several different keys.

Instruments in B-Flat.   Many band and orchestral instruments (such as the trumpet and clarinet) are pitched in B♭. This means that when the player reads the pitch C on the printed page, B♭ is the resulting pitch.

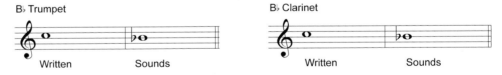

The interval of transposition for B♭ instruments is a *major second.* From concert pitch, parts for clarinet and trumpet are transposed a major second higher. Reading from a part or a full score, however, remember that the notes will sound a major second *lower* than written. Likewise, composers typically transpose the *key signature* by the same interval. If the concert key is C minor, for example, B♭ instruments will read their parts with one flat (D minor—the key a major second higher).

Beethoven opened his Symphony No. 5 with strings and B♭ clarinets in unison (the violas, cellos, and basses sound an octave lower).[1] On the full score

---

[1] Unless otherwise indicated, the clarinet in B♭ is a soprano instrument as found in the modern orchestra and band. A higher-pitched clarinet is common, however, and the word "soprano" is often reserved for the instrument in E♭ (somewhat smaller than the standard B♭ instrument).

that follows, notice that the clarinet line and the key signature are transposed a major second higher than the violin part. Likewise, the double bass part is written an octave higher than the cello so that it will sound in unison with the cellos (and not an octave below them).

When a B♭ instrument is pitched in a tenor or bass range (the bass clarinet or tenor saxophone, for example), the interval of transposition is a *major ninth* (a major second *plus an octave*). To sound concert pitch, the bass clarinet or tenor saxophone must be written a major ninth higher. Likewise, from a written part, the resulting concert pitch will be a major ninth lower. In the next example, all four instruments sound in unison. The violin plays Beethoven's motive at concert-pitch level, the B♭ clarinet is transposed a major second higher; the tenor saxophone and bass clarinet are written a major ninth higher. Notice that the key signatures of all B♭ instruments have been likewise transposed (C minor to D minor). Whether the concert key is major or minor, B♭ instruments are written in the key that has two more sharps than the concert key (3♭ + 2♯ = 1♭).

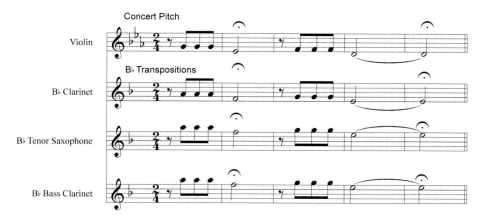

Instruments in E-Flat.   Instruments that are pitched in E♭ sound that note when C is written on their parts. If the instrument is relatively smaller (the E♭ soprano clarinet, for example), the concert pitch is higher than the notated pitch. In these cases, the interval of transposition is a minor third. For the alto saxophone (and, in wind bands, instruments such as the E♭ alto clarinet), the sounding pitch is below the notated pitch. The interval of transposition is a major sixth.

In tonal music, add three sharps to the concert key signature to transpose for E♭ instruments (3♭ + 3♯ = no sharps or flats in the next example). All three E♭ lines below will sound in unison with the violin.

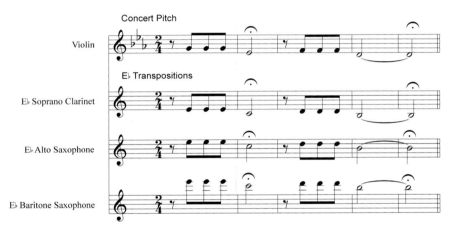

Instruments in F.   Instruments pitched in F sound a perfect fifth lower than written. The French horn is the most important of these; the English horn (an alto oboe) is also in the key of F.

Add one sharp to the concert key signature to transpose for instruments in F.

Clarinet in A.   Only one instrument in the modern orchestra is pitched in A: the clarinet. The clarinet in A is slightly longer than its B♭ counterpart and sounds a minor third lower than notated (where the B♭ instrument sounds a major second lower).

Clarinet in A

Both A and B♭ clarinets use the same fingerings. Today, most composers write only for the latter instrument, however. In the Classical and Romantic eras, the A clarinet was preferred when the concert key signature had one or more sharps; the B♭ clarinet was more often specified in flat keys. For the clarinet in A, add three flats to the concert key signature in either major or minor (E major transposes to G major, for example).

Accidentals

When key signatures are transposed correctly, an accidental in the concert key (F♯ in the key of C minor, for example) will result in an accidental in the transposition. The first two phrases of Mozart's Piano Concerto, K. 491, shown below, are transposed here for instruments in all standard keys. Notice that the F♮ in measure 5 of the flute line (and the corresponding pitch in the transpositions) is a courtesy accidental. Instruments are notated here to sound in unison with the flute; notice, however, that this notation exceeds the useable range of the baritone saxophone (see the table on page 484). While the trombone part is possible for an experienced performer, it is too high for a player of more modest abilities.

W. A. Mozart, Concerto in C Minor, K. 491
First Movement

INSTRUMENT RANGES

The following table provides instrument transpositions and ranges in the order in which they are typically included on an orchestral score. In some cases (the oboe and flute, for example), less expensive instruments lack one or more lower notes than are available on higher-priced models. On the table, these lower notes (which may or may not be available on a given instrument) are shown with solid note heads.

Woodwinds

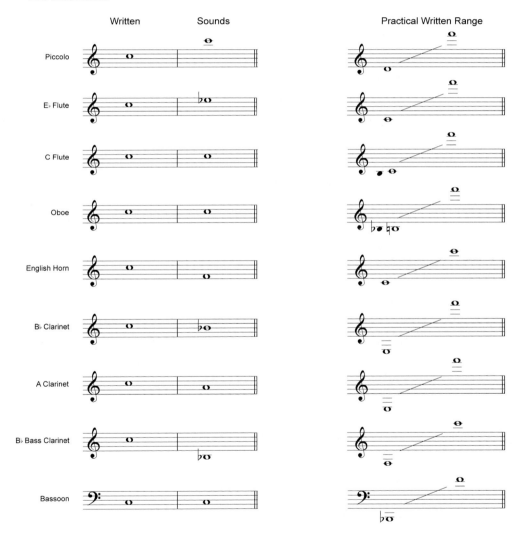

Saxophones (not typically orchestral instruments)

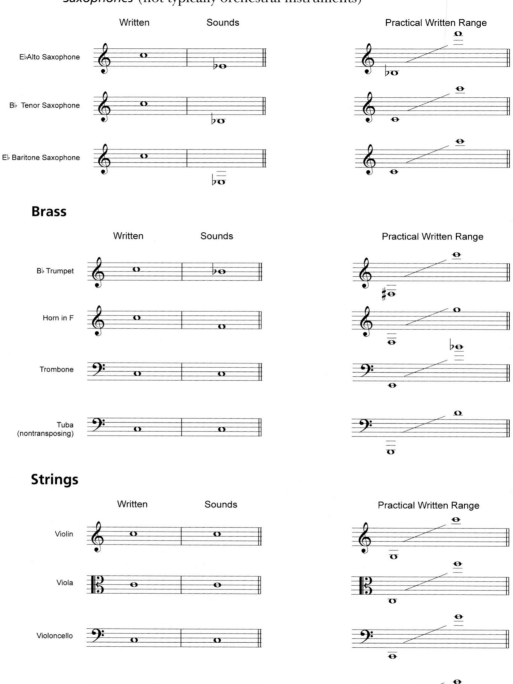

Brass

Strings

Popular Music Chord Symbols

Many different systems of chord symbols are in use today by popular and jazz musicians. In general, however, those who are familiar with any one approach can read others as well. Keep in mind that jazz and popular musicians provide harmonic identifications for pitches that might also be explained in other ways (as nonchord tones, for example, as discussed in Chapter 6). Accordingly, chord-symbol equivalents are not always available for roman-numeral symbols (and the reverse, of course).

Triad Quality

In popular music, a letter without any other accompanying symbol stands for a major triad in root position.

If the triad is minor, diminished, or augmented, other symbols are added.

minor   MI
diminished   MI(♭5)
augmented   +

Inversions.   Bass position is not usually a factor in jazz and popular music because the bass is constantly in motion and because the music is inherently melodic in concept. When composers and arrangers need to specify a bass pitch other than the root, this is indicated by a slash separating the chord and the bass.

Seventh and Ninth Chords

Composers and arrangers often add sevenths, ninths, and even elevenths to a triad (see Chapters 7, 8, and 9 of Volume II for information on the use of these materials in traditional music). A seventh above the root is indicated with a numeral 7. Note that the quality of the seventh is assumed to be *minor* unless noted otherwise (with an accidental or abbreviation). The symbol A^7, therefore, stands for a dominant seventh chord in which the key is D major or minor.

A diminished seventh chord is represented with the circle symbol (notice that the symbol for a diminished triad is Mi(♭5).

Without any other symbol, the numeral 9 refers to a *major* ninth above the root; a minor seventh is also assumed in a chord called a "dominant ninth." For other seventh/ninth combinations, quality is designated with a numeral or abbreviation and any appropriate accidental.

Added and Suspended Pitches

Added tones further enliven the harmonic vocabulary of jazz and popular musicians. Ninths and sixths are often added above the root and indicated by the appropriate number or, in more complicated symbols, with the abbreviation ADD6 or ADD9. Sixths and ninths are assumed to be major intervals above the root unless an accidental is added (♭9, for example).

Suspended pitches are carried over from the previous chord. The most common of these is a fourth above the root (where the third is usually omitted and follows in the next chord as a resolution). The designation SUS refers to the fourth, although other pitches, as designated, may be added to a chord.

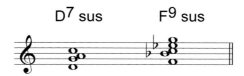

Credits

Terms Index

Composers Index